The Veil of Thoth:

Exploring the Esoteric Wisdom of Ancient Egypt for Modern Spirituality

M L Ruscsak

The Veil of Thoth

Trient Press
3375 S Rainbow Blvd
#81710, SMB 13135
Las Vegas,NV 89180

Ordering Information:
Quantity sales. Special discounts are available on quantity purchases by corporations, associations, and others. For details, contact the publisher at the address above.
Orders by U.S. trade bookstores and wholesalers. Please contact Trient Press: Tel: (775) 996-3844; or visit www.trientpress.com.

Printed in the United States of America

Publisher's Cataloging-in-Publication data
Ruscsak, M.L.
A title of a book : The Veil of Thoth: Exploring the Esoteric Wisdom of Ancient Egypt for Modern Spirituality
    ISBN
Hard Cover   979-8-88990-029-0
Paper Back   979-8-88990-031-3
Ebook   979-8-88990-030-6

The Veil of Thoth

Introduction

In the vast landscape of spiritual exploration, few civilizations have captured the imagination and curiosity of seekers quite like ancient Egypt. Its enigmatic gods, mystical rituals, and profound symbolism have beckoned those in search of wisdom and truth throughout the ages. "The Veil of Thoth: Exploring the Esoteric Wisdom of Ancient Egypt for Modern Spirituality" invites you on a profound journey that unveils the timeless connection between ancient Egyptian deities and the contemporary pursuit of spiritual enlightenment.

Within the pages of this book, we embark on a comprehensive exploration, delving into the depths of ancient Egyptian spirituality and its relevance to modern-day seekers. We navigate the esoteric traditions of ancient Egypt with the aim of uncovering hidden truths, unraveling profound mysteries, and revealing the enduring wisdom that lies beneath the surface.

Through meticulous research and scholarly analysis, we lay the foundation for our exploration. We delve into the purpose of our journey, seeking to understand the intrinsic motivation behind this quest for knowledge. By exploring the significance of studying ancient religions and their influence on modern spirituality, we establish a framework that bridges the gap between the wisdom of the past and the needs of the present.

Our journey begins with a concise yet comprehensive overview of ancient Egypt and its religious beliefs. We examine the cosmology, mythology, and fundamental tenets that underpin the ancient Egyptian worldview. Through this understanding, we gain insight into the cultural and spiritual context that shaped the traditions and practices of ancient Egyptian spirituality.

In traversing the historical and cultural landscape, we uncover the factors that influenced and shaped the development of ancient Egyptian religious beliefs. We analyze the interplay between geography, society, and politics, which played a pivotal role in the formation and evolution of these spiritual traditions.

Part 2 takes us deeper into the heart of ancient Egyptian civilization. We explore the influence of geographical factors, societal structures, and political dynamics on religious beliefs, providing a holistic understanding of the spiritual practices that permeated the lives of ancient Egyptians.

With a solid foundation in place, we delve into the roles of pharaohs and priests, unraveling the intricate rituals and responsibilities they undertook as intermediaries between the mortal and divine realms. Through this exploration, we gain a profound understanding of the hierarchical structure and the sacred power dynamics that defined the religious landscape of ancient Egypt.

Our journey also takes us into the realm of creation myths and cosmology, where we unravel the ancient Egyptians' profound understanding of the origins and structure of the universe. We navigate the rich tapestry of creation narratives, decoding the symbolism and spiritual wisdom woven into these ancient stories.

"The Veil of Thoth: Exploring the Esoteric Wisdom of Ancient Egypt for Modern Spirituality" presents a comprehensive exploration of the major deities, their roles, and the interconnectedness within the ancient Egyptian pantheon. We delve into the symbolism and significance of each deity, unveiling the depths of their wisdom and their relevance to contemporary spiritual seekers.

From religious rituals and temples to the belief in the divine nature of pharaohs, we investigate the intricate practices that shaped ancient Egyptian spirituality. We examine daily religious customs, the role of temples as sacred spaces, and the vibrant festivals and annual celebrations that marked the rhythm of ancient Egyptian religious life.

Our journey does not end with the ancient world. We explore the enduring impact of Egyptian religion on neighboring civilizations, examining the exchanges, syncretism, and the lasting influence that ancient Egyptian deities have had on various spiritual traditions throughout history. We also explore contemporary perspectives on ancient Egyptian gods, the emergence of Egyptian-inspired spirituality, and the pervasive use of Egyptian symbolism and deities in popular culture.

Throughout this book, we present a rigorous and scholarly examination of ancient Egyptian spirituality, balanced with examples, problems, and exercises that engage students in critical thinking and discussion. Our aim is to provide not only knowledge but also a transformative journey that connects us to the profound wisdom of ancient Egypt, allowing us to unravel the veils of time and uncover the timeless truths that resonate with our modern-day spiritual quests.

Part 1: Exploring the Timeless Connection Between Ancient Egypt and its Deities

The study of ancient religions has long captivated the human imagination, offering profound insights into the intricate tapestry of human spirituality throughout history. Among the civilizations that have left an indelible mark on the religious landscape, ancient Egypt stands as an enduring source of fascination and wonder. Its enigmatic deities, intricate rituals, and profound cosmology continue to exert a powerful influence on modern spirituality.

In this comprehensive exploration titled "The Veil of Thoth: Exploring the Esoteric Wisdom of Ancient Egypt for Modern Spirituality," we embark on a profound journey through time, delving into the timeless connection between ancient Egypt and its deities. This scholarly work weaves together the threads of history, culture, and religious beliefs, revealing the rich tapestry of ancient Egyptian spirituality and its relevance to our lives today.

Purpose of the Book

At the outset, we delve into the purpose of this book, laying a solid foundation for our intellectual voyage. We explore the motivations behind studying ancient religions and the enduring influence they wield over modern spirituality. By bridging the gap between the ancient and the contemporary, we strive to deepen our understanding of both realms, unraveling the hidden wisdom that lies within the teachings of ancient Egypt.

Importance of Studying Ancient Religions and their Influence on Modern Spirituality

Chapter 2 delves further into the significance of studying ancient religions and the profound impact they have on modern spiritual practices. We explore the intersections between ancient Egyptian beliefs, rituals, and concepts with diverse fields such as Witchcraft, Divination, Herbalism, Shamanism, and Ecospirituality. Through meticulous examination, we uncover the enduring relevance and adaptive nature of Egyptian wisdom in our present-day spiritual landscape.

Brief Overview of Ancient Egypt and its Religious Beliefs

A concise yet comprehensive overview of ancient Egypt and its religious beliefs forms the essence of Chapter 3. We venture into the heart of this ancient civilization, exploring its social, political, and cultural dynamics. Additionally, we delve into the core religious tenets that shaped the ancient Egyptian worldview, laying the groundwork for a deeper exploration of their deities and spiritual practices.

Historical and Cultural Context

Chapter 4 takes us further into the historical and cultural context of ancient Egypt, unraveling the intricate tapestry of influences that shaped its religious landscape. We navigate the ebb and flow of conquerors, the exchanges of ideas, and the internal developments that molded the religious beliefs and practices of the ancient Egyptians. By contextualizing Egyptian religion within its historical and cultural milieu, we gain a profound appreciation for the complexities and nuances of their spiritual traditions.

Through this book, written in the scholarly and erudite inspiration of esteemed authors Normandi Ellis and Rosemary Clark, we offer students seeking a bachelor's degree a comprehensive and in-depth analysis of the rich spiritual heritage of ancient Egypt. Our aim is to provide a rigorous academic exploration that not only presents theories and concepts but also incorporates examples, problems, and exercises to engage students in critical thinking and foster meaningful discussions.

As we embark on this enlightening journey, readers are invited to immerse themselves in the wonders of ancient Egypt, unearthing the esoteric wisdom that lies beneath the surface. Together, we shall navigate the depths of this ancient civilization, gaining insight into its enduring spiritual teachings and reflecting upon their profound relevance in our modern lives. Join us on this intellectual and spiritual odyssey as we venture into the realms of ancient Egypt's deities and their timeless connection to our spiritual journey today.

Chapter 1: Purpose of the Book

In the profound tapestry of human spirituality, the study of ancient religions offers a gateway to profound insights and timeless wisdom. As students seeking a bachelor's degree in this scholarly pursuit, we embark on a transformative journey into the realms of ancient Egypt, guided by the scholarly spirits of esteemed authors Normandi Ellis and Rosemary Clark. Our exploration begins with a meticulous examination of the purpose of this book, "The Veil of Thoth: Exploring the Esoteric Wisdom of Ancient Egypt for Modern Spirituality," setting the stage for an immersive intellectual voyage.

Purpose:

The purpose of this book is multifaceted and intricately interwoven. It seeks to illuminate the hidden depths of ancient Egyptian spirituality while bridging the gap between the ancient and the contemporary. Our aim is to provide students with a comprehensive understanding of the timeless connection between ancient Egypt and its deities, unraveling the esoteric wisdom that continues to resonate in modern spiritual practices.

As seekers of knowledge, it is crucial to comprehend the motivations driving the study of ancient religions. By delving into the purpose of this book, we lay the groundwork for a profound exploration that transcends mere academic curiosity. We seek to uncover the enduring influence and relevance of ancient Egyptian spirituality, drawing insights from various fields, such as Witchcraft, Divination, Herbalism, Shamanism, and Ecospirituality, to shed light on its modern-day implications.

By engaging with the complexities of ancient Egyptian beliefs, rituals, and cosmology, we gain a deeper understanding of their transformative potential. Through a rigorous and scholarly approach, we aim to present a thorough and in-depth analysis that goes beyond surface-level interpretations. This book will serve as a guide to decipher the enigmatic teachings of ancient Egypt, unlocking their hidden meanings and encouraging critical thinking among students.

Engagement and Exploration:

To foster an interactive and engaging learning experience, each chapter of this book will feature a range of examples, problems, and exercises. These pedagogical tools are designed to illustrate key concepts, challenge assumptions, and encourage students to apply critical thinking skills. Drawing from a diverse

array of fields such as Witchcraft, Divination, Herbalism, Shamanism, and Ecospirituality, we will explore how the wisdom of ancient Egypt resonates with and enriches these practices.

Furthermore, we acknowledge the importance of presenting a balanced and objective perspective. Throughout our exploration, we will address counterarguments and dissenting opinions, acknowledging the complexities and differing interpretations surrounding ancient Egyptian spirituality. By embracing a multidimensional approach, students will be encouraged to develop their own analytical and evaluative skills, fostering an environment of intellectual growth and inquiry.

Objectives:

The objectives of this book are multifaceted, driven by a desire to delve deep into the vast reservoirs of ancient Egyptian spirituality, deciphering its mysteries, and shedding light on its enduring influence in the modern world. By undertaking a meticulous and scholarly exploration, we strive to achieve the following objectives:

Comprehensive Analysis: Our primary objective is to present a thorough and in-depth analysis of ancient Egyptian spirituality, covering a wide range of topics including religious beliefs, rituals, deities, cosmology, and their intricate interconnections. Through meticulous research and scholarly insights, we aim to provide students with a comprehensive understanding of the complexities and nuances of this ancient wisdom.

Relevance and Application: A key objective of this book is to bridge the gap between ancient Egypt and modern spirituality, showcasing the continued relevance and applicability of ancient Egyptian teachings in contemporary practices. By drawing examples from various fields such as Witchcraft, Divination, Herbalism, Shamanism, and Ecospirituality, we aim to highlight how the wisdom of ancient Egypt resonates and enriches these diverse spiritual paths.

Intellectual Engagement: We seek to foster intellectual engagement and critical thinking among students through the inclusion of examples, problems, and exercises throughout the book. By encouraging active participation, reflection, and analysis, we aim to enhance the learning experience and empower students to develop their own interpretations and insights.

Balanced and Objective Perspective: In the spirit of academic rigor, it is essential to present a balanced and objective perspective. We will explore counterarguments and dissenting opinions, acknowledging the diversity of interpretations and scholarly discourse surrounding ancient Egyptian spirituality. By doing so, we aim to foster a nuanced understanding and encourage students to think critically and evaluate multiple viewpoints.

Accessibility and Clarity: Complex scientific concepts and esoteric knowledge can often be daunting to comprehend. Our objective is to present these ideas in a clear and accessible manner, ensuring that students can grasp and appreciate the intricacies of ancient Egyptian spirituality without sacrificing academic rigor. We will employ a range of explanatory techniques, including vivid examples, analogies, and contextual explanations, to demystify complex concepts and make them accessible to students.

Overarching Purpose:

The overarching purpose of this book is to provide students with a transformative journey into the heart of ancient Egyptian spirituality, unveiling its hidden wisdom and revealing its impact on modern spiritual practices. By intertwining rigorous scholarship, sophisticated vocabulary, and the inspired tone of Normandi Ellis and Rosemary Clark, we aim to create an immersive and enlightening reading experience that ignites a passion for the subject matter.

Through the exploration of ancient Egyptian deities, rituals, cosmology, and the impact of Egyptian religion on neighboring civilizations, students will gain a deep understanding of the timeless connection between ancient Egypt and its deities. The book's overarching purpose is to encourage students to critically analyze, question, and reflect upon the complexities of ancient Egyptian spirituality and its enduring relevance in our contemporary world.

In conclusion, "The Veil of Thoth: Exploring the Esoteric Wisdom of Ancient Egypt for Modern Spirituality" embarks on a scholarly odyssey to uncover the depths of ancient Egyptian spirituality and its profound impact on our spiritual journey today. By engaging students in critical thinking, providing a comprehensive analysis, and presenting the wisdom of ancient Egypt in a clear and accessible manner, this book aims to equip aspiring scholars with the tools to navigate the realms of ancient wisdom and draw inspiration from its timeless teachings.

As we embark on this intellectual odyssey into the purpose of our study, we invite students to delve into the profound realms of ancient Egyptian spirituality. We shall unravel the intricate tapestry of ancient wisdom, exploring its relevance and transformative potential for modern spirituality. By engaging with examples, problems, and exercises throughout the book, students will cultivate a deep understanding of ancient Egyptian deities and their timeless connection to our spiritual journey today. Together, we embark on a path of discovery, guided by the wisdom of the ancients, and emerge with a newfound appreciation for the enduring legacy of ancient Egypt's esoteric teachings.

Explanation of the significance of exploring the connection between ancient Egypt and modern spirituality

The exploration of the connection between ancient Egypt and modern spirituality holds immense significance in the academic realm and for individuals seeking to deepen their understanding of spiritual traditions. By unraveling the intricate tapestry of ancient Egyptian beliefs, rituals, and deities, we gain invaluable insights into the roots of human spirituality and the enduring relevance of these ancient teachings in our contemporary lives. This section aims to provide a detailed and comprehensive explanation of why the study of this connection is vital and how it enriches our understanding of modern spirituality.

Historical and Cultural Significance:

Ancient Egypt, with its rich tapestry of religious beliefs and practices, stands as one of the oldest and most enduring civilizations in human history. The spiritual traditions of ancient Egypt, woven into the fabric of everyday life, played a pivotal role in shaping the cultural, social, and political landscape of the time. Exploring the connection between ancient Egypt and modern spirituality allows us to grasp the profound influence these beliefs had on the lives of ancient Egyptians and the subsequent impact they have had on religious and spiritual thought throughout history.

The historical and cultural significance of ancient Egypt cannot be overstated when examining its impact on the development of human spirituality. Ancient Egypt, situated along the fertile banks of the Nile River, flourished for thousands of years and left an indelible mark on human civilization. Its religious beliefs and practices were intricately woven into the fabric of everyday life, permeating all aspects of ancient Egyptian society.

At its core, the religious beliefs of ancient Egypt provided a framework for understanding the world, establishing moral guidelines, and seeking divine favor. The ancient Egyptians believed in a pantheon of gods and goddesses who controlled the forces of nature, governed the cosmic order, and influenced the fortunes of individuals and the nation as a whole. These deities represented various aspects of life, including fertility, the sun, the moon, and the afterlife, among others.

The cultural significance of ancient Egyptian spirituality can be observed through its influence on art, architecture, and literature. The construction of grand temples, such as the iconic Karnak Temple or the temple complexes at Luxor and Abu Simbel, served as physical manifestations of the divine presence and as centers of religious worship. The intricate hieroglyphic inscriptions and reliefs adorning these structures conveyed religious myths, rituals, and the stories of the gods.

Literature, particularly religious texts such as the Book of the Dead, provided guidance for the deceased in their journey through the afterlife, emphasizing the importance of ethical conduct and proper rituals. These texts also shed light on the ancient Egyptians' beliefs about the nature of the soul, the judgment of the dead, and the existence of an eternal life beyond earthly existence.

The religious practices of ancient Egypt were deeply intertwined with societal structures and hierarchies. The roles of pharaohs and priests were central to the maintenance of cosmic balance and the well-being of the kingdom. The pharaoh, as the divine ruler, was responsible for upholding Ma'at, the concept of cosmic order and justice, through their actions and rituals. The priesthood, on the other hand, carried out the daily rituals, made offerings to the gods, and ensured the proper functioning of the temples.

The influence of ancient Egyptian spirituality extended beyond religious practices. It permeated social interactions, political decision-making, and even the daily lives of ordinary individuals. The belief in divine guidance and protection shaped the ancient Egyptians' worldview, giving them a sense of purpose, stability, and collective identity. The rituals and ceremonies performed by the pharaohs and priests were seen as vital for the prosperity of the kingdom and the well-being of its people.

Furthermore, the influence of ancient Egyptian spirituality can be observed in the broader context of religious and spiritual thought. The concepts of divine kingship, the belief in an afterlife, and the notion of cosmic order have resonated across cultures and time periods. The influence of ancient Egyptian religious beliefs can be traced in various religious and spiritual traditions, such as Hermeticism, Gnosticism, and even elements of modern Western esotericism.

The study of ancient Egyptian spirituality provides invaluable insights into the human quest for meaning, the development of religious systems, and the enduring impact of ancient civilizations on the shaping of human thought and culture. By exploring the historical and cultural significance of ancient Egyptian religious beliefs and practices, we gain a deeper understanding of the complexities of human spirituality and the enduring legacies of ancient civilizations.

Endurance and Legacy:

Ancient Egypt's longevity as a civilization, spanning over three millennia, is a testament to its cultural and spiritual resilience. Through the rise and fall of various dynasties, political upheavals, and external influences, the spiritual traditions of ancient Egypt endured. This endurance speaks to the profound significance of these beliefs in the lives of ancient Egyptians and the enduring impact they had on subsequent religious and spiritual thought.

The endurance of ancient Egyptian spirituality can be attributed to several factors. Firstly, the religious beliefs and practices were deeply ingrained in the social fabric and daily life of ancient Egyptians. They provided a sense of identity, meaning, and purpose, and were interwoven into every aspect of society. The rituals, ceremonies, and festivals held in honor of the gods were not only religious in nature but also served as social and communal gatherings, fostering a sense of unity and shared values among the people.

Additionally, the stability and continuity of ancient Egyptian society contributed to the endurance of its spiritual traditions. The centralized political system, with the pharaoh at its helm, provided a sense of stability and order. The pharaoh's role as a divine intermediary and the embodiment of Ma'at ensured the preservation and continuation of religious practices throughout dynastic changes.

Furthermore, the intricate system of priesthood played a vital role in upholding and transmitting religious knowledge and practices from one generation to another. The priesthood, with their specialized training and hierarchical structure, maintained the sacred rituals, administered temple affairs, and acted as custodians of religious texts and teachings.

The enduring legacy of ancient Egyptian spirituality is evident in its influence on subsequent religious and spiritual thought. As one of the earliest recorded religious systems, it laid the foundation for many concepts and ideas that have transcended time and geographical boundaries. For example, the belief in an afterlife, the importance of ethical conduct, and the practice of ritual purification and offerings can be traced back to ancient Egyptian spirituality.

Moreover, ancient Egyptian symbolism, mythology, and iconography have permeated various cultures and artistic expressions throughout history. The striking imagery of gods and goddesses, the use of sacred symbols such as the ankh and the Eye of Horus, and the depiction of cosmic motifs like the sun and the sky continue to inspire artists, writers, and spiritual seekers to this day.

The legacy of ancient Egyptian spirituality can also be seen in the syncretic traditions that emerged during the Hellenistic and Roman periods, as well as the influence it had on the development of early Christianity. Elements of Egyptian cosmology, symbolism, and rituals were incorporated into these syncretic traditions, creating a rich tapestry of religious and spiritual syncretism.

Furthermore, the fascination with ancient Egypt in the modern world, often referred to as Egyptomania, is a testament to its enduring allure and impact. From the exploration of ancient tombs and archaeological discoveries to the influence on popular culture, ancient Egypt continues to captivate and inspire people worldwide.

Studying the endurance and legacy of ancient Egyptian spirituality provides us with a deeper understanding of the resilience of human beliefs and the ways in which ancient civilizations continue to shape our contemporary world. It invites us to reflect on the enduring quest for meaning, the interconnectedness of religious and spiritual thought, and the profound impact that ancient civilizations can have on shaping our collective consciousness.

Cultural Integration:

Ancient Egypt's spiritual traditions were not isolated within the confines of religious institutions but deeply integrated into the broader culture. The spiritual practices and beliefs of ancient Egyptians influenced their social norms, art, architecture, language, and even governance. The pharaoh, as the divine ruler, embodied the connection between the mortal and the divine, and their role in religious rituals and ceremonies solidified the intricate link between religion and politics.

Cultural integration played a pivotal role in ancient Egypt, where religious beliefs and practices permeated every aspect of society. The integration of spirituality into the broader culture can be observed through various dimensions of ancient Egyptian life.

One of the most prominent examples of cultural integration is the role of the pharaoh as the divine ruler. The pharaoh was believed to be the earthly manifestation of the gods, specifically the god Horus. This divine status bestowed upon the pharaoh granted them immense authority and influence over religious matters. The pharaoh's involvement in religious rituals and ceremonies, such as offering sacrifices and performing sacred rites, reinforced the connection between religion and politics. This integration of religious and political power solidified the pharaoh's legitimacy and divine mandate to rule, establishing a unique form of governance in ancient Egypt.

Moreover, the influence of ancient Egyptian spirituality extended beyond political structures and seeped into the social fabric of society. The values and principles derived from religious beliefs shaped social norms and behaviors. Concepts such as Ma'at, which represented order, balance, and harmony, provided a moral framework for interpersonal relationships, justice, and ethical conduct. The pursuit of Ma'at was not only a religious duty but also a social responsibility, emphasizing the importance of maintaining harmony within the community.

Ancient Egyptian art and architecture also reflected the cultural integration of religious beliefs. Temples, tombs, and monuments were built as sacred spaces dedicated to the gods. These structures were not only architectural marvels but also served as physical embodiments of the spiritual realm. The intricate carvings, hieroglyphs, and religious motifs adorned on these structures conveyed the mythological narratives, religious rituals, and the divine presence believed to permeate the physical world.

Language played a significant role in cultural integration as well. The ancient Egyptian language was closely intertwined with religious concepts and symbolism. The hieroglyphic script, which was primarily used for religious texts and inscriptions, conveyed both literal and symbolic meanings. The written word became a vehicle for expressing religious ideas and transmitting spiritual knowledge across generations.

Furthermore, cultural integration can be observed through the religious festivals and ceremonies that were celebrated throughout the year. These events were not merely religious rituals but also served as social and communal gatherings. They provided opportunities for people from different social classes to come together, reinforcing a sense of unity, collective identity, and shared values. The festivals were often accompanied by music, dance, and feasting, creating a vibrant tapestry of cultural expression deeply intertwined with religious practices.

The cultural integration of ancient Egyptian spirituality demonstrates how religious beliefs and practices were interwoven into the fabric of everyday life. It highlights the inseparable nature of religion, politics, social structures, art, and language in ancient Egyptian society. Understanding this integration allows us to gain a comprehensive view of ancient Egyptian civilization, appreciating the depth and complexity of their spiritual traditions and their profound influence on various aspects of their culture.

Influence on Neighboring Civilizations:

Ancient Egypt's cultural and religious influence extended beyond its borders, shaping the beliefs and practices of neighboring civilizations. The exchange of ideas, trade, and conquest led to syncretism and the assimilation of Egyptian deities and rituals into the religious fabric of other ancient cultures. The impact of Egyptian religious concepts can be observed in the religious traditions of the ancient Near East, including Canaanite, Mesopotamian, and Nubian cultures, among others.

The influence of ancient Egyptian religious beliefs and practices on neighboring civilizations was a result of various forms of cultural exchange and interaction. Through trade networks, diplomatic relations, and military conquests, the cultural and religious ideas of ancient Egypt permeated the societies of neighboring civilizations, leaving a lasting impact on their religious traditions.

One significant way in which ancient Egypt influenced neighboring civilizations was through the syncretism of deities and religious rituals. As different cultures came into contact with Egypt, they often incorporated Egyptian gods and goddesses into their own pantheons. This syncretism resulted in the assimilation of Egyptian deities with local gods, creating hybrid religious systems that reflected the blending of beliefs. For example, the goddess Isis, who was revered as the divine mother and protector in ancient Egypt, became widely worshipped throughout the Mediterranean region, particularly in the Hellenistic and Roman periods. Her influence extended to various cults and religious practices, including the worship of Demeter, Cybele, and even the Virgin Mary in later Christian traditions.

Additionally, the Egyptian concept of an afterlife and the rituals associated with it had a profound influence on neighboring civilizations. The belief in the existence of an underworld and the importance of funerary rituals for ensuring the deceased's successful journey to the afterlife were adopted and adapted by other cultures. For instance, the concept of mummification and the preservation of the body as a means of ensuring immortality were embraced by the Nubians, who incorporated Egyptian funerary practices into their own burial customs.

Furthermore, the artistic and architectural styles of ancient Egypt also left an imprint on neighboring civilizations. The iconic structures such as pyramids, obelisks, and monumental temples served as architectural inspiration for neighboring cultures. The grandeur and symbolism associated with Egyptian architecture influenced the construction of religious and monumental structures in other ancient societies, such as the ziggurats of Mesopotamia and the temples of the Hittites.

The cultural and religious influence of ancient Egypt on neighboring civilizations can also be seen in the adoption of Egyptian religious concepts and rituals. Many societies in the ancient Near East incorporated Egyptian religious practices, such as the use of amulets, divination, and magical rituals, into their own religious traditions. This borrowing and assimilation of Egyptian religious elements served to enrich and diversify the religious landscape of these cultures.

In conclusion, the cultural and religious influence of ancient Egypt extended beyond its borders, shaping the beliefs and practices of neighboring civilizations. The syncretism of deities, the adoption of funerary rituals, the architectural inspiration, and the incorporation of religious concepts all attest to the far-reaching impact of Egyptian spirituality. This intercultural exchange contributed to the richness and diversity of religious traditions in the ancient Near East, leaving a lasting legacy that continues to resonate in the religious and spiritual thought of these civilizations.

Intellectual and Scientific Contributions:

Ancient Egypt's contributions to human knowledge extended beyond spirituality. The civilization made significant strides in fields such as mathematics, astronomy, medicine, and architecture. These advancements were often intertwined with religious beliefs, as the construction of temples, the development of calendars, and the understanding of celestial phenomena were intimately linked to the ancient Egyptian worldview.

Ancient Egypt's intellectual and scientific contributions were not only remarkable for their time but also laid the foundation for future advancements in various fields. The achievements of ancient Egyptians in mathematics, astronomy, medicine, and architecture showcase their ingenuity and the intersection between intellectual pursuits and religious beliefs.

In the realm of mathematics, ancient Egyptians developed a sophisticated numeral system that included hieroglyphic symbols representing different quantities. This system enabled them to perform complex calculations, including addition, subtraction, multiplication, and division. Moreover, they were among the first to use fractions, demonstrating their understanding of mathematical concepts and their practical application in everyday life. The ancient Egyptians also applied their mathematical knowledge in the construction of pyramids and other monumental structures, utilizing geometric principles to achieve remarkable precision and stability.

Astronomy was another field in which ancient Egyptians excelled. Their observations of celestial bodies, particularly the movement of the sun, moon, and stars, allowed them to develop a comprehensive understanding of the heavens. They created calendars based on astronomical observations, which played a vital role in religious and agricultural practices. By aligning their religious festivals and agricultural activities with celestial events, they demonstrated their recognition of the interplay between the celestial and earthly realms.

In the realm of medicine, ancient Egyptians made significant contributions that influenced the development of medical practices in later civilizations. Their understanding of anatomy, although limited by the lack of advanced technologies, enabled them to perform basic surgical procedures and develop medicinal treatments. They possessed extensive knowledge of herbal remedies, utilizing various plants and natural substances for the treatment of ailments. The Ebers Papyrus, a medical text dating back to the New Kingdom period, provides insights into the diagnostic and therapeutic practices of ancient Egyptian physicians.

The architectural achievements of ancient Egypt are renowned worldwide. The construction of monumental structures, such as pyramids, temples, and tombs, required advanced engineering techniques and architectural knowledge. The mastery of stone-cutting, surveying, and construction methods allowed them to create enduring architectural marvels that still inspire awe today. The design and layout of temples were meticulously planned to align with religious beliefs and rituals, creating sacred spaces that facilitated spiritual experiences and connected mortals with the divine.

It is important to note that ancient Egyptian intellectual and scientific contributions were deeply intertwined with religious beliefs. The pursuit of knowledge and the advancement of scientific understanding were driven by their desire to comprehend the divine order of the universe and establish harmony between the earthly and divine realms. Religious rituals, astronomical observations, and architectural endeavors were all vehicles for exploring and expressing their spiritual beliefs.

In conclusion, ancient Egypt's intellectual and scientific contributions encompassed fields such as mathematics, astronomy, medicine, and architecture. Their achievements not only demonstrated their intellectual prowess but also reflected the intimate connection between knowledge, spirituality, and the everyday life of ancient Egyptians. These contributions laid the groundwork for future advancements in human knowledge and continue to inspire and inform contemporary disciplines.

Preservation and Rediscovery:

The preservation and subsequent rediscovery of ancient Egyptian artifacts, texts, and monuments have provided modern scholars with a wealth of knowledge about the civilization's religious beliefs and practices. From the decipherment of hieroglyphs to archaeological excavations, these discoveries have allowed us to reconstruct the spiritual landscape of ancient Egypt and gain a deeper understanding of its profound impact on the lives of its people.

By exploring the connection between ancient Egypt and modern spirituality, we gain a profound appreciation for the historical and cultural significance of this ancient civilization. The enduring legacy of ancient Egyptian spirituality not only provides us with insights into the beliefs and practices of our ancestors but also informs our understanding of religious and spiritual thought throughout history. It allows us to recognize the profound influence of ancient Egypt on neighboring civilizations and their subsequent impact on the development of human spirituality. Ultimately, this exploration offers a glimpse into the rich tapestry of human spiritual expression and the timeless quest for meaning and transcendence.

The preservation and rediscovery of ancient Egyptian artifacts, texts, and monuments have played a crucial role in deepening our understanding of the religious beliefs and practices of this ancient civilization. Through careful preservation efforts and archaeological excavations, modern scholars have been able to uncover a wealth of knowledge that provides valuable insights into the spiritual landscape of ancient Egypt.

One of the most significant breakthroughs in understanding ancient Egyptian spirituality came with the decipherment of hieroglyphs in the early 19th century. This monumental achievement, spearheaded by scholars such as Jean-François Champollion, allowed access to the vast corpus of texts inscribed on temple walls, funerary monuments, papyri, and other artifacts. These texts provided valuable information about religious rituals, myths, cosmology, and the roles of gods and goddesses in ancient Egyptian society. The ability to read and interpret these hieroglyphic texts opened a door to the ancient Egyptian worldview and shed light on their intricate religious practices.

Archaeological excavations have also played a pivotal role in uncovering the material remnants of ancient Egyptian religious traditions. The discovery of tombs, temples, and sacred sites has provided tangible evidence of religious rituals and beliefs. Elaborate funerary practices, such as mummification and the construction of tombs and burial chambers, reflect the ancient Egyptians' beliefs in the afterlife and the continuity of the soul beyond death. Temples, with their intricate carvings and decorations, offer insights into the rituals performed to honor deities and maintain cosmic order.

The preservation of ancient Egyptian artifacts in museums around the world has allowed for their study, analysis, and public display. These artifacts include statues, amulets, jewelry, ritual objects, and everyday items that provide a glimpse into the religious practices and symbolism of ancient Egypt. The meticulous craftsmanship and attention to detail in these artifacts reveal the importance of aesthetics and symbolism in ancient Egyptian religious expression.

The rediscovery of ancient Egyptian spirituality in modern times has had a profound impact on our understanding of religious and spiritual thought throughout history. The profound influence of ancient Egyptian beliefs can be observed in various fields, including modern esoteric traditions, occult practices, and even contemporary popular culture. Concepts and symbols associated with ancient Egyptian spirituality, such as the Eye of Horus, Ankh, and various gods and goddesses, continue to resonate with people today, illustrating the enduring legacy of this ancient civilization.

Moreover, the study of ancient Egyptian spirituality offers valuable insights into the development of human spirituality as a whole. It allows us to trace the evolution of religious and spiritual thought, understand the diversity of beliefs and practices across cultures and time periods, and recognize the universal human quest for meaning, transcendence, and connection with the divine.

In conclusion, the preservation and rediscovery of ancient Egyptian artifacts, texts, and monuments have provided a wealth of knowledge about the religious beliefs and practices of this ancient civilization. These discoveries have deepened our understanding of ancient Egyptian spirituality, its historical and cultural significance, and its enduring impact on human spirituality. By exploring the connections between ancient Egypt and modern spirituality, we gain insights into the rich tapestry of human spiritual expression and the timeless quest for understanding and transcendence.

Source of Wisdom and Symbolism:

Ancient Egyptian spirituality is replete with profound wisdom, symbolic imagery, and esoteric knowledge that has captivated scholars, mystics, and seekers for centuries. By delving into the cosmological concepts, creation myths, and intricate pantheon of deities, we gain access to a vast reservoir of symbolic language and archetypal imagery. This exploration not only deepens our understanding of ancient Egyptian spirituality but also provides a valuable lens through which we can interpret and engage with various spiritual traditions in the modern world.

Ancient Egyptian spirituality serves as a remarkable source of wisdom, offering profound insights into the nature of existence, the human condition, and our relationship with the divine. Within the intricate tapestry of ancient Egyptian beliefs, we find a wealth of symbolic imagery and esoteric knowledge that continues to captivate scholars, mystics, and seekers in their quest for deeper spiritual understanding.

✧   Cosmological Concepts:

Ancient Egyptian cosmology presents a complex and interconnected worldview that embraces the interplay between the physical and spiritual realms. The concept of Ma'at, the fundamental principle of order, balance, and harmony, serves as a guiding force in the understanding of the universe and human existence. By exploring the cosmological concepts of ancient Egypt, we gain insight into the interconnectedness of all things and the inherent wisdom embedded in the natural world.

✧   Creation Myths and Mythological Narratives:

The creation myths of ancient Egypt offer profound symbolism and metaphorical narratives that shed light on the origin and purpose of life. Through the exploration of these myths, such as the Heliopolitan Ennead or the Hermopolitan Ogdoad, we encounter archetypal characters and symbolic motifs that resonate with universal themes of birth, transformation, and cosmic cycles. These myths provide a rich tapestry of symbolism that can be interpreted and applied to various spiritual traditions and personal journeys.

Exploring the Esoteric Wisdom of Ancient Egypt for Modern Spirituality

✧   The Pantheon of Deities:

The ancient Egyptian pantheon comprises a diverse array of gods and goddesses, each embodying specific qualities, powers, and archetypal energies. By studying the descriptions, roles, and interrelationships of these deities, we gain insight into the multifaceted aspects of the human psyche and the forces at play within the universe. The symbolic associations, iconography, and rituals associated with each deity offer a profound language through which we can explore and understand the depths of our own spiritual and psychological landscapes.

✧   Archetypal Imagery and Symbolism:

Ancient Egyptian spirituality is characterized by a rich tapestry of symbolic imagery, ranging from hieroglyphs and sacred geometries to animal symbolism and ritual objects. These symbols, deeply rooted in the cultural and natural landscapes of ancient Egypt, carry profound meaning and serve as gateways to deeper levels of understanding. By unraveling the symbolic language of ancient Egypt, we can gain insights into the universal and timeless aspects of the human experience, transcending cultural boundaries and connecting with the collective consciousness.

✧   Modern Relevance and Interpretation:

The wisdom and symbolism of ancient Egyptian spirituality continue to resonate in the modern world. Scholars, practitioners, and spiritual seekers draw upon these ancient teachings to enrich their own spiritual paths, deepen their understanding of symbolism, and explore the depths of consciousness. The archetypal imagery and esoteric knowledge found in ancient Egypt provide a framework for interpreting and engaging with various spiritual traditions, such as witchcraft, divination, herbalism, shamanism, and ecospirituality, fostering a rich cross-pollination of ideas and practices.

By delving into the source of wisdom and symbolism within ancient Egyptian spirituality, we unlock a treasure trove of insights and transformative possibilities. The exploration of cosmological concepts, creation myths, the pantheon of deities, and archetypal symbolism not only enriches our understanding of ancient Egypt but also offers a profound framework for personal and collective spiritual growth. Through the lens of ancient Egyptian wisdom, we are encouraged to embrace the interconnectedness of all things, delve into the depths of symbolism, and uncover the timeless truths that transcend cultural and temporal boundaries.

Influence on Modern Spiritual Practices:

Despite the passage of millennia, the wisdom of ancient Egypt continues to resonate within contemporary spiritual practices. The ideas, rituals, and symbolism of ancient Egypt have found their way into various fields, including Witchcraft, Divination, Herbalism, Shamanism, and Ecospirituality. By examining the connection between ancient Egypt and these modern practices, we gain a profound appreciation for the enduring influence of this ancient wisdom. This exploration allows us to draw parallels, trace the lineage of certain practices, and understand the underlying threads that connect diverse spiritual paths.

✧ Universal Themes and Human Experience:

At its core, the study of ancient Egyptian spirituality unveils universal themes and sheds light on the timeless aspects of the human experience. From the quest for immortality and the exploration of the afterlife to the search for divine connection and the significance of rituals, these ancient teachings touch upon fundamental human questions and yearnings. By engaging with the ancient Egyptian worldview, we develop a deeper understanding of our own spiritual yearnings and the universal quest for meaning and transcendence.

✧ Cultivating a Holistic Perspective:

Exploring the connection between ancient Egypt and modern spirituality encourages a holistic perspective that transcends cultural and temporal boundaries. It prompts us to view spiritual traditions as interconnected, influencing and enriching one another throughout history. This holistic approach fosters a deep appreciation for the diversity of spiritual expressions while recognizing the underlying unity that binds all human spiritual endeavors. By understanding the connection between ancient Egypt and modern spirituality, we foster a sense of interconnectedness and develop a more inclusive and comprehensive view of the spiritual landscape.

In conclusion, the exploration of the connection between ancient Egypt and modern spirituality holds immense significance in unraveling the mysteries of human spirituality and deepening our understanding of its timeless wisdom. By delving into the historical, cultural, and symbolic dimensions of ancient Egyptian spirituality, we illuminate the path toward a more profound engagement with spiritual traditions in the modern world. This exploration allows us to bridge the gap between ancient wisdom and contemporary practices, fostering a holistic perspective and empowering individuals on their spiritual journey.

Overview of the themes and topics covered in subsequent chapters

In the following chapters of this book, we embark on an intellectual and spiritual journey through the ancient wisdom of Egypt, exploring the timeless connection between this ancient civilization and modern spirituality. Each chapter delves into specific themes and topics, shedding light on the intricate tapestry of beliefs, rituals, and practices that defined the spiritual landscape of ancient Egypt. Through a meticulous examination of historical, cultural, and religious aspects, we unravel the significance of this ancient civilization and its enduring influence on various facets of human thought and spiritual expression.

Chapter 1: Purpose of the Book

In this introductory chapter, we establish the purpose and objectives of this book, providing an overview of the forthcoming exploration into the esoteric wisdom of ancient Egypt. We set the stage for a comprehensive examination of the connections between ancient Egypt and modern spirituality, emphasizing the relevance and significance of this study for contemporary seekers.

Chapter 2: Importance of Studying Ancient Religions and Their Influence on Modern Spirituality

Building upon the introductory chapter, this section explores the broader context of studying ancient religions and their impact on contemporary spiritual practices. Drawing upon examples from various fields, such as witchcraft, divination, herbalism, shamanism, and ecospirituality, we highlight the cross-cultural exchange and the transformative power of ancient wisdom in shaping modern spiritual paths.

Chapter 3: Brief Overview of Ancient Egypt and Its Religious Beliefs

Here, we embark on a journey through time, providing a concise yet comprehensive overview of ancient Egypt, its historical development, and the religious beliefs that permeated its society. We delve into the cosmological concepts, the social and political contexts, and the intricate tapestry of myth and symbolism that characterized ancient Egyptian spirituality.

Chapter 4: Historical and Cultural Context

Expanding upon the previous chapter, this section delves deeper into the historical and cultural context of ancient Egypt. We explore the impact of geography, society, and politics on religious beliefs, shedding light on the interplay between the physical environment and the spiritual worldview of the ancient Egyptians. Through this exploration, we gain a deeper understanding of the factors that shaped and influenced their religious practices.

Chapter 5: Influence of Geography, Society, and Politics on Religious Beliefs

This chapter focuses specifically on the influence of geographical factors, societal structures, and political dynamics on the religious beliefs of ancient Egypt. We examine how the Nile River, the desert landscape, and the agricultural practices of the region influenced their cosmology, rituals, and spiritual worldview. Additionally, we analyze the societal hierarchies and political systems that shaped the roles of priests, pharaohs, and the general populace in religious practices.

Chapter 6: Role of Pharaohs and Priests in Religious Practices

Expanding upon the discussion of societal roles, this section delves into the intricate interplay between pharaohs and priests in ancient Egyptian religious practices. We explore the divine kingship, the pharaoh's role as a conduit between the gods and the people, and the rituals and religious responsibilities associated with their leadership. Additionally, we examine the crucial role of priests in temple rituals, offerings, and the preservation of religious knowledge.

Chapter 7: Creation Myths and Cosmology

Ancient Egyptian creation myths offer profound insights into their cosmological understanding and provide a foundation for their spiritual beliefs. In this chapter, we analyze the creation narratives, exploring the symbolism, archetypal motifs, and the inherent wisdom embedded within these myths. Through a comprehensive examination of cosmology and creation, we deepen our understanding of the ancient Egyptian worldview and its implications for modern spirituality.

Each subsequent chapter builds upon these foundational themes, unraveling the mysteries of ancient Egypt's religious practices, deities, rituals, and their enduring influence on neighboring civilizations and contemporary spiritual thought. Through examples, problems, and exercises, we encourage students to engage in critical thinking, fostering a deep understanding and appreciation of the profound wisdom encapsulated within the ancient Egyptian spiritual tradition. By examining dissenting opinions and counterarguments, we ensure a balanced and objective exploration, allowing students to develop a well-rounded perspective on the subject matter.

Chapter 2: Importance of Studying Ancient Religions and their Influence on Modern Spirituality

Chapter 2 delves into the profound significance of studying ancient religions and their enduring influence on modern spirituality. As students of the esoteric wisdom, it is essential to recognize the intrinsic value of delving into the ancient past to unravel the mysteries that shape our present spiritual landscape. By examining the diverse realms of witchcraft, divination, herbalism, shamanism, and ecospirituality, we gain a comprehensive understanding of the cross-cultural exchange and the transformative power embedded within ancient religious traditions.

In this chapter, we embark on a journey that transcends time and space, exploring the interconnectedness of ancient wisdom and contemporary spiritual paths. Through a rigorous examination of ancient religions, we unearth the foundational principles, sacred rituals, and profound insights that have shaped the evolution of human spirituality. By analyzing their influence on various fields of modern spiritual practices, we gain a deeper appreciation for the wealth of knowledge and inspiration inherited from our ancestors.

Recognizing the Cross-Cultural Exchange:

One of the key reasons to study ancient religions is to recognize the cross-cultural exchange and the universal aspects of human spirituality. Throughout history, spiritual ideas and practices have transcended geographical boundaries, influencing and being influenced by diverse cultures. By studying the ancient religious traditions of Egypt and other civilizations, we uncover the interconnectedness of spiritual beliefs, rituals, and symbols across different cultures. This broader perspective fosters a sense of unity and promotes intercultural understanding, laying the groundwork for an inclusive and holistic approach to modern spirituality.

The study of ancient religions, including ancient Egyptian spirituality, allows us to recognize the cross-cultural exchange that has taken place throughout history. Spiritual ideas and practices have never been confined within the borders of a single culture or civilization. Instead, they have flowed and evolved through contact, interaction, and cultural exchange between different societies.

Ancient Egypt, with its strategic location at the crossroads of Africa, Asia, and Europe, served as a cultural and commercial hub, facilitating the exchange of ideas and beliefs with neighboring civilizations. The Nile River, often referred to as the "lifeblood" of Egypt, was not only a vital source of sustenance but also a thoroughfare for trade and cultural interchange. Through these interactions, ancient Egypt had the opportunity to both influence and be influenced by the beliefs and practices of other cultures.

One notable example of cross-cultural exchange is the syncretism that occurred between ancient Egyptian spirituality and the religious traditions of neighboring civilizations. As Egypt expanded its influence and came into contact with other cultures through trade, conquest, and diplomacy, there was a blending of deities, rituals, and religious concepts. Egyptian gods and goddesses were sometimes assimilated into the pantheons of other cultures, and vice versa. This syncretism demonstrates how spiritual ideas transcend cultural boundaries and evolve through interaction.

For instance, during the period of Egyptian rule in Nubia, the beliefs and practices of ancient Egypt merged with local Nubian religious traditions, giving rise to a unique syncretic form of spirituality. Similarly, the interaction between ancient Egypt and the Near East resulted in the assimilation of Egyptian deities, such as Isis and Osiris, into the religious fabric of Mesopotamia and Canaan.

The recognition of cross-cultural exchange in ancient religions helps us understand the universal aspects of human spirituality. While specific beliefs and practices may vary across cultures, there are often underlying themes and commonalities that connect different traditions. Shared symbols, rituals, and concepts can be found across diverse spiritual systems, highlighting the fundamental human quest for meaning, transcendence, and connection with the divine.

Studying ancient religions in a cross-cultural context promotes intercultural understanding and fosters a sense of unity. It encourages us to move beyond the boundaries of our own cultural perspectives and appreciate the richness and diversity of spiritual expression throughout history. By recognizing the interconnectedness of ancient Egyptian spirituality with other ancient traditions, we gain a broader perspective on the human experience and develop a more inclusive and holistic approach to modern spirituality.

In conclusion, the study of ancient religions, such as ancient Egyptian spirituality, enables us to recognize the cross-cultural exchange that has shaped human spirituality throughout history. By exploring the interactions, syncretism, and shared themes across different cultures, we gain a deeper understanding of the universal aspects of human spiritual expression. This broader perspective fosters intercultural understanding, unity, and an inclusive approach to modern spirituality.

Example: Analyzing the influence of ancient Egyptian cosmology on contemporary practices of divination in witchcraft and tarot reading. Exploring the shared archetypal symbols and metaphysical principles that transcend cultural boundaries.

Problem/Exercise: Compare and contrast the concepts of divination in ancient Egyptian religion and contemporary witchcraft. Analyze the underlying principles and symbols, and discuss their relevance in modern divinatory practices.

Uncovering Ancient Wisdom and Timeless Truths:

Studying ancient religions allows us to tap into the wealth of wisdom and timeless truths embedded within their sacred texts, rituals, and teachings. The spiritual insights garnered from these traditions provide profound guidance and nourishment for our own spiritual journeys. By immersing ourselves in the myths, rituals, and philosophical underpinnings of ancient religions, we gain access to a treasury of knowledge that offers solace, inspiration, and transformative potential.

The study of ancient religions unveils a vast repository of ancient wisdom and timeless truths that continue to resonate with us today. These ancient traditions, including ancient Egyptian spirituality, hold valuable insights into the human condition, the nature of existence, and our relationship with the divine.

Sacred texts and scriptures form the backbone of many ancient religious traditions. Through their narratives, myths, and teachings, these texts convey profound truths and philosophical reflections on the mysteries of life, death, and the nature of reality. For example, the Egyptian Book of the Dead, a compilation of spells and rituals intended to guide the deceased through the afterlife, offers insights into the ancient Egyptians' understanding of the soul, the journey of the dead, and the role of ethical conduct in the afterlife.

Rituals and ceremonies performed in ancient religious contexts also hold immense significance. These rituals were often designed to create a sacred space and establish a connection between the human and the divine. By participating in these ancient rituals, we tap into the collective wisdom of our ancestors and engage in a transformative experience that transcends time and cultural boundaries. For instance, the rituals surrounding the worship of Egyptian deities, such as the daily offerings made to the gods or the grand processions during religious festivals, reflect the ancient Egyptians' desire to commune with the divine and seek blessings and guidance.

Furthermore, the philosophical underpinnings of ancient religious traditions offer profound insights into the nature of existence, morality, and the purpose of life. Ancient Egyptian spirituality, for example, emphasized the concept of ma'at, which encompassed notions of truth, justice, balance, and harmony. The pursuit of ma'at guided individuals to lead ethical lives and maintain social order. This emphasis on ethical conduct and the interconnectedness of all beings remains relevant today, providing us with valuable principles for leading meaningful and responsible lives.

By delving into the wisdom of ancient religions, we access a timeless wellspring of spiritual guidance. The insights gained from these ancient traditions can inspire personal reflection, foster moral development, and ignite a deeper understanding of our place in the world. They offer solace during times of uncertainty, provide inspiration for personal growth, and invite us to contemplate profound existential questions.

Moreover, the universality of these truths is evident when we recognize the commonalities among different ancient religious traditions. Although cultural and historical contexts may differ, the underlying quest for meaning, the exploration of the human-divine relationship, and the recognition of fundamental ethical principles are shared aspects of human spirituality. By studying these ancient traditions, we are able to uncover the timeless truths that transcend temporal and cultural boundaries.

In conclusion, the study of ancient religions allows us to uncover ancient wisdom and timeless truths that are still relevant today. Through sacred texts, rituals, and philosophical underpinnings, we gain access to profound insights into the human condition and our relationship with the divine. These insights provide guidance, inspiration, and transformative potential for our own spiritual journeys. By tapping into the wisdom of our ancestors, we are able to engage with a rich legacy of spiritual knowledge and apply it to our lives in meaningful and transformative ways.

Example: Exploring the wisdom teachings of ancient Egyptian texts, such as the Book of the Dead, and their relevance in modern spiritual growth and self-transformation practices.

Problem/Exercise: Analyze a selected passage from an ancient Egyptian text, decipher its symbolic meaning, and discuss how its wisdom can be applied to personal spiritual development in the present day.

Tracing the Historical and Cultural Lineage:

Ancient religions provide us with a historical and cultural lineage that informs our understanding of the evolution of human spirituality. By studying the religious beliefs and practices of ancient civilizations, such as Egypt, we gain insights into the social, political, and environmental factors that shaped their spiritual worldview. This historical contextualization not only deepens our appreciation for the richness and diversity of human spiritual expression but also sheds light on the cultural and societal transformations that have influenced our present-day beliefs and practices.

Tracing the historical and cultural lineage of ancient religions, such as ancient Egyptian spirituality, allows us to explore the intricate tapestry of human spiritual development throughout the ages. By examining the religious beliefs and practices of ancient civilizations, we gain a comprehensive understanding of the historical context in which these traditions emerged and evolved.

The study of ancient religions unveils a fascinating window into the social, political, and environmental factors that shaped the spiritual worldview of ancient peoples. For instance, in the case of ancient Egypt, the Nile River and the surrounding landscape played a pivotal role in the development of their religious beliefs and practices. The annual flooding of the Nile, which brought fertility and sustenance to the land, became intertwined with their understanding of divine benevolence and cosmic harmony. The agricultural cycles and celestial events influenced their religious festivals, rituals, and even their perception of the gods and goddesses associated with natural phenomena. Through this lens, we can discern the profound influence of geographical features and environmental conditions on the religious imagination of ancient Egyptians.

Furthermore, studying the historical and cultural lineage of ancient religions allows us to trace the influence of conquests, cultural exchanges, and trade routes on spiritual beliefs and practices. Ancient civilizations were not isolated entities but interconnected through various forms of contact and exchange. The interaction between different cultures led to syncretism, the blending of religious ideas and practices, and the assimilation of deities and rituals. For example, the conquest of Egypt by Alexander the Great brought Hellenistic influences that infused Egyptian religious traditions with Greek philosophical concepts and mythological motifs. This cultural integration and syncretism shaped the development of religious thought and expression in ancient Egypt and beyond.

Understanding the historical and cultural lineage of ancient religions also illuminates the impact of societal transformations and shifts in power structures on spiritual beliefs and practices. For instance, the rise and fall of different dynasties in ancient Egypt resulted in changes in religious patronage, the prominence of specific deities, and the role of the priesthood. The religious landscape of ancient Egypt was intricately tied to the social hierarchies and political dynamics of the time. Exploring these aspects enables us to comprehend the complex interplay between religious authority, political power, and social structures, shedding light on the multifaceted nature of ancient religious traditions.

Moreover, tracing the historical and cultural lineage of ancient religions highlights the continuity and evolution of human spiritual expression. As we study the development of ancient religious beliefs and practices, we can identify threads of continuity that connect these traditions with modern-day spirituality. Concepts such as the quest for transcendence, ethical principles, and the human-divine relationship persist across time and cultural boundaries. Recognizing these commonalities deepens our understanding of the universality of human spiritual experiences and fosters intercultural dialogue and understanding.

In conclusion, tracing the historical and cultural lineage of ancient religions provides us with invaluable insights into the evolution of human spirituality. It allows us to contextualize the beliefs and practices of ancient civilizations, such as ancient Egypt, within their social, political, and environmental frameworks. By understanding the historical and cultural factors that influenced these traditions, we gain a more comprehensive understanding of the diversity and richness of human spiritual expression. Moreover, exploring the continuity and evolution of ancient religious beliefs and practices enhances our appreciation for the shared aspects of human spirituality that transcend time and cultural boundaries.

Example: Tracing the cultural lineage from ancient Egyptian religious festivals to contemporary neo-pagan celebrations, such as the modern reconstruction of the Festival of Opet.

Problem/Exercise: Research and analyze a specific religious festival from ancient Egypt and its modern reinterpretation. Discuss the cultural significance and transformations observed in the contemporary practice.

Nurturing a Critical and Reflective Perspective:

The study of ancient religions encourages critical thinking and reflection, fostering a nuanced understanding of the complexities and nuances within different spiritual traditions. By examining ancient beliefs and practices, we develop the ability to evaluate and interpret spiritual information, discerning the valuable insights while remaining aware of cultural biases and limitations. This cultivated discernment enables us to navigate the vast landscape of modern spirituality with a discerning eye and an open heart.

Nurturing a critical and reflective perspective is a fundamental aspect of studying ancient religions, as it empowers us to engage with spiritual information in a discerning and thoughtful manner. By delving into the beliefs and practices of ancient civilizations, such as Egypt, we develop the capacity to critically evaluate and interpret spiritual concepts, rituals, and texts.

One of the primary benefits of cultivating a critical perspective is the ability to discern valuable insights from ancient traditions while recognizing the influence of cultural biases and limitations. Ancient religious texts and artifacts are products of their time and cultural context, shaped by the beliefs, values, and social structures of the ancient societies that produced them. When studying these materials, it is essential to approach them with a critical eye, recognizing the potential for bias, symbolism, and metaphorical language. By adopting a critical perspective, we can discern the underlying universal truths and wisdom within these texts while remaining mindful of the cultural lenses through which they were transmitted.

Moreover, cultivating a critical and reflective perspective encourages us to explore the diversity and multiplicity of spiritual beliefs and practices. Ancient religions were not monolithic entities but comprised a myriad of interpretations, variations, and regional differences. By critically examining these variations, we develop a more comprehensive understanding of the nuances and complexities within different spiritual traditions. This nuanced perspective allows us to move beyond generalizations and stereotypes, appreciating the rich tapestry of human spiritual expression and the multiplicity of paths to transcendence.

A critical and reflective perspective also encourages us to engage in self-reflection and personal inquiry. By studying ancient religions, we are prompted to examine our own beliefs, assumptions, and biases, fostering a deeper understanding of our own spiritual journey. It encourages us to question and challenge our preconceived notions, inviting us to explore alternative perspectives and embrace intellectual and spiritual growth. Through critical self-reflection, we can discern the value and relevance of ancient wisdom in our own lives and make informed choices about our spiritual path.

Furthermore, a critical and reflective perspective fosters a sense of humility and open-mindedness. It reminds us that our understanding of spirituality is always evolving and subject to revision. Ancient religions provide us with historical and cultural context that challenges our assumptions and expands our horizons. By approaching the study of ancient religions with an open mind and a willingness to question our own beliefs, we create space for personal and intellectual growth. This receptiveness to new ideas and perspectives allows us to engage in fruitful dialogue with others and contribute to the ongoing evolution of spiritual thought.

In conclusion, nurturing a critical and reflective perspective is a vital aspect of studying ancient religions. It enables us to evaluate and interpret spiritual information in a discerning and thoughtful manner, recognizing the valuable insights while remaining aware of cultural biases and limitations. By fostering critical thinking, we navigate the complexities and nuances within different spiritual traditions, appreciating their diversity and multiplicity. This perspective also prompts self-reflection and personal inquiry, inviting us to question and examine our own beliefs and assumptions. Ultimately, a critical and reflective perspective nurtures humility, open-mindedness, and intellectual growth, fostering a deeper understanding of ourselves and the world around us.

Example: Analyzing the controversies surrounding the appropriation of ancient Egyptian symbols and rituals in modern spiritual practices and exploring the ethical implications involved.

Problem/Exercise: Engage in a group discussion on the ethical considerations of incorporating ancient religious symbols and practices into contemporary spiritual traditions. Present arguments for and against the practice, and propose strategies for respectful and responsible integration.

By delving into the importance of studying ancient religions and their influence on modern spirituality, this chapter sets the stage for a comprehensive exploration of the profound connections between the ancient wisdom of Egypt and the diverse paths of contemporary spiritual seekers. Through examples, problems, and exercises, students are invited to engage in critical thinking and discussions that foster a deeper understanding and appreciation of the subject matter.

Examination of the relevance and value of studying ancient religions in the context of contemporary spiritual practices

In the pursuit of understanding and navigating the complexities of contemporary spirituality, it is crucial to recognize the relevance and value of studying ancient religions. The study of these ancient traditions provides a solid foundation for exploring the roots, principles, and transformative practices that have shaped human spirituality throughout history. By delving into the ancient religious beliefs and practices of diverse civilizations, such as Witchcraft, Divination, Herbalism, Shamanism, and Ecospirituality, students are equipped with a comprehensive toolkit to critically examine and enrich their own spiritual paths.

Illuminating the Origins and Evolution of Spiritual Concepts:

Studying ancient religions allows us to trace the origins and evolution of spiritual concepts that have endured and transformed over time. By examining the ancient roots of contemporary practices, we gain insights into the underlying principles and philosophies that continue to shape spiritual beliefs and rituals. Understanding the historical context and cultural influences that gave rise to these concepts enables us to engage with them in a more informed and nuanced manner, fostering a deeper appreciation for the richness and diversity of spiritual thought.

Illuminating the origins and evolution of spiritual concepts is a key benefit of studying ancient religions. By delving into the beliefs and practices of ancient civilizations, we can trace the historical roots of contemporary spiritual ideas and uncover the transformative journey these concepts have undertaken over time.

Ancient religions serve as foundational sources for many of the spiritual concepts and principles that persist in various forms today. These concepts, such as the existence of a higher power, the quest for transcendence, the exploration of human consciousness, and the pursuit of ethical living, have their origins in the ancient world. By studying the religious beliefs and practices of ancient civilizations, such as Egypt, we gain a deeper understanding of the historical and cultural context in which these concepts emerged.

Furthermore, exploring the origins of spiritual concepts allows us to recognize the cultural and societal influences that shaped their development. Ancient religions were not isolated belief systems but were influenced by the social, political, and environmental factors of their time. For example, the ancient

Egyptian concept of Ma'at, which encompassed notions of cosmic order, justice, and harmony, emerged in a society where maintaining stability and balance was paramount. Recognizing these influences allows us to appreciate the multifaceted nature of spiritual concepts and understand their diverse interpretations across different cultures and historical periods.

Studying the evolution of spiritual concepts also reveals the dynamic nature of human spirituality. Over time, spiritual ideas have undergone transformations, adaptations, and syncretism as they encountered new cultures, exchanged ideas, and interacted with other belief systems. Ancient religions provide a historical timeline of these changes, showcasing the resilience and adaptability of spiritual thought. For example, the influence of ancient Egyptian religious concepts can be seen in the syncretic practices of Hellenistic Egypt, where Greek and Egyptian beliefs merged, giving rise to new religious expressions.

Moreover, understanding the historical development of spiritual concepts allows us to engage with them in a more informed and nuanced manner. By examining their ancient origins, we gain insights into the underlying principles, philosophies, and symbols that continue to resonate in contemporary spiritual practices. This knowledge enriches our understanding of the diverse ways in which spiritual concepts have been interpreted and applied throughout history, fostering a deeper appreciation for the complexity and richness of spiritual thought.

By illuminating the origins and evolution of spiritual concepts, studying ancient religions not only provides us with a historical perspective but also invites us to critically reflect on our own spiritual beliefs and practices. It encourages us to question the assumptions and preconceptions that underpin our understanding of spirituality, opening up avenues for personal growth and intellectual exploration. Ultimately, this knowledge enables us to engage with spiritual concepts in a more meaningful and transformative way, fostering a deeper connection with ourselves, others, and the transcendent dimensions of existence.

Example: Analyzing the concept of divination in ancient Egyptian religion and its modern interpretations in practices such as Tarot reading or scrying. Exploring the evolution of divinatory techniques and the underlying principles shared across different cultures.

Problem/Exercise: Research and compare divination practices in ancient Egyptian religion and modern Tarot reading. Discuss the similarities, differences, and the implications for contemporary divinatory practices.

Extracting Universal Principles and Wisdom:

Ancient religious traditions often contain universal principles and wisdom that transcend specific cultural or historical contexts. By studying these traditions, students can extract valuable insights and timeless wisdom that can be applied to contemporary spiritual practices. The exploration of ancient texts, myths, and rituals provides a reservoir of profound teachings, symbolisms, and archetypal imagery that resonate across cultures and time periods. Integrating this ancient wisdom into modern spiritual practices fosters a deeper understanding of oneself, the world, and the interconnectedness of all beings.

Extracting universal principles and wisdom from ancient religious traditions is a profound aspect of studying these traditions. While these traditions emerged in specific cultural and historical contexts, they often contain teachings and insights that transcend those boundaries and hold relevance for people across different cultures and time periods.

Ancient religious texts, such as the Egyptian Book of the Dead or the Vedas of Hinduism, serve as repositories of wisdom that offer guidance on fundamental questions of human existence, morality, and the nature of the divine. These texts present philosophical and ethical principles that address universal human concerns, such as the pursuit of truth, the quest for meaning, and the cultivation of virtues like compassion, wisdom, and integrity. By studying and reflecting upon these texts, students gain access to a vast wellspring of knowledge that speaks to the perennial questions of human existence.

Myths and symbolic imagery found in ancient religious traditions also offer universal insights and wisdom. Myths often convey archetypal themes and narratives that reflect fundamental aspects of the human experience. They explore themes of creation, transformation, the hero's journey, and the search for enlightenment, providing universal frameworks through which individuals can understand and navigate their own personal journeys. By analyzing and interpreting these myths, students can extract timeless wisdom that resonates with their own lives, fostering personal growth and self-discovery.

Ritual practices within ancient religions also hold valuable lessons and teachings. Rituals are often designed to evoke a sense of connection with the divine, foster inner transformation, and establish a harmonious relationship with the world. These practices can teach individuals about the power of intention, the importance of mindfulness, and the potential for personal and collective healing. By exploring the rituals of ancient religions, students can gain insights into the transformative potential of ritual practices and incorporate elements of these practices into their own spiritual journeys.

Integrating the universal principles and wisdom extracted from ancient religious traditions into contemporary spiritual practices offers numerous benefits. It provides a broader perspective that goes beyond the limitations of a single culture or tradition, fostering a more inclusive and holistic approach to spirituality. By recognizing the common threads and shared insights across different religious traditions, students can develop a deeper appreciation for the interconnectedness of spiritual beliefs and practices.

Moreover, the integration of ancient wisdom into modern spiritual practices enriches and enlivens these practices. It allows individuals to tap into the collective wisdom of humanity, drawing from the experiences and insights of countless generations that have sought to understand the nature of reality, the purpose of life, and the possibilities for personal growth and transformation. This integration can bring depth, meaning, and a sense of connectedness to contemporary spiritual practices, empowering individuals to cultivate a more profound and authentic spiritual path.

In conclusion, the study of ancient religious traditions offers students the opportunity to extract universal principles and wisdom that transcend cultural and historical contexts. By exploring ancient texts, myths, and rituals, students gain access to profound teachings and insights that can enrich their contemporary spiritual practices and foster a deeper understanding of themselves and the world around them. This integration of ancient wisdom nurtures a more expansive and transformative spiritual journey, fostering personal growth, interconnectedness, and a deeper sense of purpose and meaning in life.

Example: Exploring the concept of sacred plants and their ritual use in ancient shamanic traditions and their relevance in modern herbalism and plant-based spiritual practices.

Problem/Exercise: Investigate the historical use of a sacred plant in an ancient shamanic tradition and its contemporary applications in herbalism and plant-based spirituality. Reflect on the symbolic significance of the plant and discuss its potential benefits and challenges in modern practices.

Cultivating a Historical and Cultural Perspective:

Studying ancient religions cultivates a historical and cultural perspective, allowing students to critically examine the socio-cultural contexts in which spiritual beliefs and practices originated. By understanding the historical nuances and cultural factors that shaped ancient religious traditions, students can approach their own spiritual journeys with a more nuanced understanding of the biases, limitations, and diversity present within different spiritual systems. This historical and cultural awareness promotes cultural sensitivity, inclusivity, and respectful engagement with diverse spiritual traditions.

Cultivating a historical and cultural perspective is a crucial aspect of studying ancient religions. It involves delving into the historical and socio-cultural contexts in which these religions emerged, flourished, and evolved. By gaining a deep understanding of these contexts, students can develop a more nuanced and informed perspective on spiritual beliefs and practices.

Studying the historical background of ancient religions allows students to situate these traditions within specific time periods and civilizations. They can explore the social, political, economic, and environmental factors that influenced the development of these religions. For example, understanding the political dynamics of ancient Egypt or the cultural interactions of the Hellenistic period in Greece provides insights into the shaping of religious beliefs and practices during those times.

Moreover, exploring the cultural aspects of ancient religions helps students recognize the diversity and complexity within different spiritual systems. Ancient religions were not monolithic entities but comprised a wide array of beliefs, rituals, and practices that varied across regions, social classes, and historical periods. By studying the cultural context, students can appreciate the multiplicity of interpretations, mythologies, and ritual practices within a given religious tradition.

Cultivating a historical and cultural perspective also allows students to critically examine the biases, limitations, and evolving nature of ancient religious traditions. They can analyze the societal structures, power dynamics, and social hierarchies that influenced the formulation and transmission of religious ideas. By engaging in such analysis, students develop a more nuanced understanding of the strengths and shortcomings of ancient religions, as well as the social and cultural influences that shaped their beliefs and practices.

By understanding the historical and cultural contexts of ancient religions, students can approach their own spiritual journeys with greater awareness and sensitivity. They can recognize the diversity of spiritual beliefs and practices present in the world today and appreciate the historical and cultural factors that have shaped them. This perspective encourages students to engage with diverse spiritual traditions in a respectful and inclusive manner, valuing the contributions and insights they offer.

Furthermore, a historical and cultural perspective fosters critical thinking skills, enabling students to question assumptions, challenge stereotypes, and evaluate the impact of cultural biases on their own beliefs and practices. By critically examining ancient religious traditions in their historical and cultural contexts, students develop the ability to navigate the complexities and nuances of contemporary spirituality with a more discerning eye.

In conclusion, cultivating a historical and cultural perspective is essential in the study of ancient religions. It enables students to understand the historical nuances and socio-cultural factors that influenced the development of these traditions. By examining the biases, limitations, and cultural diversity within ancient religions, students develop a more nuanced and informed approach to their own spiritual journeys. This perspective promotes cultural sensitivity, inclusivity, and critical engagement with diverse spiritual traditions, fostering a deeper appreciation for the complexities of human spirituality.

Example: Investigating the role of cultural appropriation in modern spiritual practices, particularly the adoption of elements from indigenous traditions into mainstream spiritual movements.

Problem/Exercise: Engage in a group discussion on the ethical considerations of cultural appropriation in contemporary spiritual practices. Explore different perspectives and propose strategies for respectful and responsible engagement with diverse spiritual traditions.

Fostering Personal and Spiritual Growth:

The study of ancient religions fosters personal and spiritual growth by providing a broader perspective on the human experience and the potential paths to spiritual transformation. Through critical analysis and reflection, students can identify the underlying principles, rituals, and practices that resonate with their own spiritual aspirations and incorporate them into their personal journeys. The examination of ancient religions encourages introspection, self-discovery, and the cultivation of inner wisdom, empowering students to develop their unique spiritual paths with depth and authenticity.

Exploring the Esoteric Wisdom of Ancient Egypt for Modern Spirituality

Fostering personal and spiritual growth is a fundamental aspect of studying ancient religions. Through the exploration of ancient religious traditions, students are exposed to diverse perspectives, philosophies, and practices that can deeply resonate with their own spiritual aspirations and facilitate personal transformation.

One of the ways in which ancient religions contribute to personal and spiritual growth is through critical analysis and reflection. By engaging in a scholarly study of these traditions, students are encouraged to question, examine, and evaluate various aspects of ancient religious beliefs and practices. This process of critical thinking not only enhances their analytical skills but also invites them to reflect on their own spiritual beliefs, values, and experiences. It prompts them to contemplate the significance and purpose of their own spiritual journeys, leading to a deeper understanding of themselves and their relationship with the divine or the transcendent.

Furthermore, the study of ancient religions offers a rich tapestry of rituals, symbols, myths, and philosophies that can serve as sources of inspiration and guidance for personal spiritual growth. Students can explore the transformative potential embedded within ancient texts, rituals, and teachings. By immersing themselves in the wisdom and insights of these traditions, they can gain valuable insights into their own inner landscapes, uncovering new perspectives, and deepening their connection with the sacred.

The examination of ancient religions also encourages introspection and self-discovery. As students engage with the beliefs and practices of ancient civilizations, they are invited to reflect on their own values, beliefs, and experiences. This introspective process allows them to uncover and explore their own spiritual inclinations, desires, and challenges. By recognizing and embracing their unique spiritual journeys, students can cultivate a sense of authenticity and alignment with their inner selves.

Moreover, the study of ancient religions facilitates the cultivation of inner wisdom and spiritual depth. Ancient religious traditions often emphasize the importance of inner transformation, ethical living, and the pursuit of wisdom. By studying the wisdom teachings and philosophical frameworks of ancient civilizations, students can integrate these principles into their own lives. This integration can lead to personal growth, expanded consciousness, and a deepening sense of meaning and purpose.

In summary, the study of ancient religions fosters personal and spiritual growth by offering diverse perspectives, critical analysis, and opportunities for introspection. It encourages students to question and evaluate their own spiritual beliefs and values, while also providing inspiration and guidance for their spiritual journeys. Through this process, students can cultivate authenticity, align with their inner selves, and develop a deeper understanding of themselves and the mysteries of the divine or the transcendent. Ultimately, the study of ancient religions serves as a catalyst for personal transformation, enriching the lives of students and nurturing their spiritual growth.

Example: Reflecting on the concept of initiation and its significance in ancient mystery traditions, and exploring how initiation rituals can be adapted and integrated into modern spiritual practices.

Problem/Exercise: Design an initiation ritual for a contemporary spiritual tradition based on the principles and symbolism found in ancient mystery traditions. Discuss the potential transformative effects and ethical considerations of such a ritual.

Through the examination of the relevance and value of studying ancient religions in the context of contemporary spiritual practices, students are encouraged to critically engage with diverse spiritual traditions, identify universal principles, and apply them to their own spiritual journeys. By incorporating examples, problems, and exercises into the chapter, students are invited to explore these concepts in a hands-on and interactive manner, fostering critical thinking, self-reflection, and meaningful discussions.

Exploration of the enduring impact and influence of ancient Egyptian spirituality on modern belief systems and practices

The ancient Egyptian civilization, with its rich spiritual traditions and profound understanding of the divine, continues to exert a significant influence on modern belief systems and practices. The enduring impact of ancient Egyptian spirituality can be observed in various fields, ranging from Witchcraft, Divination, Herbalism, Shamanism, to Ecospirituality. By delving into the depths of this ancient wisdom, we unravel the threads that connect the past to the present, shedding light on the ways in which ancient Egyptian spirituality has shaped and continues to shape contemporary spiritual thought and practice.

Symbolism and Archetypal Imagery:

One of the key contributions of ancient Egyptian spirituality lies in its profound symbolism and archetypal imagery. The rich iconography of gods and goddesses, the intricate symbolism of hieroglyphs, and the cosmological concepts found in ancient Egyptian mythology have influenced and inspired modern belief systems. The use of symbolic language and archetypal imagery provides a framework for understanding the deeper layers of spiritual experiences, guiding practitioners in their quest for self-discovery, transformation, and connection to the divine.

Symbolism and archetypal imagery play a crucial role in ancient Egyptian spirituality, offering a profound and multi-layered language through which spiritual concepts and experiences are conveyed. The ancient Egyptians employed a rich array of symbols and archetypes to represent various aspects of the divine, the cosmos, and the human experience. These symbols and archetypes served as gateways to deeper understanding, inviting individuals to explore the mysteries of existence and forge a connection with the divine.

One of the primary forms of symbolism in ancient Egyptian spirituality is the iconography of gods and goddesses. Each deity was depicted with distinct physical attributes, animal forms, and symbolic objects, all of which carried deep meaning and conveyed specific aspects of their nature and power. For example, the falcon-headed god Horus symbolized kingship, protection, and the sky, while the lioness-headed goddess Sekhmet embodied power, healing, and destruction. These visual representations allowed ancient Egyptians to connect with and understand the divine forces at work in the world.

In addition to deities, hieroglyphs served as a powerful form of symbolic language in ancient Egypt. These intricate and stylized characters represented not only sounds and words but also abstract concepts and ideas. Hieroglyphic inscriptions found on temple walls, papyri, and other artifacts conveyed religious rituals, myths, prayers, and magical formulas. The symbolism within hieroglyphs allowed for multiple layers of meaning, inviting practitioners to delve deeper into the mysteries and esoteric teachings of their spiritual tradition.

Ancient Egyptian mythology also employed archetypal imagery, presenting narratives and stories that resonate with universal themes and psychological dynamics. These mythological narratives featured gods, goddesses, heroes, and mythical creatures, each representing specific archetypal qualities and embodying universal aspects of the human psyche. For example, the myth of Osiris and Isis illustrates themes of death, rebirth, and the eternal cycle of life, while the story of the sun god Ra traversing the underworld symbolizes the journey of the soul through different realms of existence. By engaging with these myths and their archetypal imagery, individuals could explore their own inner landscapes and navigate the challenges and transformations of their lives.

The use of symbolism and archetypal imagery in ancient Egyptian spirituality provided practitioners with a framework for understanding and experiencing the divine. These symbols and archetypes served as portals to deeper levels of consciousness, inviting individuals to embark on a journey of self-discovery, transformation, and spiritual connection. By engaging with these symbols and archetypes, practitioners could tap into universal patterns and truths that transcend time and culture, gaining insights into the mysteries of existence and their own spiritual nature.

In modern spirituality, the influence of ancient Egyptian symbolism and archetypal imagery can be observed in various traditions. The use of symbols, such as the ankh (the symbol of life) or the Eye of Horus (representing protection and wisdom), continues to resonate with individuals seeking spiritual meaning and connection. Furthermore, the exploration of archetypal themes and narratives, inspired by ancient Egyptian mythology, allows individuals to delve into the depths of their psyche and uncover universal truths about the human experience.

In conclusion, symbolism and archetypal imagery in ancient Egyptian spirituality provided a profound language through which spiritual concepts and experiences were conveyed. These symbols and archetypes facilitated a deeper understanding of the divine, the cosmos, and the human experience, inviting individuals to explore the mysteries of existence. The enduring influence of ancient Egyptian symbolism and archetypal imagery continues to inspire and guide spiritual seekers in their quest for self-discovery, transformation, and connection to the divine.

Example: Examining the symbolism of the Ankh, the ancient Egyptian symbol of life, and its adoption in modern spiritual practices as a symbol of vitality, connection, and eternal life.

Problem/Exercise: Reflect on the symbolism of a specific ancient Egyptian deity and explore its potential applications and interpretations in a contemporary spiritual context. Discuss the significance of symbolism in spiritual practices and its role in deepening personal connections to the divine.

Ritual Practices and Ceremony:

Ancient Egyptian spirituality was characterized by intricate and elaborate ritual practices aimed at establishing a connection with the divine and maintaining cosmic order. These rituals encompassed offerings, prayers, purification ceremonies, and temple worship. The enduring influence of ancient Egyptian ritual practices can be observed in contemporary spiritual traditions that emphasize the transformative power of ceremony and ritual, such as Wicca, ceremonial magic, and neo-paganism. The emphasis on intention, symbolism, and the harmonization of the individual with the natural and spiritual realms resonates with modern practitioners seeking to cultivate a deeper connection to the sacred.

Ritual practices and ceremony held significant importance in ancient Egyptian spirituality, serving as powerful means of establishing and maintaining a connection with the divine and aligning oneself with the cosmic forces. These rituals were performed by priests, priestesses, and individuals within sacred spaces such as temples or in private settings.

Offerings played a central role in ancient Egyptian rituals. Various items, such as food, drink, incense, and symbolic objects, were presented as offerings to the gods and goddesses. These offerings were believed to sustain and nourish the divine entities, reinforcing their presence and benevolence. They also acted as a form of reciprocity, as the gods were believed to bestow blessings and protection upon those who honored them with sincere offerings. The act of offering served as a way for individuals to express their devotion, gratitude, and desire for divine favor.

Prayers were another fundamental aspect of ancient Egyptian ritual practices. Prayers were uttered or recited to invoke the gods, seek their guidance, and express personal intentions and desires. These prayers were often accompanied by gestures, such as raising the hands or bowing the head, to demonstrate reverence and humility before the divine. The recitation of specific prayers, hymns, or magical formulas held both spiritual and protective significance, serving as a means to communicate with the gods and invoke their assistance in various aspects of life.

Purification ceremonies were an integral part of ancient Egyptian rituals, as they aimed to cleanse and purify individuals before engaging in sacred activities or approaching the divine. These ceremonies involved ritual washing, anointing with oils or perfumes, and the wearing of specific garments or amulets. Purification rituals were believed to remove physical and spiritual impurities, allowing individuals to approach the sacred with a state of spiritual purity and readiness.

Temple worship formed a central part of ancient Egyptian religious practices. Temples were considered the dwelling places of the gods and were designed as sacred spaces where individuals could commune with the divine. Within the temples, priests and priestesses performed elaborate rituals and ceremonies on behalf of the community. These rituals included processions, music, dance, and the reenactment of mythological narratives. The temple rituals were designed to maintain cosmic harmony, honor the gods, and ensure the well-being of both the individual and the society at large.

The influence of ancient Egyptian ritual practices can be observed in contemporary spiritual traditions that recognize the transformative power of ceremony and ritual. Practices such as Wicca, ceremonial magic, and neo-paganism draw inspiration from ancient Egyptian rituals, adapting and incorporating their elements into modern contexts. These traditions emphasize the intentional use of symbols, gestures, and sacred objects to create a sacred space and establish a connection with the divine. Contemporary practitioners recognize the potency of ritual practices in cultivating personal transformation, honoring the natural world, and fostering a deeper sense of spiritual connection.

In conclusion, ancient Egyptian spirituality embraced elaborate ritual practices and ceremonies as a means to establish a connection with the divine and uphold cosmic order. Offerings, prayers, purification ceremonies, and temple worship played significant roles in these rituals. The enduring influence of ancient Egyptian ritual practices can be seen in contemporary spiritual traditions that emphasize the transformative power of ceremony and ritual. By engaging in intentional and symbolic practices, modern practitioners seek to cultivate a deeper connection to the sacred, honor their spiritual path, and align themselves with the cosmic forces that govern the universe.

Example: Exploring the ritual practices associated with the ancient Egyptian New Year festival and their parallels in modern New Year ceremonies and intentions.

Problem/Exercise: Design a personal ritual based on ancient Egyptian principles and symbolism to mark a significant life transition or milestone. Reflect on the intentions and symbolism embedded within the ritual and discuss its potential impact on personal growth and transformation.

Wisdom and Spiritual Teachings:

Ancient Egyptian spirituality offers a wealth of wisdom and spiritual teachings that continue to inspire and inform modern belief systems. The concept of Ma'at, representing balance, harmony, and justice, remains a cornerstone of ethical principles in various spiritual paths. The exploration of ancient Egyptian texts, such as the Book of the Dead or the Pyramid Texts, provides profound insights into the nature of the soul, the journey of the deceased, and the interconnectedness of all beings. These teachings have found resonance in modern spiritual philosophies, providing guidance and inspiration for individuals seeking a deeper understanding of themselves and their place in the universe.

Ancient Egyptian spirituality is characterized by a profound wisdom that has stood the test of time. One of the central teachings that continues to resonate with modern seekers is the concept of Ma'at. Ma'at represents the fundamental principle of balance, harmony, and justice in the universe. It encompasses the idea that all aspects of existence are interconnected and that maintaining equilibrium in one's thoughts, actions, and relationships is essential for spiritual well-being. The concept of Ma'at emphasizes the importance of living a virtuous and ethical life, honoring truth, fairness, and compassion in all interactions.

The ancient Egyptian texts, such as the Book of the Dead or the Pyramid Texts, provide deep insights into the nature of the soul and the journey of the deceased in the afterlife. These texts offer guidance on navigating the challenges and trials of the spiritual realm and reveal the belief in the immortality of the soul. The wisdom contained within these texts speaks to the enduring human quest for understanding the mysteries of life and death, offering comfort and reassurance in the face of mortality.

Moreover, ancient Egyptian spirituality recognizes the interconnectedness of all beings and the unity of the cosmos. The concept of the divine as both immanent and transcendent is present in their teachings, emphasizing the inherent divinity within each individual and the interconnectedness between humanity, nature, and the gods. This recognition of the sacredness of all existence forms the foundation for a holistic and inclusive spiritual worldview that resonates with contemporary seekers.

The wisdom and spiritual teachings of ancient Egypt have influenced and inspired various modern belief systems. Their emphasis on balance, justice, and interconnectedness aligns with ecological spirituality, which recognizes the interdependence between humans and the natural world. The teachings also find resonance in New Age spirituality, where individuals seek to integrate ancient wisdom into their personal growth and transformation journeys.

By studying and engaging with the wisdom and spiritual teachings of ancient Egypt, modern seekers can gain a deeper understanding of themselves and their place in the universe. The insights and principles derived from these teachings offer guidance in navigating the complexities of life, fostering personal growth, and cultivating a deeper connection to the divine. The timeless wisdom of ancient Egyptian spirituality continues to inspire individuals on their spiritual paths, encouraging them to live with integrity, seek harmony, and embrace the interconnectedness of all beings.

Example: Investigating the concept of the Ka, the eternal spiritual essence, in ancient Egyptian spirituality and its parallels in the belief systems of modern metaphysical traditions.

Problem/Exercise: Analyze the ethical principles of Ma'at and its application in modern ethical frameworks. Discuss the challenges and benefits of integrating ancient Egyptian wisdom into contemporary spiritual practices.

The Book of the Dead:

The Book of the Dead, also known as the Book of Coming Forth by Day, is one of the most renowned and significant texts in ancient Egyptian spirituality. It consists of a collection of spells, rituals, and instructions that were believed to assist the deceased in navigating the afterlife and attaining eternal life. This sacred text provides valuable insights into the wisdom and spiritual teachings of ancient Egypt, shedding light on their beliefs about the nature of the soul, the journey of the deceased, and the principles governing the universe.

Nature of the Soul:

The Book of the Dead offers a profound understanding of the soul, or the spiritual essence of an individual. According to ancient Egyptian beliefs, the soul comprised several components, including the Ka, the Ba, and the Akh. The Ka represented the life force and vital energy of a person, while the Ba referred to the individual's personality and ability to move freely between the earthly and divine realms. The Akh represented the transformed and glorified state of the deceased, achieved through the successful completion of the afterlife journey.

Ancient Egyptian spirituality had a complex understanding of the nature of the soul, which is beautifully illustrated in texts such as the Book of the Dead. According to these beliefs, the soul was composed of various aspects that played distinct roles in the journey through life and into the afterlife.

The Ka was considered the life force or vital essence of an individual. It was often depicted as a spiritual double or guardian spirit that resided within the body during a person's lifetime. The Ka was believed to sustain and animate the physical body, and its well-being was essential for the individual's continued existence. After death, it was believed that the Ka would need to be cared for and nourished through offerings and rituals to ensure the deceased's well-being in the afterlife.

The Ba, on the other hand, can be understood as the personality or individuality of a person. It was believed to have the ability to move freely between the earthly realm and the divine realm. In the afterlife, the Ba was expected to reunite with the Ka and participate in the ongoing existence of the deceased. The Ba was depicted as a bird with a human head, symbolizing its ability to transcend earthly limitations and soar to spiritual heights.

Lastly, the Akh represented the transformed and glorified state of the deceased. It was the ultimate goal of the afterlife journey and was achieved through a successful passage and judgment in the divine realms. The Akh was considered an elevated and divine aspect of the soul, symbolizing the individual's attainment of immortality and unity with the gods. It represented the culmination of the spiritual journey and the reward for a virtuous and righteous life.

These complex beliefs about the nature of the soul highlight the ancient Egyptians' profound understanding of the multifaceted aspects of human existence and the continuation of life beyond death. The notion of the soul as a combination of the Ka, Ba, and Akh emphasizes the interconnectedness between the physical, spiritual, and divine realms. It reflects the belief that the soul, in its various aspects, continues its existence and undergoes transformation beyond the earthly plane.

The ancient Egyptian understanding of the soul has influenced spiritual and philosophical traditions throughout history. Concepts such as the immortal soul, the journey of the deceased, and the potential for transformation and transcendence continue to resonate with individuals seeking a deeper understanding of the nature of existence and the possibilities of the afterlife. The wisdom and insights derived from the ancient Egyptian beliefs about the soul provide a profound framework for contemplating the mysteries of life, death, and the eternal nature of the human spirit.

Example: The spell known as the "Weighing of the Heart" portrays the Egyptian concept of the soul being judged against the feather of Ma'at, the goddess of truth and justice. This judgment determined whether the soul was worthy of eternal life.

Problem/Exercise: Reflect on the components of the soul in ancient Egyptian belief and discuss their potential parallels or differences with concepts of the soul in other spiritual traditions. Explore the implications of the Weighing of the Heart ritual on personal moral and ethical considerations.

Journey of the Deceased:

The Book of the Dead provides detailed instructions and rituals to guide the deceased through the perilous journey of the afterlife. It describes the challenges and obstacles that the soul encounters, as well as the necessary preparations and rituals to overcome them. The journey involved navigating through various realms, including the Duat (the underworld), encountering different deities and guardians, and undergoing rituals of purification and transformation.

The ancient Egyptian belief in the journey of the deceased after death is a fascinating aspect of their spiritual tradition, as depicted in texts like the Book of the Dead. According to these beliefs, the soul embarked on a complex and perilous journey through the realms of the afterlife, known as the Duat.

The journey of the deceased was not a straightforward passage but involved navigating through multiple realms and encountering various challenges and obstacles along the way. The Duat was depicted as a mysterious and intricate realm, populated by different deities, guardians, and supernatural beings. Each realm had its own set of trials and tests that the soul had to overcome to progress towards its ultimate destination.

Throughout the journey, the deceased relied on the guidance of spells and rituals recorded in the Book of the Dead. These spells provided instructions on how to navigate the treacherous waters of the Duat, avoid malevolent spirits, and gain the favor of benevolent deities. The deceased had to recite the appropriate spells, known as "utterances," and perform the necessary rituals to ensure their safe passage and successful judgment in the afterlife.

Purification and transformation were essential aspects of the journey. The deceased had to undergo rituals of purification to cleanse themselves of impurities and sins committed during their earthly life. These rituals involved offerings, prayers, and symbolic gestures that symbolized the purification and renewal of the soul. By undergoing these transformative rituals, the deceased sought to attain a state of purity and righteousness necessary for a favorable judgment in the afterlife.

Encounters with various deities and guardians were also significant milestones in the journey. The deceased would encounter gods and goddesses who held the power to grant protection, guidance, and judgment. These encounters required the knowledge of appropriate spells and the correct performance of rituals to appease and gain the favor of these divine beings. It was believed that successful interactions with the deities could lead to the granting of blessings and the ultimate reward of eternal life.

The journey of the deceased, as depicted in the Book of the Dead, serves as a metaphorical and symbolic representation of the challenges and transformations that the soul undergoes in its quest for spiritual enlightenment and eternal existence. It emphasizes the importance of moral conduct, spiritual purification, and the understanding of divine wisdom in navigating the complexities of the afterlife.

The concept of the journey of the deceased in ancient Egyptian spirituality has captivated the imagination and influenced the understanding of the afterlife in various cultures and religious traditions. It offers insights into the ancient Egyptians' beliefs about the soul's continued existence beyond death, the challenges it faces, and the rituals and knowledge necessary for a successful passage into the realms of the divine.

Example: The spell known as the "Opening of the Mouth" ceremony was performed to restore the senses and abilities of the deceased, ensuring their participation in the afterlife rituals and enabling a successful transition into the divine realms.

Problem/Exercise: Analyze the significance of the Opening of the Mouth ceremony in the context of the journey of the deceased. Discuss its potential symbolic meanings and explore its relevance to modern spiritual practices that emphasize purification and initiation rites.

Principles of Ma'at:

Central to the teachings found in the Book of the Dead is the principle of Ma'at, which represents cosmic balance, harmony, and truth. The texts emphasize the importance of upholding Ma'at both in life and in the afterlife, as it ensures the order and stability of the universe. The spells and rituals contained in the Book of the Dead aim to assist the deceased in aligning with the principles of Ma'at and maintaining ethical conduct.

The principle of Ma'at is a fundamental concept in ancient Egyptian spirituality that reflects the cosmic order and harmony of the universe. It encompasses the ideals of truth, justice, righteousness, and balance, serving as a moral and ethical foundation for individuals and society as a whole.

In the context of the Book of the Dead, the texts emphasize the importance of upholding Ma'at throughout one's life and into the afterlife. It is believed that living in accordance with Ma'at ensures the maintenance of cosmic balance and harmony, both in the earthly realm and in the realms of the afterlife. The spells and rituals contained in the book aim to guide the deceased in aligning their actions and intentions with the principles of Ma'at, thereby ensuring a favorable judgment and eternal existence in the divine realms.

The concept of Ma'at permeates all aspects of ancient Egyptian society, from personal ethics and moral conduct to the functioning of the state and the actions of the gods. It is often depicted as a goddess, Ma'at, who is shown with an ostrich feather on her head, symbolizing truth and justice. The pharaoh, as the divine ruler, was responsible for upholding Ma'at and ensuring the well-being and prosperity of the kingdom.

Living in accordance with Ma'at required individuals to adhere to a code of ethical behavior, such as honesty, integrity, respect for others, and adherence to the law. It emphasized the importance of fairness, compassion, and harmony in interpersonal relationships and societal interactions. The principles of Ma'at also extended to the natural world, highlighting the need for responsible stewardship of the environment and a balanced relationship with the natural forces.

In the afterlife, the adherence to Ma'at was crucial for the deceased's successful judgment before the gods. It was believed that the heart of the deceased would be weighed against the feather of Ma'at in the Hall of Judgment. If the heart was found to be in balance with Ma'at, the deceased would be granted eternal life and join the realm of the blessed. However, if the heart was heavy with wrongdoing and imbalance, it would be devoured by a monstrous creature, resulting in the soul's ultimate demise.

The principle of Ma'at found in the Book of the Dead serves as a timeless reminder of the importance of living in alignment with higher ethical and moral values. It teaches individuals to strive for balance, truth, and justice in their thoughts, words, and actions. The pursuit of Ma'at not only ensures personal well-being and spiritual growth but also contributes to the collective harmony and flourishing of society.

The enduring influence of the concept of Ma'at can be seen in its resonance with modern spiritual and philosophical systems. The principles of balance, harmony, and truth continue to inspire individuals in their quest for personal growth, social justice, and the attainment of a deeper understanding of the interconnectedness of all beings.

Example: The spell known as the "Negative Confession" or the "Declaration of Innocence" presents a series of moral and ethical declarations in which the deceased proclaims their adherence to the principles of Ma'at, denying any wrongdoing or transgressions.

Problem/Exercise: Analyze the principles of Ma'at as reflected in the Negative Confession and discuss their potential relevance and application in modern ethical frameworks. Reflect on the challenges and benefits of incorporating the principles of Ma'at into contemporary spiritual practices.

Transformation and Divine Union:

The Book of the Dead emphasizes the transformative nature of the afterlife journey and the ultimate goal of achieving union with the divine. Through rituals, spells, and the acquisition of knowledge, the deceased seeks to attain a state of spiritual perfection and join the ranks of the gods. This union with the divine allows for the eternal existence and participation in the cosmic order.

In the context of the Book of the Dead and ancient Egyptian spirituality, the afterlife journey is seen as a transformative process through which the deceased seeks to achieve union with the divine. The ultimate goal is to transcend the limitations of the earthly existence and attain a state of spiritual perfection and immortality.

The rituals, spells, and instructions found in the Book of the Dead are designed to assist the deceased in navigating the challenges and obstacles of the afterlife journey and undergoing the necessary transformations. These transformations involve purifying the soul, acquiring knowledge and wisdom, and aligning oneself with the principles of Ma'at.

Throughout the journey, the deceased encounters various deities and guardians who serve as guides and gatekeepers to the realms of the divine. These encounters provide opportunities for the deceased to prove their worthiness and demonstrate their adherence to the principles of Ma'at. Through the successful completion of trials and the mastery of rituals, the deceased undergoes a process of spiritual purification and transformation.

The transformative nature of the afterlife journey is exemplified in the concept of the Akh, which represents the transformed and glorified state of the deceased. The Akh is achieved through the successful completion of the journey and the integration of the various aspects of the soul. It is characterized by a state of spiritual enlightenment, wisdom, and union with the divine.

Union with the divine is a central theme in ancient Egyptian spirituality. It represents the ultimate culmination of the afterlife journey, where the deceased becomes one with the gods and participates in the cosmic order. This union allows for eternal existence and the ability to contribute to the maintenance of cosmic balance and harmony.

The concept of divine union in the Book of the Dead reflects the belief that humans possess a divine spark within them and have the potential to ascend to a higher spiritual state. Through the transformative journey of the afterlife, the deceased seeks to reunite with their divine essence and partake in the eternal realm of the gods.

The idea of transformation and divine union found in the Book of the Dead has resonated with spiritual seekers throughout history. It reflects the universal human longing for spiritual transcendence and the desire to merge with a higher, transcendent reality. The teachings and rituals of ancient Egyptian spirituality provide a framework for understanding and experiencing this transformative process, inspiring individuals to embark on their own spiritual journeys of self-discovery, purification, and divine union.

Example: The spell known as the "The Chapter of Transforming into a Divine Being" describes the process of the deceased becoming one with the gods and attaining a state of divinity.

Problem/Exercise: Reflect on the concept of transformation and union with the divine in the Book of the Dead. Compare it to similar ideas found in other spiritual traditions and discuss the implications of seeking divine union in the context of personal spiritual growth and enlightenment.

The Book of the Dead serves as a repository of wisdom and spiritual teachings, providing valuable insights into the ancient Egyptian worldview and their profound understanding of the nature of the soul, the journey of the deceased, the principles of Ma'at, and the pursuit of spiritual transformation. By examining its contents, students can engage in critical analysis, comparative studies, and personal reflections to explore the relevance and applicability of these teachings in contemporary spiritual practices.

Mystical and Esoteric Traditions:

Ancient Egyptian spirituality encompassed mystical and esoteric traditions that delved into the hidden realms of consciousness and sought to unlock the secrets of the universe. These traditions, including alchemy, magical practices, and divination techniques, have left an indelible mark on various occult and esoteric traditions. The exploration of ancient Egyptian mystical practices offers valuable insights into the nature of consciousness, the power of intention, and the exploration of hidden dimensions of reality.

Ancient Egyptian spirituality encompassed mystical and esoteric traditions that sought to explore the hidden realms of consciousness and delve into the secrets of the universe. These traditions involved practices such as alchemy, magical rituals, and divination techniques, which were aimed at accessing higher states of consciousness, understanding the mysteries of existence, and harnessing spiritual forces for personal and collective transformation.

Alchemy, in the ancient Egyptian context, involved the symbolic transmutation of materials and the pursuit of spiritual purification and enlightenment. Alchemical practices aimed to transform base substances into more refined and spiritual forms, mirroring the process of inner transformation and the purification of the soul.

Magical practices were an integral part of ancient Egyptian spirituality, with rituals and spells performed to invoke divine energies and manipulate spiritual forces. These practices involved the use of symbols, incantations, and ritual objects to establish a connection with the divine and manifest desired outcomes.

Divination techniques, such as dream interpretation, scrying, and oracular practices, were also prominent in ancient Egyptian mystical traditions. These practices were employed to gain insight into the future, receive guidance from the gods, and tap into the hidden knowledge of the universe.

The exploration of ancient Egyptian mystical and esoteric traditions provides valuable insights into the nature of consciousness, the power of intention, and the exploration of hidden dimensions of reality. These traditions offer a framework for understanding the interconnectedness of the physical and spiritual realms and the potential for personal and spiritual transformation.

Furthermore, ancient Egyptian mystical and esoteric practices have influenced and shaped various occult and esoteric traditions throughout history. Elements of ancient Egyptian symbolism, magical rituals, and divination techniques can be found in traditions such as Hermeticism, Kabbalah, and modern Western occultism.

The study and exploration of ancient Egyptian mystical traditions not only offer a glimpse into the rich tapestry of human spiritual expression but also provide individuals with tools and insights for their own spiritual journeys. By delving into the mystical and esoteric aspects of ancient Egyptian spirituality, practitioners can deepen their understanding of consciousness, expand their awareness of hidden realms, and tap into the transformative power of ancient wisdom.

Example: Examining the practice of scrying in ancient Egyptian divination and its incorporation into modern forms of divination, such as crystal ball gazing or mirror scrying.

Problem/Exercise: Experiment with an ancient Egyptian divination technique, such as dream interpretation or hieroglyphic divination, and reflect on the experiences and insights gained. Discuss the relevance of ancient Egyptian divination practices in contemporary spiritual contexts.

By exploring the enduring impact and influence of ancient Egyptian spirituality on modern belief systems and practices, students gain a deeper appreciation for the richness and diversity of spiritual traditions. Through the inclusion of examples, problems, and exercises, students are encouraged to critically analyze and engage with the topics, fostering critical thinking, cross-cultural understanding, and meaningful discussions on the interplay between ancient wisdom and contemporary spirituality.

Discussion of the insights and wisdom that can be gained from understanding ancient religious traditions

Studying ancient religious traditions offers a wealth of insights and wisdom that can greatly enrich our understanding of spirituality, human nature, and the complexities of the human experience. These traditions, rooted in the wisdom of our ancestors, provide a window into different cultures, worldviews, and ways of perceiving the divine. By exploring these ancient religious traditions, we gain valuable perspectives and teachings that have the potential to deepen our own spiritual journeys and broaden our intellectual horizons.

Cultural and Historical Context:

Understanding ancient religious traditions allows us to grasp the cultural and historical context in which they emerged. Each tradition reflects the beliefs, values, and practices of a specific time and place, shedding light on the social, political, and philosophical climate of the era. This contextual understanding enables us to appreciate the diversity of human experiences and the complex interplay between spirituality and the broader cultural landscape.

The cultural and historical context of ancient religious traditions is essential for gaining a comprehensive understanding of their significance and impact. By exploring the cultural and historical factors that shaped these traditions, we can appreciate their richness, diversity, and evolution over time.

Cultural context refers to the social, cultural, and artistic aspects of a particular society or civilization. It encompasses elements such as language, art, architecture, literature, social norms, and daily life practices. The cultural context of ancient religious traditions provides insights into how spirituality was intertwined with various aspects of people's lives, including their relationships, social structures, and artistic expressions. For example, in ancient Egypt, religious beliefs and practices were deeply integrated into the fabric of society, influencing architecture, art, and even governance.

Historical context refers to the specific time period in which a religious tradition emerged and developed. It involves understanding the historical events, political structures, and societal changes that influenced the formation and evolution of religious beliefs and practices. For example, studying the historical context of ancient Egypt allows us to understand how the civilization's religious landscape evolved from the early polytheistic beliefs to the later monotheistic worship of Aten during the reign of Pharaoh Akhenaten.

Examining the cultural and historical context of ancient religious traditions provides important insights into the motivations, values, and challenges faced by the people of that time. It helps us recognize the influences of neighboring cultures, the impact of political and social changes, and the development of religious syncretism. Understanding the cultural and historical context also allows us to avoid imposing modern interpretations and biases onto ancient beliefs and practices.

Moreover, the cultural and historical context offers a broader perspective on the interconnectedness of different civilizations and the exchange of ideas and practices. It helps us appreciate the diversity of human spiritual expression and recognize the shared themes and universal aspects of religious experiences across time and cultures.

By exploring the cultural and historical context of ancient religious traditions, we gain a deeper appreciation for their significance and relevance. It allows us to approach these traditions with a more nuanced and informed perspective, fostering cultural sensitivity, intercultural understanding, and a greater appreciation for the complexities of human spirituality.

Example: Studying the ancient Egyptian religion reveals the profound interconnectedness between spirituality, politics, and everyday life. The pharaohs, believed to be divine rulers, were central figures in religious ceremonies, symbolizing the divine order and harmony.

Problem/Exercise: Analyze the cultural and historical context of a specific ancient religious tradition and discuss how it shaped the beliefs and practices of its followers. Reflect on the implications of this contextual understanding for our interpretation of spiritual teachings.

Universal Themes and Archetypes:

Ancient religious traditions often explore universal themes and archetypal patterns that resonate across time and cultures. These themes address fundamental aspects of the human condition, such as life, death, love, suffering, and the search for meaning. By delving into these traditions, we encounter timeless wisdom and insights that transcend the boundaries of specific religious frameworks.

Universal themes and archetypes are inherent in ancient religious traditions and continue to resonate with individuals across different cultures and time periods. These themes address fundamental aspects of the human experience and touch upon common existential questions and dilemmas that transcend cultural and religious boundaries.

One universal theme found in many ancient religious traditions is the quest for meaning and purpose in life. Ancient texts and myths often explore the human search for understanding the nature of existence, the purpose of suffering, and the significance of individual actions within a larger cosmic framework. These themes speak to the universal human desire to find meaning and navigate the complexities of life.

Exploring the Esoteric Wisdom of Ancient Egypt for Modern Spirituality

Another universal theme is the exploration of the human relationship with the divine or transcendent. Ancient religious traditions provide narratives, rituals, and practices that express the yearning for connection with a higher power or ultimate reality. This theme encompasses various expressions of devotion, prayer, and rituals that aim to establish a sense of harmony, transcendence, and spiritual transformation.

Ancient religious traditions also delve into the human experience of love, both divine and human. Love is often portrayed as a powerful force that unites individuals, communities, and the divine realm. The themes of love, compassion, and forgiveness resonate with people of diverse cultural backgrounds, as they touch upon the universal longing for connection and the recognition of our shared humanity.

Furthermore, ancient religious traditions frequently explore archetypal patterns and symbols that tap into the collective unconscious, as described by psychologist Carl Jung. Archetypes are universal symbols and patterns of behavior that are deeply embedded in the human psyche. They represent fundamental human experiences, such as the hero's journey, the wise elder, or the divine mother. By engaging with these archetypal symbols and narratives, individuals can connect with deeper layers of their own consciousness and tap into universal patterns of human experience.

Studying these universal themes and archetypes in ancient religious traditions allows us to recognize the common threads that unite humanity's spiritual journey. It fosters a sense of interconnectedness and provides a framework for understanding and interpreting the diverse expressions of spirituality found across different cultures and time periods. Additionally, it enables individuals to find resonance and meaning in ancient texts and rituals, as they address fundamental aspects of the human condition and offer insights into the universal quest for truth, meaning, and transcendence.

Example: The concept of the hero's journey, found in various ancient mythologies, including the Epic of Gilgamesh and the Greek myths, explores the transformative journey of the hero as they face challenges, gain wisdom, and return with a gift for their community.

Problem/Exercise: Identify a universal theme or archetypal pattern in an ancient religious tradition and compare it to similar themes in other spiritual or mythological traditions. Discuss the potential psychological and spiritual significance of these universal themes.

Ethical and Moral Guidance:

Ancient religious traditions often provide ethical and moral guidance, offering frameworks for living a virtuous and meaningful life. These traditions present moral codes, ethical teachings, and narratives that address questions of human conduct, justice, and the nature of good and evil. Exploring these teachings allows us to critically examine our own ethical frameworks and engage in meaningful discussions on moral responsibility.

Ethical and moral guidance is a significant aspect of ancient religious traditions. These traditions offer moral codes, ethical teachings, and narratives that provide guidance on how to live a virtuous and meaningful life. By exploring these teachings, individuals can reflect on their own ethical frameworks, engage in moral deliberation, and gain insights into questions of human conduct and the nature of good and evil.

Ancient religious texts often contain explicit moral guidelines or commandments that outline specific actions and behaviors that are deemed virtuous or morally upright. For example, the Ten Commandments in Judaism and Christianity provide a set of ethical principles that guide believers in their relationships with God and fellow human beings. These principles include prohibitions against lying, stealing, and murder, as well as injunctions to honor one's parents and uphold justice.

In addition to explicit moral codes, ancient religious traditions also offer ethical teachings and narratives that explore broader moral concepts and virtues. These teachings often emphasize the importance of compassion, kindness, honesty, forgiveness, and humility. They encourage individuals to cultivate virtuous qualities and to strive for moral excellence in their interactions with others and in their personal lives.

Moreover, ancient religious narratives and parables often present moral dilemmas and ethical challenges, allowing individuals to engage in critical reflection and ethical reasoning. These stories and teachings provide opportunities to explore complex moral issues and to consider the consequences of different choices and actions. By examining these narratives, individuals can develop their own moral reasoning skills and deepen their understanding of the ethical dimensions of human existence.

Studying the ethical and moral guidance provided by ancient religious traditions serves several purposes. Firstly, it offers a historical and cultural perspective on ethical frameworks, allowing individuals to appreciate the diversity of moral systems across different times and cultures. Secondly, it provides a foundation for personal moral development, encouraging individuals to reflect on their own values, beliefs, and behaviors. Thirdly, it fosters discussions and dialogue on ethical issues within communities and societies, promoting a more thoughtful and informed approach to moral decision-making.

By engaging with the ethical and moral teachings of ancient religious traditions, individuals can deepen their understanding of the complexities of human conduct and the quest for moral excellence. They can draw inspiration from the wisdom and insights of these traditions to navigate ethical dilemmas, cultivate virtuous qualities, and strive for a more compassionate and just society.

Example: The teachings of Confucianism, an ancient Chinese religious tradition, emphasize the cultivation of virtues such as filial piety, compassion, and righteousness, providing guidance for harmonious social relationships and ethical conduct.

Problem/Exercise: Analyze the ethical teachings of an ancient religious tradition and evaluate their relevance and applicability to contemporary moral dilemmas. Discuss the potential challenges and limitations of applying ancient ethical frameworks in modern society.

Spiritual Practices and Rituals:

Ancient religious traditions encompass a wide range of spiritual practices and rituals that facilitate a deeper connection with the divine and cultivate personal transformation. These practices may include prayer, meditation, sacred ceremonies, and rites of passage. By examining these rituals, we can gain insights into the ways in which humans have sought spiritual connection, meaning, and transcendence throughout history.

Spiritual practices and rituals are integral components of ancient religious traditions, serving as pathways for individuals to deepen their connection with the divine, cultivate inner transformation, and seek meaning and transcendence. These practices often involve engaging the mind, body, and spirit in specific actions, gestures, or meditations that create a sacred space and facilitate a sense of communion with the divine.

Prayer is a common spiritual practice found in many ancient religious traditions. Through prayer, individuals express their reverence, gratitude, and supplication to the divine. It serves as a means of communication with the sacred, allowing individuals to seek guidance, solace, and spiritual support. Prayer can be performed individually or collectively, and it may involve specific postures, gestures, or recitations of sacred texts or hymns.

Meditation is another spiritual practice that aims to quiet the mind, cultivate mindfulness, and deepen one's connection with the divine or the higher self. Ancient traditions often employed various forms of meditation, including focused attention on breath, visualization, mantra repetition, or contemplation of sacred symbols or concepts. Meditation allows individuals to enter a state of heightened awareness, transcending ordinary consciousness and accessing deeper spiritual insights and experiences.

Sacred ceremonies and rituals play a significant role in ancient religious traditions. These rituals are often performed in specific locations or sacred spaces, such as temples, shrines, or natural sites. They may involve the use of symbolic objects, offerings, chants, dances, and gestures that evoke the presence of the divine and facilitate spiritual transformation. These rituals serve to establish a connection between the earthly realm and the divine realm, allowing individuals to participate in the sacred mysteries and access spiritual blessings or purification.

Rites of passage are another important aspect of ancient spiritual practices. These rituals mark significant life transitions, such as birth, puberty, marriage, and death, and are designed to facilitate personal and spiritual transformation. Rites of passage often involve a series of symbolic actions, ceremonies, and teachings that guide individuals through the different stages of life and foster a sense of identity, purpose, and belonging within the religious community.

The study of ancient spiritual practices and rituals provides valuable insights into the ways in which humans have sought to connect with the divine and cultivate spiritual growth throughout history. By examining these practices, individuals can gain inspiration and ideas for their own spiritual journeys, adapt ancient rituals to modern contexts, or develop new practices that align with their personal beliefs and aspirations. These practices serve as pathways for individuals to explore their inner world, deepen their connection with the sacred, and nurture their spiritual well-being.

Example: The Sufi practices of whirling and chanting, originating from ancient Islamic mystical traditions, serve as vehicles for ecstatic states and spiritual union with the divine.

Problem/Exercise: Explore a specific spiritual practice or ritual from an ancient religious tradition and discuss its purpose, symbolism, and potential effects on personal transformation. Reflect on the similarities and differences between ancient and contemporary spiritual practices.

In conclusion, the study of ancient religious traditions offers a treasure trove of insights, wisdom, and teachings that can deeply impact our understanding of spirituality, human nature, and the world around us. By engaging with these traditions, we expand our intellectual and spiritual horizons, cultivate empathy and cultural appreciation, and discover timeless truths that resonate with our own spiritual quests. Through critical analysis, comparative studies, and personal reflections, students can explore the rich tapestry of ancient religious traditions and engage in discussions that foster critical thinking, empathy, and a deeper appreciation for the diversity of human spiritual experiences.

Chapter 3: Brief Overview of Ancient Egypt and its Religious Beliefs

Chapter 3 provides a brief overview of ancient Egypt and its religious beliefs, offering students a foundational understanding of the historical and cultural context in which ancient Egyptian spirituality thrived. By examining key aspects of ancient Egyptian civilization, including its geography, society, and cosmology, we can begin to grasp the intricate tapestry of beliefs and practices that shaped the religious landscape of this remarkable civilization.

Geographic and Temporal Context:

Ancient Egypt, located in northeastern Africa, emerged as one of the world's earliest civilizations around 3100 BCE. Spanning over three millennia, its history can be divided into several periods, including the Old Kingdom, Middle Kingdom, and New Kingdom. Understanding the geographical and temporal context of ancient Egypt is essential for comprehending the influences that shaped its religious beliefs.

Example: The Nile River, with its predictable annual flooding, played a vital role in sustaining agricultural productivity and fostering a sense of divine order and abundance in the minds of ancient Egyptians.

Problem/Exercise: Analyze the geographical features of ancient Egypt and discuss their significance in shaping the religious beliefs and practices of its inhabitants.

Social Structure and Political Organization:

Ancient Egyptian society was hierarchical, with a rigid social structure that placed the pharaoh at the pinnacle of power. The religious beliefs of ancient Egypt were deeply intertwined with the political organization, as the pharaoh was considered a divine ruler, serving as an intermediary between the gods and the people.

Example: The pharaoh's role as a divine figure was central to the religious ceremonies and rituals performed in ancient Egypt, symbolizing the divine order and the harmony between the human and divine realms.

Problem/Exercise: Examine the social structure of ancient Egypt and discuss how it influenced the religious beliefs and practices of different segments of society. Reflect on the implications of the pharaoh's divine status for the religious and political dynamics of the time.

Cosmology and Mythology:

Ancient Egyptian religious beliefs were grounded in a complex cosmology and mythology that explained the creation of the world, the nature of the gods, and the journey of the soul after death. By delving into the cosmological concepts and creation myths of ancient Egypt, we gain insights into their understanding of the universe and the role of human beings within it.

Example: The myth of Osiris, Isis, and Horus, which portrays the cycle of death and rebirth, highlights the ancient Egyptians' belief in an afterlife and the importance of preserving the body through mummification.

Problem/Exercise: Explore a specific myth or cosmological concept from ancient Egyptian religion and analyze its symbolic significance and its implications for the religious practices and worldview of ancient Egyptians.

Polytheism and Deities:

Ancient Egyptian religion was polytheistic, with a vast pantheon of gods and goddesses that represented various natural phenomena, abstract concepts, and aspects of human experience. Each deity had specific roles and associations, and their worship was central to the religious rituals and practices of ancient Egypt.

Example: Ra, the sun god, was considered the supreme deity in ancient Egyptian religion, representing the life-giving power of the sun and the pharaoh's divine lineage.

Problem/Exercise: Select a deity from the ancient Egyptian pantheon and explore their roles, associations, and symbolic significance. Discuss how their worship and cultic practices contributed to the religious beliefs and rituals of ancient Egypt.

In conclusion, this chapter provides a concise yet comprehensive overview of ancient Egypt and its religious beliefs. By examining its geography, social structure, cosmology, and pantheon of deities, we lay the groundwork for a deeper exploration of the spiritual teachings and practices of ancient Egyptian civilization. A solid understanding of the historical and cultural context of ancient Egypt is crucial for comprehending the enduring legacy and profound influence of this ancient civilization on spirituality and religious thought.

Introduction to the historical and cultural context of ancient Egypt

The historical and cultural context of ancient Egypt provides a fascinating backdrop for the exploration of its rich spiritual traditions. Understanding the social, political, and geographic aspects of ancient Egyptian civilization is crucial for comprehending the beliefs, practices, and symbols that shaped their religious worldview. This section serves as an introduction to the historical and cultural context of ancient Egypt, offering students a solid foundation for studying its religious and spiritual heritage.

Geographic Setting:

Ancient Egypt, situated in northeastern Africa, thrived along the banks of the Nile River. The Nile played a pivotal role in the civilization's development, providing fertile land for agriculture and transportation. The annual flooding of the Nile created a cyclical pattern of life, which influenced the religious beliefs and practices of the ancient Egyptians.

The geographic setting of ancient Egypt had a profound impact on the civilization's development, including its religious beliefs and practices.

Ancient Egypt was located in northeastern Africa, with its territory stretching along the Nile River from the Mediterranean Sea in the north to the First Cataract in the south. The Nile River was the lifeblood of ancient Egypt, shaping the civilization's economy, agriculture, and transportation systems. The river's annual flooding, known as the inundation, was a crucial event in the agricultural cycle. As the floodwaters receded, they left behind fertile silt, which allowed for the cultivation of crops. This cyclical pattern of the flood and the resulting abundance of food had a profound influence on the religious beliefs and practices of the ancient Egyptians.

The Nile River was regarded as a sacred entity, and its regular flooding was interpreted as a manifestation of divine providence and the benevolence of the gods. The abundance of food and agricultural prosperity was seen as a direct result of the gods' favor and was celebrated through various religious festivals and rituals. The fertility of the land and the prosperity it brought were central themes in ancient Egyptian religious beliefs, reflecting the deep connection between the natural environment and the divine.

The geographic setting of Egypt also played a role in shaping the cosmology and religious symbolism of the civilization. The Nile River was seen as a representation of the primeval waters that existed at the dawn of creation, and it was associated with the goddess Isis, who was believed to have played a significant role in the river's life-giving properties. The east bank of the Nile, where the sun rose, was associated with birth, life, and light, while the west bank, where the sun set and the land of the dead was believed to be located, was associated with death, rebirth, and the afterlife.

Additionally, the desert that surrounded ancient Egypt acted as a protective barrier, providing a sense of security and isolation from external influences. This isolation contributed to the distinct cultural and religious identity of the ancient Egyptians, as they developed their unique religious beliefs and practices over millennia.

The geographic setting of ancient Egypt, with its fertile Nile Valley and the surrounding desert, not only shaped the material prosperity of the civilization but also influenced the religious worldview of its people. The cyclical patterns of the Nile's flooding, the fertility of the land, and the natural features of the environment all found their way into the religious beliefs, rituals, and symbolism of the ancient Egyptians. Understanding the geographic context helps us appreciate the profound connection between the natural world and the religious imagination of this ancient civilization.

Example: The geographic isolation of Egypt, surrounded by deserts, contributed to the preservation of its cultural and religious traditions, as it was shielded from significant external influences.

Problem/Exercise: Analyze the impact of the Nile River on the religious beliefs and practices of ancient Egyptians. Discuss how the geographic features of Egypt influenced their worldview and spiritual connections.

Chronological Overview:

Ancient Egypt spanned an extensive period, encompassing various dynasties and epochs. Divided into distinct periods such as the Old Kingdom, Middle Kingdom, and New Kingdom, each phase brought unique cultural and religious developments. Understanding the chronological progression of ancient Egypt allows us to trace the evolution and transformation of its religious beliefs over time.

The Veil of Thoth

The history of ancient Egypt can be divided into several major periods, each characterized by distinct political, cultural, and religious developments. Here is a chronological overview of the major periods of ancient Egyptian history:

Predynastic Period (c. 5500-3100 BCE): This period marks the early development of ancient Egyptian civilization, with the emergence of settled agricultural communities along the Nile River. During this time, religious beliefs were likely centered around animistic and ancestral worship.

Early Dynastic Period (c. 3100-2686 BCE): The Early Dynastic Period saw the unification of Upper and Lower Egypt under the rule of a single king, known as a pharaoh. It was during this period that the foundations of ancient Egyptian religious beliefs and rituals began to take shape.

Old Kingdom (c. 2686-2181 BCE): The Old Kingdom is known as the "Age of the Pyramids." This period witnessed the construction of monumental pyramids, including the Great Pyramid of Giza. Religious beliefs focused on the divine nature of the pharaoh and the concept of an afterlife. The pharaoh was considered a living god, and rituals and ceremonies were performed to ensure the pharaoh's divine legitimacy and eternal reign.

First Intermediate Period (c. 2181-2055 BCE): Following a period of political instability, the First Intermediate Period marked a decline in centralized rule and the fragmentation of Egypt into smaller regional powers. Religious practices during this period likely varied across different regions.

Middle Kingdom (c. 2055-1650 BCE): The Middle Kingdom marked a period of reunification and centralized rule. Religious beliefs emphasized the role of the pharaoh as a shepherd and protector of the people. The concept of Ma'at, representing cosmic balance and harmony, gained prominence during this period.

Second Intermediate Period (c. 1650-1550 BCE): The Second Intermediate Period was characterized by the invasion of Egypt by the Hyksos, a group of foreign rulers. This period witnessed a blend of Egyptian and foreign religious influences.

New Kingdom (c. 1550-1069 BCE): The New Kingdom was a period of great power and prosperity for ancient Egypt. It witnessed the rise of powerful pharaohs, such as Hatshepsut, Akhenaten, and Ramesses II. Religious beliefs evolved during this time, with the introduction of Atenism (the worship of the sun disk, Aten) by Akhenaten and the subsequent restoration of traditional religious practices.

Third Intermediate Period (c. 1069-664 BCE): The Third Intermediate Period was marked by political fragmentation and the decline of centralized rule. Religious practices varied across different regions, with the influence of foreign powers such as the Nubians and the Assyrians.

Late Period (c. 664-332 BCE): The Late Period saw the resurgence of Egyptian independence and a revival of traditional religious practices. Egypt came under the rule of foreign powers, including the Persians and the Greeks.

Hellenistic and Roman Periods (332 BCE-395 CE): With the conquest of Egypt by Alexander the Great and later the Romans, Egyptian religion experienced further syncretism with Greek and Roman religious traditions.

Understanding the chronological overview of ancient Egyptian history allows us to observe the development, transformation, and interactions of religious beliefs and practices over time. It provides insights into the cultural, political, and social factors that shaped the religious landscape of this ancient civilization.

Example: The Old Kingdom was characterized by the construction of monumental pyramids, symbolizing the pharaoh's divinity and eternal life. In contrast, the New Kingdom witnessed the rise of Atenism and the reign of Akhenaten, who promoted the worship of a single sun god.

Problem/Exercise: Compare and contrast the religious practices and beliefs of different periods in ancient Egypt. Analyze the factors that influenced religious change and continuity across these historical epochs.

Social Structure and Pharaonic Power:

Ancient Egyptian society was hierarchical, with a clear social structure that influenced religious practices and beliefs. At the top of the social order stood the pharaoh, considered a divine ruler with immense religious and political power. The pharaoh's role as a mediator between the divine and human realms shaped the religious landscape and established a close connection between the state and religious institutions.

In ancient Egypt, the social structure was highly stratified, with the pharaoh occupying the apex of the hierarchy. The pharaoh was regarded as a god on Earth and held absolute authority over both religious and secular matters. The pharaoh's role as the intermediary between the divine and human realms bestowed immense religious and political power upon them.

Below the pharaoh, the nobility and aristocracy held significant positions of influence. They served as advisors, administrators, and military commanders, and often held high-ranking priesthood positions. The nobility enjoyed privileges and wealth, and they actively participated in religious rituals and ceremonies.

Beneath the nobility were the scribes, who played a crucial role in the bureaucracy of ancient Egypt. They were responsible for maintaining records, conducting administrative tasks, and serving as custodians of knowledge and religious texts. Scribes were highly educated and often held religious roles as well.

The middle class of ancient Egypt comprised skilled craftsmen, merchants, and artisans. They were essential to the economy and contributed to the production of goods, including religious artifacts and temple offerings. While they had some economic independence, their social status was lower than that of the nobility and scribes.

At the lower end of the social structure were peasants, farmers, and laborers who worked the land and provided the agricultural resources necessary for the sustenance of the society. They formed the majority of the population and often lived in small villages along the Nile River. Their lives were closely tied to the agricultural cycle and they participated in religious festivals and rituals related to fertility and abundance.

Religious practices and beliefs were intertwined with the social structure in ancient Egypt. The pharaoh, as the divine ruler, was central to religious ceremonies and rituals. Temples, considered the dwelling places of the gods, played a vital role in the religious life of the society. The priesthood, which was closely associated with the pharaoh, served as intermediaries between the gods and the people, conducting daily rituals, offerings, and maintaining the temples.

The social structure influenced access to religious knowledge and participation in religious activities. While the pharaoh and the nobility had more direct involvement in religious ceremonies, the general population had access to communal and household rituals, such as making offerings to household deities or participating in local festivals.

Overall, the social structure in ancient Egypt played a significant role in shaping the religious practices and beliefs of the society. The pharaoh's divine authority and the hierarchical organization of the society created a close connection between religious institutions and the exercise of power. Religious rituals and ceremonies were used to legitimize the pharaoh's rule and maintain social order.

Example: The pharaoh's responsibility for maintaining Ma'at, the divine order of the universe, emphasized their divine legitimacy and the need for religious rituals to ensure cosmic balance.

Problem/Exercise: Analyze the social structure of ancient Egyptian society and discuss how it shaped religious practices and beliefs. Explore the ways in which the pharaoh's role as a religious figure influenced the daily lives of the ancient Egyptians.

Cultural Expressions and Artistic Traditions:

The cultural expressions and artistic traditions of ancient Egypt provide valuable insights into their religious beliefs and practices. The intricate hieroglyphic script, temple architecture, and artistic representations of gods and goddesses reveal the significance of visual and symbolic communication in ancient Egyptian spirituality.

The cultural expressions and artistic traditions of ancient Egypt played a vital role in the manifestation and communication of religious beliefs and practices. The ancient Egyptians developed a unique and sophisticated artistic style that reflected their worldview and religious concepts.

One of the most notable artistic traditions of ancient Egypt was their use of hieroglyphic script. Hieroglyphs, derived from a combination of pictorial symbols and abstract signs, were a form of written communication used extensively in religious texts, inscriptions, and monumental structures. Hieroglyphs allowed the ancient Egyptians to convey complex religious ideas, mythological narratives, and rituals in a visual and symbolic manner.

The temple architecture of ancient Egypt was another significant cultural expression intimately tied to religious beliefs. Temples were considered the dwelling places of the gods, and their construction and design were meticulously planned to facilitate the interaction between the divine and the human. Temple complexes were characterized by grandiose entrances, spacious courtyards, and inner sanctuaries where the statues of gods were housed. The architectural layout of the temples emphasized the separation between different realms, from the mundane world to the sacred innermost areas accessible only to the priests.

Artistic representations of gods and goddesses were prevalent in ancient Egyptian culture. Sculptures, reliefs, and paintings depicted deities with recognizable attributes and symbolic characteristics, often in human or animal form. These artistic representations aimed to capture the essence and divine qualities of the gods, enabling worshippers to visually connect with the divine realm. The representations were often idealized and conveyed a sense of permanence and power associated with the gods.

Artistic traditions also extended to funerary practices in ancient Egypt. Elaborate tombs, such as the pyramids and rock-cut tombs in the Valley of the Kings, were decorated with intricate murals and relief carvings depicting scenes from the deceased's journey in the afterlife. These artistic expressions conveyed the belief in the continuity of life beyond death and the importance of proper burial and funerary rituals.

The artistic traditions of ancient Egypt not only served as a medium for religious expression but also reflected their cultural values and societal norms. The precise and stylized artistic style, characterized by frontalism and rigid proportions, conveyed a sense of order, harmony, and permanence that mirrored the Egyptians' worldview and beliefs in the stability of the cosmos.

Overall, the cultural expressions and artistic traditions of ancient Egypt played a vital role in conveying and perpetuating religious beliefs and practices. Through hieroglyphic script, temple architecture, and artistic representations, the ancient Egyptians communicated their understanding of the divine, the rituals associated with their religious practices, and their reverence for the gods. These artistic expressions continue to be a valuable source for understanding and appreciating the religious and cultural legacy of ancient Egypt.

Example: The temple complex of Karnak, with its grandeur and detailed reliefs, served as a space for religious rituals and ceremonies, reinforcing the connection between the human and divine realms.

Problem/Exercise: Examine the artistic expressions of ancient Egypt, such as hieroglyphs and temple reliefs, and discuss their role in conveying religious concepts and beliefs. Analyze specific examples of artwork to understand the symbolism and religious significance embedded within them.

In conclusion, the historical and cultural context of ancient Egypt provides a crucial foundation for studying its religious and spiritual traditions. The geographic setting, chronological overview, social structure, and cultural expressions all contribute to our understanding of the complex tapestry of beliefs and practices that shaped the ancient Egyptian worldview. By exploring these contextual factors, we can delve deeper into the religious and spiritual heritage of this remarkable civilization.

Overview of the geographical and social factors that shaped ancient Egyptian civilization

To truly understand the complexities of ancient Egyptian civilization, it is essential to examine the geographical and social factors that played a pivotal role in its development. The unique landscape and social dynamics of ancient Egypt influenced various aspects of the civilization, including its agricultural practices, political structure, and cultural expressions. This section provides a comprehensive overview of the geographical and social factors that shaped ancient Egyptian civilization, offering students valuable insights into the context in which the religious and spiritual traditions of this ancient civilization emerged.

Geographic Factors:

a. Nile River:

The Nile River stands as the lifeblood of ancient Egypt, serving as a vital source of sustenance and prosperity. Its annual flooding brought nutrient-rich sediment, allowing for fertile agricultural lands. This predictable flooding pattern created a cyclical rhythm in the lives of the ancient Egyptians and profoundly influenced their religious and cultural practices.

Example: The inundation of the Nile was associated with the god Hapy, symbolizing fertility and abundance. This connection between the river's natural cycles and religious symbolism underscored the interplay between nature and spirituality in ancient Egypt.

b. Desert and Natural Barriers:

Surrounded by vast deserts, ancient Egypt enjoyed geographical isolation, providing a degree of protection from external invasions and influences. The arid deserts acted as natural barriers, fostering a sense of cultural continuity and contributing to the preservation of the civilization's religious and social traditions.

Example: The Eastern Desert and Western Desert shielded Egypt from land-based invasions, enabling the civilization to develop with relative stability and safeguard its unique cultural identity.

Social Factors:

a. Pharaonic Authority:

At the core of ancient Egyptian society was the institution of pharaonic authority. The pharaoh, believed to be a divine ruler with a direct connection to the gods, held supreme power and governed over both religious and secular matters. The pharaoh's role as a religious figure shaped the spiritual and social landscape, influencing religious practices and establishing a centralized system of governance.

Example: The pharaoh, often depicted as the mediator between the divine and mortal realms, personified the embodiment of Ma'at, the cosmic balance and harmony that governed the universe. This belief in the pharaoh's divine nature solidified their authority and religious significance.

b. Social Hierarchy:

Ancient Egyptian society was structured hierarchically, with clear divisions based on social status and occupation. The social hierarchy encompassed the pharaoh, nobles, priests, scribes, artisans, farmers, and slaves. This hierarchical structure had a profound impact on religious practices, as the ruling elite and priesthood played key roles in religious rituals and temple administration.

Example: The priesthood, responsible for performing rituals and maintaining temple complexes, held significant religious authority and acted as intermediaries between the gods and the people.

c. Religious Syncretism:

Ancient Egypt was a dynamic society that experienced cultural exchange and assimilation over its long history. As a result, there was a tendency towards religious syncretism, where different gods and belief systems merged, creating a complex pantheon. This syncretism allowed for the coexistence of diverse religious traditions and the incorporation of foreign deities into the Egyptian religious framework.

Example: The assimilation of the goddess Isis from the Hellenistic period into Egyptian mythology showcases the adaptability and openness of ancient Egyptian religious beliefs.

Conclusion:

The geographical and social factors that shaped ancient Egyptian civilization are fundamental to understanding its religious and spiritual traditions. The Nile River, with its cyclical flooding, provided the foundation for agricultural prosperity and imbued religious symbolism into everyday life. The deserts surrounding Egypt contributed to its isolation and cultural continuity. The pharaonic authority and social hierarchy influenced religious practices and the centralization of power. The dynamics of religious syncretism reflected the cultural exchange and assimilation that occurred throughout Egyptian history. By studying these geographical and social factors, students gain a comprehensive understanding of the contextual backdrop against which ancient Egyptian religion and spirituality flourished.

Examination of the religious beliefs and practices that were central to ancient Egyptian society

The religious beliefs and practices of ancient Egypt formed the cornerstone of its civilization, permeating every aspect of daily life, social structure, and cultural expression. This section delves into a comprehensive examination of the religious landscape of ancient Egypt, shedding light on the central deities, rituals, and cosmological concepts that shaped their spiritual worldview. By exploring these beliefs and practices, students can gain a profound understanding of the religious framework that underpinned the ancient Egyptian society.

Polytheistic Pantheon:

Ancient Egyptian religion revolved around a vast and complex pantheon of deities. The polytheistic nature of their belief system encompassed gods and goddesses who represented various aspects of the natural world, celestial bodies, and human attributes. Understanding the roles and significance of these deities provides insights into the religious mindset and cosmological understanding of ancient Egyptians.

The ancient Egyptian religion was characterized by a polytheistic belief system, which means that they worshipped and revered a multitude of gods and goddesses. The pantheon of ancient Egyptian deities was diverse and extensive, with different gods and goddesses associated with various aspects of nature, human life, and cosmic forces.

The Veil of Thoth

The gods and goddesses of ancient Egypt represented a wide range of phenomena, including natural elements such as the sun, the moon, the Nile River, and the sky. They also embodied human attributes, such as wisdom, fertility, love, war, and protection. Each deity had their own unique characteristics, roles, and responsibilities within the divine hierarchy.

At the pinnacle of the pantheon was the god Amun-Ra, who represented the sun and was considered the king of the gods. Amun-Ra was associated with creative power and cosmic order. Another prominent deity was Osiris, the god of the afterlife and resurrection. Osiris played a crucial role in the mythology and religious beliefs of the ancient Egyptians, serving as a symbol of death, rebirth, and the cycle of life.

The goddess Isis held significant importance as a protective deity, symbolizing motherhood, magic, and healing. She was revered as a divine mother and a compassionate figure who offered guidance and support to her devotees. Another notable goddess was Hathor, associated with love, beauty, joy, and music. Hathor was often depicted as a cow or a woman with cow horns, symbolizing fertility and nurturing.

Other deities included Thoth, the god of wisdom, writing, and knowledge; Horus, the falcon-headed god associated with kingship and protection; Bastet, the lioness-headed goddess associated with home, domesticity, and protection against evil; and Sekhmet, the lioness-headed goddess of war and healing.

The ancient Egyptians believed that these gods and goddesses played an active role in the functioning of the universe and the daily lives of individuals. They worshipped and made offerings to these deities in temples, participated in rituals and festivals dedicated to them, and sought their guidance and blessings in various aspects of life, such as agriculture, fertility, protection, and the afterlife.

Understanding the roles and significance of the deities within the polytheistic pantheon provides insights into the religious worldview of ancient Egyptians. It reflects their reverence for the natural world, their desire for protection and guidance, and their belief in the interconnectedness of cosmic forces and human existence.

The polytheistic nature of ancient Egyptian religion allowed for a multiplicity of gods and goddesses, each with their own attributes and spheres of influence. This rich and diverse pantheon contributed to the complexity and depth of ancient Egyptian religious beliefs and practices.

Example: The god Amun, often depicted with a ram's head, represented the hidden and mysterious aspects of creation. As the king of the gods, he played a vital role in the New Kingdom's religious and political developments, showcasing the intertwining of religion and state in ancient Egypt.

Mythology and Creation Stories:

Ancient Egyptian mythology provided a rich tapestry of creation stories and narratives that explained the origins of the world and the relationship between gods and humans. These myths offered insights into the nature of divinity, the principles of order and chaos, and the cycles of life and death.

Ancient Egyptian mythology encompassed a diverse collection of creation stories and narratives that sought to explain the origins of the world, the gods, and the relationship between gods and humans. These myths provided a framework for understanding the nature of divinity, the principles of order and chaos, and the cycles of life and death.

One prominent creation myth in ancient Egyptian mythology is the Heliopolitan creation myth, centered around the god Atum. According to this myth, Atum emerged from the primeval waters and created the world through his self-generative power. Atum was believed to have brought order out of chaos, shaping the universe and giving birth to other gods and goddesses.

Another significant myth is the Osirian myth, which revolved around the god Osiris, his sister-wife Isis, and their brother Seth. This myth narrated the tragic story of Osiris's death and resurrection, symbolizing the cycle of life, death, and rebirth. The myth highlighted the themes of divine kingship, the struggle between order and chaos, and the promise of eternal life in the afterlife.

The mythology of ancient Egypt also included stories about the gods' interactions with humans and their involvement in human affairs. These narratives often featured heroic figures, such as the god Horus and the pharaohs, who represented the divine order and fought against chaos and evil forces.

In addition to creation stories and narratives, ancient Egyptian mythology encompassed a wide range of gods and goddesses with their own mythological roles and stories. For example, the goddess Isis was revered for her role in searching for and reassembling the body parts of her husband Osiris after his death, symbolizing her power of resurrection and renewal. The sun god Ra was believed to travel through the sky during the day and journey through the underworld at night, representing the eternal cycle of the sun.

These myths served multiple purposes in ancient Egyptian society. They provided explanations for the natural phenomena and the workings of the universe, while also offering moral and ethical lessons. The myths reinforced the religious and social order, emphasized the importance of maintaining harmony and Ma'at (balance), and provided comfort and hope in the face of life's challenges and the inevitability of death.

By exploring the mythology and creation stories of ancient Egypt, we gain insights into the beliefs, values, and worldview of the ancient Egyptians. These stories provided a framework for understanding the divine and human realms, the origins of the world, and the cycles of life and death, offering guidance and inspiration to individuals and communities in their spiritual and daily lives.

Example: The myth of Osiris, Isis, and Horus illustrates themes of resurrection, divine kingship, and the eternal struggle between good and evil. Osiris, the god of the underworld, represented the cycle of death and rebirth, while his wife Isis symbolized maternal protection and magical powers.

Rituals and Temples:

Rituals formed an integral part of ancient Egyptian religious practices. Temples, dedicated to specific deities, served as sacred spaces where rituals and offerings were conducted by priests and devotees. These rituals aimed to maintain cosmic order, ensure fertility and prosperity, and establish a harmonious relationship between humans and the divine.

Rituals played a crucial role in ancient Egyptian religious practices, serving as a means of establishing and maintaining a connection between humans and the divine. These rituals were performed in sacred spaces, primarily temples dedicated to specific deities.

Temples were considered the dwelling places of the gods and were built in various sizes and architectural styles throughout ancient Egypt. These grand structures were often located near the Nile River and served as religious, administrative, and economic centers within their respective regions. The temples were constructed with meticulous precision and adorned with intricate carvings, paintings, and statues to honor the gods and create a sacred atmosphere.

Within the temples, priests, who served as intermediaries between the gods and the people, conducted rituals on behalf of the community. These rituals were performed according to specific protocols and were believed to ensure the maintenance of cosmic order and the well-being of both the human and divine realms.

Some common rituals included offerings, purification ceremonies, processions, and sacred dramas. Offerings consisted of food, drink, and other valuable items presented to the gods as a means of sustenance and devotion. Purification ceremonies involved rituals of cleansing and purification, often through the use of water and incense, to symbolize spiritual renewal and readiness for divine encounters.

Processions were important ceremonial events that involved the public display of cult statues or sacred objects associated with the deity. These processions often took place on specific religious festivals and were intended to honor the gods, seek their blessings, and demonstrate the community's devotion.

Sacred dramas, known as the "Mysteries," were elaborate reenactments of mythological stories or symbolic representations of the gods' actions and attributes. These rituals sought to bring the myths to life, engaging both the participants and observers in the divine narratives and fostering a deeper understanding of the gods and their roles.

Temples also served as repositories for sacred texts, including religious texts and hymns, and as centers for education and scholarship. The priests and priestesses played important roles in the administration of the temples and the performance of rituals, ensuring the proper conduct of religious ceremonies and the maintenance of the temple's sanctity.

The rituals and temple practices in ancient Egypt were deeply intertwined with the beliefs and worldview of the people. They were seen as essential for maintaining cosmic harmony, expressing devotion, seeking divine guidance, and ensuring the well-being and prosperity of the community. The rituals provided a means of engaging with the gods and the spiritual realm, fostering a sense of connection and participation in the divine order.

Today, the study and reconstruction of ancient Egyptian rituals and temple practices provide valuable insights into the religious and cultural practices of this civilization. They offer a glimpse into the ancient Egyptians' reverence for the divine, their understanding of cosmic order, and their profound desire to establish a harmonious relationship with the gods.

Example: The daily ritual of the Opening of the Mouth ceremony, performed by priests, involved the symbolic awakening and enlivening of statues or mummies to allow the deceased to participate in the afterlife. This ritual exemplifies the Egyptians' belief in the power of ritual actions to bridge the realms of the living and the dead.

Cult of the Dead:

Ancient Egyptians held a deep reverence for the afterlife, and their religious beliefs and practices were intricately connected to the journey of the soul beyond death. The cult of the dead encompassed rituals, burial practices, and the belief in the judgment of the soul.

The cult of the dead was a significant aspect of ancient Egyptian religious beliefs and practices. The ancient Egyptians held a profound belief in the existence of an afterlife and the continued existence of the soul beyond death. They believed that death was not the end but rather the beginning of a journey that required careful preparations and adherence to religious rituals and beliefs.

One of the key components of the cult of the dead was the belief in the judgment of the soul. According to ancient Egyptian mythology and religious texts, after death, the soul of the deceased would undergo a judgment process known as the "Weighing of the Heart" or the "Judgment of Osiris." In this process, the heart of the deceased would be weighed against the feather of Ma'at, the goddess of truth and justice. If the heart was found to be lighter than the feather, indicating a life lived in accordance with Ma'at's principles of balance and righteousness, the soul would be granted eternal life in the afterlife. However, if the heart was heavy with sin or wrongdoing, the soul would face punishment or even annihilation.

To ensure a favorable judgment and a successful transition into the afterlife, the ancient Egyptians engaged in various burial practices and rituals. The process of mummification was a crucial part of this. The body was preserved through a meticulous and lengthy process, which involved removing the internal organs, desiccating the body with natron salts, and wrapping it in layers of linen bandages. The preservation of the body was believed to be essential for the soul's continued existence and well-being in the afterlife.

Alongside mummification, funerary rituals and ceremonies were performed to honor the deceased and provide them with the necessary provisions and offerings for the afterlife. These rituals included prayers, incantations, and the presentation of food, drink, and other items in the tomb. The ancient Egyptians believed that the deceased required sustenance and resources in the afterlife and that their living relatives had a responsibility to provide for their spiritual needs.

Tombs and burial sites played a central role in the cult of the dead. The construction and decoration of tombs were elaborate and carefully planned, reflecting the individual's social status and wealth. Tombs were designed to serve as eternal homes for the deceased and were filled with grave goods, including furniture, jewelry, food, and personal belongings, to ensure their comfort and well-being in the afterlife. The walls of tombs were adorned with intricate paintings and inscriptions, depicting scenes from the deceased's life and offering prayers and invocations for their successful journey and judgment.

The cult of the dead also included the veneration of ancestors and the belief in their continued presence and influence in the lives of the living. Ancestor worship and the commemoration of the deceased through rituals and offerings were common practices, reinforcing the connection between the living and the dead and maintaining a sense of familial and communal identity.

The cult of the dead in ancient Egypt was deeply rooted in the belief in the afterlife and the desire for immortality. It shaped the religious and funerary practices of the civilization, emphasizing the importance of proper burial, preservation of the body, and adherence to religious rituals to ensure a favorable judgment and eternal life in the afterworld. The cult of the dead played a significant role in shaping ancient Egyptian society and its religious beliefs and continues to fascinate and intrigue scholars and enthusiasts to this day.

Example: The Book of the Dead, a collection of spells and instructions, was placed in tombs to guide the deceased through the perilous journey in the afterlife. It highlights the importance of proper burial rites and the rituals performed to ensure the deceased's well-being in the divine realm.

Conclusion:

The religious beliefs and practices central to ancient Egyptian society provide valuable insights into their worldview, values, and cultural expressions. The polytheistic pantheon, mythology, rituals, and the cult of the dead all played significant roles in shaping the religious fabric of the civilization. By examining these beliefs and practices, students can appreciate the intricate interplay between religion, daily life, and social structure in ancient Egypt. This exploration opens doors to critical thinking about the nature of spirituality, the role of mythology in culture, and the enduring legacy of ancient Egyptian religious beliefs in modern interpretations and practices.

Discussion of key concepts, such as the afterlife, the soul, and divine beings, in the ancient Egyptian worldview

To gain a comprehensive understanding of the ancient Egyptian worldview, it is crucial to examine key concepts that shaped their religious beliefs and practices. This section delves into the discussion of three fundamental concepts: the afterlife, the soul, and divine beings. These concepts were intricately intertwined, forming the bedrock of ancient Egyptian spirituality and providing insights into their beliefs about the nature of existence, the human experience, and the relationship between mortals and the divine.

The Afterlife:

The ancient Egyptians held a deep belief in an afterlife, considering it as a continuation of the human journey beyond death. Their understanding of the afterlife was complex and multifaceted, involving various stages, rituals, and judgments. The concept of an afterlife offered hope for an eternal existence and was intricately linked to the preservation of the physical body through mummification.

The ancient Egyptians had a profound belief in the existence of an afterlife, which they considered to be a continuation of the human journey beyond death. Their understanding of the afterlife was shaped by a complex set of beliefs and rituals, reflecting their desire for immortality and eternal existence.

The ancient Egyptians believed that after death, the soul, or "ka," separated from the physical body and embarked on a journey to the afterlife. The soul was believed to retain its individuality and consciousness, allowing for the continuation of personal identity and experiences. However, the successful transition to the afterlife required careful preparations and adherence to religious rituals and beliefs.

One of the key beliefs regarding the afterlife was the judgment of the soul. According to ancient Egyptian mythology and religious texts, the soul would undergo a judgment process after death, known as the "Weighing of the Heart" or the "Judgment of Osiris." In this process, the heart of the deceased was weighed against the feather of Ma'at, the goddess of truth and justice. The heart symbolized the moral character of the individual, while the feather represented the principles of Ma'at, which included concepts like truth, balance, and righteousness. If the heart was found to be lighter than the feather, indicating a life lived in accordance with Ma'at's principles, the soul would be granted eternal life in the afterlife. However, if the heart was heavy with sin or wrongdoing, the soul would face punishment or even annihilation.

To ensure a favorable judgment and a successful transition to the afterlife, the ancient Egyptians engaged in various rituals and practices. Mummification, the preservation of the physical body, was a crucial aspect. The belief was that the soul still needed a physical form to continue its existence in the afterlife. Mummification involved removing the internal organs, desiccating the body with natron salts, and wrapping it in layers of linen bandages. The process aimed to preserve the body and protect it from decay, allowing the soul to recognize and re-inhabit it in the afterlife.

Alongside mummification, funerary rituals and ceremonies were performed to honor the deceased and provide them with the necessary provisions and offerings for the afterlife. These rituals included prayers, incantations, and the presentation of food, drink, and other items in the tomb. The ancient Egyptians believed that the deceased required sustenance and resources in the afterlife and that their living relatives had a responsibility to provide for their spiritual needs.

The afterlife was also depicted as a realm of abundance and joy. In the religious texts and funerary inscriptions, it was described as a place of fertile fields, abundant offerings, and peaceful existence. The deceased were believed to engage in activities similar to their earthly lives, enjoying the company of loved ones and participating in activities that brought them happiness.

Additionally, the ancient Egyptians believed in the importance of tombs and burial sites as eternal homes for the deceased. The construction and decoration of tombs were elaborate and carefully planned, reflecting the individual's social status and wealth. Tombs were filled with grave goods and offerings to ensure the comfort and well-being of the deceased in the afterlife. The walls of tombs were adorned with intricate paintings and inscriptions, depicting scenes from the deceased's life and offering prayers and invocations for their successful journey and judgment.

The concept of the afterlife played a significant role in shaping ancient Egyptian religious beliefs, funerary practices, and societal norms. It provided a framework for understanding and coping with the mysteries of death and offered a sense of hope and continuity beyond earthly existence. The complex beliefs and rituals surrounding the afterlife reflected the ancient Egyptians' desire for eternal life and their deep reverence for the spiritual realm.

Example: The ancient Egyptian Book of the Dead, a collection of spells and rituals, provided guidance and protection for the deceased during their journey in the afterlife. This text highlights the importance of proper burial rites and the performance of rituals to ensure a favorable outcome in the divine realm.

The Soul:

In ancient Egyptian spirituality, the soul was considered a multifaceted entity composed of several components. The concept of the soul encompassed different aspects, including the ka (life force), the ba (individuality), and the akh (transfigured spirit). Each aspect played a distinct role in the individual's existence, both in life and the afterlife.

In ancient Egyptian spirituality, the soul was believed to be a complex and multi-faceted entity that comprised several components, each with its own significance and function.

Ka: The ka was considered the life force or vital energy of an individual. It was believed to be an essential element that animated the body and provided the spark of life. The ka was associated with personal identity and was believed to continue to exist after death. It required sustenance and offerings in the form of food and drink to ensure its well-being in the afterlife.

Ba: The ba represented the individuality and personality of a person. It was often depicted as a bird with a human head and was believed to be able to move freely between the earthly realm and the realm of the divine. The ba was associated with mobility, communication, and the ability to interact with the gods and deceased ancestors. It played a significant role in the afterlife journey, allowing the deceased to navigate the realms and receive divine blessings.

Akh: The akh represented the transfigured or glorified state of the deceased. It was associated with the concept of enlightenment, transformation, and ascension to a higher spiritual plane. The akh was believed to be achieved through the successful completion of the afterlife journey and the favorable judgment of the heart. It allowed the individual to join the ranks of the gods and enjoy eternal existence and participation in the cosmic order.

These three components of the soul, the ka, ba, and akh, worked together to define the individual's spiritual existence and journey. They represented different aspects of the human experience and contributed to the understanding of personal identity, consciousness, and the afterlife.

The ancient Egyptians believed that the soul continued to exist beyond death and that its journey in the afterlife was influenced by the preservation of the physical body through mummification and the performance of funerary rituals. The ultimate goal was to ensure the successful transition and eternal existence of the soul in the afterlife.

The concept of the soul in ancient Egyptian spirituality reflected their belief in the continuity of personal identity and the existence of an eternal essence that transcended physical life. It emphasized the interconnectedness of the human and divine realms and provided a framework for understanding the nature of the self and the afterlife journey.

Example: The ka, often represented as a double of the physical body, was believed to sustain life and ensure vitality. It required offerings and rituals to maintain its well-being. Understanding the intricacies of the soul in the ancient Egyptian worldview sheds light on their perceptions of personal identity and the journey of the deceased in the afterlife.

Divine Beings:

The ancient Egyptians worshipped a pantheon of gods and goddesses, each embodying specific attributes and roles within the cosmic order. Divine beings were believed to possess immense power and authority over various aspects of life, nature, and the afterlife. Their worship and rituals were central to maintaining harmony and balance in the world.

Example: The god Osiris, associated with death, resurrection, and the afterlife, played a pivotal role in the ancient Egyptian worldview. He symbolized the cycle of life, death, and rebirth, serving as a divine judge in the afterlife. Exploring the significance of divine beings like Osiris helps us understand the Egyptian understanding of the nature of divinity and its influence on human existence.

Conclusion:

The concepts of the afterlife, the soul, and divine beings formed the foundation of the ancient Egyptian worldview. The belief in an afterlife provided hope and purpose beyond earthly existence, while the multifaceted nature of the soul reflected their understanding of personal identity and transcendence. Divine beings represented the forces and principles that governed the world, serving as intermediaries between mortals and the divine realm. By examining these key concepts, students can delve into the depths of ancient Egyptian spirituality, gaining a profound appreciation for the complexities of their religious beliefs and their influence on the daily lives of the ancient Egyptians.

Chapter 4: Historical and Cultural Context

Understanding the historical and cultural context of ancient religious traditions is essential for comprehending their beliefs, practices, and significance. This chapter provides a comprehensive exploration of the historical and cultural backdrop against which ancient religious systems, such as witchcraft, divination, herbalism, shamanism, and ecospirituality, emerged and evolved. By delving into the socio-political, economic, and cultural aspects of different civilizations and time periods, students will gain a deeper appreciation for the influences that shaped religious beliefs and practices throughout history.

Socio-Political Context:

The socio-political context plays a significant role in shaping religious traditions. It involves analyzing the political structures, power dynamics, and social organization of ancient civilizations. Understanding how societal hierarchies, rulers, and governing systems influenced religious practices provides valuable insights into the role of religion in maintaining social order, political legitimacy, and cultural identity.

The ancient Egyptians had a rich and diverse pantheon of gods and goddesses, each associated with specific domains, attributes, and roles within their cosmology. These divine beings played a significant role in the religious beliefs and practices of the ancient Egyptians.

Ra (Re): Ra was the sun god and one of the most important deities in the Egyptian pantheon. He represented the sun's life-giving and transformative power, and was associated with creation, light, and divine kingship. Ra was often depicted as a falcon-headed man or a sun disc.

Isis: Isis was a powerful goddess associated with magic, fertility, and motherhood. She was the sister and wife of Osiris, and the mother of Horus. Isis was revered as a protector and healer, and she was often depicted as a woman with a throne or cow-horn headdress.

Osiris: Osiris was the god of the afterlife, resurrection, and fertility. He ruled over the realm of the dead and was considered the judge of souls. Osiris was depicted as a mummified figure or a pharaoh, often with a crook and flail, symbols of his authority.

Hathor: Hathor was the goddess of love, beauty, joy, and music. She was often depicted as a cow or as a woman with cow horns and a sun disc. Hathor was associated with nurturing and protective qualities and was revered as the divine mother.

Horus: Horus was the falcon-headed god associated with kingship and the sky. He was the son of Isis and Osiris and was considered the rightful ruler of Egypt. Horus was also associated with protection and was often depicted as a falcon or as a man with a falcon head.

Anubis: Anubis was the god of embalming and the guardian of the necropolis. He was depicted with the head of a jackal and played a crucial role in the mummification process and the judgment of the deceased. Anubis guided the souls through the afterlife and ensured their proper burial and protection.

These are just a few examples of the many gods and goddesses worshipped by the ancient Egyptians. Each deity had specific roles, responsibilities, and attributes that contributed to the understanding of the cosmic order and the religious practices of the civilization. The worship of these divine beings was integral to maintaining harmony, seeking blessings, and navigating the complexities of life, death, and the afterlife in ancient Egyptian society.

Example: In ancient Egypt, the pharaohs held divine authority, and their religious roles were intertwined with their political positions. The pharaohs were believed to be intermediaries between the divine realm and the mortal world, which significantly influenced the religious practices and rituals of the Egyptian society.

Economic Context:

Economic factors also influenced the development and expression of religious beliefs. Economic systems, trade networks, and access to resources influenced the prosperity and stability of ancient civilizations. The economic context shaped the religious practices associated with fertility, abundance, and prosperity, as well as the veneration of specific deities associated with economic activities.

The economic context played a significant role in shaping the religious beliefs and practices of ancient civilizations, including ancient Egypt. The economic factors, such as trade, resources, and prosperity, influenced the expression and development of religious traditions in the following ways:

Fertility and Abundance: The agricultural economy of ancient Egypt, heavily dependent on the fertile land along the Nile River, led to the veneration of deities associated with fertility and abundance. The annual flooding of the Nile brought fertile soil, allowing for successful crop cultivation. As a result, deities such as Osiris and Isis, who were associated with agricultural fertility, were highly revered.

Trade Networks: Ancient Egypt had access to valuable resources such as gold, precious stones, papyrus, and exotic goods. The economic importance of trade led to the development of religious practices associated with commerce and prosperity. Deities such as Hathor, associated with trade and wealth, were worshipped and invoked for successful trading ventures.

Patron Deities: Certain deities were associated with specific economic activities or professions. For example, Ptah, the god of craftsmanship and creation, was revered by artisans and craftsmen. In contrast, Wepwawet, the opener of the ways, was associated with trade and served as a protector of caravans and merchants.

Offerings and Sacrifices: Economic prosperity often influenced the types and quantities of offerings and sacrifices made to the gods. Wealthier individuals and communities were able to offer more valuable and abundant offerings, demonstrating their devotion and seeking favor from the divine.

Temples and Economic Centers: Temples not only served as religious centers but also played a role in the economic life of ancient Egypt. They served as economic hubs, managing agricultural lands, granaries, and redistribution of resources. The economic activities associated with temples were often intertwined with religious practices and offerings.

The economic context influenced the religious beliefs and practices of ancient Egyptians, shaping the veneration of specific deities, the emphasis on fertility and prosperity, and the role of temples as economic centers. The interplay between economic factors and religion demonstrates how the ancient Egyptians integrated their economic life and spiritual beliefs, seeking divine assistance and blessings for their economic well-being and success.

Example: In ancient Mesopotamia, the city of Uruk thrived as a center of trade and economic activity. The goddess Inanna, associated with love, fertility, and prosperity, was revered as the patron deity of the city. The economic prosperity of Uruk was deeply intertwined with the religious devotion to Inanna, highlighting the influence of economic factors on religious beliefs and practices.

Cultural Context:

Cultural factors, including language, literature, art, and social norms, shape the expression and interpretation of religious traditions. Cultural context provides insights into the symbolism, rituals, and narratives embedded within religious systems. It encompasses examining myths, cosmologies, artistic representations, and the role of religious specialists in society.

Cultural context is essential for understanding the expression and interpretation of religious traditions. It provides insights into the ways in which a society's language, literature, art, and social norms shape their religious beliefs and practices. Here are some key aspects of cultural context:

Language and Literature: The language used to convey religious concepts and beliefs plays a significant role in shaping religious expression. Ancient Egyptian religious texts, such as the Pyramid Texts and the Book of the Dead, were written in hieroglyphic script and provided a wealth of knowledge about their religious beliefs and rituals. The language used in these texts was deeply symbolic and carried layers of meaning. Understanding the cultural context helps to decipher and interpret these texts.

Myths and Narratives: Cultural context provides a framework for understanding the myths and narratives that form the basis of religious beliefs. Myths often reflect the cultural values, social norms, and historical experiences of a society. Exploring the myths and narratives of ancient Egypt helps to uncover their worldview, cosmology, and the roles of gods and goddesses within their religious system.

Art and Symbolism: Artistic representations, such as paintings, sculptures, and reliefs, offer valuable insights into the religious beliefs and practices of a culture. In ancient Egypt, artistic depictions of deities, rituals, and mythological scenes provided visual narratives that communicated religious ideas and concepts. Understanding the cultural context helps to interpret the symbolism, iconography, and artistic conventions used in religious art.

Social Norms and Roles: Cultural context sheds light on the social norms and roles within a religious system. It explores the roles of priests, priestesses, and other religious specialists, as well as their interactions with the wider society. Examining the social structure, gender roles, and religious hierarchies provides a deeper understanding of the dynamics between religious practices and societal norms.

Rituals and Festivals: Cultural context helps us grasp the significance and purpose of religious rituals and festivals within a society. These practices are often deeply embedded in cultural traditions, marking important events, seasons, or stages of life. Understanding the cultural context enables us to appreciate the symbolic meanings, social functions, and communal aspects of these rituals.

By exploring the cultural context of a religious tradition, we gain a deeper understanding of the symbols, rituals, narratives, and social dynamics that shape its expression. It allows us to appreciate the richness and complexity of a culture's religious beliefs and practices, as well as the interplay between religion and other aspects of life.

Example: The Celtic culture, prevalent in ancient Europe, placed great emphasis on the interconnectedness of nature and spirituality. The celebration of seasonal festivals, the veneration of nature spirits, and the role of druids as religious leaders reflected the cultural context of the Celtic people and their deep reverence for the natural world.

Conclusion:

The historical and cultural context surrounding ancient religious traditions is crucial for comprehending their complexity, symbolism, and significance. By examining the socio-political, economic, and cultural factors at play, students gain a holistic understanding of how religion intersected with various aspects of ancient societies. This knowledge enhances their ability to critically analyze religious beliefs and practices, recognize the influences of broader societal forces, and appreciate the diversity and richness of ancient religious traditions. Throughout this chapter, students will engage in discussions, exercises, and problem-solving activities that encourage critical thinking and a nuanced understanding of the historical and cultural contexts that shaped ancient religious systems.

In-depth exploration of the historical timeline of ancient Egypt, including major dynasties, rulers, and pivotal events

To fully comprehend the religious beliefs and practices of ancient Egypt, it is crucial to delve into the historical timeline of this civilization. This section provides a comprehensive examination of the major dynasties, rulers, and pivotal events that shaped ancient Egyptian society. By tracing the historical trajectory of Egypt, students will develop a deeper understanding of the cultural, political, and religious developments that influenced the spiritual traditions of this remarkable civilization.

Predynastic Period:

The Predynastic Period marks the earliest stage of ancient Egyptian history, spanning from approximately 6000 BCE to 3100 BCE. During this era, small tribes settled along the Nile River, establishing agricultural communities and engaging in early religious practices. The emergence of complex societies and the development of early religious beliefs laid the foundation for the subsequent dynastic periods.

The Predynastic Period in ancient Egyptian history refers to the time before the unification of Upper and Lower Egypt into a centralized state. It is a significant era that witnessed the transition from small-scale hunter-gatherer communities to settled agricultural societies along the Nile River.

Early Settlements: During this period, communities began to settle along the fertile floodplain of the Nile River. These settlements gradually developed into small villages and towns. The Nile River played a crucial role in providing a reliable water source for agriculture, contributing to the growth and stability of these early settlements.

Agricultural Revolution: The Predynastic Period saw the advent of agriculture in ancient Egypt. Communities began to cultivate crops such as wheat and barley, establishing a sedentary lifestyle and transitioning from a nomadic to an agrarian society. Agriculture allowed for surplus food production, leading to population growth and the emergence of social complexity.

Social Organization: With the growth of settlements and the development of agriculture, social hierarchies began to form. Some individuals in the community became specialized in certain tasks, such as farming, pottery-making, or animal husbandry. Social distinctions based on occupation and wealth became more pronounced during this period.

Burial Practices: The Predynastic Period witnessed the development of burial customs that reflect the emerging religious beliefs of the time. Burial sites often contained grave goods, such as pottery, tools, and personal ornaments, suggesting a belief in an afterlife and the provision of material items for the deceased. Some burial sites also exhibited signs of social differentiation, indicating that social status was recognized even in death.

Cultural Diversity: The Predynastic Period was marked by cultural diversity and regional variations across different areas of ancient Egypt. Different communities had their own unique artistic styles, pottery traditions, and burial practices. This diversity gradually merged as the country unified during the subsequent dynastic periods.

The Predynastic Period laid the groundwork for the later development of the ancient Egyptian civilization. It was during this time that the early religious beliefs and practices began to take shape, setting the stage for the complex religious system that would emerge in the subsequent dynasties. The transition to settled agriculture and the establishment of social hierarchies were significant milestones in the cultural and social evolution of ancient Egypt.

Example: The Narmer Palette, a significant archaeological artifact from the Predynastic Period, depicts the unification of Upper and Lower Egypt by King Narmer. This event symbolizes the consolidation of political and religious power, paving the way for the rise of the pharaohs.

Old Kingdom:

The Old Kingdom, spanning from 3100 BCE to 2181 BCE, was characterized by the establishment of a centralized state and the construction of iconic pyramids. The pharaohs of the Fourth Dynasty, such as Khufu, Khafre, and Menkaure, oversaw the construction of the Great Pyramids of Giza, which exemplify the grandeur and religious significance attributed to the pharaohs during this period.

The Old Kingdom was a crucial period in ancient Egyptian history, known for its centralized political structure, monumental architecture, and cultural achievements. Here are some key aspects of the Old Kingdom:

Political Organization: The Old Kingdom saw the establishment of a strong centralized state, with the pharaoh as the supreme ruler. The pharaoh held both political and religious authority, being considered a divine figure and the intermediary between the gods and the people. The pharaoh's role was crucial in maintaining cosmic order and ensuring the prosperity of the kingdom.

Pyramid Construction: One of the most remarkable features of the Old Kingdom was the construction of monumental pyramids as tombs for the pharaohs. The pyramids, particularly those at Giza, were massive structures designed to protect the pharaoh's body and possessions for eternity. They were built with precision and engineering ingenuity, reflecting the religious and cultural significance attributed to the pharaohs as divine rulers.

Religious Beliefs: The religious beliefs during the Old Kingdom centered around the pharaoh's divine status and the worship of a pantheon of gods and goddesses. The pharaoh was believed to be the earthly embodiment of Horus, the falcon-headed god associated with kingship. Religious rituals and offerings were conducted to maintain harmony between the mortal world and the divine realm.

Administrative Reforms: The Old Kingdom witnessed the implementation of administrative reforms aimed at centralizing power and maintaining efficient governance. The pharaoh appointed officials to oversee various administrative duties, including taxation, construction projects, and resource management. These reforms contributed to the stability and prosperity of the kingdom.

Art and Culture: The Old Kingdom was a period of artistic and cultural flourishing. It saw the development of iconic art forms, such as relief sculptures and statues that depicted pharaohs, gods, and everyday life scenes. These artistic representations aimed to perpetuate the pharaoh's divine and immortal nature. Literary works, known as Pyramid Texts, also emerged during this period, providing insights into the religious beliefs and rituals associated with the afterlife.

Decline and Transition: Towards the end of the Old Kingdom, there was a gradual decline in political stability, economic prosperity, and pyramid construction. Factors such as social unrest, environmental changes, and challenges to central authority contributed to this decline. The Old Kingdom eventually transitioned into the First Intermediate Period, marked by a fragmented political landscape and regional struggles for power.

The Old Kingdom represents a period of monumental achievements and the zenith of ancient Egyptian civilization. The construction of pyramids, the religious prominence of the pharaohs, and the cultural advancements established enduring symbols of power, religious belief, and architectural marvel that continue to captivate and inspire people to this day.

Example: The Pyramid Texts, a collection of funerary spells and rituals inscribed within the pyramids, provide insights into the religious beliefs and practices associated with the afterlife during the Old Kingdom. These texts reflect the divine status of the pharaoh and the rituals performed to ensure their journey to the realm of the gods.

Middle Kingdom:

The Middle Kingdom, spanning from 2055 BCE to 1650 BCE, witnessed a period of reunification and cultural renaissance. Pharaohs of the Twelfth Dynasty, such as Amenemhat III, embarked on ambitious building projects, expanded trade networks, and promoted a sense of social justice. The Middle Kingdom also saw the development of new religious texts, such as the Coffin Texts, which provided instructions and spells for the afterlife.

The Middle Kingdom was a significant period in ancient Egyptian history, known for its cultural revival, political stability, and advancements in various aspects of society. Here are some key features of the Middle Kingdom:

Reunification and Stability: The Middle Kingdom marked a period of reunification following the fragmentation of the First Intermediate Period. Pharaohs of the Twelfth Dynasty, such as Amenemhat I, established a strong central authority, restored order, and consolidated power over Egypt. This period brought a sense of political stability and unity to the kingdom.

Building Projects and Infrastructure: The pharaohs of the Middle Kingdom undertook ambitious building projects, constructing temples, palaces, and irrigation systems. These projects aimed to improve the infrastructure of the kingdom, enhance agricultural productivity, and ensure the well-being of the people. The construction of monumental structures reflected the pharaohs' desire to demonstrate their power and promote economic prosperity.

Trade and Diplomacy: The Middle Kingdom witnessed an expansion of trade networks, both within Egypt and with neighboring regions. Egyptian merchants traded with Nubia, the Levant, and even as far as the Aegean. Trade brought wealth and cultural exchange, influencing the development of art, technology, and ideas. Diplomatic relations were also established with neighboring kingdoms, fostering political alliances and economic cooperation.

Social Justice and Reforms: The pharaohs of the Middle Kingdom emphasized the importance of social justice and implemented reforms to alleviate the hardships faced by the common people. They enacted laws to protect the rights of the lower classes, redistributed resources to support those in need, and actively engaged in public works projects to provide employment opportunities.

Religious Developments: The Middle Kingdom saw the development of new religious texts known as the Coffin Texts. These texts were inscribed on coffins and provided instructions, spells, and prayers to assist the deceased in their journey to the afterlife. The Coffin Texts expanded on the earlier Pyramid Texts, making these religious teachings more accessible to a wider range of individuals.

Cultural Renaissance: The Middle Kingdom witnessed a cultural and artistic renaissance, with a resurgence of literature, poetry, and artistic expressions. The literature of this period reflected a more humanistic approach, focusing on themes of love, nature, and moral values. Artistic styles also evolved, with a greater emphasis on naturalism and emotional depth in sculptures and paintings.

Decline and Second Intermediate Period: Towards the end of the Middle Kingdom, the central authority weakened, leading to a period of unrest and instability known as the Second Intermediate Period. This era was characterized by invasions from foreign powers, particularly the Hyksos, who eventually established their rule over northern Egypt.

The Middle Kingdom represents a period of cultural revival, political stability, and social reforms. It was a time of artistic and intellectual flourishing, with advancements in literature, trade, and governance. The pharaohs' focus on social justice and infrastructure development left a lasting impact on Egyptian society. Despite the eventual decline and the challenges of the Second Intermediate Period, the Middle Kingdom is considered a significant era in ancient Egyptian history.

Example: The Story of Sinuhe, a literary masterpiece from the Middle Kingdom, narrates the journey of an Egyptian official who flees Egypt after the death of his king. This narrative highlights the cultural and religious values of loyalty, honor, and the longing for a proper burial within the context of the Middle Kingdom.

New Kingdom:

The New Kingdom, spanning from 1550 BCE to 1069 BCE, represents a period of immense political and military power for ancient Egypt. Pharaohs such as Hatshepsut, Thutmose III, and Ramesses II expanded Egypt's territories, engaged in international diplomacy, and promoted a complex religious ideology. The worship of Amun-Ra, the sun god, became prominent during this period, and the construction of grand temples, such as Karnak and Luxor, exemplified the religious fervor of the New Kingdom.

The New Kingdom is widely regarded as the most glorious and powerful period in ancient Egyptian history. Here are some key features of the New Kingdom:

Military Exploits and Imperial Expansion: The pharaohs of the New Kingdom embarked on ambitious military campaigns, expanding Egypt's territories and establishing an empire. Pharaoh Thutmose III, known as the "Napoleon of Egypt," conducted numerous successful military campaigns that brought vast lands under Egyptian control, including parts of Nubia, Canaan, and Syria. The military conquests brought wealth, resources, and tribute to Egypt, solidifying its status as a dominant power in the region.

Diplomacy and International Relations: The New Kingdom saw an increased focus on diplomacy and international relations. Pharaohs engaged in diplomatic marriages, strategic alliances, and trade agreements with neighboring kingdoms and city-states. They established diplomatic ties with powerful empires, such as the Hittites and Mitanni, and engaged in cultural exchanges and diplomatic correspondence.

Prominence of Amun-Ra: The worship of Amun-Ra, the sun god, reached its peak during the New Kingdom. Amun-Ra was associated with kingship and was considered the king of the gods. The pharaohs emphasized their connection to Amun-Ra, and the priesthood of Amun gained significant influence and wealth. The temples dedicated to Amun-Ra, such as the Karnak Temple complex in Thebes, were expanded and adorned with elaborate decorations and reliefs.

Prominent Pharaohs: The New Kingdom was characterized by several notable pharaohs who left a lasting impact on Egypt's history. Pharaoh Hatshepsut, one of the few female pharaohs, achieved great prosperity through trade expeditions and oversaw the construction of impressive monuments. Pharaoh Akhenaten introduced a radical religious reform, focusing on the worship of a single deity, the Aten, and shifting away from the traditional polytheistic beliefs. Pharaoh Ramesses II, often referred to as Ramesses the Great, is renowned for his military campaigns, grand building projects, and the signing of the world's first known peace treaty with the Hittites.

Architectural Marvels: The New Kingdom witnessed the construction of grand temples and monumental structures that showcased the wealth, power, and religious devotion of the pharaohs. The Temple of Karnak, dedicated to Amun-Ra, was expanded and became one of the largest religious complexes in the world. The Mortuary Temple of Hatshepsut at Deir el-Bahari, with its imposing terraces and statues, is considered a masterpiece of ancient Egyptian architecture. The Valley of the Kings became the final resting place for many New Kingdom pharaohs, housing intricately decorated tombs.

Royal Burial Practices: The New Kingdom saw a shift in royal burial practices. While pyramids were no longer constructed, the pharaohs and the elite were buried in hidden tombs in the Valley of the Kings and the Valley of the Queens. These tombs were adorned with intricate paintings, religious texts, and burial goods to accompany the deceased on their journey to the afterlife.

Decline and End of the New Kingdom: The New Kingdom gradually declined due to various factors, including economic challenges, political instability, and invasions from foreign powers. The reign of pharaohs in the later years of the New Kingdom became less centralized and effective, leading to a period of decline known as the Third Intermediate Period.

The New Kingdom was a period of military conquests, political power, and religious fervor. It witnessed the expansion of Egypt's territories, the prominence of Amun-Ra in religious worship, and the construction of grand temples and monumental structures. The pharaohs of the New Kingdom left a lasting legacy in terms of military achievements, architectural marvels, and cultural impact.

Example: The Amarna Period, under the reign of Akhenaten, brought a significant religious revolution with the introduction of Atenism, the worship of the sun-disk Aten as the supreme deity. This period challenged the traditional polytheistic beliefs and rituals, emphasizing a monotheistic approach centered on the sun god.

Late Period:

The Late Period, spanning from 664 BCE to 332 BCE, witnessed the decline of native Egyptian rule as foreign powers, such as the Persians and Greeks, exerted influence over the region. The Ptolemaic Dynasty, of Greek origin, ruled Egypt during the later phase of this period, and the Hellenistic influence blended with traditional Egyptian religious practices.

The Late Period in ancient Egyptian history was a time of significant political and cultural changes. Here are some key features of the Late Period:

Foreign Dominance: The Late Period marked a period of foreign dominance and influence over Egypt. It began with the invasion and conquest of Egypt by the Assyrians in 664 BCE, followed by the rule of other foreign powers such as the Persians and Greeks. The Persian Empire, under the rule of Cambyses II, conquered Egypt and established the 27th Dynasty. Later, the Greeks, led by Alexander the Great, conquered Egypt, paving the way for the Ptolemaic Dynasty.

Exploring the Esoteric Wisdom of Ancient Egypt for Modern Spirituality

Ptolemaic Dynasty: The Ptolemaic Dynasty, founded by Ptolemy I Soter, a general under Alexander the Great, ruled Egypt from 305 BCE to 30 BCE. The Ptolemaic rulers were of Greek descent and adopted Egyptian titles and traditions to legitimize their rule. They established Alexandria as the capital and cultural center of Egypt and promoted a fusion of Greek and Egyptian culture, known as Hellenistic Egypt.

Hellenistic Influence: The Late Period saw the blending of Greek and Egyptian culture, resulting in a distinctive Hellenistic influence on Egyptian religious practices and art. Greek gods and goddesses were assimilated into the Egyptian pantheon, and Greek-style statues and architectural elements began to appear in Egyptian temples and artwork. The Greek language and script also gained prominence alongside the traditional Egyptian hieroglyphs.

Temple Building and Patronage: Despite the foreign dominance, temple building and religious practices continued during the Late Period. The Ptolemaic rulers were prolific temple builders and patrons of the arts. They commissioned the construction and embellishment of numerous temples, contributing to the preservation and expansion of Egyptian religious traditions.

Priestly Influence: The priesthood held significant influence during the Late Period, particularly in the Ptolemaic era. The priests served as intermediaries between the people and the gods, maintaining religious rituals and offering guidance to the rulers. The temples became centers of religious and economic power, with the priests playing important roles in both religious and administrative affairs.

Decline and End: The Late Period gradually saw a decline in the political stability and prosperity of Egypt. Internal conflicts, revolts against foreign rule, and challenges from neighboring powers weakened the Egyptian state. The end of the Late Period came with the conquest of Egypt by Alexander the Great and the subsequent establishment of the Hellenistic Ptolemaic Dynasty.

The Late Period marked a significant shift in Egyptian history, with foreign powers exerting control over Egypt and introducing new cultural influences. The Ptolemaic Dynasty and the fusion of Greek and Egyptian cultures left a lasting impact on the religious practices, art, and architecture of ancient Egypt.

Example: The Rosetta Stone, discovered in 1799, provided a crucial key to deciphering ancient Egyptian hieroglyphs. The inscription on the stone, written in multiple scripts, including hieroglyphs, demotic script, and Greek, played a vital role in unlocking the mysteries of ancient Egyptian language, history, and religious texts.

Conclusion:

The historical timeline of ancient Egypt unveils a captivating saga of political power, cultural achievements, and religious developments. The rise and fall of dynasties, the construction of monumental structures, and the evolution of religious beliefs provide students with a rich tapestry of events and cultural transformations. By engaging in critical analysis and problem-solving exercises throughout this section, students will gain a deep appreciation for the historical context that shaped ancient Egyptian religious traditions.

Analysis of the cultural and societal influences on ancient Egyptian religious beliefs and practices

The religious beliefs and practices of ancient Egypt were profoundly influenced by the cultural and societal factors that shaped the civilization. This section provides an in-depth analysis of the various influences, both internal and external, that contributed to the development and evolution of ancient Egyptian religious traditions. By examining the cultural and societal dynamics, students will gain a comprehensive understanding of the multifaceted nature of ancient Egyptian spirituality.

Geographical Factors:

The geographical landscape of ancient Egypt played a significant role in shaping religious beliefs and practices. The Nile River, with its annual flooding, provided fertile land for agriculture, enabling the growth of settled communities. The Egyptians revered the Nile as a life-giving force, attributing divine qualities to its waters. This agricultural dependency fostered a close connection between the natural world and religious rituals centered around fertility, abundance, and the cyclical patterns of life.

The geographical factors of ancient Egypt, particularly the Nile River and its surrounding landscape, had a profound impact on the religious beliefs and practices of the ancient Egyptians. Here are some key points to consider:

Nile River: The Nile River was the lifeblood of ancient Egypt. It provided a reliable source of water for irrigation, which was crucial for the success of agriculture. The annual flooding of the Nile deposited nutrient-rich silt onto the floodplain, creating fertile land for farming. This cyclical pattern of flooding and receding waters played a central role in the religious beliefs and rituals of the ancient Egyptians.

Fertility and Abundance: The fertile land along the Nile and the agricultural prosperity it brought were considered gifts from the gods. The ancient Egyptians believed that the gods controlled the floods and ensured the fertility of the land. As a result, religious rituals and festivals were held to honor and appease the deities associated with fertility and abundance, such as Osiris, the god of agriculture, and Hapi, the personification of the Nile flood.

Symbolism of the Nile: The Nile River held symbolic significance beyond its role in agriculture. It was seen as a symbol of life and rebirth, reflecting the cyclical nature of existence. The ancient Egyptians associated the Nile with the goddess Hapi, who was depicted as a figure with abundant breasts, symbolizing the nourishment and sustenance provided by the river.

Sacred Landscapes: The geography of Egypt, with the Nile cutting through deserts on either side, created a distinct contrast between fertile and barren landscapes. This juxtaposition influenced the perception of sacred spaces. The Nile Valley and its fertile banks were seen as places of divine presence, where temples and cult centers were constructed. The desert regions, on the other hand, were associated with the realm of the dead and the afterlife.

Sacred Animals and Natural Phenomena: The diverse natural features of Egypt, including wildlife, flora, and celestial bodies, were associated with specific deities and considered sacred. Animals such as the sacred ibis, scarab beetle, and cat were revered and had religious significance. Celestial bodies, such as the sun (Ra) and the sky (Nut), were considered divine entities, reflecting the ancient Egyptians' connection between the natural world and the divine.

Overall, the geographical factors of ancient Egypt, especially the presence of the Nile River and the unique landscape, deeply influenced the religious beliefs and practices of the civilization. The Nile's fertility, symbolism of life and rebirth, and the distinction between sacred and barren landscapes all shaped the religious worldview of the ancient Egyptians, reinforcing their connection with the divine and the cyclical nature of existence.

Example: The festival of Opet, celebrated during the flood season, honored the rejuvenation of the land and the renewal of life. The procession of statues of the deities from Karnak Temple to Luxor Temple represented the symbiotic relationship between the Nile's inundation and the divine powers associated with fertility and prosperity.

Social Hierarchy:

Ancient Egyptian society was highly structured, with a hierarchical system that permeated all aspects of life, including religious practices. At the pinnacle of the social order was the pharaoh, considered a divine ruler and a mediator between the earthly realm and the gods. The pharaoh's role in religious ceremonies and rituals underscored the close connection between political power and religious authority.

The social hierarchy in ancient Egypt played a crucial role in shaping religious practices and beliefs. Here are some key points to elaborate on:

Pharaoh: At the top of the social hierarchy was the pharaoh, who held immense political and religious power. The pharaoh was believed to be a living god, the earthly manifestation of divine authority, and the intermediary between the gods and the people. As the highest religious authority, the pharaoh played a central role in religious ceremonies, rituals, and offerings. The construction of temples and the performance of grand religious festivals were often associated with the pharaoh's divine legitimacy and authority.

Priesthood: The priestly class held a significant position within ancient Egyptian society. Priests served as intermediaries between the gods and the people, conducting rituals, making offerings, and maintaining the temples. The priesthood was organized hierarchically, with high priests overseeing temple activities and serving specific deities. The priests played a crucial role in preserving religious traditions, interpreting oracles, and providing guidance to the pharaoh and the general population.

Nobility and Elite: Below the pharaoh and the priesthood were the nobility and the elite. This social class consisted of high-ranking officials, military commanders, and members of the royal family. They often held influential positions in the government and had access to resources and privileges. The nobility and the elite were closely tied to the religious establishment, with some individuals serving as temple patrons, overseeing religious endowments, and participating in religious rituals.

Middle Class and Commoners: The middle class and commoners formed the majority of the population in ancient Egypt. This social stratum included artisans, farmers, scribes, and merchants. While they did not have the same level of access to political and religious power as the upper classes, they actively participated in religious rituals, sought the favor of specific deities for personal and communal well-being, and contributed offerings and donations to the temples.

Slaves and Servants: At the lowest rung of the social hierarchy were slaves and servants. These individuals were owned by the pharaoh, the nobility, or the temples. While they had limited agency and personal freedom, they were sometimes involved in religious activities as attendants or laborers in the temples.

The social hierarchy in ancient Egypt influenced the expression of religious practices and the dissemination of religious knowledge. The pharaoh's role as a divine ruler, the authority of the priesthood, and the involvement of the nobility and the elite in religious affairs all reinforced the close connection between political power and religious beliefs. The participation of commoners in religious rituals and their reliance on the guidance of the priesthood demonstrated the influence of religious practices on everyday life and the aspirations of individuals within the social structure.

Example: The coronation rituals of the pharaoh, such as the Heb Sed festival, demonstrated the divine legitimacy of the ruler and reaffirmed their role as a unifying force. These rituals involved complex rites performed in the presence of the gods, emphasizing the divine nature of kingship.

Influence of Mythology:

Mythology played a crucial role in shaping ancient Egyptian religious beliefs and rituals. The rich and intricate pantheon of deities reflected various natural phenomena, abstract concepts, and human experiences. Myths served as a means to explain the origins of the universe, the creation of humans, and the interactions between the gods and mortals. These narratives provided a framework for understanding the divine order and the roles and responsibilities of individuals within society.

Mythology had a profound influence on ancient Egyptian religious beliefs and practices. Here are some key points to elaborate on:

Explanation of the Universe: Egyptian mythology provided explanations for the creation of the world and the cosmos. Myths often depicted the actions of gods and goddesses in shaping the universe, from the emergence of the primeval waters to the formation of the earth and the sky. These stories helped the ancient Egyptians make sense of the world around them and understand their place within it.

Divine Interactions and Human Relationships: Myths portrayed the interactions between gods and mortals, highlighting the roles and relationships between the divine and human realms. These narratives depicted gods intervening in human affairs, granting favors, or imposing challenges. They reinforced the idea that humans had a reciprocal relationship with the gods, with offerings, prayers, and rituals serving as acts of devotion and communication.

Moral and Ethical Lessons: Myths often conveyed moral and ethical lessons, emphasizing virtues and condemning vices. They presented narratives of gods and goddesses who demonstrated qualities such as justice, wisdom, and compassion, serving as role models for human behavior. These stories provided guidance on how to lead a virtuous life, maintain social order, and uphold Ma'at, the principle of cosmic balance and harmony.

Ritual and Symbolism: Mythology influenced the development of religious rituals and the use of symbolism within ancient Egyptian religious practices. The stories of divine actions and encounters were reenacted through rituals, ceremonies, and festivals. Symbolic elements from myths, such as sacred animals, cosmic symbols, and mythological narratives, were incorporated into temple architecture, religious iconography, and sacred objects.

Identity and Belief System: Mythology played a significant role in shaping the Egyptian sense of identity and their religious worldview. Myths provided a shared narrative that connected individuals and communities, reinforcing their cultural heritage and values. They instilled a sense of belonging and collective memory, reinforcing the belief in the continuity of the divine order and the cyclical nature of life and death.

The influence of mythology in ancient Egyptian religious beliefs extended beyond mere storytelling. It shaped the understanding of the world, the relationship between the divine and mortal realms, and the moral and ethical values that guided individuals and communities. The stories and symbolism found in mythology permeated all aspects of religious life, from rituals and ceremonies to art and architecture, leaving a lasting impact on the religious landscape of ancient Egypt.

Example: The myth of Osiris, Isis, and Horus depicted the cycle of life, death, and rebirth. This narrative emphasized the importance of moral conduct, judgment in the afterlife, and the potential for resurrection and eternal life. The myth of the divine triad influenced funerary practices, rituals, and the belief in an afterlife.

Cultural Exchange and Foreign Influences:

Ancient Egypt's strategic location facilitated trade and cultural exchange with neighboring regions and civilizations. Contact with Nubia, Mesopotamia, and the Mediterranean cultures brought forth new ideas, practices, and religious beliefs that influenced the development of ancient Egyptian spirituality. Notable periods of foreign influence include the Hyksos rule and the Ptolemaic period under Greek influence.

Cultural exchange and foreign influences played a significant role in shaping ancient Egyptian spirituality. Here are some key points to elaborate on:

Trade and Contact: Ancient Egypt's geographic location along the Nile River and its proximity to various regions facilitated trade and contact with neighboring civilizations. Through trade routes and diplomatic exchanges, the Egyptians came into contact with cultures such as Nubia, Mesopotamia, and the Mediterranean civilizations. These interactions created opportunities for the exchange of goods, ideas, and religious beliefs.

Hyksos Rule: One notable period of foreign influence in ancient Egypt was the Hyksos rule during the Second Intermediate Period (c. 1650 BCE - 1550 BCE). The Hyksos, a Semitic people from the Levant, invaded and ruled parts of Egypt. During their reign, they introduced new military technologies, such as chariots and bronze weaponry, which had an impact on Egyptian warfare and military practices.

Hellenistic Influence: Another significant foreign influence occurred during the Ptolemaic period (323 BCE - 30 BCE) when Egypt was under the rule of the Greek Ptolemaic dynasty. Greek culture, language, and religious beliefs infused with Egyptian society, creating a Hellenistic blend. The worship of Greek deities, such as Zeus and Isis, became prominent, and Greek architectural styles influenced the construction of temples and monuments.

Syncretism and Adaptation: As a result of cultural exchange and foreign influences, ancient Egyptian spirituality underwent syncretism, where elements of different religious traditions were merged or adapted. For example, the goddess Isis, originally an Egyptian deity, became associated with various Greek and Mediterranean goddesses, such as Demeter and Aphrodite, through syncretism.

Cultural Borrowing: Cultural exchange also involved the borrowing and integration of religious concepts and practices. Ancient Egyptian religious traditions incorporated elements from neighboring cultures, such as Nubian and

Mesopotamian religious practices. These borrowings often occurred through trade, diplomatic interactions, and political alliances.

It is important to note that while foreign influences impacted ancient Egyptian spirituality, the Egyptians selectively adopted and adapted foreign elements to fit within their existing religious framework. They often assimilated new beliefs and practices into their own mythologies and rituals rather than completely abandoning their indigenous traditions.

Cultural exchange and foreign influences in ancient Egypt brought about changes and enrichments in religious beliefs and practices. They provided opportunities for the Egyptians to engage with different worldviews, technologies, and religious concepts, contributing to the diverse and dynamic nature of ancient Egyptian spirituality.

Example: During the reign of the pharaoh Akhenaten, the introduction of Atenism, a monotheistic belief centered on the sun-disk Aten, reflected the influence of the monotheistic religious practices of the Near East. This departure from traditional polytheism showcased the impact of cultural exchange on religious ideologies.

Funerary Beliefs and Rituals:

Ancient Egyptian religious beliefs placed great emphasis on the afterlife and the journey of the soul. The belief in an eternal afterlife and the preservation of the physical body through mummification shaped funerary practices and rituals. The construction of tombs, the burial customs, and the provision of grave goods reflected the societal belief in the continuity of life beyond death.

Funerary beliefs and rituals were of paramount importance in ancient Egyptian religious practices. Here are some key points to elaborate on:

Belief in an Afterlife: Ancient Egyptians held a deep belief in the afterlife as a continuation of the human journey beyond death. They believed that the soul, consisting of different components like the ka, ba, and akh, would endure after the physical body's demise. The afterlife was seen as a realm where the deceased would experience eternal existence and participate in the cosmic order.

Mummification: The preservation of the physical body through mummification was a crucial aspect of ancient Egyptian funerary practices. Mummification involved a complex process of embalming and wrapping the body in layers of linen bandages. It aimed to prevent decomposition and ensure the body's integrity in the afterlife, allowing the soul to recognize and reunite with its corporeal form.

Tombs and Burial Customs: Elaborate tombs were constructed as eternal homes for the deceased and served as a place of veneration and commemoration. The architecture of tombs evolved over time, from simple mastaba structures to grand pyramids and rock-cut tombs in the Valley of the Kings. The burial customs varied based on social status, with pharaohs and nobles being interred in elaborate tombs, while commoners had simpler burial sites.

Grave Goods: Alongside the deceased, grave goods were included in tombs to accompany and support the individual in the afterlife. These items ranged from practical objects, such as food, clothing, and tools, to symbolic and religious artifacts, such as amulets, statues, and offerings. Grave goods represented the belief in a continued existence and the provision of necessities and comforts in the afterlife.

Rituals and Offerings: Funerary rituals played a vital role in ensuring the deceased's smooth transition into the afterlife. Priests and family members conducted ceremonies and made offerings to nourish and sustain the soul in its journey. These rituals included prayers, incantations, and the presentation of food, drink, and symbolic items to appease and honor the gods and facilitate the deceased's transformation.

Book of the Dead: The Book of the Dead, a collection of spells and religious texts, was often included in tombs to guide and protect the deceased in the afterlife. These texts contained instructions for navigating the underworld, spells for protection against evil forces, and formulas for transformation and rebirth.

Funerary beliefs and rituals reflected the ancient Egyptians' profound reverence for the afterlife and their desire for the deceased to continue their existence in a state of peace, well-being, and spiritual fulfillment. These practices provided a means to honor the deceased, uphold cosmic order, and maintain a connection between the living and the departed.

Example: The Pyramid Texts, inscribed on the walls of royal pyramids, contained spells and rituals intended to guide the deceased pharaoh's soul through the afterlife. These texts provided a blueprint for the journey to the realm of Osiris and the attainment of immortality.

Conclusion:

The cultural and societal influences on ancient Egyptian religious beliefs and practices were multifaceted and dynamic. The geographical landscape, social hierarchy, mythology, cultural exchange, and funerary beliefs all contributed to the rich tapestry of ancient Egyptian spirituality. By critically examining these influences, students gain a deeper understanding of the complexities and interconnectedness of religious traditions and their cultural contexts. Engaging in thought-provoking exercises and discussions throughout this section will foster critical thinking and encourage students to reflect on the interplay between culture and religion in ancient Egyptian society.

Examination of the relationship between religion, politics, and daily life in ancient Egypt

The civilization of ancient Egypt was characterized by a close intertwining of religion, politics, and daily life. Religion played a central role in shaping the political structure, guiding social hierarchies, and influencing various aspects of everyday existence. This section aims to provide a thorough examination of the multifaceted relationship between religion, politics, and daily life in ancient Egypt, offering students a comprehensive understanding of how these interconnections influenced the society as a whole.

Religion and Political Legitimacy:

In ancient Egypt, religion and politics were deeply intertwined, with religious beliefs and practices providing the foundation for political legitimacy. The pharaoh, as the earthly representative of the gods, held a divine mandate to rule and maintain order. The association between religion and political power reinforced the notion of the pharaoh as a divine and all-powerful ruler, providing stability and cohesion to the society.

Religion and political legitimacy were closely intertwined in ancient Egypt, with the belief in the divine nature of the pharaoh serving as a cornerstone of political authority. Here are some key points to elaborate on:

Pharaoh as a Divine Ruler: The pharaoh was believed to be a living embodiment of the gods, possessing divine qualities and authority. As the intermediary between the gods and the people, the pharaoh played a crucial role in maintaining cosmic order and ensuring the prosperity and well-being of the kingdom. This divine association bestowed upon the pharaoh a unique legitimacy that extended beyond mere political power.

Pharaonic Titles and Titles: The pharaoh's titles and epithets emphasized their divine status and established their authority. The pharaoh was often referred to as the "Son of Ra" or the "Living Horus," linking them to the powerful solar deity Ra and the falcon-headed god Horus. These titles reinforced the pharaoh's divine lineage and reinforced their role as a mediator between the gods and the people.

Rituals and Religious Duties: The pharaoh had significant religious duties and responsibilities, performing rituals and ceremonies to appease the gods and maintain harmony in the kingdom. These rituals included offerings, processions, and temple rituals, all of which played a vital role in upholding the cosmic order and ensuring the gods' favor. By actively engaging in religious practices, the pharaoh demonstrated their commitment to fulfilling their divine role and securing political legitimacy.

Temple Construction and Patronage: The construction and patronage of temples were essential for pharaohs to demonstrate their piety and strengthen their political legitimacy. Pharaohs initiated vast building projects, erecting temples dedicated to various gods and goddesses throughout the kingdom. These temples served as centers of religious worship, and their construction symbolized the pharaoh's devotion to the gods and their ability to facilitate the divine presence within the kingdom.

Propaganda and Ideology: The association between religion and political legitimacy was reinforced through propaganda and ideology. Official inscriptions, statues, and reliefs depicted the pharaoh engaging in religious rituals and receiving the blessings of the gods, emphasizing their divine favor and legitimacy to rule. These depictions reinforced the concept of the pharaoh as a just and powerful ruler chosen by the gods.

Religious Endorsement of Policies: The pharaoh's decisions and policies were often presented as being divinely inspired or sanctioned. By aligning their actions with the religious beliefs and principles of the society, the pharaoh ensured the support and loyalty of the people. This religious endorsement of policies further solidified the pharaoh's political legitimacy and the perceived harmony between the divine and earthly realms.

In ancient Egypt, religion and political legitimacy were intricately linked, with the belief in the divine nature of the pharaoh providing the foundation for their authority and rule. The close association between religion and politics served to maintain social order, uphold cosmic harmony, and ensure the stability and prosperity of the kingdom.

Example: The coronation rituals of the pharaoh, such as the Sed festival, emphasized the divine legitimacy of the ruler and their role as the mediator between the gods and the people. These rituals reinforced the connection between religion and political authority, ensuring the acceptance and support of the ruling elite and the general population.

Temples as Political and Religious Centers:

Temples served as focal points of both religious worship and political administration in ancient Egypt. These monumental structures were not only places of religious devotion but also centers of economic activity and political authority. The priesthood, closely associated with temple institutions, wielded significant power and influence, often acting as intermediaries between the gods and the pharaoh.

Temples in ancient Egypt played a dual role as both political and religious centers. Here's a closer look at their significance in these aspects:

Religious Centers: Temples were primarily dedicated to specific gods and goddesses, serving as sacred spaces for religious rituals, ceremonies, and worship. They were believed to be the dwelling places of the deities, and their construction and maintenance were considered acts of devotion to the gods. Within the temple complex, various structures and areas served different religious functions, such as sanctuaries, offering halls, and sacred lakes.

Priesthood and Religious Authority: Temples were staffed by a hierarchical priesthood, who were responsible for the daily rituals, maintenance of the temple, and interpretation of religious texts. The priests acted as intermediaries between the gods and the people, conducting rituals and offering prayers on behalf of the community. They held considerable religious authority and were responsible for upholding the religious traditions and ensuring the proper worship of the gods.

Economic Centers: Temples were also economic powerhouses in ancient Egypt. They owned vast tracts of agricultural land, which provided income through farming and trade. The temple complexes often included workshops, granaries, and storage facilities, which contributed to the local economy. The surplus resources generated from temple activities were used to support the temple itself, maintain the priesthood, and fund religious festivals and offerings.

Political Centers: Temples exerted significant political influence in ancient Egypt. The priesthood, as religious authorities, often had close ties to the ruling pharaoh and held considerable sway over the local population. The high priests of major temples could amass significant wealth and power, which they could use to influence political decisions and policies. Temples also served as administrative centers, overseeing the distribution of resources, collection of taxes, and resolution of disputes within their territories.

Festivals and Public Gatherings: Temples were hubs of communal activity and social cohesion. Religious festivals and processions held at the temples brought together people from different social strata to celebrate and honor the gods. These events provided an opportunity for the pharaoh and local officials to interact with the populace, reinforcing their authority and fostering a sense of unity and loyalty among the people.

Education and Knowledge Centers: Temples served as centers of learning and knowledge. They were repositories of religious texts, astronomical observations, and medical knowledge. The priesthood played a role in education, passing down religious rituals, traditions, and knowledge to the next generation. Temples also provided a venue for scribes and scholars to gather and exchange ideas.

In summary, temples in ancient Egypt were not only religious sanctuaries but also multifunctional institutions with significant political, economic, and social roles. They served as religious centers where rituals and worship took place, while also acting as economic powerhouses and administrative hubs. The priesthood associated with temples held religious authority and played a crucial role in the political and social fabric of ancient Egyptian society.

Example: The Karnak Temple complex in Thebes was not only dedicated to the worship of Amun-Ra but also served as an administrative hub, controlling vast land holdings and economic resources. The high priest of Amun, known as the "God's Wife of Amun," held considerable political sway, exerting influence over the affairs of state.

Religious Festivals and Social Cohesion:

Religious festivals played a crucial role in fostering social cohesion and reinforcing communal identity in ancient Egypt. These festivals, marked by elaborate rituals and processions, brought together people from various social strata, promoting a sense of unity and shared religious experience. Such occasions provided opportunities for social interaction, trade, and the reaffirmation of societal norms and values.

Religious festivals in ancient Egypt were vibrant and significant events that played a central role in promoting social cohesion and reinforcing communal identity. Here's a closer look at their significance:

Community Gathering: Religious festivals served as occasions for the entire community to come together and participate in shared religious activities. People from different social strata, including priests, nobles, and commoners, would gather at temples or sacred sites to partake in the festivities. This brought diverse groups of individuals together, fostering a sense of collective identity and belonging.

Rituals and Ceremonies: Festivals were marked by elaborate rituals and ceremonies performed by the priesthood and worshippers. These rituals were aimed at honoring and appeasing the gods, seeking their blessings, and maintaining cosmic order. Through active participation in these rituals, individuals reaffirmed their religious beliefs and strengthened their connection to the divine.

Processions and Performances: Festivals often included grand processions, during which statues of the gods were paraded through the streets or transported to different sacred sites. These processions were accompanied by music, dance, and theatrical performances, creating a festive atmosphere and engaging the senses of the participants. Such public displays of religious devotion fostered a sense of community and shared experience.

Trade and Commerce: Religious festivals provided opportunities for trade and commerce. Temples were centers of economic activity, and during festivals, merchants and vendors would set up stalls to sell goods and offerings related to the festivities. This stimulated economic exchange and contributed to the local economy. The festivals thus served as platforms for economic interaction and growth.

Reinforcement of Social Norms: Festivals provided a platform for the reinforcement of social norms, values, and hierarchical structures. The presence of the pharaoh and nobles during the festivities reinforced their status and authority. The rituals and performances emphasized the order and harmony believed to be maintained by the gods and reflected the ideals of the society. Festivals acted as a collective reminder of the societal structure and norms, promoting social stability.

Education and Cultural Transmission: Festivals also played a role in educating the populace about religious beliefs, myths, and cultural traditions. Through rituals, performances, and storytelling, important religious narratives and teachings were imparted to the community, ensuring the transmission of cultural and religious knowledge from one generation to the next. Festivals thus served as important platforms for the preservation and dissemination of cultural heritage.

Overall, religious festivals in ancient Egypt served as occasions for communal gathering, religious devotion, economic exchange, and the reinforcement of social norms. They provided opportunities for people from different backgrounds to come together, celebrate their shared religious beliefs, and foster a sense of unity and identity within the community.

Example: The Festival of Opet, celebrated in Thebes, involved a grand procession of statues of the gods from Karnak Temple to Luxor Temple. This festival brought people together in a collective celebration of the gods, reinforcing a sense of community and shared religious devotion.

Religious Ethics and Daily Life:

Religious beliefs and ethics permeated every aspect of daily life in ancient Egypt, guiding personal conduct, social interactions, and moral values. The concept of ma'at, representing cosmic harmony and balance, formed the ethical foundation of Egyptian society. Upholding ma'at was not only an individual responsibility but also essential for the maintenance of order and the well-being of the entire community.

In ancient Egypt, religious ethics played a significant role in shaping daily life and guiding the behavior of individuals within the community. The concept of ma'at, often translated as "truth," "justice," or "balance," formed the core of the ethical framework in ancient Egyptian society. Here's a closer look at how religious ethics influenced various aspects of daily life:

Personal Conduct: Ancient Egyptians believed that living in accordance with ma'at was essential for personal well-being and spiritual growth. Individuals were expected to adhere to moral principles and exhibit virtuous behavior in their everyday lives. This included displaying honesty, integrity, and respect for others. Upholding ma'at meant avoiding actions such as lying, stealing, or causing harm to others.

Social Interactions: The principles of ma'at extended to interpersonal relationships and social interactions. Egyptians were encouraged to treat others with fairness, compassion, and empathy. They were expected to contribute positively to the community, fulfill their obligations, and maintain harmonious relationships with family, friends, and neighbors. Cooperation, loyalty, and kindness were highly valued virtues.

Justice and Law: Ma'at was closely associated with the administration of justice and the enforcement of laws in ancient Egypt. The pharaoh, as the embodiment of ma'at, was responsible for ensuring fairness and equity within society. Judicial systems were established to resolve disputes and punish wrongdoers. Concepts of righteousness, equity, and impartiality were emphasized in legal proceedings to maintain order and preserve ma'at.

Work and Profession: The ethical principles of ma'at also influenced the attitudes and behaviors in the workplace. Egyptians believed in the importance of diligence, honesty, and excellence in their chosen professions. Individuals were expected to carry out their duties with integrity and dedication, contributing to the overall well-being of the community. Hard work and craftsmanship were valued, and people were encouraged to strive for excellence in their respective fields.

Care for the Environment: The religious ethics of ancient Egypt encompassed a reverence for the natural world and the environment. Egyptians recognized the interconnectedness of humans, animals, and the divine order. They believed in the responsible stewardship of the land and its resources, emphasizing the importance of sustainable practices and avoiding actions that could disrupt the balance of nature.

Rituals and Offerings: Daily religious rituals, including prayers and offerings, were an integral part of an individual's interaction with the divine and the maintenance of ma'at. Egyptians believed that by performing these rituals and presenting offerings to the gods, they could establish a harmonious relationship with the divine and ensure the continued balance and order in the world.

The ethical principles derived from religious beliefs were not only a personal responsibility but also influenced social cohesion and the overall well-being of ancient Egyptian society. Adhering to these principles was seen as a duty to both the gods and fellow humans, contributing to the preservation of ma'at and the prosperity of the community as a whole.

Example: The Negative Confessions, recited during the judgment of the soul in the afterlife, outlined a set of moral principles that individuals were expected to follow. These principles included honesty, respect for others, and the avoidance of harmful actions. The adherence to these ethical guidelines impacted daily interactions and social relationships within the community.

Cult of the Pharaoh and State Religion:

The cult of the pharaoh and the state religion were intertwined, further solidifying the relationship between religion and politics. The deification of the pharaoh elevated their status to that of a divine being, ensuring loyalty and obedience from the population. State-sponsored religious practices, such as temple construction and endowments, showcased the pharaoh's commitment to the gods and bolstered their political authority.

In ancient Egypt, the cult of the pharaoh and the state religion were closely connected, serving to reinforce the divine status and political legitimacy of the ruler. Here's a closer look at the cult of the pharaoh and its relationship to the state religion:

Deification of the Pharaoh: The ancient Egyptians believed that the pharaoh was not only a mortal ruler but also a divine being. The pharaoh was considered to be the earthly embodiment of the gods, particularly Horus, the falcon-headed god associated with kingship. By being deified, the pharaoh acquired a divine status, representing a direct link between the divine realm and the human world. This deification elevated the pharaoh above ordinary individuals, endowing them with immense religious and political authority.

Worship of the Pharaoh: The cult of the pharaoh involved the worship and veneration of the ruler as a god. Temples and shrines were dedicated to the pharaoh, where rituals, ceremonies, and offerings were conducted to honor their divine presence. The people of Egypt were expected to show loyalty, respect, and obedience to the pharaoh as the intermediary between the gods and the mortal realm. Failure to do so was seen as a threat to the divine order and the stability of the state.

State Religion: The cult of the pharaoh was deeply intertwined with the state religion of ancient Egypt. The state sponsored and supported religious practices, particularly those associated with the pharaoh. The construction and maintenance of temples, the appointment of priests, and the allocation of resources for religious rituals were all part of the state's religious responsibilities. The pharaoh, as the divine ruler, played a central role in the religious affairs of the state and the promotion of religious unity.

Political Legitimacy: The association between the cult of the pharaoh and the state religion provided the pharaoh with political legitimacy. By being regarded as a divine ruler, the pharaoh's authority was reinforced, and their decisions and actions were perceived as being in accordance with the will of the gods. This divine mandate granted the pharaoh the right to rule, maintain order, and protect the well-being of the people. The cult of the pharaoh and the state religion served to unify the population under the pharaoh's leadership and foster a sense of loyalty and devotion.

Propagation of State Ideology: The state religion, with its focus on the cult of the pharaoh, also played a role in propagating state ideology and promoting the pharaoh's divine role. Religious texts, rituals, and artistic representations emphasized the pharaoh's connection to the gods and their role in upholding ma'at, the cosmic order. These religious practices and beliefs helped shape the narrative of the pharaoh's divine kingship and reinforce their position as the rightful ruler of Egypt.

The cult of the pharaoh and the state religion were intertwined, with the worship of the pharaoh serving as a means to consolidate political power, maintain social order, and promote religious unity within ancient Egyptian society. The religious authority of the pharaoh and the state's support of the cult reinforced the close relationship between religion and politics in the ancient Egyptian civilization.

Example: The construction of the mortuary complex at Giza, including the Great Pyramid of Khufu, demonstrated the pharaoh's dedication to religious rituals and their desire for a successful afterlife. These monumental structures served as tangible symbols of the pharaoh's power and divine connection, reinforcing their political legitimacy.

Conclusion:

The relationship between religion, politics, and daily life in ancient Egypt was complex and intertwined. Religion provided the basis for political legitimacy, shaped social hierarchies, and guided personal ethics. Temples served as centers of religious worship and political administration, while religious festivals fostered social cohesion. The cult of the pharaoh and state-sponsored religious practices further reinforced the connection between religion and politics. Understanding this intricate relationship is essential for comprehending the dynamics of ancient Egyptian society and its enduring impact on subsequent civilizations. Engaging in critical thinking exercises and discussions will encourage students to reflect on the implications of such interconnections and draw parallels with other historical and contemporary contexts.

Discussion of the archaeological and historical sources that inform our understanding of ancient Egyptian spirituality

The study of ancient Egyptian spirituality heavily relies on a wide range of archaeological and historical sources that provide valuable insights into the beliefs, rituals, and practices of this ancient civilization. These sources include texts, artifacts, temple inscriptions, tombs, and archaeological discoveries. This section aims to explore and analyze these sources, demonstrating their significance in shaping our understanding of ancient Egyptian spirituality.

Textual Sources:

Ancient Egyptian religious texts are invaluable sources of information for understanding their spiritual beliefs and practices. The most well-known and important of these texts is the Book of the Dead (also known as the Book of Coming Forth by Day), a collection of spells and rituals aimed at assisting the deceased in navigating the afterlife. This text provides detailed instructions for the journey of the soul and offers insights into the concept of the afterlife, the roles of various deities, and the importance of ethical conduct.

Ancient Egyptian religious texts are crucial sources that provide insights into the spiritual beliefs and practices of this ancient civilization. Among these texts, the most renowned is the Book of the Dead (or Book of Coming Forth by Day). Here's a closer look at textual sources in ancient Egyptian religion:

Book of the Dead: The Book of the Dead is a collection of funerary texts that were commonly placed in tombs to assist the deceased in the afterlife. It comprises a series of spells, rituals, and instructions aimed at guiding the soul through the perilous journey of the afterlife. The book emphasizes the importance of proper burial, the preservation of the body through mummification, and the recitation of specific spells to ensure a successful transition into the divine realm. It also provides information on the judgment of the soul in the Hall of Ma'at and the concept of a personal moral code.

Pyramid Texts: The Pyramid Texts are among the oldest religious texts in ancient Egypt, inscribed on the walls of pyramids during the Old Kingdom. These texts were reserved for the pharaohs and contained spells and rituals to aid them in their journey to the afterlife. The Pyramid Texts focus on the divine aspects of the pharaoh and their association with the gods, emphasizing their divine lineage and their role in the cosmic order.

Coffin Texts: The Coffin Texts, written on coffins and sarcophagi, emerged during the Middle Kingdom and were intended for a broader range of individuals. They expanded on the earlier Pyramid Texts and incorporated new spells and rituals. The Coffin Texts aimed to provide guidance and protection for the deceased in their journey through the afterlife. They also touched upon topics such as resurrection, transformation, and the identification of the deceased with various deities.

Book of Amduat: The Book of Amduat, also known as the "Book of the Hidden Chamber," is a funerary text that illustrates the nocturnal journey of the sun god, Ra, through the underworld during the twelve hours of the night. It describes the various regions and inhabitants of the netherworld, as well as the challenges and dangers faced by the sun god. The Book of Amduat reflects the belief in the cyclical nature of life, death, and rebirth, as symbolized by the journey of the sun god through the darkness of the underworld.

Hymns and Liturgical Texts: Various hymns and liturgical texts were composed to praise and worship the gods in temples. These texts expressed reverence and adoration for the deities, recounting their mythical exploits and attributes. They also played a role in public religious ceremonies, with priests reciting hymns and performing rituals to honor the gods.

These textual sources offer a glimpse into the religious beliefs, rituals, and cosmological concepts of the ancient Egyptians. They provide valuable information on the afterlife, the importance of ethical conduct, the roles of deities, and the rituals and spells performed to ensure a successful journey to the divine realm. These texts demonstrate the complexity and depth of ancient Egyptian religious thought and continue to be studied to this day, shedding light on the spiritual world of this fascinating civilization.

Example: Students can analyze specific chapters of the Book of the Dead, such as the "Weighing of the Heart" scene, and discuss the significance of each element in relation to ancient Egyptian beliefs about judgment and the afterlife.

Temple Inscriptions and Artwork:

The inscriptions found on the walls of temples and tombs provide valuable information about religious rituals, cult practices, and the relationships between deities. These inscriptions often depict scenes of offerings, prayers, and interactions between humans and divine beings. The artwork and iconography used in temple reliefs and statues also offer insights into the roles of different deities and their significance in religious ceremonies.

Temple inscriptions and artwork in ancient Egypt play a significant role in understanding religious practices, mythological narratives, and the relationships between humans and the divine. Here's a closer look at temple inscriptions and artwork:

Religious Rituals and Cult Practices: Temple inscriptions often depict scenes of religious rituals and cult practices. These inscriptions provide details about the specific ceremonies, offerings, and prayers conducted in honor of particular deities. They offer insights into the actions performed by priests and devotees, the specific items used in rituals, and the desired outcomes of these religious practices. These inscriptions can also reveal the roles and responsibilities of priests and the hierarchy within the temple.

Mythological Narratives: Temple inscriptions frequently include mythological narratives and stories, depicting the exploits and relationships of the gods and goddesses. These narratives illustrate creation myths, tales of divine intervention, and the significance of particular deities in the cosmological order. These inscriptions serve to reinforce the religious beliefs and emphasize the divine authority of the gods. They also provide important insights into the mythological framework of ancient Egyptian religion.

Divine Interactions and Symbolism: Temple inscriptions and artwork often portray interactions between humans and the divine. These scenes depict individuals making offerings, praying, or engaging in other forms of devotion to the gods. They showcase the reciprocal relationship between mortals and deities, highlighting the belief in divine intervention and the need for humans to maintain harmonious connections with the divine realm. Symbolism is also prevalent in temple artwork, with specific gestures, objects, and animals representing the attributes and characteristics of the deities.

Iconography and Representation of Deities: Temple artwork, including reliefs and statues, provides visual representations of the gods and goddesses. Specific iconography and artistic conventions were employed to depict each deity, emphasizing their distinctive attributes and symbolism. For example, the god Amun was often depicted with a tall feathered crown, symbolizing his association with air and the breath of life. These artistic representations helped worshippers identify and connect with the divine beings, reinforcing their religious beliefs and providing a visual focal point for devotion.

Offering Scenes and Divine Blessings: Temple inscriptions and artwork frequently depict scenes of offerings being presented to the gods. These scenes highlight the importance of offerings and their role in maintaining divine favor and reciprocity. They illustrate the types of offerings made, such as food, drink, or incense, and the belief that these offerings sustained the gods and ensured their blessings upon the people.

Temple inscriptions and artwork provide a wealth of information about ancient Egyptian religious practices, beliefs, and the relationships between humans and the divine. They offer a visual and textual record of rituals, mythological narratives, and the iconography associated with various deities. These sources not only deepen our understanding of ancient Egyptian religion but also serve as a testament to the artistic skill and devotion of the ancient Egyptians.

Example: Students can analyze the reliefs in the Temple of Karnak depicting the annual festival of Opet and discuss the symbolism and meaning behind the various scenes represented, as well as the significance of the festival in ancient Egyptian religious life.

Tombs and Funerary Practices:

The tombs and burial practices of ancient Egyptians provide important evidence of their beliefs regarding the afterlife and the soul's journey. The tombs of pharaohs, nobles, and common individuals offer insights into the funerary rituals, burial customs, and the inclusion of grave goods. The discovery of intact tombs, such as that of Tutankhamun, has provided a wealth of information about the religious beliefs and practices of ancient Egyptians.

Example: Students can examine the tomb of Tutankhamun and analyze the objects and inscriptions found within, discussing their significance in relation to ancient Egyptian beliefs about the afterlife and the pharaoh's role as a divine ruler.

Archaeological Discoveries:

Archaeological excavations have unearthed numerous artifacts, temples, and religious structures that contribute to our understanding of ancient Egyptian spirituality. These discoveries include temples dedicated to specific deities, statues of gods and goddesses, amulets, and ritual objects. The careful examination and analysis of these archaeological finds shed light on religious symbolism, cult practices, and the material aspects of ancient Egyptian spirituality.

Example: Students can explore the discovery of the temple complex of Amun at Karnak and discuss its architectural features, inscriptions, and the religious significance of its different sections, such as the Hypostyle Hall or the Sacred Lake.

Conclusion:

Archaeological and historical sources play a fundamental role in our understanding of ancient Egyptian spirituality. Textual sources like the Book of the Dead provide insights into the beliefs and practices surrounding the afterlife, while temple inscriptions, tomb art, and archaeological discoveries offer valuable evidence of rituals, cult practices, and the roles of deities in ancient Egyptian society. By critically examining and analyzing these sources, students can deepen their understanding of ancient Egyptian spirituality and engage in discussions about the complexities of interpreting these materials.

Part 2: Overview of Ancient Egyptian Civilization

Part 2 of this study provides a comprehensive overview of ancient Egyptian civilization, delving into its various aspects such as political organization, social structure, economy, and cultural achievements. Understanding the broader context of ancient Egyptian civilization is crucial for comprehending the religious beliefs and practices that were central to their society. This section aims to provide students with a solid foundation by exploring the historical, cultural, and geographical factors that shaped ancient Egypt.

Historical Context:

The ancient Egyptian civilization emerged around 3100 BCE and endured for over three millennia, making it one of the longest-lasting civilizations in history. This period witnessed the rise and fall of various dynasties and the rule of powerful pharaohs, each leaving their imprint on the political and religious landscape of the time. Exploring the historical context allows us to grasp the evolution and continuity of ancient Egyptian civilization.

Example: Students can examine the transition from the Predynastic period to the Early Dynastic period and analyze the political and cultural changes that occurred during this time, including the emergence of centralized political authority and the development of hieroglyphic writing.

Geographical Factors:

The geographical features of ancient Egypt significantly influenced its civilization. Situated along the banks of the Nile River, the fertile land provided the basis for agriculture, allowing the civilization to thrive. The Nile River also played a central role in transportation, trade, and religious symbolism. The surrounding deserts acted as natural barriers, protecting Egypt from invasions and fostering a sense of isolation that contributed to the preservation of their cultural traditions.

Example: Students can examine the importance of the Nile River to the ancient Egyptians and discuss how its annual flooding shaped their agricultural practices, religious beliefs, and social organization.

Cultural Achievements:

Ancient Egypt is renowned for its rich cultural achievements, which include monumental architecture, intricate art and craftsmanship, advancements in science and technology, and a sophisticated system of writing. Exploring these cultural achievements provides insight into the values, beliefs, and intellectual pursuits of the ancient Egyptians, shedding light on their worldview and spiritual practices.

Example: Students can analyze the construction of the Great Pyramid of Giza and discuss the engineering techniques employed, the religious significance of pyramid architecture, and the labor organization required for such monumental projects.

Social Structure:

The social structure of ancient Egypt was hierarchical and stratified, with the pharaoh at the apex of the society and various classes and professions occupying different positions. Understanding the social structure provides a framework for comprehending the roles of individuals within the religious context, such as the priestly class and the role of the pharaoh as both a political and religious figure.

Example: Students can explore the social hierarchy of ancient Egypt and discuss the privileges and responsibilities associated with different social roles, such as the pharaoh, nobility, scribes, priests, and commoners.

Conclusion:

This section has provided an introduction to Part 2, which focuses on the overview of ancient Egyptian civilization. By examining the historical context, geographical factors, cultural achievements, and social structure, students can gain a comprehensive understanding of the broader framework within which ancient Egyptian religious beliefs and practices developed. This understanding sets the stage for the subsequent chapters, where we will delve deeper into the religious aspects and explore the wisdom and spiritual teachings of ancient Egypt.

Chapter 5: Influence of Geography, Society, and Politics on Religious Beliefs

Chapter 5 delves into the intricate relationship between geography, society, and politics in shaping religious beliefs and practices in various ancient civilizations, including but not limited to witchcraft, divination, herbalism, shamanism, and ecospirituality. Understanding the profound impact of these factors on the religious landscape allows us to appreciate the complexity and diversity of ancient spiritual traditions. This section provides a comprehensive introduction to the influence of geography, society, and politics on religious beliefs, highlighting their interplay and significance.

Influence of Geography:

Geography serves as a crucial backdrop for understanding religious beliefs and practices. The natural environment, including the landforms, climate, and resources available, shapes the religious cosmology and the ways in which individuals interact with the divine. Whether it be the sacred mountains and forests in shamanic traditions or the elemental forces of water, air, fire, and earth in witchcraft and herbalism, geography provides the foundation upon which these beliefs are constructed.

Example: Students can explore the significance of sacred sites in different religious traditions, such as the veneration of Mount Olympus in ancient Greek religion or the association of caves and rivers with spiritual power in shamanic practices.

Influence of Society:

Society, with its norms, values, and social structures, significantly influences religious beliefs and practices. The social fabric shapes the organization of religious institutions, the roles of religious practitioners, and the ways in which rituals and ceremonies are conducted. Additionally, societal factors such as gender dynamics, social hierarchy, and cultural diversity impact the interpretation and expression of religious beliefs.

Example: Students can examine the gender roles and rituals in witchcraft traditions, analyzing the influence of societal expectations on the roles of witches and the use of divination practices within specific cultural contexts.

Influence of Politics:

Political systems and power structures exert a profound influence on religious beliefs and practices. Rulers and political elites often seek to legitimize their authority through religious affiliations, leading to the establishment of state religions and the promotion of specific religious practices. Conversely, religious movements and ideologies can challenge political authority and shape societal dynamics. The intertwining of politics and religion can create tensions, conflicts, and changes in the religious landscape.

Example: Students can explore the influence of political leaders, such as pharaohs in ancient Egypt or emperors in ancient Rome, on the religious beliefs and rituals of their respective civilizations, and analyze the ways in which political motivations shape religious practices.

Conclusion:

This section has provided an introduction to Chapter 5, which focuses on the influence of geography, society, and politics on religious beliefs. By examining the intricate interplay between these factors, we gain a deeper understanding of the contextual factors that shape spiritual traditions in diverse ancient civilizations. It is through the lens of geography, society, and politics that we can unravel the complexity of religious belief systems and appreciate the dynamic relationship between human cultures and their spiritual practices. In the subsequent chapters, we will delve into specific case studies and explore the multifaceted influences on religious beliefs within different historical and cultural contexts.

Examination of how the geographical features of ancient Egypt, such as the Nile River and the surrounding landscape, influenced religious beliefs and practices

Ancient Egypt, with its unique geographical features, played a pivotal role in shaping the religious beliefs and practices of its civilization. The Nile River, a lifeline for the ancient Egyptians, and the surrounding landscape had a profound impact on their understanding of the divine, their rituals, and their cosmology. In this section, we will explore how these geographical elements influenced religious beliefs and practices in ancient Egypt, drawing examples from witchcraft, divination, herbalism, shamanism, and ecospirituality.

The Nile River: The Nile River was the backbone of ancient Egyptian civilization, providing fertile land, water for irrigation, and transportation. Its annual flooding cycle, marked by inundation and recession, shaped the religious worldview of the Egyptians. They viewed the Nile as a divine entity, personifying the life-giving force that sustained their agricultural society.

Example: Students can examine the role of the Nile River in witchcraft traditions, where the river's ebb and flow are associated with cycles of life, death, and rebirth, and explore how witches used divination methods to predict the river's behavior for agricultural planning.

Fertility and the Black Land: The fertile land along the banks of the Nile, known as the Black Land, was essential for agricultural productivity. The Egyptians believed that the gods and goddesses resided in the land and controlled its fertility. The annual flooding of the Nile brought nutrient-rich sediment, ensuring abundant harvests and reinforcing the connection between the natural world and the divine.

Example: Students can analyze the significance of herbs and plants in herbalism, exploring how the agricultural fertility provided by the Nile influenced the selection and use of specific plants in medicinal and spiritual practices.

Deserts and Sacred Spaces: The surrounding deserts, contrasting with the fertile Nile Valley, held a profound spiritual significance in ancient Egypt. The deserts were seen as liminal spaces, representing chaos, danger, and the realm of the unknown. It was in these desolate areas that religious rituals, such as shamanic journeys or initiation ceremonies, often took place, as they were believed to bring individuals closer to the divine and facilitate spiritual transformation.

Example: Students can examine the role of shamanic practices in navigating the desert landscapes of ancient Egypt and discuss the transformative experiences associated with such journeys.

Cosmic Symbolism: The geographical features of Egypt, such as the river, the deserts, and the celestial bodies visible in the clear skies, were seen as reflections of the cosmic order. The Nile represented the celestial river in the heavens, connecting the earthly realm to the divine realm. The desert was associated with the primordial chaos that the gods had to overcome to establish order and balance in the world.

Example: Students can explore the cosmological beliefs of ancient Egyptians, analyzing the symbolism of the river and the desert in relation to the celestial bodies, and discussing how these concepts influenced religious rituals and practices.

Conclusion:

The geographical features of ancient Egypt, including the Nile River, the surrounding landscape, and the deserts, played a significant role in shaping religious beliefs and practices. These elements influenced the Egyptians' understanding of the divine, their rituals, and their cosmology. By studying the impact of geography on religious beliefs and practices, we gain insights into the deep connection between humans and their environment, and the ways in which cultural and natural landscapes intertwine in shaping spiritual traditions. Through examples drawn from various fields such as witchcraft, divination, herbalism, shamanism, and ecospirituality, we can develop a comprehensive understanding of the intricate relationship between geography and religious beliefs in ancient Egypt.

Analysis of the social structures and hierarchies that shaped religious traditions, including the roles of different social classes and the priesthood

The religious traditions of ancient Egypt were intricately intertwined with the social structures and hierarchies that permeated their society. The roles and positions of different social classes, as well as the influential priesthood, played a significant role in shaping religious beliefs, practices, and the overall religious landscape. In this section, we will delve into an analysis of these social structures and hierarchies, drawing examples from witchcraft, divination, herbalism, shamanism, and ecospirituality, to gain a comprehensive understanding of their impact on ancient Egyptian religious traditions.

Social Classes: Ancient Egyptian society was structured hierarchically, with distinct social classes that held varying degrees of influence and privilege. At the pinnacle of the social order were the pharaohs and the royal family, who were believed to have divine authority and were central figures in religious rituals and ceremonies. Below them were the nobility, comprising high-ranking officials, priests, and military leaders, who enjoyed considerable power and held important religious roles.

Example: Students can examine the role of divination in different social classes, discussing how the pharaohs and the nobility sought oracles and divination methods to guide their decisions, while lower social classes, such as peasants, might rely on alternative divination practices, such as dream interpretation or consulting local seers.

Priesthood: The priesthood held a central position in ancient Egyptian religious life. The priests served as intermediaries between the divine and the human realm, conducting rituals, performing sacrifices, and maintaining the temples dedicated to various deities. They played a crucial role in upholding religious traditions, interpreting sacred texts, and ensuring the proper performance of rituals.

Example: Students can explore the hierarchical structure within the priesthood, discussing the different priestly ranks and roles, from the high priest of a particular temple to the lower-ranking priests responsible for specific tasks such as purification rituals or offerings.

Ritual Specialists: Alongside the formal priesthood, there were also ritual specialists who held important positions in religious practices. These individuals, such as magicians, healers, or scribes, possessed specialized knowledge and skills related to magic, divination, and religious texts. They often served the community by providing spiritual guidance, healing, or engaging in magical practices.

Example: Students can analyze the role of herbalists in ancient Egyptian society, examining how their expertise in medicinal plants and their association with healing influenced their status within the social hierarchy and their connection to religious practices.

Commoners and Slaves: The majority of the population in ancient Egypt consisted of commoners and slaves who played essential roles in sustaining the economy and supporting the religious activities of the upper classes. Although they had limited access to higher religious positions, they actively participated in communal rituals and festivals, seeking the favor of the deities and engaging in personal religious practices.

Example: Students can discuss the concept of ecospirituality within the context of ancient Egypt, exploring how the commoners' connection to the natural world, such as farming, animal husbandry, or daily encounters with sacred sites, influenced their spiritual beliefs and practices.

Counterargument: It is important to note that while social structures and hierarchies influenced religious traditions in ancient Egypt, there were also instances of individuals from lower classes rising to prominent religious positions or gaining recognition for their spiritual insights. These exceptions challenge the notion of strict social determinism in religious practices and emphasize the complexity of the ancient Egyptian religious landscape.

Conclusion:

The social structures and hierarchies in ancient Egypt played a pivotal role in shaping religious traditions. The social classes, priesthood, and various ritual specialists all contributed to the religious landscape, with each group having distinct roles and responsibilities. While the upper classes and priesthood held significant influence, commoners and slaves actively participated in religious rituals and fostered their own spiritual practices. By examining examples from witchcraft, divination, herbalism, shamanism, and ecospirituality, we can gain a multifaceted understanding of how social structures and hierarchies impacted religious beliefs and practices in ancient Egypt. Additionally, it is crucial to consider dissenting opinions and exceptions that challenge the notion of a rigid social determinism, allowing for a more nuanced analysis of the complex interplay between society and religion in ancient Egyptian civilization.

Exploration of the political dynamics and the relationship between religious authority and political power in ancient Egypt

The civilization of ancient Egypt witnessed a unique and intricate interplay between religious authority and political power. The pharaoh, as the divine ruler, held immense political influence, and religious institutions played a significant role in legitimizing and supporting the ruling regime. In this section, we will embark on an exploration of the political dynamics and the complex relationship between religious authority and political power in ancient Egypt, drawing examples from witchcraft, divination, herbalism, shamanism, and ecospirituality, to provide a comprehensive understanding of this intriguing connection.

Divine Kingship: At the heart of ancient Egyptian political dynamics was the concept of divine kingship. The pharaoh, believed to be a living deity, served as the intermediary between the gods and the mortal realm. The ruling pharaohs were not only political leaders but also religious figures, embodying the divine and ensuring the prosperity and harmony of the kingdom.

Example: Students can examine the role of witchcraft and divination in political decision-making processes, discussing how the pharaohs sought supernatural guidance to legitimize their authority and make crucial judgments, such as predicting the outcome of battles or determining the most favorable time for construction projects.

State Religion: The state religion of ancient Egypt played a vital role in consolidating political power. The pharaoh, along with the priesthood, was responsible for maintaining and promoting religious practices and rituals dedicated to the state gods. These religious institutions served to reinforce the pharaoh's divine status and maintain social order.

Example: Students can analyze the role of herbalism and shamanism in supporting the political agenda of the ruling regime, exploring how plants and natural substances were associated with divine powers and used in religious rituals to ensure the pharaoh's well-being and protection.

Temples and Cults: Temples were central to the religious and political landscape of ancient Egypt. They served as centers of worship, economic hubs, and administrative institutions. The priesthood played a crucial role in the maintenance and operation of these temples, thereby exerting significant political influence.

Example: Students can investigate the role of ecospirituality in the management of temple lands and resources, discussing how the agricultural practices tied to temple estates supported both religious and political objectives, ensuring the sustenance of the temple community and contributing to the economic stability of the kingdom.

Foreign Relations: Political dynamics in ancient Egypt were not limited to internal affairs but also extended to foreign relations. The pharaohs' religious authority played a vital role in diplomatic interactions and alliances with other nations. The perceived divine status of the pharaohs provided them with an elevated position and facilitated diplomatic negotiations.

Example: Students can explore how the practice of divination influenced diplomatic decision-making, discussing how the interpretation of celestial events or oracles guided the pharaohs' foreign policies and helped establish alliances or prevent potential conflicts.

Counterargument: It is important to acknowledge that not all aspects of political power in ancient Egypt were intertwined with religion. While religious authority played a significant role, other factors, such as military strength, economic resources, and geographic considerations, also influenced political dynamics.

Conclusion:

The political dynamics in ancient Egypt were deeply intertwined with religious authority, with the pharaohs' divine kingship and the support of religious institutions serving to consolidate and legitimize their rule. The state religion, temples, priesthood, and religious practices all played crucial roles in maintaining political power and social order. By examining examples from witchcraft, divination, herbalism, shamanism, and ecospirituality, we gain insights into how these practices intersected with political decision-making, diplomacy, and the overall governance of ancient Egypt. However, it is important to recognize that political power in ancient Egypt was a multifaceted phenomenon, influenced by various factors beyond religious authority.

Exercises:

Analyze the role of divination in ancient Egyptian foreign relations, highlighting specific examples and discussing the implications for diplomatic decision-making.

Compare and contrast the political dynamics in ancient Egypt with those of another ancient civilization, such as Mesopotamia or Greece, focusing on the role of religion in each society.

Investigate the impact of political power on religious beliefs and practices among different social classes in ancient Egypt, using evidence from archaeological findings and historical records.

Discuss the potential challenges and limitations of relying on religious authority for political legitimacy, considering both the advantages and disadvantages for the ruling regime.

These exercises aim to engage students in critical thinking, promote discussion, and encourage a deeper understanding of the complex relationship between religious authority and political power in ancient Egypt.

Chapter 6: Role of Pharaohs and Priests in Religious Practices

Chapter 6 delves into the fascinating realm of ancient Egyptian religious practices, focusing specifically on the significant roles played by the pharaohs and priests. Within the context of witchcraft, divination, herbalism, shamanism, and ecospirituality, this chapter offers a comprehensive analysis of the unique positions held by these individuals and the profound influence they exerted on religious beliefs and rituals in ancient Egypt. By exploring their roles in depth, we can gain a deeper understanding of the intricate relationship between the ruling elite and the religious institutions that shaped the spiritual landscape of this ancient civilization.

The Pharaoh: The pharaoh held the most elevated position in both political and religious domains, embodying the divine on earth and serving as the intermediary between humanity and the gods. The pharaoh's role extended beyond mere leadership; they were considered divine beings and were entrusted with the responsibility of maintaining cosmic balance and ensuring the prosperity of the kingdom.

Example: To comprehend the significance of the pharaoh's role, students can examine the practice of divination and how the pharaoh's participation in divinatory rituals helped guide decision-making processes. By studying specific instances of divination, such as the interpretation of celestial omens or the consultation of oracles, students can grasp the direct involvement of the pharaoh in religious practices and the influence of their actions on the belief systems of ancient Egyptians.

The Priesthood: The priesthood played an indispensable role in the religious landscape of ancient Egypt, acting as intermediaries between the gods and the people. They held the responsibility of performing rituals, maintaining temples, and administering religious practices. The priests possessed specialized knowledge of religious texts, rituals, and cosmological beliefs, enabling them to communicate with the divine and fulfill their sacred duties.

Example: Students can explore the practice of herbalism and its connection to the priestly role. By examining the use of herbs and plants in religious rituals, such as purification ceremonies or offerings, students can understand how priests utilized their knowledge of herbal properties to engage with the spiritual realm and enhance the efficacy of religious practices.

Rituals and Offerings: The pharaohs and priests played central roles in conducting elaborate rituals and making offerings to the gods. These rituals were performed to maintain cosmic order, seek divine favor, and ensure the well-being of the kingdom and its inhabitants. The religious practices carried out by the pharaohs and priests were seen as essential for upholding the harmony of the divine and mortal realms.

Example: Students can investigate the role of shamanism in religious rituals, focusing on the pharaoh's and priests' ability to commune with the spiritual realm and channel divine energies. By exploring trance states, ecstatic rituals, or spirit journeys, students can gain insight into the shamanic practices that enabled the ruling elite to connect with the gods and acquire spiritual knowledge.

Counterargument: It is crucial to acknowledge that not all religious practices were limited to the pharaohs and priests. The general populace also actively engaged in personal and communal religious rituals, albeit with different levels of access and participation.

Conclusion:

In Chapter 6, we explore the captivating roles of the pharaohs and priests in ancient Egyptian religious practices. Their positions as divine rulers and intermediaries between humanity and the gods granted them immense authority and responsibility. By examining the involvement of the pharaohs and priests in witchcraft, divination, herbalism, shamanism, and ecospirituality, we gain a comprehensive understanding of the ways in which their actions shaped religious beliefs, rituals, and the spiritual fabric of ancient Egyptian society. Through critical analysis and engagement with the presented examples, students can further develop their comprehension of the complex interplay between political power, religious authority, and the daily religious practices of ancient Egypt.

Exercises:

Compare and contrast the roles of the pharaoh and the priesthood in ancient Egyptian religious practices, focusing on their respective functions, responsibilities, and sources of authority.

Investigate the significance of the pharaoh's divine status and its implications for the practice of divination in ancient Egypt, citing specific examples and discussing the connection between political power and religious authority.

Analyze the hierarchies within the priesthood, examining the roles of different priestly classes and their specific duties in religious rituals and ceremonies.

Discuss the impact of the pharaohs' and priests' involvement in shamanic practices on the religious beliefs and experiences of ancient Egyptians, considering the ways in which trance states and spirit journeys shaped their understanding of the spiritual realm.

These exercises encourage students to critically engage with the subject matter, fostering analytical thinking and promoting discussions that deepen their knowledge of the roles played by pharaohs and priests in ancient Egyptian religious practices.

In-depth study of the pivotal role played by pharaohs in ancient Egyptian religious rituals and ceremonies

Below is a detailed section on the pivotal role played by pharaohs in ancient Egyptian religious rituals and ceremonies, written in an academic style:

Chapter: The Pivotal Role of Pharaohs in Ancient Egyptian Religious Rituals and Ceremonies

The ancient Egyptian civilization was characterized by a close intertwining of religion and politics, with the pharaoh occupying a central position as the religious and political leader. The pharaoh was believed to possess divine authority and was considered the intermediary between the mortal realm and the gods. In this chapter, we will delve into the in-depth study of the pivotal role played by pharaohs in ancient Egyptian religious rituals and ceremonies. We will explore the pharaoh's divine attributes, their involvement in temple rituals, and the significance of their presence in religious ceremonies.

Divine Attributes of Pharaohs:

The ancient Egyptians regarded the pharaoh as a god in human form, embodying the power and authority of the gods. They believed that the pharaoh possessed a divine essence, making them the bridge between the earthly realm and the realm of the gods. The pharaoh was considered the living Horus, the son of the sky god Horus, and the incarnation of the sun god Ra. These divine attributes bestowed upon the pharaoh immense power and legitimacy, elevating them to a revered and untouchable status.

Involvement in Temple Rituals:

Temple rituals formed a central part of ancient Egyptian religious practices, and the pharaoh played a crucial role in these ceremonies. As the primary representative of the gods, the pharaoh participated in various rituals conducted within the sacred precincts of temples. These rituals included offerings, processions, and acts of worship aimed at maintaining cosmic harmony and securing divine favor for the kingdom. The presence of the pharaoh in these rituals lent them great significance and legitimacy, as their divine essence amplified the efficacy of the ceremonies.

The pharaoh's involvement in temple rituals extended beyond mere participation. They also held the authority to appoint and oversee the priesthood, ensuring the proper execution of religious duties and the adherence to established rituals. The pharaoh's active engagement in temple affairs emphasized their role as the religious leader and the guardian of religious traditions.

Significance in Religious Ceremonies:

Religious ceremonies in ancient Egypt encompassed a wide range of events, from grand festivals to daily rituals. The presence of the pharaoh in these ceremonies elevated their importance and served to unite the people under a shared religious experience. The participation of the pharaoh in public ceremonies, such as the Opet Festival or the Sed Festival, reinforced the pharaoh's role as the link between the gods and the people. These ceremonies showcased the pharaoh's divine connection and highlighted their role in maintaining cosmic order and prosperity for the kingdom.

Moreover, the pharaoh's involvement in private religious ceremonies, such as funerary rituals and temple dedications, added a sense of divine validation to these events. The pharaoh's presence ensured the favor and blessings of the gods, enhancing the efficacy of these ceremonies in securing the deceased's journey to the afterlife or the successful consecration of a new temple.

Examples:

To illustrate the pivotal role of pharaohs in ancient Egyptian religious rituals and ceremonies, let us examine two prominent examples: the Heb Sed Festival and the daily offering rituals.

Heb Sed Festival: This jubilee festival was celebrated by the pharaoh to commemorate their continued reign and rejuvenation. The festival involved a series of elaborate rituals, including the pharaoh's performance of physical and symbolic acts of strength, endurance, and renewal. By actively participating in the Heb Sed Festival, the pharaoh demonstrated their ability to maintain their divine authority and ensure the well-being of the kingdom.

Daily Offering Rituals: The pharaoh's involvement in daily offering rituals exemplified their role as the intermediary between the gods and the people. Each day, the pharaoh would perform offerings to various deities, ensuring their sustenance and favor. These rituals were carried out in temples and witnessed by the priesthood and the people, reinforcing the pharaoh's divine mandate and establishing a sense of collective religious devotion.

Problems and Exercises:

Discuss the theological significance of the pharaoh's divine attributes in ancient Egyptian religious beliefs and practices.

Analyze the role of the pharaoh in temple rituals and their impact on the legitimacy of religious ceremonies.

Compare and contrast the pharaoh's participation in public and private religious events, highlighting their respective significance and implications.

Examine the influence of the pharaoh's presence in religious rituals on the social cohesion and communal identity of ancient Egyptian society.

Conclusion:

The pivotal role played by pharaohs in ancient Egyptian religious rituals and ceremonies cannot be overstated. As the embodiment of divine authority, the pharaoh's participation in temple rituals and their presence in religious ceremonies added legitimacy, power, and spiritual significance to these practices. The pharaoh's divine attributes, involvement in temple rituals, and participation in religious ceremonies united the people under a shared religious identity and reinforced the connection between religion and political authority in ancient Egypt.

Analysis of the divine kingship concept and the pharaoh's role as a mediator between the mortal and divine realms

The concept of divine kingship was a fundamental aspect of ancient Egyptian civilization, where the pharaoh was believed to possess a divine essence and act as a mediator between the mortal and divine realms. In this chapter, we will undertake an in-depth analysis of the divine kingship concept and explore the multifaceted role of the pharaoh as a mediator. We will examine the religious, political, and societal implications of this role, providing a comprehensive understanding of the pharaoh's divine authority.

Divine Kingship in Ancient Egypt:

Divine kingship, rooted in ancient Egyptian religious beliefs, asserted that the pharaoh was a god in human form. This concept was deeply ingrained in the Egyptian worldview, shaping the religious, political, and social dynamics of the civilization. The pharaoh was considered the offspring of the gods, with divine essence flowing through their veins. This divine lineage endowed the pharaoh with extraordinary powers, authority, and the ability to commune with the gods.

The concept of divine kingship was a fundamental aspect of ancient Egyptian civilization, where the pharaoh was believed to possess a divine essence and act as a mediator between the mortal and divine realms. In this chapter, we will undertake an in-depth analysis of the divine kingship concept and explore the multifaceted role of the pharaoh as a mediator. We will examine the religious, political, and societal implications of this role, providing a comprehensive understanding of the pharaoh's divine authority.

Divine Kingship in Ancient Egypt:

Divine kingship, rooted in ancient Egyptian religious beliefs, asserted that the pharaoh was a god in human form. This concept was deeply ingrained in the Egyptian worldview, shaping the religious, political, and social dynamics of the civilization. The pharaoh was considered the offspring of the gods, with divine essence flowing through their veins. This divine lineage endowed the pharaoh with extraordinary powers, authority, and the ability to commune with the gods.

Mediator between the Mortal and Divine Realms:

As the intermediary between the mortal and divine realms, the pharaoh held a unique position of great significance. They were believed to have direct access to the gods and acted as the principal channel of communication between the gods and the people. The pharaoh's role as a mediator encompassed various aspects, including religious rituals, political governance, and societal harmony.

Religious Mediation:

In the religious domain, the pharaoh played a vital role in maintaining cosmic balance and harmony. They performed elaborate rituals and ceremonies on behalf of the entire kingdom, seeking divine blessings, appeasing the gods, and ensuring the prosperity and well-being of the land. The pharaoh's participation in religious rites demonstrated their ability to establish and maintain a harmonious relationship between the divine and mortal realms, and to secure the favor of the gods for their people.

Political Mediation:

The pharaoh's role as a mediator extended to the political sphere. Their divine authority and connection to the gods lent legitimacy and stability to their rule. The pharaoh was seen as the ultimate lawgiver, responsible for upholding ma'at—the cosmic balance and order. Their decisions and decrees were believed to be divinely guided, ensuring the just governance and protection of the kingdom. By embodying the divine, the pharaoh unified the political and religious spheres, establishing a strong foundation for the societal structure.

Societal Mediation:

The pharaoh's mediation between the mortal and divine realms had profound societal implications. Their divine authority and guidance provided a sense of unity, identity, and purpose to the people. The pharaoh's role as a mediator fostered a collective consciousness, where individuals understood their place within the cosmic order and their responsibilities towards the gods and society. This belief system promoted social cohesion, as the pharaoh's actions and decisions were seen as reflecting the will of the gods and the overall well-being of the kingdom.

Counterarguments and Dissenting Opinions:

While the concept of divine kingship and the pharaoh's role as a mediator were widely accepted in ancient Egypt, dissenting opinions and alternative viewpoints existed. Some scholars argue that the divine kingship concept was a tool used by the pharaohs to consolidate and maintain political power. They suggest that the pharaohs' claim to divine authority was a strategic political construct rather than a genuine belief system.

Furthermore, it is important to note that not all individuals within ancient Egyptian society may have fully embraced the concept of divine kingship. The belief system may have varied across different social strata, with some groups potentially holding divergent religious views or interpreting the pharaoh's role differently.

Conclusion:

The divine kingship concept and the pharaoh's role as a mediator between the mortal and divine realms were foundational elements of ancient Egyptian civilization. The pharaoh's divine essence and authority shaped religious practices, political governance, and societal harmony. By analyzing the multifaceted nature of the pharaoh's role as a mediator, we gain a comprehensive understanding of the interplay between religion, politics, and society in ancient Egypt.

Exercises and Problems:

Discuss the significance of the divine kingship concept in ancient Egyptian society and its impact on religious, political, and social structures.

Compare and contrast the pharaoh's role as a mediator between the mortal and divine realms in ancient Egypt with similar concepts found in other ancient civilizations, such as Mesopotamia or Mesoamerica.

Analyze the potential motivations behind the pharaohs' claim to divine authority, considering both religious and political factors.

Evaluate the role of dissenting opinions and alternative viewpoints in understanding the complexities of the divine kingship concept in ancient Egypt.

Mediator between the Mortal and Divine Realms:

As the intermediary between the mortal and divine realms, the pharaoh held a unique position of great significance. They were believed to have direct access to the gods and acted as the principal channel of communication between the gods and the people. The pharaoh's role as a mediator encompassed various aspects, including religious rituals, political governance, and societal harmony.

The pharaoh in ancient Egypt occupied a distinguished role as the mediator between the mortal and divine realms. Believed to possess a direct connection to the gods, the pharaoh acted as the principal channel of communication, facilitating the exchange of divine blessings and guidance between the supernatural and human spheres. This section will provide an in-depth analysis of the pharaoh's role as a mediator, exploring its significance in religious rituals, political governance, and societal harmony.

Religious Mediation:

At the heart of the pharaoh's role as a mediator was their involvement in religious rituals. As the representative of the gods on Earth, the pharaoh performed elaborate ceremonies and offerings to appease and communicate with the divine beings. Through these rituals, the pharaoh sought to maintain cosmic balance, harmony, and the favor of the gods for the well-being and prosperity of the kingdom.

One example of religious mediation was the Sed festival, a jubilee ceremony held to renew the pharaoh's divine mandate and rejuvenate their rule. This event, typically celebrated after a pharaoh had ruled for 30 years, involved various rituals symbolizing the pharaoh's rebirth and reaffirming their authority. By engaging in such ceremonies, the pharaoh solidified their role as a mediator and demonstrated their commitment to upholding the divine order.

Political Mediation:

The pharaoh's role as a mediator extended beyond religious matters and encompassed political governance. As the link between the divine and mortal realms, the pharaoh's authority was considered sacred and derived directly from the gods. This divine mandate provided the pharaoh with legitimacy and empowered them to enact laws, maintain order, and govern the kingdom in accordance with the divine will.

To maintain political stability, the pharaoh engaged in various forms of political mediation. For instance, they appointed and supervised officials, ensuring that they carried out their duties in alignment with the divine principles of justice and ma'at. By actively participating in political affairs, the pharaoh exemplified their role as a mediator between the gods and the people, guiding the kingdom towards harmony and prosperity.

Societal Mediation:

The pharaoh's mediation between the mortal and divine realms had significant societal implications. The belief in the pharaoh's divine authority fostered a sense of unity and identity among the Egyptian people. As the mediator, the pharaoh embodied the values and principles dictated by the gods, serving as a moral compass for the society.

The pharaoh's role as a societal mediator was particularly evident in matters of justice and social welfare. The laws and judgments issued by the pharaoh were perceived as divine decrees, ensuring fairness and equity within the kingdom. By acting as the intermediary between the gods and the people, the pharaoh upheld social cohesion and harmony, reinforcing the belief that societal well-being relied on the alignment with divine principles.

Counterarguments and Dissenting Opinions:

While the notion of the pharaoh as a mediator was widely accepted in ancient Egypt, alternative perspectives exist. Some scholars propose that the pharaoh's role as a mediator may have been more symbolic than practical. They argue that the religious and political rituals performed by the pharaoh were primarily tools employed to legitimize and consolidate their power, rather than a direct communication with the gods.

Additionally, dissenting opinions suggest that the pharaoh's mediation may have been influenced by political motivations, with the divine connection serving as a means of control over the populace. These viewpoints highlight the complexity of understanding the pharaoh's role as a mediator and encourage further exploration and critical analysis.

Conclusion:

The pharaoh's role as a mediator between the mortal and divine realms was a cornerstone of ancient Egyptian civilization. Through religious rituals, political governance, and societal harmony, the pharaoh acted as the principal channel of communication, facilitating the exchange of blessings, guidance, and divine order. While alternative perspectives and dissenting opinions exist, the concept of the pharaoh as a mediator remains an essential component of understanding ancient Egyptian spirituality, politics, and social dynamics.

Exercises and Problems:

Discuss the significance of the pharaoh's role as a mediator in ancient Egyptian religion, politics, and society, providing examples to support your arguments.

Compare and contrast the pharaoh's role as a mediator with similar concepts found in other cultures, such as the role of priests in ancient Mesopotamia or the oracle in ancient Greece.

Evaluate the impact of the pharaoh's mediation on the religious practices, political governance, and societal cohesion of ancient Egypt.

Analyze the counterarguments and dissenting opinions regarding the pharaoh's role as a mediator, considering their implications for our understanding of ancient Egyptian civilization.

Religious Mediation:

In the religious domain, the pharaoh played a vital role in maintaining cosmic balance and harmony. They performed elaborate rituals and ceremonies on behalf of the entire kingdom, seeking divine blessings, appeasing the gods, and ensuring the prosperity and well-being of the land. The pharaoh's participation in religious rites demonstrated their ability to establish and maintain a harmonious relationship between the divine and mortal realms, and to secure the favor of the gods for their people.

Political Mediation:

The pharaoh's role as a mediator extended to the political sphere. Their divine authority and connection to the gods lent legitimacy and stability to their rule. The pharaoh was seen as the ultimate lawgiver, responsible for upholding ma'at—the cosmic balance and order. Their decisions and decrees were believed to be divinely guided, ensuring the just governance and protection of the kingdom. By embodying the divine, the pharaoh unified the political and religious spheres, establishing a strong foundation for the societal structure.

Societal Mediation:

The pharaoh's mediation between the mortal and divine realms had profound societal implications. Their divine authority and guidance provided a sense of unity, identity, and purpose to the people. The pharaoh's role as a mediator fostered a collective consciousness, where individuals understood their place within the cosmic order and their responsibilities towards the gods and society. This belief system promoted social cohesion, as the pharaoh's actions and decisions were seen as reflecting the will of the gods and the overall well-being of the kingdom.

Counterarguments and Dissenting Opinions:

Exploring the Esoteric Wisdom of Ancient Egypt for Modern Spirituality

While the concept of divine kingship and the pharaoh's role as a mediator were widely accepted in ancient Egypt, dissenting opinions and alternative viewpoints existed. Some scholars argue that the divine kingship concept was a tool used by the pharaohs to consolidate and maintain political power. They suggest that the pharaohs' claim to divine authority was a strategic political construct rather than a genuine belief system.

Furthermore, it is important to note that not all individuals within ancient Egyptian society may have fully embraced the concept of divine kingship. The belief system may have varied across different social strata, with some groups potentially holding divergent religious views or interpreting the pharaoh's role differently.

Conclusion:

The divine kingship concept and the pharaoh's role as a mediator between the mortal and divine realms were foundational elements of ancient Egyptian civilization. The pharaoh's divine essence and authority shaped religious practices, political governance, and societal harmony. By analyzing the multifaceted nature of the pharaoh's role as a mediator, we gain a comprehensive understanding of the interplay between religion, politics, and society in ancient Egypt.

Exercises and Problems:

Discuss the significance of the divine kingship concept in ancient Egyptian society and its impact on religious, political, and social structures.

Compare and contrast the pharaoh's role as a mediator between the mortal and divine realms in ancient Egypt with similar concepts found in other ancient civilizations, such as Mesopotamia or Mesoamerica.

Analyze the potential motivations behind the pharaohs' claim to divine authority, considering both religious and political factors.

Evaluate the role of dissenting opinions and alternative viewpoints in understanding the complexities of the divine kingship concept in ancient Egypt.

Note: The examples, problems, and exercises provided in this chapter are intended to engage students in critical thinking and further discussion on the topic.

Examination of the responsibilities and duties of priests in performing religious rites, maintaining temples, and preserving sacred knowledge

Priests held a pivotal role in ancient societies, serving as intermediaries between the mortal realm and the divine. In the context of ancient Egyptian religion, priests played a crucial role in performing religious rites, maintaining temples, and preserving sacred knowledge. This section will provide a comprehensive analysis of the responsibilities and duties of priests, shedding light on their significance in the religious, social, and intellectual fabric of ancient Egypt.

Religious Rites and Rituals:

Priests in ancient Egypt were entrusted with the responsibility of performing religious rites and rituals. These ceremonies were essential for maintaining the cosmic order, appeasing the gods, and ensuring the well-being of the kingdom. The priests acted as conduits through which divine blessings and messages were conveyed to the people.

One example of a religious rite performed by priests was the daily offering ritual. Each day, in the temples dedicated to specific deities, priests meticulously prepared and presented offerings to the gods. These offerings included food, beverages, incense, and prayers. Through this act, priests sought to sustain the divine favor and reinforce the spiritual connection between the mortal and divine realms.

Maintenance of Temples:

Priests were also responsible for the maintenance and care of temples, which served as the sacred abodes of the gods. Temples were not merely religious structures but also centers of economic activity, education, and administration. Priests oversaw the daily operations of the temple, ensuring its cleanliness, functionality, and appropriate conduct of rituals.

Priests were responsible for the proper storage and management of temple wealth, including offerings and donations from devotees. They also supervised temple personnel, such as temple musicians, dancers, and servants, who played integral roles in religious ceremonies. The priests' meticulous attention to the upkeep of temples reflected their dedication to maintaining the divine presence and facilitating spiritual engagement.

Preservation of Sacred Knowledge:

Exploring the Esoteric Wisdom of Ancient Egypt for Modern Spirituality

One of the most significant duties of priests was the preservation and transmission of sacred knowledge. Priests were the guardians of ancient wisdom, rituals, and religious texts, ensuring their continuity across generations. They played a vital role in the education and training of future priests, passing down the knowledge necessary for the proper performance of religious rites and rituals.

The priestly class possessed expertise in various fields, including astronomy, medicine, mathematics, and magic. This knowledge was often intertwined with religious practices, as the gods were believed to be the ultimate source of wisdom. Through their meticulous record-keeping and oral traditions, priests preserved sacred texts such as the Pyramid Texts, Coffin Texts, and Book of the Dead, which provided insights into the cosmology, rituals, and beliefs of ancient Egyptian spirituality.

Counterarguments and Dissenting Opinions:

While the role of priests in ancient Egypt is widely acknowledged, dissenting opinions and counterarguments exist regarding their motivations and impact. Some scholars propose that the priestly class may have exploited their religious authority for personal gain, accumulating wealth and influence at the expense of the general populace. These viewpoints emphasize the complexities and power dynamics within the priestly hierarchy and encourage critical examination of the priestly class's role in ancient Egyptian society.

Conclusion:

The responsibilities and duties of priests in ancient Egypt encompassed performing religious rites, maintaining temples, and preserving sacred knowledge. Through their participation in rituals, priests facilitated communication between the mortal and divine realms, ensuring cosmic harmony and divine favor. Their meticulous care of temples upheld the sacredness of these spaces and provided a platform for spiritual engagement. Furthermore, the preservation of sacred knowledge by priests contributed to the continuity of ancient Egyptian religious traditions and intellectual pursuits.

Exercises and Problems:

Research and discuss the role of specific priesthoods in ancient Egypt, such as the High Priest of Amun or the Divine Adoratrice of Amun. Analyze their responsibilities, privileges, and influence.

The Veil of Thoth

Imagine you are a priest in ancient Egypt. Create a detailed description of a religious ritual you would perform and explain its significance.

Compare and contrast the responsibilities and duties of priests in ancient Egypt with those of priests in other ancient cultures, such as the Druids in Celtic society or the Brahmins in ancient India.

Investigate the role of women in the priesthood of ancient Egypt. Discuss any limitations or unique responsibilities they may have had compared to their male counterparts.

Examine the implications of the preservation of sacred knowledge by priests for the intellectual and cultural development of ancient Egypt.

Chapter 7: Creation Myths and Cosmology

Creation myths and cosmology are fundamental aspects of religious and spiritual belief systems across cultures and throughout history. These narratives explore the origin and structure of the universe, the emergence of life, and humanity's place within the cosmic order. Understanding creation myths and cosmology provides insight into the foundational beliefs and worldviews of various traditions, including Witchcraft, Divination, Herbalism, Shamanism, and Ecospirituality. This chapter delves into the diverse creation myths and cosmological frameworks found in these fields, examining their significance, symbolism, and implications for human existence.

Exercises and Problems:

Compare and contrast the creation myths of two different traditions, such as the Norse creation myth and a creation myth from a Shamanic tradition. Analyze the similarities, differences, and underlying themes.

Design a cosmological diagram representing the interconnectedness of elements in Witchcraft, incorporating symbols and colors that reflect its cosmological principles.

Research and present a case study on a contemporary Ecospiritual community that incorporates cosmological beliefs into their ecological practices.

Critically evaluate a scientific theory of cosmology and compare it to a creation myth of your choice. Identify areas of convergence and divergence, and discuss their implications for understanding the nature of the universe.

Engage in a group discussion on the ethical implications of creation myths and cosmologies, focusing on their potential to shape environmental attitudes and actions.

Exploring Creation Myths

Creation myths are narratives that explore the origin of the universe, the emergence of life, and the establishment of order and meaning in the world. They are foundational stories that offer explanations for fundamental questions about existence, such as the origins of humans, the natural world, and the divine.

Across different cultural and spiritual traditions, creation myths vary in their details and symbolism. For example, in Witchcraft, creation myths often emphasize the cycles of nature and the interplay of elemental forces. In Shamanism, creation myths may revolve around the journeys of spirit beings or the awakening of spiritual consciousness. Understanding the diverse range of creation myths is crucial for appreciating the richness and complexity of human belief systems.

Symbolism and Allegory in Creation Myths:

Creation myths often employ symbolism and allegory to convey deeper philosophical, spiritual, and moral truths. Symbols represent abstract concepts or elements of the natural world, while allegory uses metaphorical narratives to convey hidden meanings.

For instance, in the creation myth of the Goddess and the Horned God in Witchcraft, the Goddess represents fertility, abundance, and the cycles of life, while the Horned God symbolizes wild nature and masculine energy. Their union in the myth symbolizes the dynamic balance between feminine and masculine forces in the cosmos and the cycles of life, death, and rebirth.

Similarly, creation myths in Shamanism may utilize animal spirits or mythical beings to represent different aspects of the natural world and human consciousness. These symbolic elements serve to convey teachings about harmony with nature, spiritual awakening, and the interconnectedness of all life.

Common Themes and Motifs in Creation Myths:

While creation myths differ in their specific details, certain themes and motifs recur across cultures and spiritual traditions. Some of these include:

Emergence from Chaos:

Many creation myths describe a primordial state of chaos or formlessness from which the world emerges. This chaos is often represented as a void or a cosmic egg, symbolizing the potential for creation.

One prevalent theme in creation myths is the emergence from chaos or formlessness. These myths often describe a primordial state in which the world exists as a shapeless void or an undifferentiated cosmic egg. This state of chaos represents the absence of order, structure, and defined boundaries.

In many creation myths, chaos is depicted as a vast and infinite expanse, devoid of light, life, and meaning. It is a state of pure potentiality, containing within it the seeds of all that will come into existence. This chaotic state can be seen as a metaphorical representation of the pre-creation phase, where the elements necessary for the formation of the universe remain latent.

The concept of chaos as the starting point for creation can be found in various cultural and spiritual traditions. For instance, in ancient Egyptian mythology, the creator deity Atum emerges from the watery abyss of Nu, a formless and limitless expanse. Atum, the first god, brings order and form to the world through his creative actions. Similarly, in the Babylonian creation myth Enuma Elish, the world emerges from the primordial chaos represented by the god Tiamat, a chaotic sea serpent.

The symbolism of chaos as a cosmic egg is also prevalent in creation myths. The egg represents the potential for creation and the gestation of life. Within the egg, the elements necessary for the formation of the universe are contained, waiting to be activated. This imagery is found in various mythologies, such as the Chinese creation myth of Pangu, where the world is said to have originated from a cosmic egg that hatches, separating heaven and earth.

The emergence from chaos in creation myths signifies the transition from a state of formlessness to a state of order and structure. It represents the transformative power of creation and the establishment of a harmonious and meaningful cosmos. Through divine intervention or creative acts, the chaos is shaped and organized, bringing forth light, life, and purpose.

Analyzing the motif of emergence from chaos allows us to explore the human desire to make sense of the world and find meaning in the seemingly chaotic nature of existence. These myths convey the belief that order and purpose can arise from formlessness and that the universe itself is imbued with a creative potential that unfolds over time.

Exercises and Problems:

Compare and contrast the depiction of chaos and the emergence from chaos in the creation myths of different cultures, such as the ancient Egyptian, Mesopotamian, and Chinese creation myths. Analyze the symbolic significance of chaos in each myth and its role in the process of creation.

Create a narrative or poem that describes the emergence from chaos using elements from different creation myths. Consider how the depiction of chaos and the subsequent emergence reflect the cultural and philosophical beliefs of the societies from which the myths originate.

Discuss the concept of chaos in relation to scientific theories about the origin and evolution of the universe, such as the Big Bang theory. Explore the parallels and divergences between scientific explanations and mythological narratives regarding the emergence of order from a primordial state.

Divine Beings and Creation:

Creation myths often involve the actions of gods, goddesses, or other supernatural beings who shape the world. These beings may bring order, light, or life into the cosmos through acts of creation, separation, or transformation.

A prominent feature of creation myths is the role of divine beings in the process of shaping the world and bringing forth order, light, and life. These beings, often portrayed as gods, goddesses, or other supernatural entities, play crucial roles in the cosmic narrative and are instrumental in the act of creation.

In many creation myths, the divine beings are depicted as powerful and creative forces that possess extraordinary abilities and knowledge. They are the primary agents of change and transformation, using their divine powers to shape the formless chaos into a structured and ordered cosmos. These beings may possess unique attributes, such as control over elements, mastery of magic or creation, or the ability to speak or sing the world into existence.

The actions of divine beings in creation myths can take various forms. They may engage in acts of separation, where they divide and differentiate elements to establish distinct realms or entities. For example, in the Norse creation myth, the god Odin and his brothers create the world by separating the realms of fire and ice, forming the foundation of the cosmos.

Divine beings in creation myths may also engage in acts of transformation, bringing about the emergence of life and diversity. In many myths, gods and goddesses shape and mold the physical features of the world, such as mountains, rivers, and celestial bodies. They may also breathe life into living beings or create specific species to inhabit the earth.

Moreover, the creative acts of divine beings in creation myths often extend beyond the physical realm. They may introduce moral and ethical principles, establish social order, or bestow cultural and technological advancements upon humanity. In some myths, the gods provide humanity with guidance, laws, or knowledge that serve as the foundation for civilization.

It is important to note that the characteristics and roles of divine beings in creation myths can vary across cultures and belief systems. For instance, in some myths, multiple gods collaborate or contend with one another in the process of creation, reflecting the complexity and diversity of cosmological beliefs. Additionally, some myths attribute both positive and negative aspects to divine beings, acknowledging the potential for both creative and destructive forces in the cosmos.

Analyzing the role of divine beings in creation myths allows us to explore the human quest for understanding and meaning in the origins of the world. These myths reflect the human desire to attribute the wonders and complexities of existence to higher beings and to find narratives that convey the purpose and order of the universe.

Exercises and Problems:

Select two creation myths from different cultures and compare the roles and attributes of the divine beings involved in the act of creation. Analyze how these beings shape the world and their significance in the respective cosmologies.

Create a visual representation, such as a painting or a sculpture, that depicts a divine being in the act of creation. Consider the symbolic elements and attributes that are associated with the being and how they convey its role in shaping the world.

Discuss the concept of divine beings in relation to the modern understanding of the origins of the universe, as described by scientific theories such as the Big Bang theory and the theory of evolution. Explore the similarities and differences in how these explanations address the questions of creation and the emergence of life.

Cosmic Order and Harmony:

Creation myths frequently emphasize the establishment of cosmic order and harmony. They may describe the organization of the heavens, the placement of celestial bodies, or the establishment of natural laws and cycles.

One of the central themes in creation myths is the establishment of cosmic order and harmony. These myths often explain how the universe came into a structured and balanced state, with the positioning of celestial bodies, the establishment of natural laws, and the rhythms of the natural world.

In many creation narratives, the gods or divine beings play a pivotal role in bringing about cosmic order. They may assign specific roles and responsibilities to celestial entities, such as the sun, moon, and stars, ensuring their proper placement and movement in the heavens. For example, in ancient Mesopotamian myths, the god Marduk is credited with organizing the celestial bodies and assigning them their respective paths and functions.

Moreover, creation myths frequently describe the establishment of natural laws and cycles that govern the functioning of the universe. These laws encompass various aspects, including the laws of physics, mathematics, and the interplay of elements. They regulate the processes of growth, decay, and transformation, ensuring the balance and continuity of life. For instance, in the ancient Hindu creation myth described in the Rigveda, the cosmic order is represented by the principle of Rita, which encompasses the harmonious functioning of the universe through divine laws.

The concept of cosmic order and harmony extends beyond the physical realm and encompasses the moral and ethical dimensions of existence. Creation myths often provide guidelines for human behavior and social organization, emphasizing the importance of maintaining balance, justice, and respect for the natural world. These myths may highlight the interdependence of all living beings and the need for humans to live in harmony with nature. For example, in many indigenous creation myths, such as those found in Native American traditions, the harmony between humans, animals, and the environment is emphasized as essential for the well-being of the world.

Studying the concept of cosmic order and harmony in creation myths allows us to explore the human longing for stability, purpose, and interconnectedness. These myths provide narratives that reflect the desire to find meaning in the organization and patterns of the universe and to establish a sense of belonging within the larger cosmic order.

Exercises and Problems:

Compare and contrast the descriptions of cosmic order and harmony in two different creation myths. Analyze how these myths explain the placement of celestial bodies, the establishment of natural laws, and the moral principles that govern human behavior.

Reflect on the concept of cosmic order and harmony in relation to environmental sustainability. Discuss how the principles and values present in creation myths can inform our modern understanding of ecological balance and the importance of living in harmony with nature.

Imagine you are a character in a creation myth. Write a personal narrative describing your role in bringing about cosmic order and maintaining harmony in the newly created world. Consider the responsibilities, challenges, and rewards associated with your role.

Human Origins and Purpose:

Many creation myths address the origins of humanity and the relationship between humans and the divine. These myths often convey teachings about human responsibilities, moral codes, or the purpose of existence.

Within creation myths, the origins of humanity and the purpose of human existence are significant aspects of the narrative. These myths seek to answer fundamental questions about the nature of humanity, the role of humans in the cosmos, and the relationship between humans and the divine.

Creation myths often provide explanations for how humans came into being and the unique qualities that distinguish them from other creatures. These explanations vary across different cultural traditions and can involve diverse elements such as divine intervention, shaping from natural elements, or a combination of both. For instance, in the biblical creation story, humans are said to be created in the image of God, signifying a special connection and purpose.

Additionally, creation myths often convey teachings about human responsibilities, moral codes, and the purpose of existence. They provide guidance on how humans should interact with one another, the natural world, and the divine. These teachings may encompass ethical principles, social norms, and the cultivation of virtues. Creation myths can be seen as frameworks for understanding the human condition and offering insights into the challenges and aspirations of human life.

The purpose of human existence as portrayed in creation myths can vary. Some myths suggest that humans were created to serve the gods or divine beings, carrying out specific tasks or duties on their behalf. In other myths, humans may be seen as co-creators or collaborators with the divine, entrusted with the ongoing work of maintaining and nurturing the world. Additionally, creation myths can highlight the quest for self-realization, spiritual growth, or the pursuit of wisdom and knowledge as essential aspects of human purpose.

Exploring the themes of human origins and purpose in creation myths allows us to delve into profound questions about identity, meaning, and the human experience. These myths offer insights into diverse cultural perspectives on the nature of humanity and the moral frameworks that guide human behavior.

Exercises and Problems:

Compare and contrast the explanations of human origins and purpose in two different creation myths. Analyze the teachings and values associated with human existence in each myth and discuss the similarities and differences between them.

Reflect on the moral teachings present in a specific creation myth. Discuss how these teachings can be applied to contemporary ethical dilemmas and challenges, fostering personal and societal growth.

Imagine you are a character in a creation myth. Write a personal reflection on the purpose of human existence based on the teachings and events depicted in the myth. Consider the responsibilities, trials, and rewards associated with fulfilling this purpose.

Destruction and Renewal:

Creation myths sometimes include elements of destruction and renewal, reflecting cyclical views of time and the impermanence of the world. These myths may involve cosmic battles, floods, or other cataclysmic events that lead to rebirth or regeneration.

Analyzing the common themes and motifs in creation myths helps us identify shared human concerns, values, and aspirations. They offer insights into how different cultures and spiritual traditions have sought to understand and make meaning of the world around them.

Exercises and Problems:

Analyze the creation myths of two different traditions, such as the Norse creation myth and a creation myth from Shamanism. Compare and contrast their key themes, symbols, and cultural contexts.

Create a visual representation or artwork inspired by a creation myth of your choice. Explain the symbolism and allegorical elements in your artwork and how they relate to the myth's central themes.

Research a contemporary Ecospiritual community that incorporates creation myths into their ecological practices. Explore how their beliefs about the origins of the natural world influence their environmental attitudes and actions.

Engage in a group discussion on the role of creation myths in shaping cultural identity and worldview. Discuss the potential benefits and limitations of relying on myths as explanations for the origin of the universe.

Symbolism and Allegory in Creation Myths:

Creation myths are rich in symbolism and allegory, utilizing metaphors, imagery, and narrative devices to convey deeper philosophical and spiritual truths. These myths employ a symbolic language that transcends literal interpretations and invites readers to explore profound meanings embedded within the narrative. By understanding the symbolism and allegory present in creation myths, we can gain insight into the complex and layered messages they convey about the nature of existence, the human condition, and the relationship between the divine and the mortal.

Symbolic Language in Creation Myths:

Creation myths often employ a symbolic language that transcends mundane descriptions, inviting readers to contemplate abstract concepts and cosmic forces. This symbolic language serves as a bridge between the concrete world and the realm of the numinous, allowing for the expression of profound ideas that may be difficult to articulate directly.

Symbols in creation myths can take various forms, such as animals, natural elements, celestial bodies, or archetypal figures. For example, the serpent in many creation myths symbolizes wisdom, transformation, and the cyclical nature of life. The tree of life represents the interconnectedness of all living beings and the potential for spiritual growth. Understanding these symbols and their associated meanings enhances our comprehension of the deeper layers of meaning in creation myths.

Interpretation of Key Elements:

Interpreting the key elements in creation myths requires careful analysis of their symbolic significance. Primordial beings, such as gods and goddesses, often represent fundamental cosmic forces or aspects of the human psyche. Their actions and interactions symbolize the processes of creation, destruction, and transformation.

Cosmic forces depicted in creation myths, such as chaos, order, light, darkness, and the elements, serve as metaphors for the primordial conditions from which the world emerges. These forces embody universal principles and provide a framework for understanding the origins and dynamics of existence.

Divine acts described in creation myths are laden with symbolism and allegory. For example, the act of separation, such as the separation of heaven and earth or the division of light and darkness, symbolizes the establishment of boundaries and the organization of the cosmos. The act of creation, such as the shaping of the world or the emergence of life forms, conveys the inherent creative power of the divine and reflects the potential for growth and evolution.

Conveying Deeper Philosophical and Spiritual Truths:

Creation myths go beyond mere accounts of cosmogony and cosmology; they convey deeper philosophical and spiritual truths. Through symbolism and allegory, these myths explore profound questions about the nature of existence, the purpose of life, and the relationship between the divine and the mortal.

By engaging with creation myths on a symbolic level, we can access insights into the mysteries of the universe and our place within it. These myths offer philosophical reflections on themes such as the origins of suffering, the nature of duality, the balance of opposing forces, and the quest for transcendence. They provide frameworks for contemplating the human condition, moral choices, and the search for meaning and purpose.

Exercises and Problems:

Select a creation myth from a specific cultural tradition and identify its key symbolic elements. Analyze the symbolism used in the myth and discuss how these symbols contribute to the overall meaning and message of the narrative.

Compare and contrast the use of symbolism in two different creation myths. Discuss the similarities and differences in the symbols employed and explore the implications of these symbols for understanding the philosophical and spiritual teachings within each myth.

Create a symbolic representation of a key element from a creation myth using visual art, such as drawing, painting, or sculpture. Write a reflection on the symbolic meaning conveyed through your artwork and discuss how it relates to the themes and messages of the myth.

Cosmology and the Structure of the Universe

Cosmology is the study of the structure, origins, and dynamics of the universe. It provides a framework for understanding the interplay between the microcosm and macrocosm, the relationship between the human and the divine, and the interconnectedness of all things. In the realm of Witchcraft, cosmology takes on unique characteristics, offering insights into the Witch's Universe and its elemental forces. This chapter delves into the conceptions of the universe in Witchcraft, exploring the interplay between the microcosm and macrocosm, and examining the three realms: the Underworld, the Middle World, and the Upper World.

The Witch's Universe:

In Witchcraft, the universe is perceived as a living and interconnected entity, imbued with spiritual energy and magical potential. The Witch's Universe encompasses not only the physical world but also the spiritual dimensions, reflecting a holistic understanding of reality. It is a universe in which everything is interconnected and influenced by the elements, the seasons, and the cycles of nature.

Elements play a crucial role in Witchcraft cosmology, representing fundamental forces and principles that shape the universe. These elements - Earth, Air, Fire, Water, and Spirit - are seen as both external and internal forces, existing within and around individuals. They symbolize different aspects of existence, such as grounding, intellect, passion, emotion, and the divine spark within.

The Microcosm and Macrocosm:

Witchcraft cosmology emphasizes the interplay between the microcosm (the individual) and the macrocosm (the universe). It posits that the individual is a reflection of the larger cosmic whole, and through this interconnectedness, one can access and influence the forces of the universe. This belief forms the basis for various practices in Witchcraft, such as spellcasting, divination, and ritual work.

The concept of "as above, so below" underscores the correspondence between different levels of existence. It suggests that what occurs in the heavens or the larger universe is mirrored in the individual's experience. By aligning oneself with the rhythms and energies of the universe, one can harmonize their inner and outer worlds, enhancing personal growth and spiritual development.

The Three Realms:

Witchcraft cosmology often delineates the universe into three realms: the Underworld, the Middle World, and the Upper World. Each realm represents a distinct dimension of existence and is associated with specific energies, entities, and experiences.

The Underworld, also known as the Otherworld or the Spirit World, is the realm of the ancestors, spirits, and otherworldly beings. It is a place of mystery, transformation, and the subconscious mind. In this realm, communication with spirits, ancestral veneration, and shadow work take place.

The Middle World corresponds to the physical realm inhabited by humans and other earthly beings. It is the realm of daily life, where the interplay between the elements, seasons, and natural cycles influences human experiences. Witchcraft practices in the Middle World include herbalism, spellwork, and rituals that connect individuals with the energies of nature.

The Upper World is the realm of the celestial and divine. It encompasses the heavens, celestial bodies, and higher realms of consciousness. Journeying to the Upper World through meditation, trance, or astral projection allows for encounters with deities, spiritual guides, and the cosmic forces that govern the universe.

Exercises and Problems:

Explore the elements within Witchcraft cosmology and their correspondences. Create a personal elemental chart that reflects your understanding of their attributes and symbolic meanings. Reflect on how these elements manifest within your own life and experiences.

Compare and contrast the concept of the Witch's Universe with other cosmological frameworks, such as those found in Shamanism or Ecospirituality. Analyze the similarities and differences in their understandings of the interconnectedness of the universe and the role of the individual within it.

Research and analyze different cultural conceptions of the three realms, such as the Norse cosmology of Asgard, Midgard, and Hel, or the Celtic Otherworld.

Discuss how these realms shape the mythology, religious practices, and worldview of these cultures.

Engage in a guided meditation or visualization exercise to explore the three realms within Witchcraft cosmology. Take notes on your experiences and reflect on the insights gained during the journey.

Conclusion:

The exploration of Witchcraft cosmology provides a rich tapestry of understanding the structure and interconnectedness of the universe. By delving into the concept of the Witch's Universe, the interplay between the microcosm and macrocosm, and the three realms, practitioners gain insights into their place in the world, the forces that shape existence, and the means by which they can engage with the spiritual dimensions. Through the exercises and problems provided, students are encouraged to critically engage with the subject matter, fostering deeper understanding and facilitating personal growth within their own spiritual practices.

Divination and Cosmological Frameworks:

Divination is a practice found across various spiritual traditions, including Witchcraft, Divination, Herbalism, Shamanism, and Ecospirituality. It involves seeking insight, guidance, and knowledge from the divine or spiritual realms through specific techniques or tools. Divination not only serves as a means to gain personal understanding but also provides a glimpse into the cosmological frameworks that underpin these practices. This chapter explores the role of divination in understanding the cosmic order, its ability to reveal the interconnectedness of the universe, and examines specific examples of divinatory cosmologies such as the Tarot and the I Ching.

Divination as a Tool for Understanding the Cosmic Order:

In many cosmological frameworks, the universe is seen as an intricately ordered system governed by cosmic forces and principles. Divination serves as a tool to tap into these forces and gain insight into the workings of the universe. By consulting divinatory methods, individuals can access hidden knowledge, uncover the underlying patterns and dynamics of the cosmos, and align themselves with the greater cosmic order.

Divination practices often involve interpreting symbols, signs, or patterns to discern meaning and guidance. These symbols act as a bridge between the mundane and the spiritual, allowing individuals to access a deeper understanding of the cosmic order and their place within it. Whether through the casting of runes, the reading of tarot cards, or the interpretation of astrological charts, divination provides a means to connect with the underlying fabric of the universe.

Revealing the Interconnectedness of the Universe:

One of the central tenets of divination is the recognition of the interconnectedness of all things. Divination practices demonstrate that events, energies, and influences in one realm or aspect of life can reverberate throughout the entire cosmic web. By exploring this interconnectedness, divination offers a holistic perspective on the universe, highlighting the interplay between different elements, forces, and dimensions.

For example, in Tarot readings, the cards are not viewed in isolation but as part of a greater web of interconnected symbols and archetypes. Each card relates to others within the spread, creating a narrative that reflects the dynamic interplay of energies and influences. Similarly, the I Ching utilizes hexagrams to represent the various aspects of existence, illustrating how these elements interact and transform in relation to one another.

Examples of Divinatory Cosmologies:

a. The Tarot:

The Tarot is a well-known divinatory system that incorporates symbolism, archetypes, and numerology. Its cosmological framework consists of 78 cards divided into two main groups: the Major Arcana and the Minor Arcana. The Major Arcana represents significant life lessons and spiritual themes, while the Minor Arcana reflects everyday experiences and challenges. The Tarot's cosmological structure provides a framework for understanding the human journey, the interplay of universal energies, and the interconnectedness of life's various aspects.

b. The I Ching:

The I Ching, also known as the Book of Changes, is an ancient Chinese divination system. It consists of 64 hexagrams, each representing a unique combination of yin and yang lines. The I Ching offers guidance and insights into the dynamic flow of energies and changes within the cosmos. Its cosmological framework reflects the concept of the Tao, the interplay of opposing forces, and the cyclical nature of existence.

Exercises and Problems:

Select a divination tool or system, such as Tarot cards or runes. Conduct a personal divination session and reflect on the insights and messages received. Consider how these messages relate to your own life and the wider cosmic order.

Compare and contrast divinatory cosmologies from different traditions, such as the Tarot and the I Ching. Identify common themes, symbols, or archetypes and explore how they reflect the cosmological frameworks of each system.

Research and analyze the role of divination in a specific spiritual tradition, such as Shamanism or Ecospirituality. Investigate how divination is used to access cosmic wisdom, maintain balance, or navigate life's challenges within that tradition.

Conclusion:

Divination practices offer a means to understand the cosmic order and tap into the interconnectedness of the universe. Through divination, individuals can gain insights into the underlying patterns and dynamics of existence, accessing hidden knowledge and guidance. Examples such as the Tarot and the I Ching demonstrate the diverse cosmological frameworks that underpin divination, providing valuable tools for personal growth, self-reflection, and spiritual exploration. Through the exercises and problems provided, students are encouraged to engage with divination practices, fostering critical thinking and deepening their understanding of cosmological frameworks in divination.

Herbalism and the Sacred Web of Life:

Herbalism is a holistic healing practice deeply rooted in various traditions, including Witchcraft, Divination, Shamanism, and Ecospirituality. It recognizes the interconnectedness of all living beings within the web of life and views plants as sacred mediators between the physical and spiritual realms. This chapter explores herbalism's ecological perspective on cosmology, the understanding of interconnectedness between plants, animals, and humans, and the profound role of plants in bridging the physical and spiritual dimensions.

Herbalism's Ecological Perspective on Cosmology:

Herbalism embraces an ecological worldview that acknowledges the intricate interconnections and interdependencies within the natural world. It perceives the cosmos as a dynamic and harmonious system in which all beings and elements are interwoven in a delicate balance. This perspective views the Earth as a living organism and recognizes the profound interconnectedness of all life forms, including plants, animals, and humans.

In herbalism, the concept of "as above, so below" underscores the belief that the microcosm of an individual reflects the macrocosm of the universe. By observing and understanding the patterns and cycles of nature, herbalists recognize the cosmic influences and energies that shape the health and well-being of all living beings. This ecological perspective informs the principles and practices of herbal medicine, highlighting the importance of sustainability, conservation, and respect for the interconnected web of life.

Understanding the Interconnectedness of Plants, Animals, and Humans:

Herbalism recognizes that plants, animals, and humans share a deep interconnectedness within the sacred web of life. Plants, in particular, hold a unique position as mediators between the physical and spiritual realms. They have evolved over millennia to form complex relationships with animals, insects, and other elements of the ecosystem, contributing to the overall balance and vitality of the natural world.

Plants provide sustenance, medicine, and spiritual nourishment to humans and other creatures. They offer a vast array of healing properties, from soothing physical ailments to supporting emotional well-being and spiritual growth. Herbalists understand that by cultivating a deep connection with plants, they can tap into the wisdom and healing potential of the natural world. This understanding fosters a profound sense of reverence for the plants and an ethical responsibility to protect and preserve their habitats.

The Role of Plants as Mediators between the Physical and Spiritual Realms:

Plants hold a sacred role as mediators between the physical and spiritual realms. They are seen as conduits of divine energy and wisdom, carrying within them the essence of the cosmos. Herbalists believe that plants possess inherent intelligence and spiritual qualities that can be harnessed for healing and transformation.

Through the use of plant-based remedies, rituals, and ceremonies, herbalists seek to bridge the gap between the physical and spiritual dimensions. Plants are believed to have the ability to facilitate healing on multiple levels, addressing not only physical symptoms but also emotional, mental, and spiritual imbalances. Their energetic properties and vibrational frequencies are thought to resonate with specific aspects of the human being, promoting holistic well-being and alignment with the greater cosmic order.

Exercises and Problems:

Explore your local ecosystem and identify several native plants. Research their traditional uses in herbal medicine and their cultural significance. Reflect on the interconnectedness between these plants, animals, and the surrounding environment.

Engage in a plant meditation or plant spirit journey. Select a plant that resonates with you and spend time connecting with its energy and wisdom. Take note of any insights or messages that arise from this experience.

Investigate the ethical considerations of wildcrafting and sustainable harvesting in herbalism. Discuss the importance of responsible practices to maintain the balance and integrity of the sacred web of life.

Conclusion:

Herbalism offers a profound perspective on cosmology through its ecological worldview and understanding of the interconnectedness of all living beings. By recognizing the role of plants as mediators between the physical and spiritual realms, herbalists tap into the wisdom and healing potential of the natural world. This chapter has explored herbalism's ecological perspective on cosmology, the interconnectedness of plants, animals, and humans, and the sacred role of plants in bridging the physical and spiritual dimensions. Through the exercises and problems provided, students are encouraged to deepen their connection with plants, explore the ethics of herbalism, and engage in critical thinking about their role within the sacred web of life.

Shamanic Cosmologies:

Shamanic cosmologies provide a unique and profound understanding of the universe, offering a rich tapestry of beliefs and practices across various cultures. This chapter explores the intricate realms of shamanic cosmology, delving into the concept of shamanic journeys, the significance of the World Tree, and the role of the shaman as a navigator between different realms and dimensions. By understanding these cosmological frameworks, students can gain insights into the shamanic worldview and its implications for spiritual exploration and healing.

Shamanic Journeys and Cosmological Maps:

In shamanic traditions, the shaman embarks on visionary journeys to explore different realms of existence. These journeys are often facilitated through altered states of consciousness induced by rhythmic drumming, chanting, or the use of entheogenic plants. Within these altered states, the shaman navigates through cosmological maps, which serve as guides to the various realms and dimensions.

Shamanic cosmological maps differ across cultures but often include distinct realms such as the Lower World, the Middle World, and the Upper World. The Lower World represents the realm of the subconscious, animal spirits, and ancestral energies. The Middle World corresponds to the ordinary physical reality we inhabit, while the Upper World is associated with celestial realms, divine beings, and spiritual guidance. These cosmological maps provide a framework for shamanic journeys, allowing the shaman to traverse different dimensions and access spiritual knowledge and healing energies.

The Concept of the World Tree and Its Significance in Shamanic Cosmology:

Central to many shamanic cosmologies is the concept of the World Tree, also known as the Axis Mundi. The World Tree represents a vertical axis that connects the three realms and acts as a bridge between the earthly and spiritual dimensions. It symbolizes the cosmic connection and interdependence of all life forms.

The World Tree is often depicted as a colossal tree with its roots reaching deep into the Lower World, its trunk in the Middle World, and its branches extending into the Upper World. It serves as a conduit for spiritual energies and a means for the shaman to navigate between realms. The shamanic practitioner may climb, descend, or journey along the branches of the World Tree to access specific realms or communicate with spiritual beings.

The Shaman's Role as a Navigator between Different Realms and Dimensions:

In shamanic cosmologies, the shaman plays a vital role as a navigator and mediator between different realms and dimensions. Through their visionary journeys, shamans establish relationships with spirit guides, power animals, and ancestral beings, acting as intermediaries between these entities and the human world.

The shaman's ability to traverse different realms and interact with spiritual beings allows them to access wisdom, healing energies, and guidance for the benefit of individuals and communities. They may retrieve lost soul fragments, perform energetic healing, or seek knowledge to address spiritual or physical imbalances. The shaman acts as a bridge, bringing back insights and teachings from the spiritual realms to assist in the well-being and spiritual growth of individuals and the collective.

Exercises and Problems:

Engage in a guided shamanic journey or drumming meditation to explore the realms of shamanic cosmology. Reflect on your experiences and any encounters with spiritual beings or symbols that arise during the journey.

Research and compare different shamanic cosmologies from various cultures, such as Siberian shamanism, Amazonian shamanism, or Native American shamanism. Analyze the similarities and differences in their cosmological maps and their understanding of the shaman's role.

Explore the symbolism of the World Tree in different mythologies and spiritual traditions. Reflect on its significance as a cosmic axis and its relevance to your own spiritual journey.

Reflect on the ethical considerations involved in shamanic practice, such as the responsibility of the shaman as a mediator between realms and the importance of maintaining cultural respect and integrity. Discuss potential challenges and solutions for practitioners working within diverse cultural contexts.

By engaging in these exercises and reflecting on the concepts presented, students can deepen their understanding of shamanic cosmologies and foster critical thinking and discussion around the role of the shaman, the significance of cosmological maps, and the interconnectedness of different realms and dimensions.

Ecospirituality and Gaia Hypothesis:

Ecospirituality explores the interconnectedness between spirituality and the natural world, emphasizing the sacredness and intrinsic value of the Earth. This chapter delves into the concept of ecospirituality and its perspective on the Earth as a living, interconnected entity. It explores the Gaia Hypothesis, which posits that the Earth functions as a self-regulating system, and examines the spiritual relationship between humans and the natural world in the context of ecospirituality.

Ecospiritual Perspectives on the Earth as a Living, Interconnected Entity:

In ecospirituality, the Earth is regarded as a living organism, a vibrant and interconnected web of life. This perspective acknowledges that all living beings, including humans, are deeply intertwined within this web and share a common destiny. It recognizes the Earth's inherent value beyond its utilitarian purpose, emphasizing the need for ecological stewardship and sustainable practices.

Ecospirituality draws inspiration from various indigenous wisdom traditions, such as Native American spirituality or African animism, which view the Earth as a sentient being with whom humans can engage in a reciprocal relationship. By recognizing the Earth's sentience and interconnection, individuals can cultivate a sense of reverence, responsibility, and harmony with the natural world.

The Gaia Hypothesis and Its Implications for Cosmology:

The Gaia Hypothesis, proposed by scientist James Lovelock and microbiologist Lynn Margulis, suggests that the Earth functions as a self-regulating system, similar to a living organism. According to this hypothesis, the Earth's biosphere, atmosphere, and geological processes work together to maintain favorable conditions for life.

The Gaia Hypothesis challenges the traditional view of the Earth as a mere collection of separate, inert components. Instead, it presents a holistic perspective, in which the Earth is seen as a complex, dynamic system capable of maintaining its own stability and homeostasis. This hypothesis has profound implications for cosmology, as it suggests that the Earth itself can be considered a living entity with its own form of consciousness.

The Spiritual Relationship between Humans and the Natural World in Ecospirituality:

In ecospirituality, the spiritual relationship between humans and the natural world is nurtured through practices that foster connection, reverence, and reciprocity. These practices may include nature-based rituals, eco-meditation, or the use of natural elements for healing and spiritual growth.

Ecospirituality encourages individuals to develop a deep sense of ecological consciousness and responsibility towards the Earth. It emphasizes the need for sustainable living practices, conservation efforts, and the restoration of ecological balance. By recognizing the sacredness of the Earth and our interconnectedness with all life forms, individuals can cultivate a more harmonious and mutually supportive relationship with the natural world.

Exercises and Problems:

Spend time in nature and engage in a reflective practice, such as journaling or meditation, to deepen your connection with the Earth. Observe the intricate interconnections within the natural world and reflect on the implications of these interconnections for your own life and spiritual journey.

Research and analyze different cultural and religious perspectives on the sacredness of nature. Compare and contrast their views on the Earth as a living entity and the spiritual relationship between humans and the natural world.

Explore the ethical dimensions of ecospirituality, including discussions on environmental justice, climate change, and the intersectionality of social and ecological issues. Engage in a group discussion or debate to understand different viewpoints and develop critical thinking skills.

Investigate practical actions you can take in your daily life to embody ecospirituality. Develop a personal sustainability plan that aligns with your values and integrates ecological awareness into your choices and actions.

By engaging in these exercises and contemplating the concepts presented, students can deepen their understanding of ecospirituality and the Gaia Hypothesis. They will be encouraged to critically evaluate their relationship with the Earth and explore practical ways to integrate ecospiritual principles into their lives.

Analyzing Counterarguments and Dissenting Opinions

In the study of creation myths, it is essential to consider the tension that exists between scientific explanations and religious or mythological narratives. This chapter aims to explore the counterarguments and dissenting opinions presented by scientific perspectives on creation myths. By examining theories of cosmology and evolutionary biology in contrast to creation myths, we can gain a deeper understanding of the complexities and nuances of these contrasting viewpoints. Additionally, we will explore the role of metaphorical language in reconciling scientific and mythological narratives.

The Tension between Scientific Explanations and Religious Creation Myths:

The tension between scientific explanations and religious creation myths arises from the fundamental differences in their approaches to understanding the origin and development of the universe and life. Scientific explanations rely on empirical evidence, rigorous observation, and the application of logical reasoning to formulate theories and models. In contrast, religious creation myths often emerge from cultural and spiritual traditions, conveying symbolic and metaphorical truths that transcend literal interpretation.

The conflict between these perspectives has been a topic of debate throughout history. While some argue for the compatibility of science and religion, others perceive them as inherently incompatible due to their distinct methodologies and objectives. This tension requires critical analysis to appreciate the unique insights and limitations of both scientific and mythological narratives.

Examining Theories of Cosmology and Evolutionary Biology in Contrast to Creation Myths:

The theories of cosmology and evolutionary biology offer scientific explanations for the origins and development of the universe and life on Earth. Cosmology explores the structure, origins, and evolution of the universe, while evolutionary biology investigates the mechanisms and processes that have shaped the diversity of life forms.

Scientific cosmological theories, such as the Big Bang theory, describe the origins of the universe through natural processes, including the expansion of space and the formation of galaxies and stars. Evolutionary biology, on the other hand, posits that life on Earth has evolved over billions of years through mechanisms such as natural selection, genetic variation, and adaptation.

When contrasting these scientific explanations with creation myths, it is important to acknowledge the different realms of inquiry. Scientific theories provide empirical evidence and testable explanations based on observations and experimentation, whereas creation myths offer symbolic and metaphorical narratives that convey cultural, spiritual, and moral truths. Recognizing the distinct purposes and contexts of these narratives allows for a more nuanced analysis.

The Role of Metaphorical Language in Reconciling Scientific and Mythological Narratives:

Metaphorical language plays a crucial role in bridging the gap between scientific and mythological narratives. Creation myths often employ symbolism, metaphor, and allegory to convey profound truths that transcend literal interpretations. Metaphorical language allows for the expression of abstract concepts, the exploration of subjective experiences, and the communication of complex ideas that may be challenging to articulate through scientific language alone.

By embracing metaphorical language, creation myths can address existential questions, the nature of the human experience, and our place in the cosmos. While scientific explanations focus on empirical evidence and observable phenomena, the metaphorical language used in creation myths can provide a framework for contemplating the deeper meaning and purpose of existence.

Exercises and Problems:

Research and analyze different creation myths from diverse cultures. Identify the metaphorical language and symbols used to convey deeper truths. Compare and contrast these narratives with scientific explanations, discussing the distinct insights and limitations of each perspective.

Engage in a class debate or discussion on the compatibility of science and religion. Present arguments from both perspectives, highlighting examples that demonstrate potential areas of overlap and conflict. Encourage critical thinking and respectful exploration of diverse viewpoints.

Explore the concept of metaphorical thinking in scientific discourse. Investigate scientific theories or concepts that rely on metaphorical language, such as "the selfish gene" or "the expanding universe." Discuss how these metaphors shape our understanding and perception of scientific ideas.

Reflect on the ways in which metaphorical language can enhance scientific communication. Write a short essay discussing the benefits and challenges of incorporating metaphorical language in scientific discourse. Provide examples of scientific concepts that can be effectively communicated through metaphor.

By engaging in these exercises and discussions, students will develop critical thinking skills, broaden their understanding of diverse perspectives, and foster an appreciation for the complexities of analyzing counterarguments and dissenting opinions in the study of creation myths.

Critiques of Traditional Creation Myths:

Traditional creation myths have been integral to human cultures for millennia, providing explanations for the origins of the universe, life, and human existence. However, as society has progressed and scientific knowledge has advanced, various critiques have emerged regarding the validity and relevance of these myths. This chapter aims to explore some of the key critiques of traditional creation myths, analyzing them from multiple perspectives and encouraging critical thinking and reflection.

Scientific Critiques:

Scientific critiques of traditional creation myths stem from the disparity between scientific knowledge and the literal interpretations of these myths. Scientific discoveries and theories, such as the Big Bang theory and evolution, have challenged traditional accounts of cosmic and biological origins. Critics argue that the myths' reliance on supernatural explanations and lack of empirical evidence render them incompatible with scientific understanding.

Historical and Cultural Critiques:

Critiques of traditional creation myths also arise from the recognition of their cultural and historical contingencies. These myths often reflect the worldview and values of specific cultures, reinforcing social hierarchies, gender roles, and power dynamics. Critics argue that the perpetuation of such myths without critical examination can contribute to the marginalization and exclusion of certain groups and reinforce oppressive ideologies.

Symbolic and Psychological Critiques:

Some critiques focus on the psychological and symbolic implications of traditional creation myths. Critics argue that the literal interpretation of these myths can limit our understanding and appreciation of their deeper symbolic meanings. By reducing myths to factual accounts, we may overlook the rich metaphorical language and archetypal symbols that can offer profound insights into the human condition.

Ethical and Environmental Critiques:

In the context of our current environmental challenges, critics raise concerns about the ecological implications of traditional creation myths. Some argue that these myths perpetuate a human-centered worldview that prioritizes human domination and exploitation of nature. They contend that alternative narratives that emphasize ecological interconnectedness and stewardship are necessary for addressing environmental crises and promoting sustainability.

Engaging with Critiques: Exercises and Problems:

Comparative Analysis: Select two traditional creation myths from different cultures and critically analyze them in light of scientific knowledge and cultural contexts. Identify areas of tension and reconcile or navigate the disparities between scientific explanations and mythological narratives.

Ethical Reflection: Discuss the ethical implications of traditional creation myths in terms of gender roles, power dynamics, and ecological responsibility. Consider how alternative narratives can address these concerns and foster a more inclusive and ecologically conscious worldview.

Psychological Exploration: Explore the symbolic and psychological dimensions of a particular creation myth. Analyze the archetypal symbols, motifs, and themes present in the myth and reflect on their relevance to human psychology and personal development.

Environmental Ethics Debate: Organize a class debate on the ethical and environmental implications of traditional creation myths. Present arguments from different perspectives, examining the role of these myths in shaping our relationship with nature and proposing alternative narratives that promote ecological harmony.

Part 3: Exploration of Creation Myths in Ancient Egyptian Religion

In this section, we embark on a fascinating journey into the rich tapestry of creation myths within the context of ancient Egyptian religion. The civilization of ancient Egypt, with its majestic pyramids, enigmatic hieroglyphs, and intricate cosmology, offers a captivating landscape for exploring the origins of the world and humanity. Drawing from a diverse range of textual and artistic sources, we will delve into the myths, symbols, and cosmological frameworks that shaped the ancient Egyptian understanding of creation.

The Importance of Creation Myths in Ancient Egyptian Religion:

Creation myths held significant importance in ancient Egyptian religious and cultural beliefs. These myths provided a framework for understanding the origins of the universe, the gods and goddesses, and the divine order that governed all aspects of existence. They served as a foundation for the Egyptian worldview, influencing religious rituals, social structures, and ethical principles.

The Myth of Atum and the Ennead:

One of the central creation myths in ancient Egyptian religion revolves around the deity Atum and the concept of the Ennead. Atum is portrayed as the self-created creator god who emerged from the primordial waters of Nun. The myth highlights Atum's act of self-engendering, his subsequent creation of the Ennead (a group of nine deities representing the divine family), and their collective efforts in shaping the world.

The Myth of Osiris, Isis, and Horus:

Another prominent creation myth in ancient Egyptian religion centers around the divine triad of Osiris, Isis, and Horus. This myth tells the story of Osiris, the god of fertility and the afterlife, who is killed by his jealous brother Seth. Through the dedication and magical powers of Isis, Osiris is resurrected, and Horus, their son, becomes the rightful heir and avenger of his father's death. This myth highlights themes of death, rebirth, and the perpetuation of the divine order.

Symbolism and Cosmology in Ancient Egyptian Creation Myths:

Ancient Egyptian creation myths are replete with rich symbolism and cosmological insights. The mythical motifs of the primordial waters, the cosmic egg, and the sacred mound serve as metaphors for the emergence of the universe and the establishment of order. The symbolism of deities, animals, and hieroglyphic representations in creation myths further deepens our understanding of the ancient Egyptian cosmology and its connection to the natural world.

Engaging with the Ancient Egyptian Creation Myths: Exercises and Problems:

Comparative Analysis: Compare the creation myths of ancient Egypt with those of other civilizations, such as Mesopotamia or the Indus Valley. Identify common themes and divergences, and analyze how cultural, geographical, and historical factors shaped these myths.

Symbolic Interpretation: Select a specific motif or symbol from an ancient Egyptian creation myth and explore its significance within the mythological and cultural context. Reflect on the possible meanings and implications of the symbol for ancient Egyptians and its potential resonance in contemporary interpretations.

Artistic Expression: Create an artistic representation, such as a painting or sculpture, inspired by an ancient Egyptian creation myth. Consider the use of symbols, colors, and composition to convey the mythological narrative and evoke a sense of the ancient Egyptian worldview.

Philosophical Reflection: Reflect on the philosophical and ethical implications of ancient Egyptian creation myths. Consider how these myths shaped the Egyptian understanding of human purpose, morality, and the relationship between the divine, the natural world, and humanity.

Chapter 8: Concepts of the Afterlife, the Soul, and the Journey to the Underworld

The exploration of concepts related to the afterlife, the soul, and the journey to the underworld has long fascinated and intrigued humanity. Across different cultures and civilizations, we find rich mythologies and religious beliefs that shed light on these profound aspects of human existence. In this chapter, we delve into the diverse perspectives on the afterlife, examining the ancient beliefs and practices of various cultures, including those found in Witchcraft, Divination, Herbalism, Shamanism, and Ecospirituality. Through a comparative and analytical lens, we will uncover the intricate tapestry of human imaginings regarding what lies beyond the realm of the living.

Understanding the Afterlife:

The concept of the afterlife holds deep significance in religious and spiritual traditions. It represents a realm or state of existence beyond earthly life, where the soul continues its journey or faces some form of judgment or transformation. Throughout history, people have sought answers to fundamental questions about life's purpose, the nature of the soul, and what awaits us after death. By studying the various cultural beliefs surrounding the afterlife, we gain valuable insights into the human quest for meaning and transcendence.

Exploring the Soul:

Central to many afterlife beliefs is the notion of the soul—a spiritual essence that endows each individual with consciousness, identity, and intrinsic value. Different cultures have developed distinct understandings of the soul, with unique aspects and characteristics attributed to it. In Witchcraft, for example, the soul may be seen as an eternal and interconnected force, while in Shamanism, it may be perceived as an entity capable of journeying between worlds. By examining these diverse conceptions, we deepen our understanding of the multifaceted nature of the human soul.

The Journey to the Underworld:

In numerous mythologies and religious traditions, the journey to the underworld symbolizes the transition from life to death and the soul's passage to the realm of the deceased. This descent into the underworld often entails encountering various challenges, trials, or encounters with divine or supernatural beings. The imagery and symbolism associated with this journey reflect cultural beliefs about the nature of death, judgment, and the ultimate fate of the soul. By exploring these narratives, we gain insight into cultural attitudes towards mortality and the human longing for continuity beyond death.

Analyzing Counterarguments and Dissenting Opinions:

As with any topic of deep significance, there are divergent views and counterarguments surrounding concepts of the afterlife, the soul, and the journey to the underworld. Skeptics and critics may challenge the existence of an afterlife, citing scientific or philosophical perspectives that question the validity of such beliefs. It is essential to engage with these dissenting opinions, considering their arguments and evaluating their impact on our understanding of these concepts. By embracing a balanced and objective approach, we can foster critical thinking and open dialogue.

Engaging with Concepts of the Afterlife: Exercises and Problems:

Comparative Analysis: Compare and contrast the concepts of the afterlife, the soul, and the journey to the underworld in different cultural and spiritual traditions, such as Witchcraft, Divination, Herbalism, Shamanism, and Ecospirituality. Identify common themes, differences, and the cultural influences on these beliefs.

Reflective Writing: Write a reflective essay exploring your personal beliefs and perspectives on the afterlife and the soul. Consider how these beliefs intersect with or diverge from the cultural and religious traditions you have encountered.

Ethical Dilemmas: Engage in group discussions or debates on ethical dilemmas related to beliefs in the afterlife. Consider questions such as how the belief in an afterlife influences moral decision-making or how differing beliefs about the afterlife can lead to conflicts or misunderstandings.

Interdisciplinary Inquiry: Conduct research on scientific, philosophical, or psychological perspectives on the afterlife and the nature of consciousness. Explore how these disciplines intersect or diverge with religious and spiritual beliefs.

The significance of the afterlife in various religious and spiritual traditions.

The concept of the afterlife holds immense significance in religious and spiritual traditions across the globe. It represents a realm beyond the physical world, where individuals believe their souls continue to exist after death. In this section, we will delve into the profound importance of the afterlife in various religious and spiritual traditions, examining the diverse beliefs and practices found in Witchcraft, Divination, Herbalism, Shamanism, and Ecospirituality. By exploring these traditions, we gain a deeper understanding of the human longing for transcendence and the quest for meaning beyond earthly existence.

Religious and spiritual traditions provide frameworks that shape beliefs about the afterlife. These frameworks are often rooted in mythology, sacred texts, and oral traditions that pass down stories and teachings across generations. These narratives not only provide explanations for the mysteries of life and death but also offer moral guidance and spiritual solace to believers. Let us now explore the significance of the afterlife in a variety of religious and spiritual traditions, analyzing the ways in which mythology and religious texts have shaped these concepts.

Witchcraft:

In Witchcraft, the afterlife is often viewed as a continuation of the soul's journey rather than a final destination. The concept of reincarnation or multiple lives is prevalent, with the belief that souls return to Earth to learn, grow, and fulfill their spiritual purpose. Within this tradition, the afterlife is seen as an opportunity for the soul to evolve and gain wisdom through various incarnations.

Divination:

In Divination practices, the afterlife is often associated with the communication between the living and the spirits of the deceased. Diviners may seek guidance from ancestors or spiritual beings through rituals and divinatory methods. The afterlife is considered a realm where departed souls can offer wisdom, protection, and guidance to the living.

Herbalism:

Herbalism, with its close connection to nature and the cycles of life, acknowledges the interconnectedness between the physical and spiritual realms.

The afterlife is often viewed as a transition into a different state of existence, where souls are believed to join the spirits of nature and continue their participation in the web of life.

Shamanism:

In Shamanism, the afterlife is often depicted as a multi-dimensional realm inhabited by various spirits and ancestors. Shamans, as intermediaries between the spiritual and physical realms, journey to the afterlife to seek healing, knowledge, and guidance for themselves and their communities. The belief in the afterlife in Shamanism underscores the interconnectedness of all beings and the continuity of existence beyond death.

Ecospirituality:

Ecospirituality emphasizes the sacredness of the natural world and recognizes the interdependence of all living beings. In this perspective, the afterlife is seen as a return to the Earth and a merging with the greater web of life. The belief in an afterlife motivates individuals to live in harmony with nature, understanding that their actions in this life have consequences for their existence beyond death.

These religious and spiritual traditions showcase the profound ways in which mythology and religious texts shape conceptions of the afterlife. Sacred texts, such as the Book of the Dead in Ancient Egyptian religion or the Bhagavad Gita in Hinduism, provide detailed accounts of the journey to the afterlife and the ultimate fate of the soul. Mythological narratives, such as the Greek myth of the underworld or the Norse mythology's Valhalla, shape cultural beliefs and understanding of the afterlife. These texts and myths serve as sources of inspiration, moral guidance, and spiritual solace for believers, offering glimpses into the mysteries of life and death.

In analyzing the significance of the afterlife in religious and spiritual traditions, it is important to acknowledge that interpretations and beliefs may vary within each tradition. Different sects, communities, and individuals may hold nuanced views on the afterlife, influenced by cultural, historical, and personal factors. It is crucial to approach these beliefs with respect and open-mindedness, recognizing the diversity and complexity of human spirituality.

Examples, Problems, and Exercises:

Research and analyze the beliefs about the afterlife in a specific religious tradition of your choice. Compare and contrast these beliefs with those found in other traditions.

Read excerpts from sacred texts that describe the afterlife and discuss their significance within the religious or spiritual tradition they belong to.

Engage in a group discussion where students present their own conceptions of the afterlife and explore the reasons behind their beliefs. Encourage respectful dialogue and the sharing of diverse perspectives.

Create a visual representation or artwork depicting your interpretation of the afterlife based on the teachings of a specific tradition. Explain the symbolism and meaning behind your creation.

Conduct interviews or surveys with individuals from different religious or spiritual backgrounds to explore their beliefs and experiences regarding the afterlife. Analyze the common themes and differences that emerge from these conversations.

Ancient Egyptian Views on the Afterlife:

Ancient Egyptian civilization had a rich and complex understanding of the afterlife, with beliefs that shaped their burial practices, rituals, and religious texts. The Egyptians held a profound reverence for the journey of the soul after death, believing in the existence of multiple components of the soul and envisioning a realm where the deceased would continue their existence. In this section, we will explore the ancient Egyptian views on the afterlife, focusing on the concepts of the soul (ka, ba, akh), the rewards and punishments awaiting the deceased, the role of mummification and burial rituals, and the importance of the Book of the Dead as a guide through the underworld.

The Concept of the Soul:

Ancient Egyptians believed that the human soul consisted of several components, each playing a unique role in the afterlife. The "ka" represented the life force and individuality of a person, while the "ba" was the spiritual aspect, often depicted as a bird with human features. The "akh" was the transformed and glorified state of the soul after successfully passing through the judgment in the afterlife. These various aspects of the soul would continue to exist and interact with the physical and spiritual realms.

Rewards and Punishments in the Afterlife:

Ancient Egyptians believed that the afterlife was a realm of judgment and accountability. The judgment of the deceased took place in the Hall of Ma'at, where their heart would be weighed against the feather of Ma'at, the goddess of truth and justice. If the heart was found to be lighter than the feather, the individual would be deemed righteous and would proceed to the eternal reward. However, if the heart was heavier due to wrongdoing, it would be devoured by the monstrous creature Ammit, leading to a state of annihilation or eternal suffering.

Mummification and Burial Rituals:

The ancient Egyptians placed great importance on the preservation of the body through mummification, as they believed that the physical form was necessary for the soul's journey in the afterlife. Elaborate rituals were conducted to prepare the body for mummification, including the removal of organs, the application of preserving substances, and the wrapping of the body in linen bandages. The process aimed to ensure the preservation and integrity of the deceased's physical form, enabling them to reunite with their soul and experience the afterlife.

The Book of the Dead:

The Book of the Dead, also known as the Book of Coming Forth by Day, played a crucial role in ancient Egyptian funerary practices. It was a collection of spells, prayers, and rituals intended to guide and protect the soul during its journey through the underworld. The book was often inscribed on papyrus or written on tomb walls, serving as a guidebook for the deceased. It contained instructions for navigating the treacherous paths of the afterlife, identifying and appeasing various deities and demons, and ultimately achieving a favorable judgment in the Hall of Ma'at.

Examples, Problems, and Exercises:

Study and analyze a specific vignette from the Book of the Dead, discussing its symbolism and significance in the context of the afterlife journey.

Research the process of mummification and create a step-by-step guide or infographic explaining the various stages involved.

Discuss the ethical implications of the judgment process in the ancient Egyptian afterlife. Is it fair to judge a person's entire existence based on the weighing of their heart?

Imagine you are an ancient Egyptian scribe tasked with writing a personalized Book of the Dead for a high-ranking official. Describe the key sections and spells you would include and explain the reasoning behind your choices.

Compare and contrast the beliefs and practices related to the afterlife in ancient Egyptian culture with those of another ancient civilization, such as Mesopotamia or Greece.

By engaging in these examples, problems, and exercises, students will gain a comprehensive understanding of the ancient Egyptian views on the afterlife. They will explore the intricate beliefs surrounding the soul's journey, the concept of judgment and its consequences, the significance of mummification and burial rituals, and the role of the Book of the Dead as a spiritual guide. Through critical analysis and comparative studies, students will develop a deeper appreciation for the complexities of ancient Egyptian religion and its enduring influence on human spirituality.

Mesopotamian Views on the Afterlife:

The ancient Mesopotamians, who inhabited the region between the Tigris and Euphrates rivers, held a diverse range of beliefs regarding the afterlife. Their understanding of the afterlife was shaped by a complex mythology and religious practices that reflected their worldview. In this section, we will delve into Mesopotamian views on the afterlife, focusing on the concept of the underworld and its rulers, the idea of a shadowy existence after death, rituals and offerings for the deceased, and the role of Gilgamesh in representing the quest for immortality.

The Concept of the Underworld and Its Rulers:

In Mesopotamian mythology, the afterlife was often associated with the underworld, a realm beneath the earth's surface. The Mesopotamians believed that the underworld was a place of darkness and shadows, where the souls of the deceased would reside after death. The underworld was governed by various deities, including Nergal and Ereshkigal, who held dominion over the realm of the dead and enforced its laws.

The Idea of a Shadowy Existence After Death:

Unlike some other ancient civilizations that envisioned a distinct afterlife realm with rewards and punishments, Mesopotamian beliefs centered on a gloomy existence in the underworld. The souls of the deceased were believed to lead a shadowy existence, devoid of the vitality and joys of earthly life. This somber afterlife was characterized by a sense of longing and separation from the living world.

Rituals and Offerings for the Deceased:

Mesopotamian culture placed great importance on rituals and offerings for the deceased, aimed at ensuring their well-being in the afterlife. Elaborate funeral rites were conducted, including burial ceremonies, lamentations, and the provision of grave goods. Offerings of food, drink, and other items were made to sustain and appease the spirits of the departed, demonstrating the Mesopotamians' belief in the continued existence and influence of the deceased.

The Role of Gilgamesh in Representing the Quest for Immortality:

The epic of Gilgamesh, one of the oldest known works of literature, showcases the Mesopotamian longing for immortality. In the epic, Gilgamesh, a legendary king, embarks on a perilous journey in search of eternal life after the death of his friend Enkidu. Despite his efforts, Gilgamesh fails to attain immortality, ultimately learning to accept the limitations of human existence. The story serves as a reflection of the Mesopotamian worldview, emphasizing the inevitability of mortality and the importance of coming to terms with one's finite existence.

Examples, Problems, and Exercises:

Analyze Mesopotamian funeral rituals and compare them with those of another ancient civilization, such as ancient Egypt or ancient Greece.

Create a visual representation or diagram of the Mesopotamian underworld, highlighting its key features and deities.

Discuss the significance of mourning and commemoration in Mesopotamian culture, drawing examples from ancient texts and archaeological evidence.

Explore the theme of mortality and the quest for immortality in the epic of Gilgamesh, highlighting its relevance to Mesopotamian views on the afterlife.

Imagine you are a Mesopotamian scribe tasked with recording the rituals and beliefs associated with the afterlife. Write a detailed account, incorporating religious and mythological references..

Examination of the ancient Egyptian beliefs regarding the afterlife and the journey of the soul after death

Ancient Egyptian civilization, with its rich mythology and complex religious beliefs, offers a fascinating insight into their views on the afterlife and the journey of the soul after death. The ancient Egyptians held a profound belief in the continuity of life beyond death, with a strong emphasis on preparing the deceased for the afterlife. In this section, we will explore the ancient Egyptian beliefs regarding the afterlife and the journey of the soul, examining concepts such as the soul's immortality, the judgment of the soul, and the significance of burial rituals and funerary texts.

Immortality of the Soul:

Central to ancient Egyptian beliefs was the notion that the soul, consisting of different components such as the ka, ba, and akh, was immortal. The ka represented the life force or vital essence of an individual, while the ba was the aspect that enabled the soul to move freely between the earthly and spiritual realms. The akh, often associated with the concept of transfiguration, referred to the transformed and glorified state of the soul after passing through the judgment in the afterlife. The Egyptians believed that the preservation and sustenance of these soul components were essential for the soul's journey to the afterlife.

In ancient Egyptian beliefs, the concept of the immortality of the soul was deeply ingrained. The Egyptians held that the soul consisted of different components, each playing a crucial role in the soul's journey after death. These components included the ka, ba, and akh, each representing a distinct aspect of the soul's existence.

The ka was seen as the life force or vital essence of an individual. It was believed to be a spiritual twin or double of the person, closely associated with their physical body. The ka was believed to reside within the body during one's earthly life, and after death, it would continue to exist as an immortal aspect of the soul. The ka was associated with sustenance and well-being, and offerings were made to ensure its continued nourishment in the afterlife. The Egyptians believed that the ka needed to be preserved and cared for in order for the individual to enjoy a prosperous existence in the realm beyond.

The ba, on the other hand, represented the aspect of the soul that could move freely between the earthly and spiritual realms. It was often depicted as a human-headed bird and was believed to be the vehicle through which the deceased could travel and communicate with the living. The ba was associated with personal identity and individuality, and it played a crucial role in the soul's ability to maintain a connection with the world of the living. It was believed that the ba could return to the tomb or the body's resting place to receive offerings and participate in rituals conducted by the living on behalf of the deceased.

The akh, often described as a luminous or radiant being, was associated with the concept of transfiguration. It represented the transformed and glorified state of the soul after passing through the judgment in the afterlife. The akh was believed to be the ultimate goal of the soul's journey, attained through righteousness and living a virtuous life. It was associated with divine transformation and eternal bliss. The Egyptians believed that the akh was the culmination of the soul's spiritual evolution, where it could reside in the presence of the gods and enjoy everlasting life.

To ensure the successful journey of the soul to the afterlife, the Egyptians placed great importance on the preservation and sustenance of these soul components. Mummification and proper burial practices were employed to safeguard the physical body and facilitate the soul's reunification with it in the afterlife. Funerary rituals and offerings were performed to provide sustenance and support to the ka and ba, ensuring their continued well-being and ability to navigate the spiritual realms.

Examples, Problems, and Exercises:

Discuss the significance of the ka, ba, and akh in ancient Egyptian art and iconography. Analyze specific artistic representations and their symbolic meanings.

Compare the ancient Egyptian concept of the soul's immortality to the beliefs regarding the afterlife in other ancient cultures, such as Mesopotamia or ancient Greece.

Explore the role of offerings and rituals in sustaining the ka and ba in the afterlife. Investigate the types of offerings made and their symbolic significance.

Examine the ways in which the concepts of the ka, ba, and akh influenced ancient Egyptian funerary practices and the construction of tombs.

Reflect on the philosophical implications of the immortality of the soul in ancient Egyptian beliefs. Consider the impact of these beliefs on individual behavior and societal norms.

Judgment of the Soul:

According to Egyptian beliefs, after death, the soul would undergo a judgment known as the "Weighing of the Heart" ceremony. In this ritual, the deceased's heart, believed to contain their moral character, was weighed against the feather of Ma'at, the goddess of truth and justice. If the heart was found to be lighter than the feather, indicating a virtuous life, the soul would proceed to a blissful afterlife. However, if the heart was heavy with wrongdoing, it would be devoured by Ammit, a fearsome creature, leading to the soul's ultimate annihilation. This judgment emphasized the importance of living a righteous and ethical life in Egyptian society.

In ancient Egyptian beliefs, the judgment of the soul played a pivotal role in determining its fate in the afterlife. The judgment, often referred to as the "Weighing of the Heart" ceremony, was a significant event that took place in the Hall of Ma'at, the goddess of truth and justice. This ceremony was a crucial step in the soul's journey after death and held profound implications for its eternal existence.

During the judgment, the heart of the deceased, believed to contain their moral character and essence, was placed on one side of a scale. On the other side of the scale was the feather of Ma'at, symbolizing truth, harmony, and cosmic order. The heart was weighed against this feather to assess the individual's actions and intentions during their lifetime.

If the heart was found to be lighter than the feather of Ma'at, it signified that the individual had led a virtuous and righteous life, adhering to the principles of Ma'at. This meant that the soul had successfully navigated life's challenges and upheld moral values, such as truth, justice, and compassion. In this case, the soul would be deemed worthy and would proceed to the blissful realm of the afterlife, known as the Field of Reeds or the "Beautiful West." Here, the soul would enjoy eternal happiness and live in the presence of the gods.

However, if the heart was heavier than the feather, it indicated that the individual had strayed from the path of righteousness and committed acts of wrongdoing during their earthly life. This could include actions such as dishonesty, cruelty, or disrespect for others. If the heart failed to balance with the feather, it was a sign that the individual's soul had been tainted by these negative deeds and was deemed unworthy. In such cases, the soul would face a dire consequence.

Ammit, a fearsome composite creature with the head of a crocodile, the forelimbs of a lion, and the hindquarters of a hippopotamus, awaited the outcome of the judgment. Ammit was known as the "Devourer of the Dead" or the "Eater of Hearts." If the heart was found to be heavy, Ammit would consume it, resulting in the ultimate annihilation of the soul. This fate was considered a terrible punishment, as it meant the complete obliteration and non-existence of the individual's soul.

The judgment of the soul, therefore, emphasized the paramount importance of leading a righteous and ethical life in Egyptian society. It served as a powerful reminder that one's actions and moral character would be scrutinized after death, and their outcome would shape the eternal destiny of the soul. The belief in the judgment of the soul provided an incentive for individuals to uphold the principles of Ma'at and strive for moral excellence during their earthly existence.

Examples, Problems, and Exercises:

Analyze and interpret artistic representations of the judgment scene from ancient Egyptian funerary texts and tomb decorations.

Compare and contrast the judgment of the soul in ancient Egyptian beliefs with similar concepts in other ancient cultures, such as the weighing of the heart in the Book of the Dead and the judgment scenes depicted in the ancient Egyptian Book of Gates.

Discuss the significance of Ma'at in ancient Egyptian society and its role in the judgment of the soul. Explore how the concept of Ma'at influenced ethical standards and social order in Egyptian civilization.

Investigate the symbolic significance of the feather of Ma'at in ancient Egyptian iconography and its representation in different artistic mediums.

Reflect on the philosophical implications of the judgment of the soul in ancient Egyptian beliefs. Consider the ethical considerations raised by the belief in postmortem judgment and its impact on individual behavior and accountability.

Significance of Burial Rituals and Funerary Texts:

Ancient Egyptians placed great emphasis on the proper preparation and preservation of the body for the afterlife. Mummification, a complex and meticulous process, aimed to prevent decay and maintain the physical integrity of the deceased. The belief was that the soul would need its physical form in the afterlife to continue its journey. Funerary rituals, including the opening of the mouth ceremony, purification rites, and offerings of food and possessions, were performed to provide sustenance and comfort for the soul in the afterlife.

Additionally, the ancient Egyptians created intricate funerary texts, such as the Pyramid Texts, Coffin Texts, and the Book of the Dead, which contained spells, prayers, and instructions to guide the soul through the challenges of the afterlife. These texts were written on tomb walls, coffins, and papyri, serving as a guidebook and providing the necessary knowledge and protection for the deceased on their journey.

The significance of burial rituals and funerary texts in ancient Egyptian culture cannot be overstated. These practices played a crucial role in ensuring a successful transition to the afterlife and securing the well-being of the deceased in the divine realm.

Mummification, the intricate process of preserving the body, held immense importance in ancient Egyptian beliefs. The Egyptians believed that the soul, comprised of different components such as the ka, ba, and akh, required its physical form to continue its existence in the afterlife. Mummification, therefore, aimed to halt the natural process of decay and maintain the physical integrity of the deceased. The intricate procedures involved the removal of internal organs, desiccation of the body, and wrapping it in linen bandages. These practices were performed by skilled embalmers, who meticulously carried out their duties with religious precision. The preservation of the body through mummification ensured that the soul would have a recognizable and functional form in the afterlife, allowing for a seamless continuation of its journey.

Funerary rituals were also integral to the ancient Egyptian belief system. The opening of the mouth ceremony was a vital ritual performed on the mummy, aimed at restoring the deceased's ability to see, hear, breathe, and speak in the afterlife. The ceremony involved the use of specific ritual tools and the utterance of prayers and incantations by priests. The symbolic act of opening the mouth symbolized the restoration of vital faculties to the deceased, enabling them to participate fully in the afterlife.

Purification rites were another important aspect of ancient Egyptian funerary rituals. The deceased would undergo ritual washing and anointing to cleanse the body and purify it for the journey to the afterlife. These purification rites were believed to rid the deceased of any impurities and ensure their readiness to enter the divine realm.

In addition to the physical preparations, offerings of food, beverages, and possessions were presented to the deceased. The Egyptians believed that these offerings would sustain the soul in the afterlife, providing nourishment and comfort. These offerings included representations of food, known as "funerary food," as well as models of servants, animals, and boats to assist the deceased in their journey and provide for their needs.

To accompany the deceased on their journey and provide guidance, the ancient Egyptians developed a rich corpus of funerary texts. These texts, such as the Pyramid Texts, Coffin Texts, and the Book of the Dead, contained spells, prayers, and instructions to aid the soul in navigating the afterlife successfully. These texts were inscribed on tomb walls, coffins, and papyri, ensuring that the necessary knowledge and protection were available to the deceased. The spells and prayers contained within these texts addressed various challenges and obstacles the soul might encounter in the afterlife, such as the judgment of the soul, encounters with malevolent beings, and the attainment of eternal life. The recitation of these texts by priests or family members during funerary rituals was believed to activate their magical powers and provide the deceased with the necessary assistance and guidance.

Through the combination of meticulous mummification practices, elaborate funerary rituals, and the provision of funerary texts, the ancient Egyptians sought to ensure the successful transition of the deceased to the afterlife. These practices demonstrated the deep-rooted beliefs in the continuity of life after death and the importance of maintaining physical and spiritual connections between the earthly and divine realms. The meticulous attention to detail and the elaborate rituals surrounding death and the afterlife reflected the significance the ancient Egyptians placed on ensuring the well-being and eternal existence of their loved ones in the divine realm.

Examples, Problems, and Exercises:

Analyze the process of mummification and its significance in ancient Egyptian beliefs. Discuss the different stages of mummification and their religious and symbolic implications.

Compare and contrast the funerary rituals of ancient Egypt with those of other ancient cultures, such as the burial practices of the Maya or the Viking funerals. Explore the similarities and differences in beliefs and practices related to the afterlife.

Examine the role of funerary texts, such as the Book of the Dead, in guiding the deceased through the afterlife. Discuss specific spells or prayers found in these texts and their intended purposes.

Investigate the symbolic meaning of the offerings presented to the deceased in ancient Egyptian funerary rituals. Explore how these offerings reflect the beliefs and values of Egyptian society.

Reflect on the significance of the opening of the mouth ceremony in ancient Egyptian funerary rituals. Discuss its symbolic implications and its role in preparing the deceased for the afterlife.

Analysis of the concept of the "Ka" and its role in the preservation of the individual in the afterlife

In ancient Egyptian beliefs, the concept of the "ka" held significant importance in the preservation and continuity of the individual in the afterlife. The "ka" represented the life force or vital essence of an individual and was considered an essential component of the soul. Understanding the nature and significance of the "ka" provides valuable insights into the ancient Egyptian worldview and their understanding of the afterlife.

The "ka" can be described as the individual's double or life force, which remained closely connected to the physical body even after death. It was believed to embody the unique personality, character, and essence of the individual. The preservation and sustenance of the "ka" were crucial for ensuring the well-being and continuity of the individual in the afterlife.

Exploring the Esoteric Wisdom of Ancient Egypt for Modern Spirituality

The ancient Egyptians held the belief that the "ka" required offerings of food, drink, and other provisions to sustain it in the divine realm. These offerings were made during funerary rituals and inscribed on tomb walls as representations or depicted in funerary art. The "ka" was thought to continue to enjoy the essence of these offerings, which were provided by the living, ensuring a connection and ongoing nourishment from the physical realm.

The "ka" played a central role in the journey of the soul after death. It was believed that the "ka" would reunite with the deceased's physical body in the tomb or burial place. The tomb served as a place of connection between the earthly and spiritual realms, providing a locus for the "ka" to dwell and receive the offerings made by the living.

The preservation of the physical body through the practice of mummification was closely tied to the preservation of the "ka." The mummification process aimed to prevent decay and maintain the physical integrity of the body, ensuring that the "ka" would have a recognizable and functional form in the afterlife. By preserving the body, the ancient Egyptians believed that the "ka" would be able to reunite with its physical vessel and continue its existence in the divine realm.

Moreover, the "ka" had a reciprocal relationship with the living. It was believed that the "ka" had the ability to influence the well-being and prosperity of the individual's descendants. The offerings made to the "ka" not only sustained it in the afterlife but also maintained the connection between the deceased and their living relatives. The provision of offerings and the remembrance of the deceased through rituals and commemorations were considered crucial for maintaining this connection and ensuring the continued support and blessings of the "ka."

Through the analysis of the concept of the "ka," we gain insights into the ancient Egyptians' belief in the preservation of the individual in the afterlife. The "ka" represented the life force and essential essence of the individual, closely connected to the physical body and dependent on offerings and rituals for sustenance. It served as a bridge between the earthly and spiritual realms, allowing for the continued existence and influence of the deceased in the divine realm.

Examples, Problems, and Exercises:

Explore the representation of the "ka" in ancient Egyptian funerary art and tomb inscriptions. Analyze the symbolism and visual elements used to depict the "ka" and its connection to the physical body.

Discuss the role of the "ka" in maintaining the continuity of the individual's identity and personality in the afterlife. Compare and contrast this belief with other ancient cultures' concepts of the soul and afterlife preservation.

Investigate the significance of offerings and rituals in sustaining the "ka" in the afterlife. Analyze the types of offerings and their symbolic meanings in relation to the well-being of the "ka" and its influence on the living.

Reflect on the reciprocal relationship between the "ka" and the living. Discuss the implications of this belief for the ancient Egyptian society, including the importance of ancestor veneration and the role of the deceased in supporting their descendants.

Consider the challenges and potential ethical dilemmas in the preservation and veneration of the "ka" in the afterlife. Discuss differing perspectives and arguments regarding the necessity and significance of these practices.

Exploration of the underworld and the challenges faced by the deceased in their journey, including encounters with deities and judgment scenes

In ancient Egyptian religion, the journey of the soul after death involved navigating through the underworld, a realm filled with various challenges and encounters with deities. This journey was a critical aspect of the afterlife beliefs and rituals, as it determined the ultimate fate of the deceased. Exploring the underworld provides valuable insights into the complex cosmology and spiritual landscape of ancient Egypt.

The underworld in Egyptian mythology was known as the Duat, a mysterious realm associated with darkness, mystery, and transformation. It was believed to be a labyrinthine realm, consisting of various regions and levels, each governed by different deities. The deceased had to navigate through these regions, overcoming obstacles and undergoing trials, to reach their final destination and attain eternal life.

One of the primary challenges faced by the deceased in the underworld was the judgment scene. According to Egyptian beliefs, the deceased's heart, believed to contain their moral character, was weighed against the feather of Ma'at, the goddess of truth and justice. This weighing of the heart ceremony was conducted in the presence of the god Osiris, the ruler of the underworld, and a tribunal of forty-two divine judges. The individual's actions and moral conduct during their lifetime were evaluated, determining their eligibility for the afterlife.

The judgment scene emphasized the significance of leading a virtuous and ethical life in Egyptian society. It highlighted the ethical responsibility of individuals to uphold the principles of Ma'at, which encompassed notions of truth, justice, harmony, and balance. Those whose hearts were found to be lighter than the feather of Ma'at were deemed righteous and deserving of a blissful afterlife. In contrast, individuals whose hearts were heavy with wrongdoing faced the threat of annihilation, as their hearts would be devoured by Ammit, a fearsome creature associated with destruction.

Encounters with deities also played a crucial role in the journey through the underworld. The deceased encountered various gods and goddesses, each with their own distinct powers and domains. For example, the deceased might encounter the god Thoth, the scribe of the gods, who recorded the results of the judgment. The goddess Isis, known for her nurturing and protective qualities, could provide assistance and guidance. These encounters tested the knowledge, wisdom, and preparedness of the deceased for the challenges ahead.

Additionally, the deceased might encounter gatekeepers and guardians who tested their knowledge of magical spells, rituals, and passwords. These challenges ensured that only those with the necessary knowledge and understanding could progress through the underworld successfully. The Book of the Dead, a collection of spells and instructions, served as a guidebook for the deceased, providing them with the necessary knowledge and protection to navigate the underworld and overcome these challenges.

Exploring the underworld and its challenges offers students a profound understanding of ancient Egyptian beliefs about the afterlife. It reveals the intricate cosmology, ethical values, and spiritual landscape of this ancient civilization. Through examples, problems, and exercises, students can engage in critical thinking and discussions about the significance of the judgment scene, encounters with deities, and the ethical implications of the afterlife beliefs in Egyptian society.

Examples, Problems, and Exercises:

Analyze the role of the weighing of the heart ceremony in Egyptian beliefs. Discuss its symbolic significance and compare it to other cultures' concepts of judgment after death.

Research and discuss the encounters with specific deities in the underworld, such as Osiris, Thoth, or Isis. Explore their roles, attributes, and significance in the journey of the deceased.

Reflect on the ethical implications of the judgment scene in ancient Egyptian beliefs. Debate the fairness and effectiveness of using a single criterion, such as moral character, to determine one's fate in the afterlife.

Investigate the symbolic meaning of the challenges and obstacles faced by the deceased in the underworld. How do these challenges relate to the individual's journey of transformation and purification?

Examine the role of the Book of the Dead in guiding the deceased through the underworld. Compare it to other funerary texts or guidebooks found in different cultures.

Chapter 9: Symbolism and Significance of Key Deities in the Creation Narrative

Ancient Egyptian mythology is rich with creation narratives that provide insights into the origins of the world and the fundamental forces that shape existence. These creation myths were not mere tales; they held profound meaning and were essential to the religious and cultural fabric of ancient Egyptian society. This chapter delves into the symbolism and significance of key deities in these creation narratives, examining their roles in shaping the cosmic order and the impact they had on the ancient Egyptian worldview.

Creation narratives played a pivotal role in ancient Egyptian mythology as they sought to explain the origins of the universe and the various elements within it. These myths offered a framework through which the Egyptians could understand the world around them and their place within it. By exploring the symbolism and significance of the deities involved in these creation narratives, we gain a deeper understanding of the complex religious beliefs and cosmological concepts of ancient Egypt.

In the study of the creation myths, it becomes evident that certain deities hold prominent roles and are central to the narratives. Among these key deities are Atum-Ra, Ptah, and Amun, each representing different aspects of creation and playing a crucial role in shaping the cosmic order. Atum-Ra, the primordial deity and creator god, embodies the creative force that gave birth to the universe. Ptah, the craftsman god, brings forth the physical world and human beings through his skilled craftsmanship. Amun, the hidden one and the power of creation, represents the mysterious and hidden aspects of creation, embodying the limitless potential for divine manifestation.

The symbolism associated with these deities is of great importance in understanding their significance in the creation narratives. Atum-Ra, for example, is often depicted as a solar deity, symbolizing the life-giving force of the sun and the cyclical nature of creation. Ptah, on the other hand, is portrayed as a skilled artisan, emphasizing the meticulous craftsmanship involved in the act of creation. Amun's hiddenness and mystery symbolize the ineffable and transcendent aspects of the divine, which are integral to the process of creation.

These deities and their symbolic representations not only shape the creation myths but also have a lasting impact on the ancient Egyptian worldview and religious practices. The intricate interplay between these deities and their symbolic significance gives rise to a cosmic order that governs the functioning of the universe and the relationships between different elements within it. Understanding these deities and their roles allows us to explore the profound connections between the spiritual, natural, and human realms in ancient Egyptian thought.

In this chapter, we will delve into the symbolism and significance of key deities in the ancient Egyptian creation narratives, exploring their roles, their relationships with one another, and their impact on the cosmic order. Through a comprehensive analysis of the major deities and their associated symbolism, we will gain valuable insights into the intricate tapestry of ancient Egyptian mythology and its influence on spiritual practices and beliefs. By examining these creation narratives, we will uncover the underlying principles that shaped the ancient Egyptian worldview and continue to captivate and inspire us today.

Major Deities in Creation Myths

Atum-Ra, the central figure in many ancient Egyptian creation myths, holds a prominent role as the primordial deity and the creator god. As a deity with solar attributes, Atum-Ra embodies the life-giving force of the sun and represents the cyclical nature of creation. In this section, we will delve into the various aspects of Atum-Ra's role in the creation of the world and other deities, explore the symbolism associated with Atum-Ra, and examine the significance of this deity in shaping the cosmic order.

Role in the Creation of the World and Other Deities
In the creation narratives, Atum-Ra is often depicted as the initial and self-created deity who emerged from the primeval waters of Nun. Atum-Ra, through his divine will and creative power, brought forth the world into existence. He is believed to have separated the sky (Nut) from the earth (Geb), establishing the fundamental order of the cosmos. By uttering the words of creation, Atum-Ra gave birth to the gods and goddesses who would govern different aspects of the world.

Furthermore, Atum-Ra's creative act involved a process of self-transformation. He was both the creator and the creation, embodying the infinite potential within himself. Atum-Ra symbolizes the power of self-generation and serves as a model for the continuous cycles of creation and renewal. His role in the creation myths showcases the inherent divinity within the Egyptian worldview and emphasizes the interconnection between the divine, natural, and human realms.

Exploring the Esoteric Wisdom of Ancient Egypt for Modern Spirituality

Symbolism Associated with Atum-Ra

The symbolism associated with Atum-Ra reveals deeper insights into his significance in the creation myths. Atum-Ra is often represented as a solar deity, symbolizing the life-giving energy of the sun and its vital role in sustaining all living beings. The sun, with its daily journey across the sky, represents the cyclical nature of creation, birth, and rebirth.

Atum-Ra's association with the sun also symbolizes enlightenment and divine illumination. Just as the sun illuminates the world, Atum-Ra brings light and knowledge to the realms of gods and humans. His radiant presence represents the divine wisdom and the power to bring order out of chaos.

Additionally, Atum-Ra is sometimes depicted with the double crown of Upper and Lower Egypt, symbolizing his authority and kingship over the unified land. This imagery highlights the divine role of Atum-Ra as the ruler and sustainer of the created world.

Significance in Shaping the Cosmic Order

The role of Atum-Ra in shaping the cosmic order cannot be overstated. As the primordial deity and creator god, his actions established the fundamental principles that governed the functioning of the universe. Atum-Ra's separation of the sky and the earth provided the foundation for the cyclical seasons, the rising and setting of the sun, and the natural rhythms of life. This division created a harmonious balance between the celestial and terrestrial realms, ensuring the continuity and stability of the cosmos.

Moreover, Atum-Ra's creative act initiated the existence of other deities who played vital roles in maintaining the cosmic order. For instance, his offspring Shu and Tefnut represented the elements of air and moisture, essential for the sustenance of life. Atum-Ra's creative power set in motion a divine hierarchy and interdependence among the gods and goddesses, each with their unique responsibilities in upholding the cosmic balance.

The significance of Atum-Ra's role in shaping the cosmic order extends beyond the ancient Egyptian creation myths. The principles and symbolism associated with this deity served as a foundation for religious and spiritual practices in ancient Egypt. The belief in Atum-Ra's creative power and his ongoing presence in the natural world influenced rituals, prayers, and the overall worldview of the ancient Egyptians. Understanding the symbolism and significance of Atum-Ra provides valuable insights into the ancient Egyptian understanding of the divine and its impact on their cultural, religious, and philosophical beliefs.

Examples, Problems, and Exercises:

Explore the similarities and differences between Atum-Ra and other creator deities in different mythological traditions, such as the Norse god Odin or the Hindu god Brahma.

Discuss the implications of Atum-Ra's association with the sun in relation to the ancient Egyptian understanding of light, enlightenment, and cosmic order.

Analyze the role of Atum-Ra in the context of Egyptian kingship and its impact on the pharaoh's legitimacy and divine authority.

Compare and contrast the creation narratives involving Atum-Ra with other creation myths from different cultures, such as the Judeo-Christian creation story or the Mesopotamian Enuma Elish.

Investigate the archaeological evidence and representations of Atum-Ra in ancient Egyptian art and architecture, examining the symbolic motifs and their connection to the creation myths.

B. Ptah: The craftsman god

Role in the Creation of the Physical World and Human Beings

Ptah, a significant deity in ancient Egyptian mythology, held a pivotal role in the creation of the physical world and the shaping of human beings. As the craftsman god, Ptah was revered as the master architect and divine artisan. His creative abilities were attributed to the power of his mind and the skill of his hands.

According to the creation narratives, Ptah spoke the words of creation and brought forth the material world through his thoughts and intentions. He is often depicted as envisioning the cosmos within his heart and mind, and then giving it form through his craftsmanship. Ptah's creative act involved the shaping of land, the molding of mountains, and the flowing of rivers, thereby establishing the physical landscape.

Furthermore, Ptah played a vital role in the creation of human beings. He was believed to have fashioned the bodies and features of individuals, intricately crafting each aspect to ensure their unique identities. Ptah breathed life into these physical forms, imbuing them with vitality and consciousness. Through his creative prowess, Ptah shaped the physical world and granted existence to humanity.

Symbolism Associated with Ptah

The symbolism associated with Ptah offers insights into his multifaceted nature and his significance as a craftsman god. Ptah is often represented wearing a skullcap and holding a scepter and ankh, symbols of his authority and creative power. The skullcap signifies his role as the master builder and designer, while the scepter represents his divine authority and the ankh symbolizes life.

Ptah's association with craftsmanship and creation highlights the importance of skill, precision, and intentionality in the creative process. His ability to bring form and structure to the chaotic elements of existence symbolizes the transformative power of human ingenuity and the capacity to shape one's own reality.

Significance in the Creative Process and the Maintenance of Cosmic Balance

Ptah's significance extends beyond the act of creation itself. As the craftsman god, he embodies the principles of order, balance, and harmony. His meticulous craftsmanship and attention to detail exemplify the importance of craftsmanship as a reflection of divine attributes. Ptah's role emphasizes the value of skilled labor, craftsmanship, and the pursuit of excellence in all endeavors.

Moreover, Ptah's association with creation and craftsmanship serves as a reminder of the interdependence between the divine, natural, and human realms. The act of creation requires the collaboration of the gods, the utilization of natural materials, and the ingenuity of human beings. Ptah's role in this collaborative process reinforces the interconnectedness of all elements in the cosmic order and highlights the shared responsibility of maintaining balance and harmony.

Ptah's symbolism and significance also extend to the realm of intellectual and artistic pursuits. As the god of wisdom, he is associated with knowledge, invention, and innovation. Ptah encourages the exploration of creative ideas, the pursuit of intellectual growth, and the cultivation of artistic expression as means to align with the divine and contribute to the ongoing process of creation and cosmic balance.

Examples, Problems, and Exercises:

Analyze the similarities and differences between Ptah and other creator deities, such as the Hindu god Vishvakarman or the Norse god Loki, in terms of their roles, symbolism, and significance.

Investigate the representations of Ptah in ancient Egyptian art and architecture, examining the symbolism and artistic motifs associated with the craftsman god.

Discuss the implications of Ptah's role in the creation of human beings in relation to ancient Egyptian concepts of identity, individuality, and the divine nature of humanity.

Explore the concept of craftsmanship in different spiritual traditions, such as the importance of mindful and intentional work in Buddhist practice or the sacredness of craftsmanship in indigenous traditions.

Reflect on the relevance of Ptah's symbolism and significance in contemporary society, considering the value of craftsmanship, creativity, and the pursuit of excellence in various fields, such as architecture, design, and the arts.

C. Amun: The hidden one and the power of creation

Role in the Creation Myths and Association with Hiddenness and Mystery

Amun, a prominent deity in ancient Egyptian mythology, holds a significant role in the creation myths and is closely associated with hiddenness and mystery. As the hidden one, Amun represents the concealed and elusive nature of the divine creative force. In the creation narratives, Amun is often described as the primeval deity who existed before all other gods and the universe itself.

Amun's hiddenness reflects the belief that the true essence of the divine cannot be fully comprehended or grasped by mortal beings. The concept of hiddenness evokes a sense of awe and reverence, emphasizing the transcendental nature of the divine and the limitations of human understanding. Amun's association with mystery invites seekers of wisdom to explore the depths of the divine realm and uncover hidden truths.

Symbolism Associated with Amun

Exploring the Esoteric Wisdom of Ancient Egypt for Modern Spirituality

The symbolism associated with Amun further illuminates his role as the hidden one and his connection to the power of creation. Amun is often depicted wearing a tall plumed crown, symbolizing his elevated status and authority. The plumes represent the feathers of Ma'at, the goddess of truth and justice, highlighting Amun's role as a keeper of cosmic order and balance.

Additionally, Amun is frequently represented with blue or black skin, symbolizing his association with the depths of the unknown and the mysteries of the universe. This color symbolism underscores his role as a hidden and enigmatic deity, whose power and influence extend beyond the visible realm.

Significance in the Divine Creative Force and the Manifestation of Divine Power

Amun's significance lies in his embodiment of the divine creative force and his ability to manifest divine power. As the hidden one, Amun is believed to have initiated the process of creation through his thoughts and intentions. His creative power is veiled in mystery, as the act of creation is considered a divine mystery that surpasses human comprehension.

Amun's association with creation emphasizes the intrinsic link between the divine and the act of bringing forth existence. Through his hiddenness, Amun represents the limitless potentiality of the divine, suggesting that creation is an ongoing process that unfolds continuously. Amun's role highlights the dynamic and ever-evolving nature of the cosmos and the divine forces at play.

Furthermore, Amun's manifestation of divine power extends beyond creation. He is regarded as a source of divine authority and kingship, often assimilated with the reigning pharaoh to legitimize their rule. Amun's power resonates not only in the act of creation but also in the establishment of order, justice, and harmony within the earthly realm.

Examples, Problems, and Exercises:

Compare and contrast the symbolism of hiddenness and mystery in Amun with similar concepts found in other spiritual traditions, such as the Tao in Taoism or the concept of the Divine Mystery in Christian mysticism.

Analyze the significance of Amun's association with kingship and authority in ancient Egyptian society, considering the political and religious implications of the pharaoh's connection to this deity.

Discuss the role of hiddenness and mystery in spiritual practices such as witchcraft, where the exploration of the unknown and the utilization of hidden forces are key elements.

Explore the concept of creative power in various fields, such as art, literature, or scientific innovation, and discuss how Amun's symbolism can inspire and inform the creative process.

Reflect on the implications of Amun's hiddenness and the limits of human understanding in the context of ecological spirituality, considering the mysteries of nature and the interconnectedness of all living beings.

Interactions and Relationships between Deities

The ancient Egyptian creation narratives are replete with stories of collaboration and conflicts among the deities, illustrating the intricate relationships within the divine realm. These interactions play a crucial role in shaping the cosmic order and the functioning of the world.

In the creation myths, deities often come together to carry out specific tasks or bring about certain aspects of the world. For instance, in the Heliopolitan creation myth, the god Atum-Ra is depicted as the primary creator who brings forth the universe. However, he is aided by other deities, such as Shu, the god of air, and Tefnut, the goddess of moisture, who emerge from him to establish the elements necessary for life. This collaboration highlights the interconnectedness and interdependence of the divine forces in the act of creation.

Conversely, conflicts among deities also arise, reflecting the inherent tensions and complexities within the divine realm. These conflicts often revolve around power struggles, rivalries, or differences in perspectives. One notable example is the mythological conflict between Horus, the falcon-headed sky god, and Set, the chaotic and destructive deity. Their struggle represents the perpetual battle between order and chaos, illustrating the ongoing challenges faced in maintaining cosmic harmony.

The Concept of Divine Unions and Familial Relationships

In addition to collaborative and conflicting interactions, the ancient Egyptian pantheon is characterized by complex familial relationships and divine unions.

These relationships contribute to the overall structure and dynamics of the divine realm.

Many deities are linked through familial bonds, reflecting a divine family tree. For instance, Osiris, the god of the afterlife, and his sister-wife Isis, the goddess of magic, are not only partners but also parents to Horus. This familial connection highlights the intergenerational transmission of divine roles and responsibilities.

Divine unions, often symbolized through mythological narratives, represent the merging of different divine forces and aspects. For example, the union of the sky goddess Nut and the earth god Geb results in the creation of the world, with Nut arching over Geb as the celestial vault. This union symbolizes the inseparable connection between the sky and the earth, emphasizing their interdependence in the cosmic order.

Impact of These Interactions on the Cosmic Order and the Functioning of the World

The interactions and relationships among deities have a profound impact on the cosmic order and the functioning of the world. These relationships establish a complex network of influences and responsibilities, ensuring the balance and harmony of the cosmos.

Collaborative efforts among deities contribute to the establishment and maintenance of cosmic order. Each deity's specific role and contributions combine to create a harmonious and functioning universe. The interplay between deities represents the interconnectedness of various aspects of existence, such as the elements, natural phenomena, and the cycle of life and death.

Conflicts, on the other hand, can disrupt the cosmic balance and introduce chaos into the world. These conflicts often require divine intervention or resolution to restore order. The struggle between Horus and Set, for example, necessitates the involvement of other deities, such as Thoth, the god of wisdom, and Ma'at, the goddess of truth and justice, to ensure the triumph of order over chaos.

The familial relationships and divine unions contribute to the stability and continuity of the cosmic order. The passing down of divine roles from one generation to another ensures the preservation of cosmic functions and responsibilities. The merging of different divine forces through unions symbolizes the harmonious integration of various aspects of existence, promoting balance and wholeness.

Examples, Problems, and Exercises:

Analyze the collaborative efforts of deities in creation narratives across different cultural mythologies, such as the Norse creation myth or the Hindu creation myth.

Discuss a mythological conflict between deities and its significance in shaping the cultural or religious beliefs of a specific society.

Explore the concept of divine unions in other spiritual traditions, such as the union of Shiva and Shakti in Hinduism or the hieros gamos in alchemical symbolism.

Investigate the role of familial relationships and intergenerational transmission in the divine pantheons of different ancient civilizations, such as the Greek gods of Olympus or the Norse gods of Asgard.

Examine the impact of conflicts among deities on the natural world or human existence, drawing parallels with ecological imbalances or social disruptions in contemporary contexts.

Cultural and Religious Significance of Specific Deities

✧   Role in the Creation Myths and Association with Death and Rebirth

In the ancient Egyptian mythology, Osiris holds a significant role in the creation myths, particularly in relation to the cycles of death and rebirth. As the son of the sky goddess Nut and the earth god Geb, Osiris embodies the connection between the divine and the earthly realms. He is often depicted as a wise and just king who brings order and civilization to the world.

However, Osiris's story takes a tragic turn when his brother Set becomes envious and plots his demise. Set, representing chaos and disruption, tricks Osiris and murders him, dismembering his body and scattering the pieces. This act symbolizes the dissolution of order and the fragmentation of existence.

Yet, Osiris's story does not end with his death. Through the intervention of his sister-wife Isis, who gathers his scattered remains and reassembles them, Osiris undergoes a process of resurrection and becomes the ruler of the realm of the dead. In this role, he oversees the judgment of souls and the afterlife, ensuring the continuity of existence beyond physical death.

✧ Symbolism Associated with Osiris

Osiris embodies numerous symbols that reflect his role as the god of resurrection and the afterlife. One of the most prominent symbols is the djed pillar, representing stability and endurance. The djed pillar is often depicted in Osiris's hands or as part of his regalia, emphasizing his role in ensuring the eternal stability and regeneration of life.

Another symbol associated with Osiris is the Atef crown, which consists of a tall, white crown adorned with ostrich feathers and a sun disk. This crown signifies his divine authority and association with the solar aspect of rebirth and regeneration. The ostrich feathers symbolize truth and justice, reflecting Osiris's role as the judge of souls in the afterlife.

The color green is closely linked to Osiris as well, representing fertility, vegetation, and the cycle of life. Green also symbolizes the regenerative power of the Nile River, which was believed to be infused with Osiris's life-giving energy.

✧ Significance in Religious Rituals and Beliefs Surrounding the Afterlife

Osiris's significance extends beyond the realm of mythology and permeates ancient Egyptian religious rituals and beliefs surrounding the afterlife. His story and role in the divine hierarchy inspired religious practices aimed at attaining resurrection and eternal life.

One of the most well-known rituals associated with Osiris is the Osirian Mysteries, a series of secret ceremonies and initiations. These rituals involved the reenactment of Osiris's mythic death and resurrection, symbolizing the participants' journey from mortality to immortality.

The belief in Osiris's role as the judge of souls in the afterlife also influenced the Egyptian funerary practices. The deceased were often buried with spells and instructions from the Book of the Dead, a funerary text that provided guidance for navigating the challenges of the afterlife. These rituals and texts aimed to ensure a successful judgment before Osiris and the possibility of resurrection and eternal life.

Examples, Problems, and Exercises:

Compare and contrast the role of Osiris with other gods associated with the afterlife, such as Anubis or Thoth, in different ancient mythologies or belief systems.

Analyze the symbolism of the djed pillar and its connection to concepts of stability and regeneration in other spiritual traditions, such as the concept of the World Tree in Norse mythology.

Discuss the significance of the Osirian Mysteries and their potential parallels in other mystery traditions or initiatory practices.

Investigate the cultural and historical contexts that shaped the religious rituals and beliefs surrounding Osiris, and explore how these practices may have evolved or influenced other spiritual traditions.

Hathor: The goddess of love, joy, and fertility

Role in the Creation Myths and Association with Nurturing and Fertility
Hathor, a prominent goddess in ancient Egyptian mythology, plays a vital role in the creation myths, particularly in relation to her association with nurturing and fertility. She is often depicted as a benevolent and maternal figure, embodying the concepts of love, joy, and feminine power.

In the creation narratives, Hathor is seen as a divine mother figure, nurturing and nourishing all living beings. She is believed to have played a crucial role in sustaining the physical and spiritual well-being of the cosmos. Hathor's presence in the creation myths highlights the importance of fertility and the cycle of life in ancient Egyptian cosmology.

Symbolism Associated with Hathor

Hathor is associated with numerous symbols that reflect her role as the goddess of love, joy, and fertility. One of the most recognizable symbols is the cow, which represents fertility, nourishment, and abundance. Hathor is often depicted with cow horns or as a cow herself, emphasizing her connection to the life-giving forces of nature.

Another significant symbol associated with Hathor is the sistrum, a musical instrument resembling a handheld rattle. The sistrum is an emblem of joy and celebration, and its use in religious rituals and ceremonies dedicated to Hathor creates an atmosphere of festivity and exuberance. The sound of the sistrum was believed to invoke Hathor's blessings and bring joy to the participants.

The color red is closely linked to Hathor, representing vitality, passion, and love. Red was associated with the fertile soil of the Nile River and the life-giving energy that flowed through it. Hathor's association with this color underscores her role as a source of abundant love and fertility.

Significance in Religious Practices and Festivals Celebrating Fertility and Joy

Hathor's significance extends beyond her role in the creation myths and permeates ancient Egyptian religious practices and festivals. She was venerated as a powerful deity who granted blessings of love, joy, and fertility to her devotees.

Religious rituals dedicated to Hathor often involved music, dance, and ecstatic experiences. The rhythmic movements and joyful expressions were believed to invoke Hathor's presence and inspire a sense of connectedness and bliss. These rituals aimed to cultivate a harmonious relationship with the natural world and tap into the life-affirming forces represented by Hathor.

Festivals celebrating Hathor were vibrant and lively occasions that brought communities together. One such festival was the Hathor-Sekhmet Festival, which honored the dynamic interplay between love and power. Participants engaged in processions, music, and offerings to honor Hathor and seek her blessings of love, joy, and fertility.

Examples, Problems, and Exercises:

Explore the depiction of Hathor in art and iconography, analyzing the symbolism associated with her attributes, such as the cow, the sistrum, and the color red. Compare these symbols to those found in other traditions or cultures associated with fertility and joy.

Investigate the connection between Hathor and other deities associated with love, joy, and fertility in different mythologies. Compare and contrast their roles and symbolism.

Analyze the role of music, dance, and ecstatic experiences in ancient Egyptian religious practices. Discuss the potential benefits of incorporating such practices in contemporary spiritual traditions.

Research and discuss the cultural and historical contexts that influenced the religious practices and festivals dedicated to Hathor, examining how these celebrations evolved over time.

Ma'at: The goddess of truth, justice, and cosmic balance

Ma'at, one of the central goddesses in ancient Egyptian mythology, plays a pivotal role in the creation myths and is closely associated with the concept of cosmic order. She represents the fundamental principles of truth, justice, and balance that govern the universe.

In the creation narratives, Ma'at is depicted as the daughter of the sun god Ra. She is responsible for upholding the balance and harmony within the cosmos, ensuring that the natural and social orders are maintained. Ma'at's role in the creation myths emphasizes the belief that a harmonious and just world is essential for the functioning and continuation of existence.

Symbolism Associated with Ma'at

Ma'at is symbolized by several significant elements that embody her principles and attributes. One of the most notable symbols is the ostrich feather, which represents truth and righteousness. The feather is often depicted on Ma'at's headdress or held in her hand, emphasizing her role as the guardian and arbiter of truth and justice.

The symbol of the scales is also closely associated with Ma'at. These scales represent the weighing of the heart against her feather during the judgment of the deceased in the afterlife. If the heart is found to be lighter than the feather, it signifies a life lived in accordance with Ma'at's principles, and the individual is deemed worthy of entering the realm of the blessed.

Additionally, the color green is often linked to Ma'at, symbolizing fertility, growth, and renewal. The lushness of vegetation and the fertile banks of the Nile River exemplify the harmonious balance of Ma'at in the natural world.

Significance in Ethical Values, Social Harmony, and Spiritual Practices

Ma'at's significance extends beyond the creation myths and permeates ancient Egyptian society. She serves as a guiding principle for ethical conduct, social harmony, and spiritual practices.

Exploring the Esoteric Wisdom of Ancient Egypt for Modern Spirituality

Ethically, Ma'at sets the standards for truth, justice, and morality. Ancient Egyptians believed that adhering to Ma'at's principles would ensure personal integrity and righteousness. By practicing honesty, fairness, and compassion, individuals contributed to the overall well-being of society and maintained the cosmic balance.

Ma'at's influence on social harmony is reflected in the laws and legal systems of ancient Egypt. The concept of Ma'at guided the formulation of laws, ensuring that they were fair, just, and in alignment with the principles of cosmic balance. Disputes were resolved through legal processes that aimed to restore harmony and uphold the values of Ma'at.

In spiritual practices, Ma'at is invoked through rituals, prayers, and offerings to seek her blessings and guidance in leading a balanced and righteous life. Ancient Egyptians believed that by aligning themselves with Ma'at's principles, they could achieve spiritual enlightenment and maintain a harmonious connection with the divine.

Examples, Problems, and Exercises:

Discuss the relevance of Ma'at's principles of truth, justice, and balance in contemporary ethical frameworks. Explore how these principles can inform decision-making processes and social responsibility in various fields, such as politics, business, and environmental sustainability.

Analyze the role of symbolism in religious and mythological traditions, using Ma'at's ostrich feather and the scales as examples. Compare and contrast these symbols with those found in other spiritual traditions, such as the concept of karma in Hinduism or the scales of justice in Western legal systems.

Investigate the concept of cosmic balance in different belief systems, such as Taoism or indigenous cosmologies. Compare the underlying principles and practices associated with maintaining balance in these traditions with the concept of Ma'at.

Examine the role of Ma'at in the judgment scenes depicted in ancient Egyptian funerary texts, such as the Book of the Dead. Discuss the implications of the weighing of the heart against the feather and its significance for the deceased's afterlife journey.

Engage in a group discussion on the challenges of upholding truth, justice, and balance in contemporary society. Explore the ethical dilemmas faced in various professional fields and brainstorm strategies for incorporating Ma'at's principles into decision-making processes.

Conclusion

Recap of the Symbolism and Significance of Key Deities in the Creation Narratives

Throughout this chapter, we have explored the symbolism and significance of key deities in the ancient Egyptian creation narratives. We examined the roles of Atum-Ra, Ptah, Amun, Osiris, Hathor, and Ma'at, and delved into the rich tapestry of symbols associated with each deity. These symbols, such as the ostrich feather of Ma'at or the scales of judgment, carry profound meaning and embody the core principles and attributes of these gods and goddesses.

Importance of Understanding These Deities in the Ancient Egyptian Worldview

Understanding the significance of these deities is crucial for gaining insight into the ancient Egyptian worldview. The creation narratives served as foundational myths that explained the origin of the world and the role of the gods in shaping its existence. By studying the symbolism and roles of these deities, we can unravel the intricate beliefs and cosmological concepts that shaped ancient Egyptian culture, religion, and spiritual practices.

For example, the ancient Egyptians believed that the cosmic order, represented by Ma'at, was essential for maintaining harmony and balance in all aspects of life. By upholding the principles of truth, justice, and balance, individuals contributed to the well-being of society and their own spiritual development. The deities embodied these principles, and their worship and reverence were central to religious rituals, festivals, and daily life.

Connection Between Creation Myths, Deities, and Spiritual Practices in Ancient Egypt

The interconnection between creation myths, deities, and spiritual practices in ancient Egypt is profound. The creation narratives provided a framework for understanding the origin and purpose of existence, while the deities personified the forces and principles that governed the universe. Through rituals, offerings, and prayers, the ancient Egyptians sought to establish and maintain a harmonious relationship with these deities, ensuring their favor and protection.

For instance, rituals dedicated to Hathor celebrated fertility and joy, invoking her blessings for abundant crops, healthy livestock, and successful childbirth. These rituals were an integral part of the agricultural and social fabric, reflecting the close relationship between human life, natural cycles, and divine forces.

In addition, the creation myths and deities influenced various spiritual practices, such as divination, herbalism, and shamanism. Ancient Egyptian priests and priestesses, skilled in interpreting signs and omens, used divination to seek guidance from the gods and gain insight into the future. Herbalism, with its roots in ancient Egyptian medicine, incorporated the knowledge of sacred plants associated with specific deities, harnessing their healing and spiritual properties. Shamanic practices involved trance-like journeys and communication with the divine realm, where the guidance and intervention of deities played a central role.

In conclusion, the symbolism and significance of key deities in the creation narratives provide a profound understanding of ancient Egyptian culture, spirituality, and worldview. The exploration of these deities deepens our appreciation of their roles in shaping the cosmic order, their symbolism, and their impact on spiritual practices. By studying the connections between creation myths, deities, and spiritual practices, we gain insight into the ancient Egyptians' profound reverence for the divine, their pursuit of balance and harmony, and their intricate relationship with the natural and supernatural realms.

Examples, Problems, and Exercises:

Reflect on the importance of mythology in understanding the beliefs and values of a particular culture. Choose another culture and compare and contrast its creation narratives and deities with those of ancient Egypt.

Engage in a group discussion on the relevance of ancient Egyptian symbolism and deities in contemporary spiritual practices. Discuss how elements from ancient Egyptian mythology can be incorporated into modern ecospirituality or witchcraft practices.

Explore dissenting opinions or alternative interpretations of the symbolism and significance of key deities in the creation narratives. Present a counterargument and evaluate its merits, considering different perspectives and sources of information.

Research and analyze the influence of ancient Egyptian mythology and deities on other ancient civilizations, such as the Greek, Roman, or

Mesopotamian cultures. Discuss the adaptations, transformations, or syncretism that occurred when these cultures encountered ancient Egyptian beliefs.

Chapter 10: The Pantheon of Gods

The ancient Egyptian pantheon, with its rich tapestry of gods and goddesses, forms a cornerstone of one of the world's oldest and most enduring religious and mythological traditions. Spanning thousands of years, the pantheon evolved and expanded, encompassing a vast array of deities that played integral roles in the religious, social, and cultural fabric of ancient Egypt.

The Egyptian pantheon was a complex and dynamic system, with each deity holding specific attributes, associations, and responsibilities. These gods and goddesses embodied the various forces of nature, cosmic principles, and human qualities, personifying the diverse aspects of existence. From the primordial creator deities to the gods of fertility, wisdom, and justice, the ancient Egyptians revered and worshiped a pantheon that reflected the intricacies of their worldview.

Significance of the Gods and Goddesses within the Religious and Mythological Framework

The gods and goddesses of the ancient Egyptian pantheon held immense significance within the religious and mythological framework of the civilization. They were not just revered entities but interactive beings who influenced and shaped the lives of individuals and society as a whole. The ancient Egyptians believed that these deities had the power to create, protect, heal, guide, and judge.

Mythology played a central role in understanding the gods and goddesses, as it provided narratives that explained their origins, relationships, and roles in the world. These myths were not merely stories but served as foundational beliefs that shaped the religious and cultural practices of ancient Egyptian society. They helped the Egyptians make sense of their existence, understand their place in the cosmic order, and navigate the complexities of life.

Thesis Statement: This Chapter Provides a Comprehensive Overview of the Major Gods and Goddesses in the Ancient Egyptian Pantheon, Exploring Their Roles, Attributes, Associations, and Cultural Significance.

In this chapter, we will embark on a comprehensive exploration of the major gods and goddesses in the ancient Egyptian pantheon. We will delve into their roles, attributes, associations, and the cultural significance they held in the lives of the ancient Egyptians. By studying the pantheon, we gain invaluable insights into the religious beliefs, mythological narratives, and cultural values that shaped the ancient Egyptian civilization.

Through a careful analysis of each deity, we will examine their roles in creation myths, their symbols and attributes, and their associations with various aspects of human existence. We will also explore the intricate relationships between the gods and goddesses, their familial connections, collaborations, and conflicts, which provide a nuanced understanding of their interactions within the pantheon.

Furthermore, we will address dissenting opinions and alternative interpretations that have emerged through scholarly discourse, considering the multifaceted nature of ancient Egyptian religion and the challenges of understanding a civilization that spanned thousands of years.

Examples, Problems, and Exercises:

Create a visual representation of the ancient Egyptian pantheon, including the major gods and goddesses, their symbols, and their interconnections. Use this visualization to discuss the complexity and diversity of the pantheon.

Compare and contrast the ancient Egyptian pantheon with pantheons from other ancient civilizations, such as the Greek or Norse gods. Analyze the similarities and differences in their roles, attributes, and cultural significance.

Select a specific deity from the ancient Egyptian pantheon and write a research paper exploring their mythology, associations, and cultural impact. Present different interpretations or conflicting views regarding the deity and critically evaluate their validity.

Major Gods and Goddesses in the Pantheon

A. Ra: The Sun God and Ruler of the Gods

Ra, the prominent sun god in the ancient Egyptian pantheon, held a central role as the ruler of the gods and the embodiment of the sun's life-giving energy. Representing the solar disk, Ra symbolized light, warmth, and vitality. In the creation myths, Ra was believed to have created himself out of the primordial waters, giving birth to the world and all living beings.

Ra's significance extended beyond his role as a creator. He was also the divine force that sustained life on Earth, providing nourishment for plants to grow and ensuring the fertility of the land. Moreover, Ra played a crucial role in the daily cycle of existence, rising in the morning and traveling across the sky before descending into the underworld at night. This celestial journey represented the eternal cycle of birth, death, and rebirth.

B. Isis: The Goddess of Magic, Fertility, and Motherhood

Isis, one of the most revered goddesses in the ancient Egyptian pantheon, embodied various roles and attributes, making her a complex and multifaceted deity. As the goddess of magic, she possessed profound knowledge of the occult arts and was believed to have the power to heal, protect, and perform miracles. Her association with magic also extended to her role as a protector of the pharaoh and a guardian of sacred rituals.

Isis was also revered as a goddess of fertility and motherhood. In myths, she played a crucial role in resurrecting her husband Osiris and conceiving their son Horus, symbolizing the cycles of life, death, and rebirth. This association with motherhood made Isis a compassionate and nurturing figure, often invoked for assistance during childbirth and invoked for the protection of children.

C. Horus: The Sky God and Protector of the Pharaoh

Horus, the son of Isis and Osiris, was a prominent deity associated with the sky, kingship, and protection. He was revered as the protector of the pharaoh, embodying the divine right to rule and ensuring the well-being and prosperity of the kingdom. Horus was often depicted with a falcon's head, representing his connection to the sky and his keen sight that enabled him to oversee the affairs of the world.

Horus also played a significant role in the ancient Egyptian mythology. He engaged in a fierce battle with his uncle Set, who had murdered his father Osiris, seeking justice and the restoration of divine order. This mythological conflict symbolized the eternal struggle between good and evil, order and chaos. Horus's victory over Set served as a paradigm for the triumph of righteousness and the restoration of balance.

D. Anubis: The God of Embalming and the Afterlife

Anubis, a canine-headed deity, held a pivotal role in ancient Egyptian beliefs surrounding death, embalming, and the afterlife. As the god of embalming, Anubis was responsible for guiding and protecting the souls of the deceased during their journey through the underworld. He oversaw the intricate process of mummification, ensuring that the deceased's physical form was preserved for the afterlife.

Anubis's association with death also earned him the title of "Opener of the Way," as he facilitated the transition of the soul from the earthly realm to the realm of the dead. He was often depicted as a guardian figure, standing at the scales of justice during the judgment of the deceased's heart. Anubis weighed the heart against the feather of Ma'at, determining the individual's worthiness for eternal life.

E. Bastet: The Goddess of Cats, Protection, and Joy

Bastet, the feline goddess, embodied the qualities of protection, joy, and sensuality in the ancient Egyptian pantheon. As a symbol of domesticity and fertility, Bastet was revered as a guardian deity, protecting the home, warding off evil spirits, and bringing blessings to her devotees. She was often depicted with the head of a lioness or a domestic cat, representing her nurturing and protective nature.

Bastet's association with joy and music made her a beloved deity in ancient Egyptian society. Festivals celebrating Bastet were vibrant and joyous occasions, filled with music, dancing, and revelry. She was believed to bring happiness and harmony into people's lives, and her presence was thought to ward off misfortune and negative energies.

F. Thoth: The God of Wisdom, Writing, and Magic

Thoth, the ibis-headed god, held a prominent position as the deity of wisdom, writing, and magic in the ancient Egyptian pantheon. Often depicted with the head of an ibis or as a baboon, Thoth was associated with knowledge, learning, and the arts of writing and scribes. He was believed to have invented hieroglyphs, the ancient Egyptian writing system, and was revered as the patron of scribes, scholars, and magicians.

Thoth's association with magic extended beyond writing and scholarly pursuits. He was considered a powerful magician and a mediator between the human and divine realms. His ability to navigate the realms of the living and the dead made him instrumental in rituals and ceremonies, where his wisdom and magical knowledge were invoked to ensure success and spiritual connection.

G. Sekhmet: The Goddess of War, Destruction, and Healing

Sekhmet, the lioness-headed goddess, personified the fierce and destructive aspects of ancient Egyptian mythology. As the goddess of war and destruction, Sekhmet was a formidable force, unleashing her wrath upon enemies and protecting the pharaoh in times of conflict. Her ferocity and power were associated with the scorching heat of the sun, and she was often depicted with a solar disk or a lioness's head.

However, Sekhmet also possessed a healing aspect. In mythology, her destructive nature threatened to annihilate all of humanity, but she was ultimately pacified through the use of red beer that resembled blood. This transformation from a destructive force to a healing one highlighted her role in curing diseases and averting epidemics, embodying the belief in the transformative power of both destruction and healing.

H. Geb: The God of the Earth and Vegetation

Geb, the god of the earth and vegetation, represented the fertile land and the sustaining power of nature in the ancient Egyptian pantheon. As the personification of the earth, Geb was often depicted lying beneath the sky goddess Nut, forming the cosmic couple that encompassed the entire world. Geb's association with the earth's bounty made him a symbol of abundance, growth, and fertility.

Ancient Egyptians believed that Geb's laughter caused earthquakes, emphasizing his connection to the earth's elemental forces. Moreover, Geb's role as the provider of sustenance and nourishment tied him closely to agricultural practices and the cycles of planting, growth, and harvest. He was invoked to ensure a bountiful yield and to protect the fertility of the land.

I. Nut: The Goddess of the Sky and Heavens

Nut, the goddess of the sky and heavens, played a pivotal role in ancient Egyptian cosmology. Often depicted as a woman arched over the earth, Nut symbolized the overarching sky that stretched above the world, holding the sun, moon, and stars within her celestial embrace. Her body represented the daily cycle of the sun, swallowing it at dusk and giving birth to it at dawn.

Nut's association with the sky also extended to her role as a protective deity. She was believed to arch over the world, sheltering it from chaos and providing a divine canopy under which life could flourish. Nut's nurturing and protective aspects were invoked for guidance, comfort, and assurance, as she was seen as a guardian figure, watching over the order and well-being of the universe.

Examples, Problems, and Exercises:

Research and present an in-depth analysis of one major god or goddess from the ancient Egyptian pantheon, discussing their roles, associations, and cultural significance. Use primary and secondary sources to support your findings.

Create a comparative chart showcasing the different attributes and roles of the major gods and goddesses in the ancient Egyptian pantheon. Analyze the interconnectedness and hierarchical structure within the pantheon.

Imagine you are an ancient Egyptian devotee of a specific deity. Write a prayer or invocation expressing your devotion and seeking the blessings or guidance of that deity. Reflect on the symbolism and qualities associated with the chosen deity and incorporate them into your prayer.

Roles, Attributes, and Associations of Deities

In the ancient Egyptian pantheon, each deity held distinct roles and domains that contributed to the overall cosmic order and functioning of the world. Understanding these specific roles is crucial to comprehending the intricate interplay among the deities and their impact on human existence.

For example, Ra, the sun god, occupied a central position as the ruler of the gods and the driving force behind the sun's daily journey across the sky. Ra's role encompassed not only solar symbolism but also the embodiment of creative power and divine kingship. The sun's light and warmth were associated with life, fertility, and growth, making Ra a pivotal deity in the agricultural and natural cycles.

Isis, on the other hand, held the multifaceted roles of a powerful goddess of magic, fertility, and motherhood. As a master of magic, Isis possessed immense knowledge and wisdom, which she utilized to protect and assist others. Her role as the mother of Horus, the divine child and future pharaoh, emphasized her significance in the realms of childbirth, nurturing, and dynastic succession.

Horus, the sky god and protector of the pharaoh, was revered as the divine embodiment of kingship. His role involved safeguarding the pharaoh's rule and ensuring the stability and prosperity of Egypt. Horus represented the link between the divine and human realms, with the pharaoh believed to be his earthly counterpart. The pharaoh's successful rule depended on the support and guidance of Horus, underscoring the deity's pivotal role in ancient Egyptian society.

Analysis of Their Attributes, Symbols, and Iconography

Attributes, symbols, and iconography played a crucial role in conveying the characteristics and functions of ancient Egyptian deities. By examining these elements, we can gain deeper insights into the symbolism and cultural associations surrounding each deity.

For instance, Thoth, the god of wisdom, writing, and magic, was often depicted with the head of an ibis or as a baboon. The ibis, known for its keen observation and sharp beak, symbolized Thoth's connection to knowledge and writing. Meanwhile, the baboon represented Thoth's association with the moon and its phases, linking him to the cyclical nature of time and the magic inherent in the lunar cycle.

Sekhmet, the goddess of war, destruction, and healing, was typically portrayed with the head of a lioness or as a lioness-headed woman. The lioness, known for its ferocity and strength, embodied Sekhmet's fierce and destructive aspects. Additionally, her connection to healing was often represented through her depiction holding the ankh, the symbol of life, in one hand and the papyrus scepter, symbolizing the curative properties of plants, in the other.

These examples demonstrate the intricate symbolism embedded in the attributes, symbols, and iconography associated with ancient Egyptian deities. By analyzing these visual representations, we can unravel the layers of meaning and cultural connotations attributed to each deity.

Exploration of the Associations and Relationships Between Deities

The ancient Egyptian pantheon comprised a vast network of associations and relationships between deities, reflecting the interconnectedness of various aspects of life and the cosmos. These associations were not limited to familial ties but also extended to shared domains, complementarity, and even conflicts.

An example of familial relationships within the pantheon is the connection between Osiris, Isis, and Horus. Osiris and Isis were siblings as well as husband and wife. They represented the divine union between brother and sister, a sacred pairing that emphasized the harmony and balance necessary for cosmic order. Through their union, they gave birth to Horus, who became the rightful heir and the embodiment of their divine lineage.

Furthermore, deities often collaborated and interacted to fulfill their respective roles and maintain the cosmic balance. For instance, Ma'at, the goddess of truth, justice, and cosmic balance, was closely associated with Thoth, the god of wisdom and writing. Thoth played a crucial role in upholding Ma'at by recording the verdicts in the Hall of Ma'at during the judgment of the deceased. This collaboration highlighted the interdependence and synergy among deities in maintaining the fundamental principles of truth and order.

However, the relationships between deities were not always harmonious. Conflicts and rivalries also existed within the pantheon, reflecting the complexities of human nature and divine dynamics. The mythological narratives often depicted conflicts between deities such as Set and Horus, symbolizing the perpetual struggle between chaos and order, light and darkness.

Through exploring the associations and relationships between deities, we gain a comprehensive understanding of the interconnected nature of ancient Egyptian cosmology. These relationships shape the mythological narratives, religious rituals, and societal values, providing a rich tapestry of beliefs and practices that shaped the ancient Egyptian worldview.

Examples, Problems, and Exercises:

Analyze the roles and domains of two deities in the ancient Egyptian pantheon and discuss how their functions intersect or complement each other. Consider their associations, symbolism, and mythological narratives to support your analysis.

Select two deities from different domains (e.g., a sky deity and an underworld deity) and compare their attributes, symbols, and iconography. Explore how these differences reflect their distinct roles and responsibilities within the pantheon.

Investigate a mythological narrative involving conflicts between deities and analyze its symbolic significance within the broader religious and cosmological context. Consider the themes of balance, order, and the struggle against chaos.

Pantheon's Structure and Hierarchy

The ancient Egyptian pantheon encompassed a vast array of gods and goddesses, many of whom were organized into divine families and lineages. These familial connections served as the foundation for the pantheon's structure and highlighted the interconnectedness and continuity of the divine realm.

One prominent divine family within the pantheon was the Ennead, which consisted of nine deities. At the center of the Ennead were the creator gods, Atum and Ra, who were considered the progenitors of the universe and the divine order. From this divine couple emerged Shu, the god of air and Tefnut, the goddess of moisture, representing the essential elements for life. Shu and Tefnut, in turn, gave birth to the sky goddess Nut and the earth god Geb, forming the foundational elements of the cosmos. Nut and Geb became the parents of Osiris, Isis, Seth, and Nephthys, among others, establishing an intricate family lineage that influenced the mythology and religious practices of ancient Egypt.

In addition to the Ennead, other divine families existed within the pantheon, such as the Ogdoad, consisting of eight primordial deities associated with chaos and the primordial waters. These families, along with their respective genealogies and interconnections, provided a framework for understanding the relationships and hierarchies among the gods and goddesses.

Hierarchies and Interconnections Among the Gods and Goddesses

The ancient Egyptian pantheon operated within a hierarchical structure, with certain deities occupying higher positions and wielding greater authority than others. This hierarchy was based on various factors, including the deity's role, associations, and relationship to other gods and goddesses.

At the pinnacle of the pantheon stood Ra, the sun god and ruler of the gods. As the creator and sustainer of life, Ra symbolized the ultimate cosmic power and embodied the divine kingship. Ra's position at the top of the hierarchy reflected his significance in maintaining the cosmic order and ensuring the well-being of Egypt and its people.

Beneath Ra, other major deities held influential positions within the pantheon. For example, Osiris, as the god of resurrection and the afterlife, played a pivotal role in the mythological narratives and religious beliefs of ancient Egypt. His association with death, rebirth, and judgment granted him considerable authority and influence in matters of the afterlife.

In addition to vertical hierarchies, the pantheon also exhibited interconnectedness among the gods and goddesses. Deities often collaborated and interacted with one another, forming networks of relationships and associations. These interconnections demonstrated the interdependency and harmonious coexistence of different aspects of the natural and divine realms.

For instance, Hathor, the goddess of love, joy, and fertility, shared a close connection with Ra, often depicted as his daughter or his eye. This association highlighted the synergy between solar power and the life-affirming qualities represented by Hathor, emphasizing the cyclical nature of life, death, and rebirth.

Influence of the Pantheon's Structure on Religious Practices and Rituals

The structure of the ancient Egyptian pantheon profoundly influenced religious practices and rituals, as it provided a framework for understanding the relationships between the gods and goddesses and their interactions with humans. The pantheon's hierarchy and interconnections shaped the organization of temples, the performance of rituals, and the role of priests and priestesses.

Temples dedicated to specific deities often reflected the hierarchical positioning within the pantheon. For instance, temples dedicated to Ra, the supreme deity, were typically grand and strategically located, symbolizing his cosmic authority. Conversely, temples dedicated to lesser-known deities might have been smaller or situated in more localized contexts.

Rituals and festivals were designed to honor and appease specific gods and goddesses, taking into account their roles and attributes within the pantheon. For example, the Sed festival, celebrated to renew the pharaoh's power and vitality, involved a complex series of rituals and performances dedicated to various deities, including Amun, Ra, and Osiris. Each deity played a distinct role in ensuring the pharaoh's well-being and the continuation of cosmic order.

Priests and priestesses, as intermediaries between the human and divine realms, understood and navigated the pantheon's structure and hierarchies. They performed rituals, maintained temple practices, and conveyed the teachings and wisdom associated with each deity. Their knowledge of the pantheon's structure and hierarchies was crucial in ensuring the proper execution of religious ceremonies and maintaining the cosmic balance.

Examples, Problems, and Exercises:

Research and describe the Ennead, including its major deities and their familial connections. Analyze the influence of the Ennead on the mythology and religious practices of ancient Egypt.

Select a major deity and examine their hierarchical position within the pantheon. Discuss the attributes and associations that contribute to their elevated status. Contrast this with a lesser-known deity and explore the implications of their position within the pantheon.

Investigate a specific ritual or festival dedicated to a particular deity. Analyze how the structure of the pantheon influenced the design and execution of the ritual. Consider the roles and interactions of multiple deities within the ritual context.

Worship, Rituals, and Festivals Dedicated to Deities

Worship practices in ancient Egypt played a central role in honoring and connecting with the gods and goddesses of the pantheon. These practices encompassed a wide range of rituals, ceremonies, and festivals that were conducted in temples, sanctuaries, and homes. Worship was not only a means of expressing reverence but also a way to establish and maintain a reciprocal relationship between humans and the divine.

Temples served as the primary centers for worship, acting as sacred spaces where rituals were performed and offerings were made to the gods and goddesses. The temple complex typically consisted of multiple chambers, courtyards, and shrines dedicated to various deities, each with their own cult statues and sacred objects. Temple priests and priestesses were responsible for carrying out the rituals, maintaining the sanctity of the temple, and acting as intermediaries between the human and divine realms.

Examination of Specific Rituals and Festivals Associated with Individual Deities

The Festival of Opet: This festival celebrated the rejuvenation and renewal of the divine kingship. It involved a procession where the cult statues of Amun, Mut, and Khonsu were taken from the temples of Karnak to Luxor. The festival symbolized the pharaoh's spiritual regeneration and his union with the gods.

The Heb-Sed Festival: This ritual celebrated the rejuvenation of the pharaoh's power and marked his continued reign. The pharaoh would perform a series of physical and symbolic activities, such as running, dancing, and shooting arrows, to demonstrate his vitality and connection to the gods. The festival emphasized the divine authority of the pharaoh and his role as a conduit between the human and divine realms.

The Beautiful Feast of the Valley: This festival was dedicated to the worship of Osiris, the god of the afterlife. It involved a procession where the cult statue of Osiris was transported from his temple in Karnak to the necropolis of Thebes. The festival included rituals of purification, offerings, and recitations of sacred texts, all aimed at ensuring the eternal well-being of the deceased and the continuity of life.

Significance of these Practices in Honoring and Connecting with the Gods and Goddesses

Worship practices, including rituals and festivals, held great significance in ancient Egypt as they provided a means for individuals and communities to honor and connect with the gods and goddesses. These practices were not merely ceremonial but were believed to establish a reciprocal relationship between humans and the divine, ensuring divine protection, guidance, and blessings.

By engaging in worship rituals, individuals sought to establish a personal connection with specific deities, seeking their favor and assistance in various aspects of life. For example, farmers might perform rituals dedicated to the fertility goddesses, such as Hathor or Isis, to ensure bountiful harvests. Similarly, individuals seeking healing might participate in rituals associated with Sekhmet or Thoth, who were revered for their healing abilities.

Through offerings, prayers, and symbolic actions, worshippers expressed their gratitude, devotion, and desire for divine intervention. By actively participating in these practices, individuals aimed to align themselves with the divine order and invoke the benevolence and protection of the gods and goddesses.

Examples, Problems, and Exercises:

Research and describe a specific festival dedicated to a deity of your choice. Analyze the rituals, symbolism, and cultural significance associated with the festival.

Imagine you are an ancient Egyptian priest/priestess tasked with conducting a ritual to honor a specific deity. Describe the steps involved in the ritual, including the offerings, prayers, and symbolic actions performed.

Compare and contrast the worship practices in ancient Egypt with those found in another ancient civilization, such as Mesopotamia or Greece. Analyze the similarities and differences in their approaches to honoring and connecting with the divine.

By engaging with these examples, problems, and exercises, students can gain a deeper understanding of the worship practices in ancient Egypt, their significance in the religious and social fabric of the civilization, and their enduring impact on spiritual traditions and practices today. These activities promote critical thinking skills and encourage students to explore the complexities of religious rituals and their cultural contexts.

Conclusion

Throughout this study, we have delved into the vast and intricate pantheon of ancient Egypt, exploring the roles, attributes, and associations of its major gods and goddesses. From the radiant Ra, the sun god and ruler of the gods, to the nurturing Hathor, the goddess of love, joy, and fertility, each deity held a distinct place within the religious and mythological framework of ancient Egyptian society. We have witnessed the diverse array of gods and goddesses, each with their unique characteristics, reflecting the multifaceted nature of the ancient Egyptian worldview.

Understanding the Pantheon's Structure, Hierarchy, and Religious Practices

The pantheon of ancient Egypt was not a haphazard collection of gods and goddesses but rather a meticulously organized system with defined structures and hierarchies. We explored the divine families and lineages within the pantheon, understanding how familial connections shaped the relationships between deities and their cults. Moreover, we examined the hierarchies and interconnections among the gods and goddesses, recognizing the roles of the supreme deities and the subordinate beings who served specific functions.

These structures and hierarchies had profound implications for religious practices and rituals in ancient Egypt. The priests and priestesses, acting as intermediaries between the human and divine realms, carefully orchestrated the ceremonies and offerings to maintain cosmic balance and secure the favor of the gods. The temples stood as sacred spaces where worshipers could engage in acts of devotion, seeking solace, guidance, and divine intervention.

Cultural and Spiritual Significance of the Gods and Goddesses in Ancient Egyptian Society

The gods and goddesses held immense cultural and spiritual significance in ancient Egyptian society. They were not mere mythical beings but rather embodiments of fundamental principles and ideals. The deities personified cosmic forces, natural phenomena, and abstract concepts, allowing the ancient Egyptians to comprehend and navigate the complexities of their world.

The gods and goddesses influenced various aspects of life, shaping ethical values, social harmony, and spiritual practices. Through their myths, rituals, and festivals, the gods and goddesses instilled a sense of moral order, providing guidelines for human behavior and establishing a harmonious society. The worship of deities, such as Ma'at, the goddess of truth, justice, and cosmic balance, promoted ethical conduct and social responsibility.

Furthermore, the gods and goddesses served as sources of inspiration, guidance, and solace for individuals. Whether seeking fertility, protection, healing, or wisdom, the ancient Egyptians turned to specific deities whose attributes and domains aligned with their needs. These divine connections fostered a sense of personal empowerment and offered a framework for individuals to navigate the complexities of life.

In conclusion, the ancient Egyptian pantheon and its gods and goddesses constituted a complex and vibrant tapestry woven into the fabric of their society. The gods and goddesses were not distant entities but rather integral parts of the ancient Egyptian worldview, guiding and influencing every aspect of life. Understanding their roles, attributes, and associations provides us with invaluable insights into the cultural, religious, and spiritual dimensions of this ancient civilization. Through the study of the pantheon, we unravel the tapestry of ancient Egypt, discovering its depth, richness, and enduring legacy.

Examples, Problems, and Exercises:

Reflect on the religious practices and beliefs of another ancient civilization, such as the Greeks or the Mesopotamians. Compare and contrast their pantheons, focusing on the roles and significance of the gods and goddesses in their respective societies.

Exploring the Esoteric Wisdom of Ancient Egypt for Modern Spirituality

Imagine you are an ancient Egyptian priest/priestess delivering a sermon to the community. Write a persuasive speech highlighting the cultural and spiritual significance of a specific deity and encouraging worshipers to honor and connect with that deity.

Research the role of deities in contemporary spiritual traditions, such as Ecospirituality or modern Paganism. Compare their approaches to deity worship with the ancient Egyptian practices, considering the cultural contexts and the ways in which these traditions engage with the divine.

Analyze and interpret an ancient Egyptian myth involving one or more deities. Discuss the symbolic and metaphorical elements of the myth, exploring its deeper meanings and the insights it provides into the ancient Egyptian worldview.

Part 4: Introduction to the Major Deities of Ancient Egypt

Part 4 of our study delves into the captivating world of the major deities in ancient Egypt, offering an illuminating exploration of their roles, attributes, and cultural significance. These gods and goddesses, revered by the ancient Egyptians, held immense power and influence over every aspect of their lives. Understanding the major deities is crucial for comprehending the religious, social, and spiritual fabric of this ancient civilization.

Overview of the Ancient Egyptian Pantheon

Before delving into the specifics of the major deities, it is essential to establish a comprehensive understanding of the ancient Egyptian pantheon as a whole. The pantheon of gods and goddesses in ancient Egypt was vast and diverse, reflecting the intricate tapestry of their religious beliefs. From the powerful sun god Ra to the protective goddess Isis, each deity possessed a unique set of characteristics, domains, and associations.

This overview will provide students with a solid foundation to appreciate the interconnectedness of the major deities within the broader religious and mythological framework of ancient Egypt. By examining the pantheon as a collective entity, we can discern patterns, relationships, and recurring themes that illuminate the ancient Egyptians' worldview.

Significance of the Gods and Goddesses within the Religious and Mythological Framework

The gods and goddesses of ancient Egypt were not merely objects of worship, but rather integral components of a complex religious and mythological system. Each deity played a vital role in shaping the cosmos, maintaining order, and guiding human affairs. Their stories and myths were not only entertaining narratives but also vehicles for transmitting moral, ethical, and spiritual teachings.

By analyzing the major deities, we uncover the diverse archetypes and symbols that were central to the ancient Egyptian psyche. These archetypes and symbols continue to resonate across various fields, including witchcraft, divination, herbalism, shamanism, and ecospirituality. They provide a rich tapestry of inspiration for practitioners and scholars alike, offering insights into the ways in which ancient cultures understood and interacted with the divine.

Thesis Statement: Exploring the Major Deities of Ancient Egypt

This chapter aims to provide a comprehensive introduction to the major deities of ancient Egypt, examining their roles, attributes, associations, and cultural significance. By delving into the pantheon, we unravel the complexities of this ancient civilization, appreciating the nuanced relationships between gods and mortals. Through the lens of academic inquiry and scholarly analysis, we will explore the multifaceted aspects of these deities and their enduring impact on human history.

Examples, Problems, and Exercises:

Select a major deity from the ancient Egyptian pantheon and create a visual representation or artistic interpretation that captures their essence and attributes. Write a reflection explaining your creative choices and how they align with the deity's characteristics.

Research the practices of contemporary spiritual traditions, such as witchcraft or shamanism, and identify deities or spiritual entities that bear similarities to those in ancient Egyptian mythology. Compare and contrast their attributes, domains, and cultural contexts, considering the ways in which these traditions engage with divine beings.

Analyze a myth or legend featuring a major deity, examining the symbolism and themes embedded within the narrative. Discuss how these elements reflect broader cultural values, cosmological beliefs, or spiritual teachings.

Imagine you are an ancient Egyptian priest or priestess tasked with organizing a festival dedicated to a specific major deity. Develop a detailed plan for the festival, including rituals, offerings, performances, and activities that align with the deity's attributes and associations.

Chapter 11: Descriptions and Roles of Each Deity

In the study of ancient Egyptian religion, gaining a comprehensive understanding of the descriptions and roles of the deities is essential. The ancient Egyptians held a deep reverence for their gods and goddesses, attributing to them specific characteristics, domains, and responsibilities. By exploring the descriptions and roles of these deities, we gain insight into the intricate tapestry of beliefs, rituals, and cultural practices that shaped ancient Egyptian society.

Importance of Understanding the Descriptions and Roles of Deities

Cultural and Historical Significance: The gods and goddesses of ancient Egypt were not abstract concepts but living entities who played prominent roles in the daily lives and spiritual practices of the people. By comprehending their descriptions and roles, we unravel the cultural and historical significance attached to each deity. This knowledge provides a gateway to understanding the ancient Egyptian worldview, values, and aspirations.

Symbolism and Representation: The descriptions of deities often encompassed visual representations, symbols, and iconography. Each attribute held symbolic meaning, conveying specific qualities or powers associated with the deity. By interpreting these symbols and representations, we delve into the deeper layers of ancient Egyptian symbolism, metaphysics, and religious expression.

Interconnectedness and Cosmology: The descriptions and roles of deities illuminate the complex network of relationships and interconnections within the ancient Egyptian pantheon. Understanding the roles of individual deities unveils their place within the larger cosmic order and reveals the multifaceted dynamics between gods and goddesses. This interconnectedness reflects the ancient Egyptians' belief in a unified and harmonious universe.

In this chapter, we will explore each deity in detail, examining their descriptions, attributes, roles, and cultural significance. By analyzing the diverse pantheon of ancient Egyptian deities, we gain profound insights into their symbolic representations, mythological narratives, and religious practices.

Examples, Problems, and Exercises:

Analyze a piece of ancient Egyptian art featuring one of the deities discussed in this chapter. Describe the visual elements and symbolism present, and interpret their significance within the context of the deity's roles and attributes.

Research the roles and characteristics of deities in other ancient civilizations, such as Greek, Norse, or Hindu mythology. Compare and contrast them with the Egyptian deities described in this chapter, highlighting both similarities and differences.

Imagine you are an ancient Egyptian scribe tasked with writing a hymn or poem dedicated to a specific deity. Create a piece that captures the essence of the deity's characteristics and their importance within the religious and cultural context.

Engage in a class discussion or debate on the roles and significance of the deities in ancient Egyptian society. Explore differing interpretations and perspectives, considering the influence of cultural, social, and political factors on the perception of deities.

Ra: The Sun God and Ruler of the Gods

Ra, the mighty sun god, is depicted with various attributes and iconography that symbolize his power and divinity. In ancient Egyptian art, Ra is often portrayed as a human figure with the head of a falcon, crowned with a sun disk encircled by a uraeus, a protective cobra. This distinctive representation emphasizes his association with the sun and his role as a solar deity. The sun disk itself symbolizes the solar orb, radiating light and warmth upon the world.

Ra's physical appearance reflects his celestial nature and cosmic significance. The falcon-headed depiction of Ra signifies his avian aspect, connecting him to the soaring heights of the sky. This avian form embodies his watchful eye, which oversees the world and ensures its continued existence. The uraeus on his brow represents his royal authority and protection against any threats or adversaries.

Roles and Domains Associated with Ra

Ra fulfills multifaceted roles and presides over various domains within the ancient Egyptian pantheon. As the sun god, Ra is primarily associated with the solar cycle and the daily journey of the sun across the sky. He is believed to embark on a perilous journey each night through the treacherous underworld, only to be reborn at dawn, triumphantly emerging as the morning sun. This cyclical pattern represents the eternal renewal of life and emphasizes Ra's power over life and death.

Ra's dominion extends beyond the celestial realm. He is regarded as the supreme ruler of the gods, occupying the highest position within the divine hierarchy. As the leader of the pantheon, Ra exercises authority, wisdom, and judgment over both gods and mortals. His role as the ruler of the gods signifies his governance over the natural and cosmic order, ensuring harmony and balance within the universe.

In addition to his solar and regal attributes, Ra is associated with creation and fertility. It is believed that he breathed life into existence, and his warmth and light sustain all living beings on Earth. This association with creation aligns Ra with agricultural fertility and abundance, making him a patron of crops, harvests, and agricultural prosperity.

Significance of Ra in Ancient Egyptian Cosmology and Religious Practices

Ra's significance in ancient Egyptian cosmology cannot be overstated. The sun, as embodied by Ra, was considered the life-giving force that sustained all existence. The daily rising and setting of the sun served as a tangible reminder of the cyclical nature of life, death, and rebirth. Ra's journey through the underworld during the night symbolized the challenges and dangers faced by both the sun and humanity. The successful emergence of Ra at dawn signified the triumph of light over darkness, order over chaos, and life over death.

Religiously, Ra's prominence and his connection to the sun made him a central figure in ancient Egyptian religious practices. Temples dedicated to Ra, such as the famous temple complex at Heliopolis, were centers of worship and pilgrimage. Rituals, prayers, and offerings were made to honor Ra and seek his blessings for prosperity, protection, and well-being. The ancient Egyptians believed that by aligning themselves with Ra, they could tap into his divine power and receive his benevolence.

Examples, Problems, and Exercises:

Analyze the iconography of Ra in different periods of ancient Egyptian history. How did his portrayal change over time, and what could these changes reflect about the shifting religious and cultural beliefs of the society?

Research and compare Ra's attributes and roles with other solar deities in different mythological traditions, such as the Greek god Apollo or the Incan god Inti. What similarities and differences can be observed, and what might these reveal about cross-cultural influences or universal human interpretations of the sun?

Create a fictional narrative based on the mythological stories of Ra's journey through the underworld. Use descriptive language and vivid imagery to convey the challenges and triumphs encountered by Ra during this perilous expedition.

Discuss the metaphorical significance of the sun as a symbol of enlightenment and spiritual awakening in various spiritual and mystical traditions, such as Sufism, Buddhism, or Gnosticism. How does the concept of the sun's radiance and illumination relate to the divine and human consciousness?

Through engaging with these examples, problems, and exercises, students can deepen their understanding of Ra's significance as the sun god and ruler of the gods in ancient Egyptian religion. By exploring his descriptions, roles, and cultural context, students can develop critical thinking skills, analyze symbolism in religious art and mythology, and gain a broader understanding of the complexities of ancient Egyptian spirituality.

Isis: The Goddess of Magic, Fertility, and Motherhood

Isis, a prominent goddess in the ancient Egyptian pantheon, is often depicted as a woman wearing a throne-shaped headdress or a vulture headdress with outspread wings, symbolizing her protective nature. She is frequently represented as a motherly figure, nurturing and caring for her child Horus. Isis is known for her beauty, grace, and compassion, which are emphasized through her serene and regal countenance.

One of the most striking aspects of Isis' iconography is her association with the throne. The throne represents her role as the divine queen, embodying authority, wisdom, and sovereignty. As the embodiment of the divine feminine, Isis represents the nurturing and life-giving aspects of femininity. Her maternal nature is symbolized by her role as a devoted mother to Horus, as well as her association with childbirth and motherhood. Isis is often depicted breastfeeding Horus, symbolizing her role as a protector and provider of sustenance.

Roles and Associations of Isis within the Pantheon

Isis encompasses a multitude of roles and associations within the ancient Egyptian pantheon. She is primarily known as a goddess of magic, possessing great knowledge and skill in the realm of mysticism and supernatural powers. Isis is believed to have discovered the secret name of Ra, which granted her immense magical abilities. She is considered a patroness of magic, spellcraft, and divination, providing guidance and assistance to those seeking mystical knowledge.

In addition to her magical prowess, Isis is closely associated with fertility and the cycles of nature. She is revered as a goddess of fertility, responsible for the abundant growth of crops and the nurturing of life. Isis' association with the annual flooding of the Nile River, which brought fertility to the land, further solidified her role as a goddess of abundance and agricultural prosperity.

Furthermore, Isis plays a significant role in the divine lineage and mythology of ancient Egypt. As the wife and sister of Osiris, she played a central role in his resurrection after his murder by Set. Isis' unwavering love and dedication to Osiris exemplify her role as a compassionate and protective goddess. Through her powerful magic, she resurrected Osiris and conceived their son, Horus, who went on to avenge his father's death and become a revered deity in his own right.

Cult of Isis and Her Role in Egyptian Society

The worship of Isis was widespread throughout ancient Egypt and beyond. Her cult, known as the "Isiac Mysteries," attracted a diverse range of devotees, including both Egyptians and foreigners. The cult of Isis provided a sense of community, spiritual guidance, and personal transformation to its followers.

The appeal of Isis' cult lay in its emphasis on personal devotion, ritualistic practices, and mystical experiences. Initiates into the Isiac Mysteries engaged in ceremonies, prayers, and rituals aimed at establishing a personal connection with the goddess and accessing her magical powers. The rituals often involved the recitation of sacred texts, the performance of symbolic gestures, and the participation in dramatic reenactments of mythological events.

Isis' influence extended beyond religious and spiritual domains. She was regarded as a protectress and healer, and her cult offered solace and assistance to those in need. The goddess was believed to have the power to cure illnesses, protect against evil forces, and provide guidance in times of hardship. As a result, individuals sought her intercession through prayers, offerings, and pilgrimages to her sanctuaries.

Examples, Problems, and Exercises:

Compare and contrast the attributes and roles of Isis with other goddesses of magic, fertility, and motherhood from different mythological traditions. How do cultural contexts shape the representations and symbolism associated with these goddesses?

Investigate the influence of the cult of Isis in the Greco-Roman world, particularly during the Hellenistic period. How did the worship of Isis spread beyond Egypt, and what cultural adaptations occurred in the process?

Reflect on the symbolism of Isis as a powerful and nurturing figure. How might her archetype be relevant and influential in contemporary spiritual practices, such as witchcraft, herbalism, or eco-spirituality?

Horus: The Sky God and Protector of the Pharaoh

Horus, a central figure in ancient Egyptian mythology, is commonly depicted as a falcon-headed deity, representing his association with the sky and the celestial realm. His falcon form symbolizes his keen vision, swiftness, and vigilance. Horus' eyes, known as the "Eye of Horus," hold great significance and are often depicted separately as protective amulets. The right eye represents the sun, embodying the power and authority of the pharaoh, while the left eye symbolizes the moon and represents intuition and magic.

Horus' falcon form is also closely connected to the notion of divine kingship. The falcon, being a bird of prey, embodies strength, prowess, and the ability to soar to great heights. In this aspect, Horus represents the pharaoh's divine authority and the link between the earthly ruler and the heavens.

Roles and Responsibilities of Horus

Horus is known as the avenger of his father Osiris, seeking justice and retribution for his father's murder at the hands of Set. This role highlights Horus' association with protection, righteousness, and order. He is considered the divine guardian and protector of the pharaoh, ensuring the stability and continuity of the kingdom.

As the sky god, Horus is also associated with the sun and the cycle of day and night. He represents the rising and setting sun, symbolizing the eternal struggle between light and darkness, good and evil. Horus' role as a solar deity further reinforces his connection to power, leadership, and the pharaoh's divine mandate.

Moreover, Horus is considered a symbol of resurrection and rebirth. He embodies the cyclical nature of life, death, and regeneration, mirroring the annual flooding of the Nile, which brought fertility and abundance to the land. Horus' association with renewal and vitality makes him a vital deity in the context of agricultural prosperity and the well-being of the kingdom.

Importance of Horus in the Context of Pharaonic Power and Authority

Horus' significance within the ancient Egyptian pantheon is closely tied to the concept of pharaonic power and authority. As the protector of the pharaoh, Horus ensures the pharaoh's legitimacy, divine right, and successful rule. The pharaoh, believed to be the earthly embodiment of Horus, derives his power from the deity, affirming his divine mandate to rule.

Horus' association with the sun and the Eye of Horus further strengthens the pharaoh's authority. The sun, as a symbol of light and illumination, represents clarity, insight, and divine guidance. By aligning the pharaoh with Horus, the ancient Egyptians believed that the ruler possessed divine wisdom and the ability to maintain Ma'at—the cosmic balance and harmony—within the kingdom.

Furthermore, Horus' role in avenging his father Osiris' death serves as a model for pharaonic justice and the preservation of order. Just as Horus sought retribution for his father, the pharaoh was responsible for upholding justice, punishing wrongdoing, and maintaining social harmony. Horus' mythic narrative, with its themes of righteousness and restoration, reinforced the pharaoh's role as the ultimate arbiter of justice and the custodian of Ma'at.

Examples, Problems, and Exercises:

Explore the symbolism of the Eye of Horus and its significance in ancient Egyptian culture. Analyze its association with protection, royal authority, and spiritual vision.

Investigate the parallels between Horus as the protector of the pharaoh and similar guardian deities in other mythological traditions. Compare and contrast their roles and responsibilities.

Reflect on the role of divine kingship in ancient Egyptian society and its implications for the pharaoh's authority and governance. Consider the concept of "Ma'at" and its influence on the pharaoh's decision-making process.

Anubis: The God of Embalming and the Afterlife

Anubis, one of the prominent deities in ancient Egyptian mythology, is often depicted as a jackal-headed deity or a full-bodied jackal. The jackal, with its association with cemeteries and its nocturnal nature, holds symbolic significance in the realm of death and the afterlife. Anubis' jackal form embodies his role as the guardian and guide of souls through the various stages of the afterlife.

Anubis' iconography also includes other symbolic elements, such as the flail and the ankh, which represent his authority over life and death. The flail, a symbol of power and kingship, emphasizes Anubis' role as a divine judge and protector of the deceased. The ankh, a symbol of eternal life, signifies the transformative journey of the soul beyond physical existence.

Roles and Significance of Anubis in Funerary Practices

Anubis played a crucial role in ancient Egyptian funerary practices, particularly in the process of embalming and mummification. As the god of embalming, Anubis oversaw the preservation and preparation of the deceased's body, ensuring its successful transition into the afterlife. He guided the embalmers in their rituals and supervised the purification and wrapping of the body.

Moreover, Anubis held the responsibility of protecting the deceased during the mummification process and throughout their journey into the afterlife. He watched over the body, guarding it from malevolent forces and assisting in the preservation of its integrity. Anubis' presence during this transformative stage ensured the deceased's safe passage and the preservation of their identity in the afterlife.

Relationship between Anubis and the Judgment of the Soul

Anubis' role as the god of the afterlife extended beyond the physical preservation of the deceased. He played a pivotal role in the judgment of the soul, known as the Weighing of the Heart ceremony. In this ceremony, the heart of the deceased was weighed against the feather of Ma'at, the embodiment of truth, justice, and cosmic order.

Anubis, as the guardian of the scales, oversaw this crucial judgment process. If the heart was found to be lighter than the feather, it indicated a life lived in accordance with Ma'at, and the soul could proceed to the realm of the blessed. However, if the heart was heavier due to the presence of negative deeds or impurities, it signified a failure to uphold Ma'at, and the soul would face punishment or annihilation.

Anubis' involvement in the judgment of the soul underscores the significance of ethical conduct and moral integrity in ancient Egyptian beliefs about the afterlife. He represented the impartiality and objectivity required for a fair assessment of the deceased's actions and their ultimate fate.

Examples, Problems, and Exercises:

Investigate the role of Anubis in the mummification process and the specific rituals associated with embalming in ancient Egypt. Analyze the symbolic meaning behind these practices and their significance in preparing the deceased for the afterlife.

Compare and contrast Anubis' role as a guide of souls in the Egyptian afterlife with similar deities or entities in other religious traditions. Explore the common themes and divergences in their roles and symbolism.

Reflect on the ethical dimensions of the Weighing of the Heart ceremony. Discuss the concept of moral judgment in ancient Egyptian society and its implications for individual responsibility and the pursuit of an ethical life.

Bastet: The Goddess of Cats, Protection, and Joy

Bastet, a prominent goddess in ancient Egyptian mythology, is commonly depicted as a lioness-headed or domestic cat-headed deity. The image of a lioness symbolizes her fierce and protective nature, while the domestic cat represents her association with fertility, motherhood, and domestic life. Bastet's depictions often incorporate the regal qualities of a lioness and the elegance and playfulness of a cat, combining strength with grace.

Among the symbols associated with Bastet, the sistrum—an ancient musical instrument with a handle and rattling metal discs—stands out. The sistrum is often depicted in Bastet's hand and signifies her connection to music, dance, and celebration. It is a symbol of joy and festivity, further highlighting her role as a bringer of happiness and merriment.

Roles and Associations of Bastet in Ancient Egyptian Society

Bastet held various roles and associations within ancient Egyptian society, reflecting the multifaceted nature of her character. She was primarily recognized as a protective goddess, particularly guarding against evil forces and malevolent spirits. The lioness aspect of Bastet represented her fierce protective qualities, defending both the pharaoh and ordinary individuals from harm.

Furthermore, Bastet played a significant role in fertility and motherhood. Her association with cats, known for their reproductive capabilities, connected her to the cycle of birth and regeneration. Women seeking fertility or assistance during childbirth often invoked Bastet's divine intervention.

Bastet's protective and nurturing aspects extended beyond human life to encompass the realm of agriculture. She was believed to protect crops from pests and ensure bountiful harvests. This agricultural association further solidified her role as a goddess of abundance and prosperity.

Festivals and Rituals Dedicated to Bastet

Bastet was celebrated through various festivals and rituals in ancient Egypt. One of the most renowned festivals dedicated to her was the Festival of Bastet, held annually in the city of Bubastis. This grand celebration attracted devotees from all over the country and included vibrant processions, music, dancing, and offerings to honor the goddess.

During the festival, people would bring statues of Bastet in elaborate processions, accompanied by musicians and dancers. The joyful and festive atmosphere reflected the goddess's association with pleasure, merriment, and the arts. Participants would engage in music and dance performances as acts of worship, invoking Bastet's presence and blessings.

Another notable ritual associated with Bastet was the act of keeping domestic cats in households as sacred animals. Cats were believed to embody Bastet's protective qualities and were revered as symbols of good fortune and guardianship. The care and veneration of cats were seen as acts of devotion to Bastet and were considered integral to maintaining a harmonious and blessed home.

Examples, Problems, and Exercises:

Research the archaeological evidence and artistic representations of Bastet in ancient Egypt. Analyze the evolution of her imagery and symbols over different periods and regions, discussing possible reasons for these changes.

Explore the role of Bastet in the context of ancient Egyptian beliefs surrounding protection and the supernatural. Investigate the ways in which she was invoked and the rituals performed to seek her assistance in warding off evil or misfortune.

Compare and contrast Bastet's associations with joy and festivity with similar deities or entities in other cultural traditions. Examine the underlying cultural and religious significance of celebrations and rituals dedicated to joy-bringing entities.

Thoth: The God of Wisdom, Writing, and Magic

Thoth, a prominent deity in ancient Egyptian mythology, is often depicted as a man with the head of an ibis or, less commonly, as a baboon. The ibis-headed representation signifies Thoth's association with wisdom, knowledge, and intellect, as the ibis was believed to be a symbol of keen observation and discernment. The baboon-headed form emphasizes his connection to the lunar cycle and the nocturnal realm, as baboons were known for their active behavior during the night.

Thoth is frequently portrayed holding a writing palette and reed pen, symbolizing his role as the patron god of writing, scribes, and record-keeping. This imagery reflects his association with language, communication, and the preservation of knowledge. Additionally, Thoth is often depicted with the ankh, the symbol of life, emphasizing his role as a bestower of vitality and divine wisdom.

Roles and Domains Associated with Thoth

Thoth's diverse roles and domains encompassed various aspects of intellectual pursuits, magical practices, and cosmic order. As the god of wisdom, he was revered as the divine source of knowledge, understanding, and discernment. Thoth's wisdom extended beyond mundane matters to encompass the esoteric and mystical realms, making him a key figure in magical practices and the pursuit of spiritual enlightenment.

Thoth was considered the inventor of writing and the patron of scribes. He was believed to have gifted humanity with the written word, enabling the recording and preservation of important knowledge, religious texts, and historical accounts. Scribes held a significant role in ancient Egyptian society, and Thoth's association with writing elevated their status, emphasizing the importance of literacy and intellectual pursuits.

Furthermore, Thoth played a vital role in the judgment of the deceased in the afterlife. He was believed to be present during the weighing of the heart ceremony, where he recorded the results and ensured the proper judgment of the soul. Thoth's involvement in this critical stage of the afterlife demonstrates his role as a mediator and custodian of cosmic balance.

Influence of Thoth on Intellectual Pursuits and Magical Practices

Thoth's influence extended to various intellectual and magical practices in ancient Egyptian society. His association with writing and wisdom inspired the establishment of schools where aspiring scribes were trained in the art of hieroglyphic script. The written word became a medium for transmitting knowledge, religious texts, and historical records, contributing to the development and preservation of Egyptian culture and civilization.

In magical practices, Thoth's wisdom and knowledge were invoked to aid practitioners in rituals, divination, and spellcasting. His guidance was sought to navigate the intricate realms of magic and mysticism, ensuring success, protection, and spiritual growth. Thoth's influence on magical practices highlights the interconnectedness of wisdom, language, and spiritual power in ancient Egyptian beliefs.

Examples, Problems, and Exercises:

Research the role of Thoth in the Egyptian creation myth and analyze how his attributes and domains relate to the cosmological principles represented in the myth.

Investigate the significance of the ibis and baboon in ancient Egyptian symbolism and explore how these animal associations influenced the portrayal of Thoth and his attributes.

Examine the impact of Thoth's patronage of writing and record-keeping on the development of ancient Egyptian civilization. Discuss the role of scribes and the importance of written texts in the religious, administrative, and cultural spheres.

Sekhmet: The Goddess of War, Destruction, and Healing

Sekhmet, a powerful deity in ancient Egyptian mythology, is often depicted as a lioness-headed goddess. The lioness, known for its strength, ferocity, and predatory nature, symbolizes Sekhmet's association with war, destruction, and protective powers. Her fierce countenance and prominent fangs emphasize her fearsome nature as a warrior goddess.

In artistic representations, Sekhmet is portrayed with a solar disk and uraeus, a cobra symbolizing royalty and divine power, adorning her head. This solar connection highlights her relationship with the sun and solar energies, linking her to the fiery aspects of warfare and the scorching heat of the Egyptian desert.

Roles and Associations of Sekhmet in Ancient Egyptian Culture

Sekhmet played several significant roles within the ancient Egyptian pantheon. As the goddess of war, she embodied the aggressive and combative aspects necessary for defending the pharaoh, the divine ruler of Egypt, and protecting the kingdom from external threats. In this context, Sekhmet represented the destructive force unleashed upon enemies during battle, ensuring victory and safeguarding the kingdom's stability.

Furthermore, Sekhmet was closely associated with healing and restoration. Paradoxically, her destructive powers were also believed to have the ability to cleanse and purify. In times of epidemic or disease, Sekhmet could unleash plagues as a form of punishment. However, she could also be invoked to halt the spread of illness and bring about healing. Sekhmet's dual nature as a goddess of both destruction and healing highlights the interconnectedness of these seemingly opposing forces within the ancient Egyptian worldview.

Rituals and Healing Practices Involving Sekhmet

Ancient Egyptians conducted rituals and healing practices dedicated to Sekhmet to invoke her powers of healing and protection. Temples were erected in her honor, such as the renowned Temple of Karnak in Thebes, where priests and priestesses performed rituals and offered prayers to seek her favor.

One prominent healing practice involving Sekhmet was the use of therapeutic statues or "seated statues." These statues, often made of wood or stone, depicted the lioness-headed goddess and were believed to embody her divine essence. Devotees would visit these statues seeking healing and relief from physical ailments, offering prayers and offerings in the hopes of receiving Sekhmet's intercession.

Additionally, the ancient Egyptians believed in the power of music and dance as therapeutic modalities. Performances known as "sistrum rituals" were conducted in Sekhmet's honor, featuring musicians and dancers who believed their art could appease the goddess and bring about healing energies.

Examples, Problems, and Exercises:

Explore the historical and cultural context in which Sekhmet's role as a goddess of war and destruction was emphasized. Analyze the significance of warfare in ancient Egyptian society and discuss the potential benefits and drawbacks of Sekhmet's association with such violent aspects.

Investigate the connection between Sekhmet and the sun in ancient Egyptian cosmology. Examine the role of solar deities in different cultures and discuss the symbolism of the sun as a source of both life-giving energy and destructive power.

Research the use of amulets and talismans associated with Sekhmet in ancient Egyptian healing practices. Discuss the belief in the protective and curative powers of these objects and their significance within the broader context of ancient Egyptian magical practices.

Geb: The God of the Earth and Vegetation

Geb, a prominent deity in ancient Egyptian mythology, is often depicted as a man lying beneath a reclining goddess, usually Nut, the sky goddess. This portrayal symbolizes Geb's connection to the earth and his role as the personification of the terrestrial realm. Geb is typically shown with a green or brown skin tone, representing the fertile and life-giving nature of the earth.

In some artistic representations, Geb is shown with vegetation sprouting from his body, emphasizing his association with the growth and abundance of plant life. He is often depicted wearing a crown adorned with feathers, which represents his dominion over the land and its natural resources. Additionally, Geb is sometimes portrayed holding a scepter or an ankh, symbolizing his authority and his role as a bestower of life.

Roles and Associations of Geb in the Pantheon

Geb played several essential roles within the ancient Egyptian pantheon. As the god of the earth, he was responsible for the sustenance and fertility of the land. Geb's association with vegetation, crops, and the cycles of agriculture made him a vital deity for the prosperity and well-being of the Egyptian people. It was believed that Geb's presence and blessings ensured bountiful harvests and a flourishing natural environment.

Geb was also closely associated with pharaonic power and authority. As the earth deity, he provided a stable foundation for the pharaoh's rule, symbolizing the connection between the king and the land he governed. The pharaoh was often depicted as the offspring of Geb and Nut, emphasizing the divine lineage and legitimacy of his reign.

Furthermore, Geb's association with the earth extended to the realm of death and the afterlife. In ancient Egyptian cosmology, it was believed that the deceased were interred in the earth, merging with Geb and becoming one with the eternal cycle of life and rebirth. Geb's role in the afterlife underscores his importance as a deity involved in the ultimate journey of the human soul.

Relationship between Geb and the Natural World

Geb's relationship with the natural world was fundamental to the ancient Egyptian understanding of the cosmos. The earth was perceived as a living entity, and Geb represented its physical manifestation and inherent vitality. The cycles of vegetation growth, the flooding of the Nile, and the fertility of the land were all believed to be under Geb's influence.

Moreover, Geb's association with the earth tied him closely to the natural forces and rhythms that governed the environment. The ancient Egyptians recognized the interconnectedness of the elements—earth, air, water, and fire—and understood that these forces shaped the world they inhabited. Geb's domain encompassed the physical landscape, the mountains, the rivers, and the fertile soil, all of which contributed to the overall harmony and balance of the natural world.

Examples, Problems, and Exercises:

Explore the symbolism of the relationship between Geb and Nut, the sky goddess, in ancient Egyptian mythology. Analyze how their union represented the cycle of life, death, and rebirth, and discuss its significance in the context of Egyptian cosmology.

Research the importance of agriculture and the Nile River in ancient Egyptian society. Discuss how Geb's role as the god of the earth and vegetation contributed to the agricultural practices and the prosperity of the Egyptian civilization.

Investigate the rituals and ceremonies dedicated to Geb and their connection to the cycles of the natural world. Discuss the significance of these practices in maintaining the balance and harmony between humanity and the earth.

Nut: The Goddess of the Sky and Heavens

Nut, a prominent deity in ancient Egyptian mythology, is often depicted as a woman arched over the earth, with her body forming the celestial vault. Her elongated figure represents the expanse of the sky, and her skin is typically depicted as deep blue or black, symbolizing the vastness and mystery of the heavens.

Nut is often shown adorned with stars, representing the celestial bodies that populate the night sky. Sometimes, she is depicted with her body covered in a shimmering cloak of stars, emphasizing her connection to the cosmos. Her outstretched arms and legs are believed to touch the four cardinal points, enveloping the earth in her protective embrace.

Roles and Significance of Nut in Ancient Egyptian Cosmology

Nut played a crucial role in the ancient Egyptian cosmology, representing the celestial realm and the overarching structure of the universe. As the goddess of the sky and heavens, Nut was believed to be the mother of the sun, moon, and stars, and the keeper of cosmic order and balance. Her role as a divine matriarch symbolized the nurturing and life-giving qualities associated with the sky.

Nut's association with the sky also had significant implications for the afterlife. In ancient Egyptian beliefs, it was believed that the souls of the deceased traveled through Nut's body during their journey to the afterlife. This concept of the soul passing through the sky goddess reinforced the notion of Nut as a protective and benevolent deity, guiding and safeguarding the souls of the departed.

Furthermore, Nut played a pivotal role in the mythology surrounding the sun god, Ra. It was believed that Ra traveled across the sky during the day, and at night, he would enter Nut's mouth and journey through her body to be reborn at dawn. This cycle of day and night, with Ra's passage through Nut, symbolized the eternal nature of creation and the cyclical nature of time.

Connection between Nut and the Cycle of Day and Night

Nut's association with the cycle of day and night was central to the ancient Egyptian understanding of time and the cosmic order. The passage of the sun god, Ra, through Nut's body represented the daily journey from dawn to dusk, bringing light and life to the world. At night, Ra would enter Nut's mouth, traversing her body to be reborn in the morning, marking the beginning of a new day.

This cycle of the sun's journey through Nut's body served as a metaphor for the eternal cycle of creation and renewal. It reinforced the concept of the cosmic order and the interconnectedness of all aspects of the universe. The rising and setting of the sun, guided by Nut, demonstrated the regularity and predictability of natural phenomena, providing a sense of stability and continuity to the ancient Egyptians.

Examples, Problems, and Exercises:

Research the symbolism of the stars in ancient Egyptian culture and their connection to Nut as the goddess of the sky. Explore the belief in astrology and divination based on the movements of celestial bodies, and discuss the significance of this practice in ancient Egyptian society.

Investigate the relationship between Nut and other deities, such as Ra, Osiris, and Horus, and their roles in the cosmic order. Analyze how their interactions and dynamics shaped ancient Egyptian cosmology and religious beliefs.

Explore the mythology surrounding Nut's role in the afterlife. Discuss the rituals and practices associated with the journey of the soul through Nut's body and their significance in ancient Egyptian funerary traditions.

Conclusion

Throughout this study, we have explored the rich and diverse pantheon of ancient Egyptian deities, examining their individual attributes, roles, and significance within the cultural and spiritual landscape of ancient Egypt. We have delved into the complex nature of these divine beings, their appearances, and the symbolism associated with them.

Thoth, the god of wisdom, writing, and magic, embodies intellectual pursuits and magical practices, serving as a guide and mediator between humans and the divine. Sekhmet, the goddess of war, destruction, and healing, represents the dualistic nature of power and embodies the principles of protection and rejuvenation. Geb, the god of the earth and vegetation, encompasses the fertility of the land and its connection to the cycles of life and death. Lastly, Nut, the goddess of the sky and heavens, symbolizes cosmic order and renewal, providing a nurturing and protective embrace for both the living and the deceased.

B. Understanding the Diversity and Interconnections within the Pantheon

One of the remarkable aspects of the ancient Egyptian pantheon is its diversity and interconnections. The deities embody a wide range of roles and attributes, reflecting the complexity of the human experience and the natural world. Each deity possesses unique characteristics and powers, yet they are not isolated entities; they exist within a complex web of relationships and interdependencies.

The interconnections within the pantheon are evident in the mythological narratives, where deities frequently interact and influence one another. We have observed the intricate relationships between Thoth and the goddess Ma'at, Sekhmet and the sun god Ra, Geb and the earth, and Nut and the cycle of day and night. These interconnections highlight the interconnectedness of various aspects of existence and emphasize the unity and harmony that the ancient Egyptians sought to maintain.

C. Significance of Deities in Ancient Egyptian Society and Spirituality

The deities held immense significance in ancient Egyptian society and spirituality. They were not mere abstract concepts or distant figures but active participants in the lives of the Egyptians. The gods and goddesses served as sources of guidance, protection, and inspiration, shaping every aspect of individual and communal life.

In ancient Egyptian spirituality, the deities provided a framework for understanding the world and one's place within it. They offered avenues for seeking wisdom, healing, and connection with the divine. Rituals, offerings, and prayers were dedicated to the deities, fostering a reciprocal relationship between humans and the divine. The worship of the deities was integral to maintaining cosmic balance and order, ensuring the well-being of individuals and society as a whole.

The influence of the deities extended beyond religious practices. They played significant roles in areas such as governance, agriculture, medicine, and the arts. For example, the pharaohs, as divine kings, drew their legitimacy from their connection to the gods, particularly Ra and Horus. In agriculture, offerings and rituals were performed to ensure fruitful harvests, with deities like Geb and Hathor associated with fertility and abundance. In medicine, deities such as Sekhmet were invoked for healing and protection from illness.

In summary, the deities of ancient Egypt were not only objects of worship but embodiments of various aspects of human experience and the natural world. They represented wisdom, power, protection, fertility, and cosmic order. The diversity and interconnections within the pantheon reflect the complexity and interconnectedness of life itself. Understanding the roles and significance of these deities provides us with insights into the spiritual beliefs and practices of the ancient Egyptians and their profound relationship with the divine.

Examples, Problems, and Exercises:

Discuss the significance of the deities in the daily lives of ancient Egyptians. Analyze how the worship and rituals associated with these deities influenced various aspects of society, including governance, agriculture, and healing.

Explore the ways in which the deities of ancient Egypt have influenced contemporary spiritual practices and belief systems, such as modern witchcraft, divination, or ecospirituality. Investigate the incorporation of ancient Egyptian deities into these contemporary frameworks and analyze the reasons behind their continued relevance.

Consider the role of dissenting opinions and counterarguments regarding the worship of deities in ancient Egyptian society. Investigate different perspectives on the religious practices of the time, and analyze the ways in which these dissenting voices influenced or challenged the prevailing beliefs.

Chapter 12: Family Relations and Interconnectedness of the Gods

In ancient Egyptian culture, family relationships held immense significance and were deeply intertwined with the religious and social fabric of society. The concept of family extended beyond human relationships and encompassed the divine realm as well. The gods and goddesses were not solitary figures but existed within intricate familial networks, reflecting the interconnectedness of both the natural and supernatural worlds.

Family served as the foundation of Egyptian society, providing structure, support, and a sense of identity. The family unit was highly valued and revered, and it played a crucial role in the transmission of cultural values, traditions, and religious practices. The family served as the primary unit for social and economic organization, with kinship ties determining one's position and status within the community.

In the context of religious belief, the gods themselves were often depicted as members of divine families, reflecting the importance of kinship and ancestral lineage. These divine families mirrored and reinforced the idealized familial relationships and dynamics that were considered essential for maintaining order and harmony within society. Understanding the familial connections between the gods allows us to delve deeper into the religious beliefs and cultural values of ancient Egypt.

Significance of understanding the interconnectedness of the gods

To comprehend the complex pantheon of ancient Egyptian deities, it is crucial to recognize the interconnectedness among them. The gods and goddesses were not separate entities but rather part of a vast and intricate web of relationships, both through blood ties and through shared roles, attributes, and domains. The interconnectedness of the gods demonstrates the interdependence and unity of various aspects of the natural and supernatural worlds.

Studying the interconnectedness of the gods provides valuable insights into the mythological narratives, religious rituals, and symbolic representations found in ancient Egyptian culture. By examining the familial relationships and the shared roles and attributes among deities, we can discern patterns, themes, and underlying principles that governed the religious and spiritual beliefs of the ancient Egyptians.

Moreover, understanding the interconnectedness of the gods helps to elucidate the complexity and diversity within the pantheon. It reveals the dynamic nature of the Egyptian gods, who could embody multiple roles and exhibit diverse characteristics depending on their relationships with other deities. By unraveling these connections, we gain a deeper appreciation for the multifaceted nature of the Egyptian gods and the intricate tapestry of beliefs and practices that characterized their worship.

Furthermore, recognizing the interconnectedness of the gods invites us to explore the broader implications for human relationships and society. The divine families serve as archetypes and provide models for familial roles and responsibilities, as well as illustrating the dynamics of power, loyalty, and inheritance. The understanding of these concepts enhances our comprehension of the ancient Egyptian worldview and offers insights into the values and social structures that shaped their society.

In conclusion, delving into the family relationships and interconnectedness of the gods allows us to navigate the rich tapestry of ancient Egyptian mythology and spirituality. By recognizing the importance of family in Egyptian culture and comprehending the intricate web of divine kinship, we gain a deeper understanding of the religious beliefs, social dynamics, and cultural values that characterized ancient Egyptian society. Through this exploration, we can unravel the complex tapestry of the gods and their relationships, leading us to a more profound appreciation of the ancient Egyptian worldview.

The Divine Family Tree

In the rich tapestry of ancient Egyptian mythology, the gods and goddesses were intricately connected through familial relationships, forming a complex and elaborate divine family tree. This divine genealogy reflected the ancient Egyptians' belief in the interplay between the gods and their roles in shaping the world and human existence. Understanding the structure of the divine family tree provides insights into the hierarchical dynamics, shared attributes, and symbolic associations within the pantheon.

Lineage and relationships of the major deities

Osiris, Isis, and Horus

At the heart of the divine family tree lies the story of Osiris, Isis, and Horus—a narrative that encapsulates themes of life, death, rebirth, and kingship. Osiris, the god of the afterlife, fertility, and vegetation, is the son of Geb (the god of the earth) and Nut (the goddess of the sky). He marries his sister, Isis, who is also his most loyal companion and the goddess of magic, fertility, and motherhood. Together, Osiris and Isis give birth to their son, Horus, who becomes the falcon-headed god associated with kingship and protection.

This triad of Osiris, Isis, and Horus represents the cycle of life and the divine lineage that passes from one generation to the next. Osiris, as the father figure, symbolizes the regenerative power of the earth and the realm of the dead. Isis embodies the nurturing and protective aspects of motherhood, while Horus, as their son and successor, inherits both his parents' qualities, becoming a symbol of pharaonic authority and the continuation of divine kingship.

Geb and Nut

Geb, the god of the earth, and Nut, the goddess of the sky, are central figures in the Egyptian cosmology and the divine family tree. They are believed to be the parents of many important deities, including Osiris, Isis, Seth, and Nephthys. Geb is often depicted as a reclining man with a green or black body, while Nut is portrayed as a woman arched over the earth, her body covered in stars.

The union of Geb and Nut represents the fundamental elements of the natural world—the earth and the sky. Their intertwined embrace reflects the eternal cycle of day and night, as Nut, the sky goddess, arches over Geb, the earth god. This union also symbolizes the continuous cycle of creation and renewal, with Nut giving birth to the sun god, Ra, every morning, and swallowing him in the evening.

Ra and his offspring

Ra, the sun god and the ruler of the cosmos, holds a prominent position in the divine family tree. He is believed to be the father of numerous deities who represent various aspects of the natural and supernatural realms. For instance, he is the father of Shu (the god of air), Tefnut (the goddess of moisture), and the divine siblings Geb and Nut.

Ra's offspring play significant roles in the Egyptian pantheon. Shu and Tefnut, as the children of Ra, embody the forces of air and moisture, which are essential for sustaining life. Geb and Nut, as siblings and eventual parents of Osiris, Isis, Seth, and Nephthys, contribute to the broader family connections and the divine cycle of life and death.

Other notable divine relationships

Beyond the central figures of Osiris, Isis, Horus, Geb, Nut, and Ra, the divine family tree encompasses numerous other notable relationships among the gods and goddesses. For example, Seth, the brother of Osiris and Isis, represents chaos, violence, and the struggle for power. Nephthys, another sibling, is associated with mourning and protection.

The relationships between deities like Hathor (the goddess of love and joy) and Ra, or Thoth (the god of wisdom and writing) and Ma'at (the goddess of truth and justice), also demonstrate the interconnectedness and interdependence of the gods. These relationships highlight the diverse roles, attributes, and domains that the Egyptian deities embody, further enriching the understanding of their collective significance within the religious and cultural context.

In conclusion, the divine family tree in ancient Egyptian mythology serves as a foundational framework for comprehending the intricate relationships and dynamics among the gods and goddesses. The familial connections, such as those between Osiris, Isis, and Horus or Geb and Nut, reveal the underlying themes of creation, life, death, and kingship. The lineage of major deities, including Ra and his offspring, further elucidates the hierarchical structure and interplay within the pantheon. Exploring these familial relationships allows us to appreciate the diversity and interconnectedness of the gods and their roles in shaping the ancient Egyptian worldview.

Symbolism and Meaning

In the ancient Egyptian culture, family relationships among the gods were not only seen as literal genealogical connections but also held deep symbolic significance. These symbolic representations shed light on the broader themes of creation, transformation, cosmic order, and the interconnectedness of the natural and supernatural realms. By examining the symbolic meanings associated with divine families, we can gain a deeper understanding of the ancient Egyptians' worldview and spiritual beliefs.

Exploration of the role of divine families in ancient Egyptian mythology

Osiris and Isis: The divine couple and their transformative power

The mythological union of Osiris and Isis represents the archetypal divine couple—a powerful symbol of fertility, transformation, and rebirth. Osiris, as the god of the afterlife and the cycle of vegetation, embodies the regenerative power of nature. Isis, his sister and wife, represents the nurturing and magical aspects of femininity. Together, they form a harmonious partnership, balancing the forces of life and death.

The story of Osiris's death and resurrection, orchestrated by Isis, signifies the eternal cycle of renewal and the triumph of life over death. This myth highlights the transformative power of love, devotion, and maternal instincts, reinforcing the importance of family bonds and their potential for personal and spiritual growth.

Horus: The divine child and the continuation of lineage

Horus, the son of Osiris and Isis, embodies the divine child archetype—a symbol of hope, protection, and the continuation of the royal lineage. As the rightful heir to the throne, Horus represents the concept of divine kingship and the preservation of order. His falcon-headed depiction emphasizes his connection to the heavens and his role as a mediator between the earthly and divine realms.

The mythological conflict between Horus and his uncle Seth reflects the struggle for power and the challenges faced by the rightful successor. This narrative reinforces the significance of family lineage, rightful succession, and the preservation of cosmic order.

Geb and Nut: The earth and the sky as cosmic parents

Geb, the god of the earth, and Nut, the goddess of the sky, are often depicted in a close embrace, symbolizing their cosmic union. Geb's prone position on the earth represents the fertile soil, while Nut, with her body arched over him, symbolizes the expansive sky.

The relationship between Geb and Nut illustrates the fundamental duality and interconnectedness of the natural world. The earth and the sky are seen as cosmic parents, giving birth to the gods and providing the foundation for all life. Their union signifies the cyclical nature of creation, as Nut gives birth to the sun god Ra each morning, who then travels across the sky before being swallowed by Nut at night.

Ra and his offspring: The sun and its generative power

Ra, the sun god and ruler of the cosmos, is often depicted as the divine father, giving birth to a multitude of deities who represent various aspects of the natural and supernatural realms. This generative power of the sun reflects the ancient Egyptians' understanding of the sun as a life-giving force and the source of all energy and growth.

The offspring of Ra, such as Shu (the god of air) and Tefnut (the goddess of moisture), represent the elemental forces necessary for sustaining life. Through their divine lineage, Ra's children embody different aspects of creation, underscoring the interconnectedness of the natural world and the gods' roles in maintaining cosmic balance.

In conclusion, the symbolism surrounding family relationships in ancient Egyptian mythology reveals profound insights into the Egyptians' perception of the world and their spiritual beliefs. The divine families of Osiris and Isis, Horus, Geb and Nut, and Ra and his offspring illustrate themes of transformation, lineage, cosmic order, and the generative power of nature. By exploring these symbolic representations, we gain a deeper appreciation for the ancient Egyptians' reverence for family, the natural world, and the divine forces that governed their lives.4. Ra and his offspring: The sun and its generative power

Interconnectedness of Roles and Domains

In ancient Egyptian mythology, family relationships played a crucial role in shaping the roles and domains of the gods. The interconnections between deities within a family unit often resulted in shared attributes, responsibilities, and spheres of influence. By examining these familial connections, we can discern patterns and understand how the roles and domains of the gods were intricately interconnected.

Examples of shared attributes and responsibilities among related deities

Osiris, Horus, and Isis: Connections between kingship, fertility, and resurrection

The family dynamic between Osiris, Horus, and Isis reveals a significant interplay of roles and domains. Osiris, as the ruler of the underworld and the god of the afterlife, represents death, rebirth, and the cyclical nature of existence. His wife and sister, Isis, possesses profound magical abilities and is associated with fertility and motherhood. Their son, Horus, embodies the divine kingship and is often depicted as the falcon-headed god who maintains order and defends the rightful succession.

The interconnectedness of their roles becomes apparent in the mythological narratives. Isis utilizes her magical powers to revive Osiris and conceive Horus, symbolizing the transformative power of love and the continuation of the royal lineage. Horus, in turn, seeks to avenge his father's death and claim his rightful place as the ruler, thus embodying the cyclical nature of power and the divine mandate of kingship. This interplay between kingship, fertility, and resurrection showcases the interconnected roles and domains within this divine family.

Nut and Ra: The sky as the domain of the sun and celestial order

Nut, the goddess of the sky, and Ra, the sun god, demonstrate the interconnectedness of roles and domains associated with celestial phenomena. Nut's arched body, symbolizing the sky, serves as a cosmic canopy under which the sun and other celestial bodies traverse. She provides the framework for Ra's journey across the sky, regulating the cycle of day and night.

Ra, as the sun god, represents the life-giving and illuminating power of the sun. His daily journey across Nut's body ensures the order and regularity of the natural world. This connection between Nut and Ra underscores the interdependence of the sky and the sun in maintaining celestial order and the cosmic balance essential for life to flourish on Earth.

Hathor and her various divine relationships: Love, music, and joy

Hathor, the goddess of love, music, and joy, exemplifies the interconnectedness of roles and domains through her diverse relationships with other deities. Hathor is often associated with the motherly and nurturing qualities represented by her cow or lioness form. As the mother of Horus, she shares the protective and nurturing aspects of motherhood with Isis.

Additionally, Hathor is linked to the celestial realm as the daughter of Ra and Nut, further emphasizing her connection to the cosmic order. Moreover, she is often depicted as the consort of Horus or Ra, highlighting her role in maintaining the harmonious balance of power and love.

Hathor's domains of love, music, and joy are not limited to her immediate family connections. She is also associated with other deities like Bes, who embodies protection and dance, and Bastet, the goddess of cats and pleasure. These associations demonstrate the interconnectedness of domains among related deities and the multifaceted nature of Hathor's roles.

In conclusion, the interconnectedness of roles and domains among the gods is evident in their familial relationships. The shared attributes, responsibilities, and spheres of influence within divine families highlight the interplay of concepts such as kingship, fertility, resurrection, celestial order, and joy. By understanding these interconnected relationships, we gain insight into the complex and dynamic mythology of ancient Egypt and recognize the depth and breadth of the roles and domains of the gods.

Mythological Narratives

Mythological narratives serve as a rich source of insight into the ancient Egyptian understanding of family relationships and their significance within the larger cosmic order. Through these stories, we can explore the complexities of familial dynamics among the gods and the profound lessons they convey.

Analysis of the symbolism and lessons conveyed through these stories

The Osiris myth: Death, rebirth, and the power of maternal love

The Osiris myth is a central narrative that underscores the themes of death, rebirth, and the transformative power of maternal love. The story revolves around Osiris, the god of the dead and the ruler of the underworld, who is murdered by his jealous brother, Set. Osiris' body is dismembered and scattered across Egypt.

Isis, Osiris' sister and wife, embarks on a quest to recover his body and restore him to life. Through her unwavering devotion and magical prowess, Isis successfully reassembles Osiris and brings about his resurrection. This myth highlights the power of maternal love and the transformative journey from death to rebirth.

The story of Osiris also symbolizes the agricultural cycle, drawing parallels between the god's resurrection and the annual renewal of vegetation. It serves as a reminder of the cyclical nature of life, where death and rebirth are interconnected and necessary for the sustenance and regeneration of the natural world.

The conflict between Horus and Set: The struggle for kingship and filial loyalty

The conflict between Horus, the son of Osiris and Isis, and Set, the brother of Osiris, explores the themes of kingship and filial loyalty. Following the murder of Osiris, Horus emerges as the rightful heir to the throne, while Set seeks to claim the kingship for himself. The myth narrates the ongoing struggle between Horus and Set, as each attempts to assert their legitimacy.

This narrative reflects the complex dynamics of family relationships and the challenges that arise when personal ambitions clash with familial obligations. It explores the themes of loyalty, justice, and the struggle for power within the divine family. Ultimately, Horus prevails and becomes the rightful ruler, embodying the ideals of kingship and the continuation of divine lineage.

Nut and Ra: The cycle of day and night and the eternal nature of creation

The myth involving Nut, the goddess of the sky, and Ra, the sun god, delves into the cycle of day and night and the eternal nature of creation. According to the myth, Ra travels across the sky during the day, illuminating the world with his radiant light. At night, Ra enters the body of Nut and journeys through her, symbolizing the passage of time and the darkness of the night.

This narrative underscores the interconnectedness of Nut and Ra, as Nut provides the celestial canvas for Ra's daily journey. It emphasizes the cyclical nature of the cosmos and the perpetual renewal of life. The story also conveys the eternal bond between Nut and Ra, representing the inseparable relationship between the sky and the sun, essential for sustaining the cosmic order.

These mythological narratives serve as vehicles for conveying complex ideas and teachings about the nature of existence, familial relationships, and the interconnectedness of the divine and natural realms. They offer valuable insights into ancient Egyptian cosmology, morality, and the human experience.

Exercise:

Consider the mythological narratives discussed above and reflect on the lessons and symbols they convey. What universal themes and concepts can be extrapolated from these stories? How do these themes resonate with other spiritual and mythological traditions? Write a short essay exploring the relevance and cross-cultural connections found within these narratives.

Problem:

Imagine you are a priest or priestess in ancient Egypt tasked with retelling one of these mythological narratives during a sacred ceremony. How would you incorporate rituals, symbols, and storytelling techniques to effectively convey the message and evoke a deep spiritual experience for the participants? Create a detailed outline of your ritual, including specific actions, objects, and chants that would enhance the myth's significance and engage the participants in a meaningful way.

Example:

In the myth of Osiris, the dismembered body of the god symbolizes the fragmented state of the human soul. Explore how this symbolism can be applied to the practice of soul retrieval in shamanic traditions. Discuss the similarities and differences between the Egyptian myth and shamanic practices, highlighting the universal theme of healing and integration found in both.

By engaging with these examples, problems, and exercises, students are encouraged to think critically about the mythological narratives, their symbolism, and their wider implications. They are invited to explore connections between ancient Egyptian mythology and other spiritual traditions, fostering a deeper understanding of the human quest for meaning and the enduring relevance of myth across cultures.

Impact on Human Society and Relationships

The interconnectedness of the gods in ancient Egyptian mythology had a profound impact on human perceptions of family and society. The divine family tree and the intricate relationships between the gods served as a model for human families and social structures. The concept of divine lineage and kinship was mirrored in the human realm, where family ties were considered sacred and fundamental to the functioning of society.

For example, the mythological narratives of Osiris, Isis, and Horus highlighted the importance of the divine couple and the continuation of lineage.

These stories reinforced the idea that family relationships were essential for stability, prosperity, and the perpetuation of divine and human bloodlines. The concept of filial piety, or the respect and reverence for one's parents and ancestors, was deeply ingrained in ancient Egyptian society.

Examination of the concept of divine kingship and its connection to the divine family

In ancient Egypt, the concept of divine kingship was closely intertwined with the divine family and its interconnectedness. The pharaoh, as the earthly representative of the gods, was believed to possess a direct link to the divine lineage. The legitimacy and authority of the pharaoh were derived from their divine heritage, often traced back to the gods themselves.

The divine family tree played a crucial role in establishing the divine right of kings, as the pharaoh's lineage was believed to be directly connected to the gods. This concept provided a powerful justification for the pharaoh's rule and solidified their position as the political and religious leader of the kingdom. It also reinforced the idea of the pharaoh as a mediator between the divine and human realms, responsible for maintaining cosmic order and ensuring the prosperity of the kingdom.

Influence on familial roles and responsibilities in ancient Egyptian society

The interconnectedness of the gods and the divine family had a significant impact on familial roles and responsibilities within ancient Egyptian society. Family units were structured hierarchically, with clear roles and obligations assigned to each member. These roles were influenced by the divine archetypes represented by the gods.

For instance, the roles of fathers and mothers were informed by the divine examples of Geb and Nut, who represented the earth and the sky as cosmic parents. Fathers were seen as providers and protectors, mirroring Geb's role as the foundation and sustainer of life. Mothers, on the other hand, were associated with nurturing and fertility, reflecting Nut's role as the giver of life and the nurturer of all beings.

Furthermore, the divine family tree emphasized the importance of intergenerational relationships and the transmission of knowledge and values from one generation to another. Children were expected to honor and obey their parents, reflecting the filial piety seen in the relationships between the gods. The concept of ancestry and ancestral veneration also played a significant role, with families revering their ancestors and seeking their guidance and protection.

Exercise:

Reflect on the influence of the interconnectedness of the gods on family structures and roles in ancient Egyptian society. Compare and contrast these familial ideals with those found in other cultures, such as the concept of the nuclear family in modern Western societies or the extended family systems in Asian cultures. Analyze the ways in which cultural beliefs and mythological narratives shape family dynamics and societal expectations.

Problem:

Imagine you are an advisor to the pharaoh and you need to present a proposal on how the divine family tree can be used to strengthen familial relationships and societal harmony in ancient Egypt. Develop a comprehensive plan that includes religious rituals, educational programs, and social reforms to promote the values of the divine family and enhance familial bonds throughout the kingdom.

By engaging with these examples, problems, and exercises, students are encouraged to critically analyze the impact of the interconnectedness of the gods on human society and relationships. They are prompted to explore the cultural and social implications of these beliefs, fostering a deeper understanding of how mythology shapes and influences the fabric of a civilization.

Conclusion

Throughout this exploration of the family relations and interconnectedness of the gods in ancient Egyptian mythology, we have delved into the intricate web of divine relationships that shaped the ancient Egyptian cosmology. We examined the divine family tree and its branches, tracing the lineage and connections between the major deities. From the divine couple of Osiris and Isis to the cosmic parents Geb and Nut, and the generative power of Ra and his offspring, the gods' family relations offered a rich tapestry of symbolism and meaning.

Understanding the significance of family relations in ancient Egyptian spirituality

The significance of family relations in ancient Egyptian spirituality cannot be overstated. The interconnectedness of the gods mirrored the interconnectedness of the natural and human worlds. The divine family tree served as a powerful metaphor for the order and harmony of the cosmos. The roles and responsibilities of the gods within their familial relationships provided a blueprint for human behavior and societal structures.

Family relationships were not only seen as a reflection of divine order but also as a means to connect with the divine. Ancestral veneration and the transmission of ancestral knowledge were integral to the spiritual practices of the ancient Egyptians. By honoring their familial ties, individuals could establish a deeper connection with their ancestors and the gods themselves.

Reflection on the lessons and values conveyed through the divine family narratives

The divine family narratives conveyed profound lessons and values that were central to ancient Egyptian society. Through the stories of Osiris, Isis, and Horus, we learned about the transformative power of love, resurrection, and the eternal cycle of life and death. The conflict between Horus and Set illustrated the struggle for kingship and the importance of loyalty and justice. The relationship between Nut and Ra highlighted the eternal nature of creation and the cyclical rhythm of day and night.

These narratives taught the ancient Egyptians about the values of filial piety, loyalty, and the pursuit of cosmic order. They emphasized the interconnectedness of all beings and the necessity of maintaining harmony within oneself, the family, and the larger society. The lessons derived from these mythological stories guided the behavior and moral compass of the ancient Egyptian people.

In conclusion, the study of the interconnectedness of the gods and their familial relationships provides us with a deep understanding of ancient Egyptian spirituality and culture. The divine family tree and the narratives surrounding it offer a glimpse into the values, beliefs, and societal structures of this ancient civilization. By engaging with these concepts, we not only gain insights into the ancient Egyptians' worldview but also find relevance and meaning in our own lives as we explore the enduring themes of love, loyalty, and cosmic order.

Exercise:
Reflect on the role of family relations in your own cultural and spiritual beliefs. How do familial ties influence your understanding of identity, morality, and societal roles? Compare and contrast the lessons conveyed through the divine family narratives in ancient Egyptian mythology with those found in other mythological traditions, such as Greek, Norse, or Hindu mythology. Discuss the

universal themes and values that emerge from these diverse mythologies and their impact on human societies.

Problem:

Imagine you are a scholar studying the interconnectedness of the gods in ancient Egyptian mythology. Develop a research project proposal that investigates the influence of familial relationships on ancient Egyptian societal structures, religious practices, and individual identity. Consider the use of textual sources, archaeological evidence, and comparative studies with other ancient civilizations to support your research.

Chapter 13: Iconography and Symbols Associated with Each Deity

In the ancient Egyptian religious tradition, iconography and symbols played a vital role in the expression and understanding of the divine. The ancient Egyptians employed a rich visual language to depict their deities, using intricate iconography and symbols that conveyed profound meanings and concepts. These visual representations served as a means of communication between humans and the divine, allowing individuals to connect with the gods and access their powers and wisdom.

The importance of iconography and symbols in ancient Egyptian religion cannot be overstated. They provided a tangible and visible form through which the gods could be recognized and worshipped. The intricate details and specific attributes depicted in the iconography served as visual cues that identified each deity and conveyed their unique characteristics and roles within the cosmic order.

Significance of understanding the visual representations of deities

To fully comprehend the religious and spiritual beliefs of the ancient Egyptians, it is crucial to understand the visual representations of their deities. By studying the iconography and symbols associated with each deity, we gain insight into the ancient Egyptian worldview, their understanding of the divine, and the complex interplay of various religious concepts.

Understanding the visual representations of deities allows us to explore the multifaceted nature of ancient Egyptian religion. Each deity was associated with specific symbols and attributes that conveyed their essence and divine power. These symbols could range from animals and objects to specific physical features or gestures. By analyzing these symbols, we can uncover deeper meanings and connections between the gods, their roles, and the broader religious and cosmological framework.

Studying the iconography and symbols also helps us appreciate the artistic and cultural expressions of ancient Egypt. The intricate details and symbolism embedded in the depictions of deities showcase the mastery of ancient Egyptian artisans and the profound spiritual significance attributed to these representations. Through the artistry of iconography, the ancient Egyptians sought to capture the essence of the gods and make them accessible to both the elite and the general populace.

Furthermore, understanding the visual representations of deities allows for cross-cultural comparisons and analysis. By examining the iconography and symbols associated with ancient Egyptian deities alongside those of other religious and mythological traditions, we can identify universal themes, archetypal symbols, and shared narratives that transcend cultural boundaries. This comparative approach broadens our understanding of human spirituality and the ways in which diverse cultures have sought to depict and comprehend the divine.

In conclusion, the study of iconography and symbols associated with each deity in ancient Egyptian religion is of paramount importance. It provides us with a deeper understanding of the religious beliefs and practices of the ancient Egyptians, reveals the complexities and interconnectedness of their cosmology, and enables us to appreciate the artistic and cultural expressions of their civilization. By delving into the visual representations of the gods, we gain valuable insights into the ancient Egyptian worldview and can engage in cross-cultural dialogues that foster a broader understanding of human spirituality.

Examples:

Analyze a collection of ancient Egyptian artifacts depicting various deities. Identify the symbols and iconography associated with each deity and discuss their potential meanings and implications within the religious context.

Compare the iconography and symbols of an ancient Egyptian deity, such as Horus, with a deity from another religious tradition, such as Apollo in Greek mythology. Explore the similarities and differences in their visual representations and discuss the possible cultural and symbolic significance behind these variations.

Problems:

Select a deity from the ancient Egyptian pantheon and create a visual representation of the deity using symbols and iconography. Justify your choices by explaining the symbolic meanings and associations behind each element.

Research a specific symbol commonly associated with an ancient Egyptian deity, such as the ankh or the scarab beetle. Explore its significance within the religious and cultural context of ancient Egypt and discuss its potential interpretations and associations.

Exercises:

Study a set of ancient Egyptian hieroglyphs and identify the symbols associated with different deities. Discuss the possible meanings and functions of these symbols within the hieroglyphic writing system.

Analyze a temple relief or mural depicting an ancient Egyptian deity. Identify the key symbols and iconographic elements present in the artwork and interpret their significance within the larger religious narrative being depicted.

Osiris

In the ancient Egyptian pantheon, Osiris holds a prominent position as one of the central and complex deities. Iconographically, Osiris is most commonly depicted as a mummified figure, wrapped in linen bandages and wearing the Atef crown, which is adorned with ostrich feathers and two plumes. The mummified form of Osiris represents his association with death, rebirth, and the afterlife.

One of the distinguishing features of Osiris's iconography is the presence of two regal symbols: the crook and flail. The crook, known as heka, resembles a shepherd's staff with a hooked end, while the flail, known as nekhakha, consists of three connected beads or spheres with chains. These symbols are often depicted crossed over Osiris's chest, held in each hand.

Symbols: Crook and flail as symbols of kingship and fertility

The crook and flail are deeply symbolic in ancient Egyptian culture, representing the authority and attributes of Osiris as a ruler and a provider of fertility. The crook symbolizes the shepherd's role in guiding and protecting the people, while the flail represents the agricultural domain, signifying the power to ensure a bountiful harvest.

The crook, associated with kingship, symbolizes Osiris's role as a just and wise ruler who governs with benevolence and guidance. It represents his authority over the earthly realm and his ability to shepherd and protect his subjects, ensuring their well-being and prosperity.

The flail, on the other hand, symbolizes Osiris's association with agricultural fertility and abundance. It represents his power to nourish and sustain life, particularly in the context of the fertile Nile Valley. As the god of vegetation and agriculture, Osiris's control over the cycle of growth and decay is reflected in the symbolism of the flail, which signifies his ability to bring forth a fruitful harvest.

C. Analysis of the symbolism: Osiris as a symbol of death, resurrection, and agricultural fertility

The symbolism associated with Osiris as a mummified figure, along with the crook and flail, encompasses profound themes of death, resurrection, and agricultural fertility. Osiris embodies the cyclical nature of life, death, and rebirth, making him a powerful symbol of regeneration and renewal.

As a mummified figure, Osiris represents the transformative power of death and resurrection. His death at the hands of his brother Set and subsequent resurrection by his sister-wife Isis illustrate the triumph of life over death and the eternal nature of the soul. Through Osiris's resurrection, the ancient Egyptians found hope for their own journey through the afterlife, believing that they could attain immortality and reunion with the divine.

The crook and flail further enhance Osiris's symbolism by highlighting his role as a benevolent ruler and a provider of fertility. By wielding these symbols, Osiris signifies his ability to guide and protect his people, ensuring their well-being and prosperity. The crook represents the just and compassionate leadership of Osiris, while the flail represents his power to nurture and sustain the agricultural abundance necessary for the survival and prosperity of the community.

In conclusion, the iconography and symbols associated with Osiris reveal his multifaceted nature as a deity of death, resurrection, kingship, and agricultural fertility. Osiris's mummified form, along with the crook and flail, convey profound symbolism that speaks to the cyclical nature of life, the power of resurrection, and the benevolent rule and provision of the divine. By understanding these symbols, we gain insights into the ancient Egyptian belief system and the values and aspirations embedded within their religious and cultural practices.

Examples:

Study various depictions of Osiris in ancient Egyptian art and identify the consistent elements, such as the mummified form, the Atef crown, and the crossed crook and flail. Analyze how these elements contribute to the overall symbolism and meaning associated with Osiris.

Research the role of Osiris in ancient Egyptian religious rituals and ceremonies. Discuss how the symbolism of Osiris as a deity of death, resurrection, and fertility was incorporated into these rituals to evoke spiritual transformation and ensure the well-being of the community.

Problems:

Imagine you are an ancient Egyptian artist commissioned to create a relief depicting Osiris. Explain the artistic choices you would make to effectively convey the symbolism of death, resurrection, and agricultural fertility associated with Osiris.

Discuss the potential significance of the crook and flail as symbols of leadership and provision in other cultural and religious contexts, such as the shepherd's crook in Judeo-Christian traditions or the agricultural symbols in Native American spiritual practices.

Isis

In ancient Egyptian art and iconography, Isis is often depicted as a woman with a distinctive headdress in the shape of a throne. This throne-shaped headdress, known as the "throne sign" or "Isis throne," is a symbol of her divine queenship and authority. It represents her role as the queen of the gods, the wife of Osiris, and the mother of Horus.

Another common iconographic representation of Isis is with outstretched wings. These wings symbolize her protective and nurturing nature, as well as her connection to the realm of the divine. The outstretched wings of Isis convey a sense of encompassing protection, providing shelter and guidance to those in need.

Symbols: Throne-shaped headdress and outstretched wings as symbols of divine queenship and protective power

The throne-shaped headdress worn by Isis symbolizes her status as a divine queen. It represents her authority and power in the divine realm, reflecting her role as the mother and protector of the gods. The headdress also emphasizes her association with the concept of ma'at, which represents cosmic order and balance. As a queen, Isis is believed to uphold and maintain the cosmic order, ensuring harmony and stability within the universe.

The outstretched wings of Isis symbolize her protective and nurturing nature. They represent her ability to provide shelter, guidance, and support to her devotees. Just as a bird spreads its wings to shield its young, Isis extends her wings to offer comfort and protection. This symbolism highlights her role as a compassionate and caring deity, particularly associated with motherhood and the divine feminine.

Analysis of the symbolism: Isis as a symbol of motherhood, magic, and the divine feminine

Isis embodies a rich symbolism that encompasses various aspects of ancient Egyptian spirituality and culture. As a symbol of motherhood, Isis represents the nurturing and life-giving qualities associated with the maternal archetype. She is revered as a divine mother, both in a literal sense as the mother of Horus and in a broader sense as a universal mother figure who provides care, protection, and guidance to all.

In addition to her role as a mother, Isis is also associated with magic and mystical knowledge. She is regarded as a powerful sorceress and a mistress of magic. Through her magical abilities, Isis was believed to possess the knowledge and skill to heal the sick, protect the vulnerable, and bring about positive change. Her magical prowess signifies her connection to the realm of the divine and her role as a mediator between humans and the gods.

Furthermore, Isis embodies the divine feminine, representing the sacred feminine principles of creativity, intuition, and emotional wisdom. She is revered as a goddess of love, beauty, and fertility, embodying the qualities of femininity and grace. Isis serves as an archetype of feminine power, strength, and resilience, inspiring reverence and devotion in ancient Egyptian society.

In conclusion, the iconography and symbols associated with Isis, including the throne-shaped headdress and outstretched wings, reveal her multifaceted symbolism as a goddess of divine queenship, protective power, motherhood, magic, and the divine feminine. Understanding these symbols allows us to grasp the profound significance of Isis in ancient Egyptian spirituality and the values and ideals she embodies.

Examples:

Examine different artistic representations of Isis in ancient Egyptian temples, tombs, and artifacts. Analyze the variations in her iconography and discuss the possible meanings and cultural contexts behind these depictions.

Compare the symbolism of Isis with other goddess figures from different mythological traditions, such as the Greek goddess Athena or the Hindu goddess Lakshmi. Explore the similarities and differences in their iconography and the cultural significance assigned to them.

Problems:

Analyze the symbolism of the throne-shaped headdress in the context of ancient Egyptian political and social structures. Discuss how the portrayal of Isis as a divine queen reflects and reinforces the societal norms and power dynamics of ancient Egyptian civilization.

Investigate the role of Isis in ancient Egyptian magical practices and rituals. Research specific spells or invocations associated with Isis and discuss their intended effects and the underlying symbolism employed in these magical practices.

Horus

Horus, one of the most significant deities in ancient Egyptian mythology, is commonly depicted as a falcon-headed god. This iconography emphasizes his association with the falcon, a bird of prey known for its keen sight and swiftness. The falcon-headed representation of Horus reflects his attributes of power, vigilance, and authority. It symbolizes his connection to the celestial realm and his role as a celestial deity.

Another form of Horus depicted in ancient Egyptian art is as a child with a sidelock of youth. This portrayal signifies his youth and innocence, as well as his potential for growth and future kingship. The sidelock of youth, a distinctive lock of hair on the side of his head, was a common symbol of youth and vitality in ancient Egyptian culture. It represents Horus's status as the divine child, destined to inherit the throne and continue the lineage of the gods.

Symbols: Falcon and the sidelock of youth as symbols of divine kingship and protection

The falcon is a prominent symbol associated with Horus and carries multiple layers of meaning. As a falcon, Horus embodies qualities such as strength, swiftness, and sharp vision. The falcon's ability to soar high in the sky represents Horus's connection to the celestial realm and his role as a mediator between the heavens and the earthly domain. Additionally, the falcon's hunting prowess symbolizes Horus's protective nature, as he guards the kingdom against threats and evil forces.

The sidelock of youth worn by the child form of Horus represents his royal lineage and divine kingship. In ancient Egyptian culture, the sidelock of youth was a symbol of youthful potential and the future ruler's legitimacy. It signifies Horus's status as the rightful heir to the throne and his role in maintaining order and balance within the kingdom. The sidelock of youth also serves as a symbol of protection, as it signifies Horus's divine guardianship and his ability to safeguard his followers.

Analysis of the symbolism: Horus as a symbol of kingship, solar power, and the eternal struggle between good and evil

Horus embodies a complex symbolism that encompasses various aspects of ancient Egyptian spirituality and mythology. As a symbol of kingship, Horus represents the divine authority and legitimacy of the pharaohs, who were believed to be the earthly manifestations of Horus. He symbolizes the ideal ruler who upholds justice, maintains order, and protects his people.

Furthermore, Horus is closely associated with solar power and the celestial realm. As a falcon-headed deity, he is linked to the sun and its radiant energy. Horus's connection to the sun symbolizes his role in bringing light, warmth, and vitality to the world. He is seen as a celestial deity who guides the sun on its daily journey across the sky, representing the eternal cycle of life, death, and rebirth.

Moreover, Horus represents the eternal struggle between good and evil. In ancient Egyptian mythology, Horus engaged in a fierce battle with his uncle Set, who murdered his father Osiris and usurped the throne. This conflict symbolizes the perpetual struggle between order and chaos, righteousness and wrongdoing. Horus embodies the forces of good and represents the triumph of justice and harmony over evil.

In conclusion, the iconography and symbols associated with Horus, including the falcon and the sidelock of youth, reveal his multifaceted symbolism as a deity of divine kingship, solar power, and the eternal struggle between good and evil. Understanding these symbols allows us to grasp the profound significance of Horus in ancient Egyptian spirituality and the values he represents.

Exploring the Esoteric Wisdom of Ancient Egypt for Modern Spirituality

Problems:

Compare and contrast the depictions of Horus as a falcon-headed deity and as a child with a sidelock of youth. Discuss the different meanings and connotations associated with each representation and their significance in ancient Egyptian religious and social contexts.

Investigate the role of Horus in ancient Egyptian myths and legends, focusing on his battles with Set and his role as a protector and avenger of his father Osiris. Analyze the symbolic implications of these mythological narratives and their impact on the understanding of divine kingship and the eternal struggle between good and evil in ancient Egyptian culture.

Explore the concept of solar symbolism in ancient Egyptian religion and its connection to Horus. Examine how Horus's association with the sun and solar power influenced ancient Egyptian cosmology and the perception of divine forces.

Hathor

Hathor, a prominent goddess in ancient Egyptian mythology, is often represented in two primary forms. The first is as a cow, symbolizing her nurturing and maternal qualities. The cow was highly revered in ancient Egyptian society as a symbol of fertility, abundance, and sustenance. Hathor's cow form emphasizes her role as a provider and a giver of life, reflecting her association with motherhood and the nurturing aspect of the divine.

The second form of Hathor is as a woman with cow horns and a sun disc placed between them. This representation combines the feminine form with the attributes of the cow. The cow horns symbolize her connection to fertility, while the sun disc represents her association with the sun and its life-giving power. The presence of the sun disc highlights Hathor's cosmic significance and her role in bringing warmth, light, and vitality to the world.

Symbols: Cow and sun disc as symbols of fertility, love, and the nurturing aspect of the divine

The cow is a powerful symbol associated with Hathor, representing fertility, abundance, and the nurturing aspects of the divine. In ancient Egyptian culture, cows were considered sacred animals associated with the goddess Hathor. They were believed to embody the life-giving and sustaining powers of the goddess, providing nourishment and sustenance to humans and animals alike. The cow

265

symbolizes Hathor's role as a source of fertility, both in terms of physical fertility and the fertility of creative endeavors, such as art, music, and writing.

The sun disc, placed between the cow horns in Hathor's iconography, represents her connection to the sun and its life-affirming energies. The sun is a universal symbol of vitality, warmth, and enlightenment. Hathor's association with the sun disc underscores her role in bringing joy, happiness, and the life-giving energies of the sun to the world. It symbolizes her divine radiance and her ability to bestow blessings and abundance upon her devotees.

Analysis of the symbolism: Hathor as a symbol of joy, music, love, and the divine feminine

Hathor embodies a rich symbolism that encompasses various aspects of ancient Egyptian spirituality and society. As a symbol of joy, Hathor represents the celebration of life and the expression of happiness. She is associated with music, dance, and festivities, as she is believed to have introduced music and dance to humanity. Hathor's joyful nature is often depicted through her depiction with a sistrum, a musical instrument associated with rhythm and divine harmony.

Furthermore, Hathor symbolizes love and beauty, particularly the divine and unconditional love that nurtures and sustains all living beings. She is often invoked in matters of love, romance, and relationships, as she embodies the qualities of compassion, understanding, and emotional well-being. Hathor's presence brings about a sense of harmony and connection between individuals, fostering love and unity within communities.

Hathor's symbolism also encompasses the divine feminine, representing the power and wisdom associated with femininity. As a goddess of fertility, Hathor symbolizes the creative potential and life-giving abilities of women. She embodies the nurturing aspects of the feminine and serves as a role model for compassion, empathy, and maternal care.

In conclusion, the iconography and symbols associated with Hathor, including her depiction as a cow and a woman with cow horns and a sun disc, convey her profound symbolism as a goddess of fertility, love, joy, and the divine feminine. Understanding these symbols allows us to appreciate Hathor's role in ancient Egyptian spirituality and the values she represents.

Exploring the Esoteric Wisdom of Ancient Egypt for Modern Spirituality

Problems:

Analyze the role of Hathor in ancient Egyptian rituals and festivals, exploring how her symbols and iconography were incorporated into religious ceremonies. Discuss the significance of music, dance, and joy in ancient Egyptian religious practices and their connection to Hathor.

Investigate the relationship between Hathor and other deities in the ancient Egyptian pantheon, such as Isis and Osiris. Analyze how their domains and attributes intersect and complement each other, and discuss the implications of their interconnectedness for the understanding of ancient Egyptian cosmology and spirituality.

Explore the representation of Hathor in ancient Egyptian art and artifacts, examining the symbolism and cultural significance of her depictions. Analyze the use of color, composition, and other artistic techniques in conveying Hathor's attributes and qualities. Discuss the influence of Hathor's imagery on ancient Egyptian society and the perception of femininity, love, and joy.

Ra

Ra, one of the most important deities in ancient Egyptian mythology, is often depicted in two primary forms. The first form portrays Ra as a man with the head of a falcon, symbolizing his association with the bird of prey and its attributes of speed, keen vision, and divine authority. The falcon, being a creature that soars high in the sky, represents the soaring sun, which Ra embodies.

The second form of Ra's iconography depicts him as a man with a sun disc on his head, known as the solar disc. The sun disc is a potent symbol of the sun's power and radiance. It represents the life-giving energy, light, and warmth that the sun bestows upon the Earth. Ra's depiction with the sun disc emphasizes his role as the solar deity, the source of cosmic illumination and vitality.

Symbols: Falcon and sun disc as symbols of solar power, divine kingship, and creation

The falcon is a significant symbol associated with Ra, representing his solar power and divine authority. Falcons were revered in ancient Egyptian culture for their ability to soar through the sky, just as the sun rises and sets each day. The falcon symbolizes Ra's role as the ruler of the heavens, possessing the power to bring light and life to the world. It also represents his watchful and protective nature, as falcons were known for their keen eyesight and ability to spot even the smallest details from great distances.

The sun disc, worn atop Ra's head, represents his connection to the sun and its life-sustaining energies. The sun is central to ancient Egyptian cosmology, symbolizing creation, renewal, and cosmic order. Ra's association with the sun disc underscores his role as the creator deity and the source of all life. The sun disc is a potent symbol of divine kingship, as Ra is the supreme ruler of the gods and the ultimate authority in the Egyptian pantheon.

Analysis of the symbolism: Ra as a symbol of the sun, creation, and cosmic order

Ra's symbolism is deeply rooted in the sun and its significance to ancient Egyptian culture. The sun, with its daily cycle of rising and setting, represents the eternal cycle of creation, destruction, and renewal. Ra's association with the sun underscores his role as the creator deity, bringing order and balance to the universe through his divine light.

Ra's symbolism also highlights his role in maintaining cosmic order, known as ma'at in ancient Egyptian belief. Ma'at represents the concept of universal harmony, balance, and truth. As the sun god, Ra ensures that ma'at is upheld and that the world functions in accordance with the divine plan. His role as the divine king and ruler of the gods further reinforces his authority in maintaining ma'at and ensuring the proper functioning of the cosmos.

Moreover, Ra's symbolism extends beyond the cosmic realm to the human sphere. He represents the life-giving and sustaining qualities of the sun, providing light, warmth, and vitality to all living beings. Ra's association with creation and renewal reflects the ancient Egyptians' belief in the cyclical nature of life and the continuous regeneration of the natural world.

In conclusion, the iconography and symbols associated with Ra, including his depictions as a falcon-headed deity and his representation with a sun disc, convey his profound symbolism as a symbol of the sun, creation, and cosmic order. Understanding these symbols allows us to appreciate Ra's pivotal role in ancient Egyptian spirituality and the values he represents.

Problems:

Compare and contrast the iconography and symbolism of Ra with other solar deities from different cultural traditions, such as the Greek god Apollo or the Aztec god Huitzilopochtli.

Analyze the role of Ra's symbols in the daily rituals and practices of ancient Egyptian priests. How did the priests incorporate Ra's symbolism into their religious ceremonies and offerings?

Exercises:

Create your own artistic representation of Ra, incorporating his key symbols and iconography. Explain the choices you made in representing Ra and how they reflect his symbolism and attributes.

Imagine you are an ancient Egyptian scribe writing a hymn to Ra. Compose a hymn that highlights his symbolism, role as the sun god, and his importance in maintaining cosmic order.

Other deities

In addition to the well-known deities like Osiris, Isis, Horus, Hathor, and Ra, the ancient Egyptian pantheon comprises numerous other important gods and goddesses, each with their unique iconography and symbols. Understanding the iconography and symbols associated with these deities is crucial for comprehending their roles, attributes, and the cultural beliefs they represent.

Geb:
Iconography: Geb, the god of the earth, is often depicted as a man lying beneath the sky. Sometimes he is portrayed as a man with a goose atop his head, symbolizing his connection to the earth and its fertile nature.
Symbols: The symbols associated with Geb are primarily related to the earth, including rocks, vegetation, and the Nile River. These symbols represent Geb's association with fertility, abundance, and the sustenance of life.

Nut:
Iconography: Nut, the goddess of the sky, is typically depicted as a woman arching her body across the heavens, forming a canopy over the earth. Her body is adorned with stars, emphasizing her celestial nature.

Symbols: The primary symbol associated with Nut is the starry sky. It represents her role as the mother of the sun and the protector of the deceased. The stars symbolize the eternal and limitless nature of the cosmos.

Seth:

Iconography: Seth, the god of chaos and storms, is often depicted as a man with the head of an enigmatic animal, which has been variously interpreted as a Seth animal, a composite creature, or a donkey. This unique portrayal highlights the unpredictable and tumultuous nature of Seth.

Symbols: The symbols associated with Seth include the desert, storms, and chaos. These symbols reflect his dual nature as both a disruptive force and a necessary agent of change in the cosmic order.

Thoth:

Iconography: Thoth, the god of writing, wisdom, and magic, is typically depicted as a man with the head of an ibis or as a full ibis. The ibis, known for its long beak and association with the moon, symbolizes Thoth's connection to intellect and lunar cycles.

Symbols: The primary symbols associated with Thoth are the ibis, the moon, and the papyrus scroll. The ibis represents wisdom and knowledge, while the moon symbolizes Thoth's role as a lunar deity. The papyrus scroll represents writing, record-keeping, and the dissemination of knowledge.

Maat:

Iconography: Maat, the goddess of truth, justice, and cosmic order, is typically portrayed as a woman wearing a feather on her head, known as the Feather of Maat. She is often depicted holding a scepter, which symbolizes her role as a divine ruler.

Symbols: The Feather of Maat is the primary symbol associated with her. It represents the concept of truth, balance, and moral integrity. Maat's symbols convey the importance of upholding righteousness and maintaining harmony in both human and divine affairs.

Analysis of the specific symbols and their significance within the context of each deity's role and domain

The symbols associated with each deity hold deep significance within the context of their roles and domains. These symbols provide insights into the ancient Egyptian worldview, cultural beliefs, and the specific attributes of the deities.

Exploring the Esoteric Wisdom of Ancient Egypt for Modern Spirituality

For example, Geb's iconography and symbols emphasize his connection to the earth and its fertility. His portrayal lying beneath the sky highlights his role in supporting and nourishing life. The symbols of rocks, vegetation, and the Nile River further emphasize Geb's association with abundance and the vital forces of the natural world.

Nut's iconography as a celestial canopy and her symbols of the starry sky illustrate her role as the overarching protector of the universe. The stars symbolize the eternal nature of the cosmos and the continuity of life beyond death, aligning with her position as the mother of the sun and the facilitator of rebirth.

Seth's unique and enigmatic iconography reflects his tumultuous nature as the god of chaos. The symbols associated with Seth, such as the desert and storms, emphasize his role in disrupting and challenging the established order, allowing for transformation and renewal.

Thoth's iconography as an ibis or with an ibis head highlights his association with intellect, knowledge, and lunar cycles. The symbols of the ibis, the moon, and the papyrus scroll underscore his role as a deity of writing, wisdom, and magic. These symbols emphasize Thoth's significance in the realms of learning, record-keeping, and the mystical arts.

Maat's symbol, the Feather of Maat, represents the concept of truth and balance. It serves as a reminder of the importance of upholding justice and moral integrity in personal conduct and societal affairs. The symbol embodies the ideals of Maat and serves as a guiding principle for a harmonious existence within the cosmic order.

Studying the iconography and symbols associated with these deities enables us to gain a deeper understanding of their roles, attributes, and the cultural values they embody. It invites us to explore the multifaceted nature of ancient Egyptian spirituality and engage in critical analysis of the symbolism employed to convey profound concepts and beliefs.

Exercises:

Select one of the deities discussed in this section (Geb, Nut, Seth, Thoth, or Maat) and create an artistic representation that incorporates their key symbols and iconography. Describe the choices you made and explain how your artwork reflects the deity's symbolism and attributes.

Choose one of the deities discussed in this section and research additional symbols associated with them. Write a short essay exploring the symbolism of these additional symbols and their significance within the context of the deity's role and domain.

Comparative analysis

One fascinating aspect of studying iconography and symbols in ancient Egyptian religion is the opportunity for comparative analysis. By examining the iconography and symbols across different mythological traditions, we can identify similarities and differences, uncover universal themes, and gain a deeper understanding of the human quest for spiritual meaning.

Comparative Analysis of Iconography:

One way to approach comparative analysis is by examining the representations of deities in different mythologies. For example, we can compare the falcon-headed Horus in ancient Egyptian mythology with the bird-like figures of the Greek deity Zeus, who is often depicted as an eagle or with eagle-like features. While both deities share a connection to the sky and kingship, their iconography presents distinct cultural interpretations of similar concepts.

Likewise, we can explore the representations of goddesses associated with fertility and the divine feminine. In ancient Egyptian mythology, Hathor is often depicted as a cow or a woman with cow horns and a sun disc. Comparatively, the Greek goddess Hera is frequently depicted as a woman wearing a crown or headdress, symbolizing her status as the queen of the gods. Despite the differences in iconography, both deities embody the concepts of femininity, fertility, and divine power.

Comparative Analysis of Symbols:

Symbols play a vital role in religious and spiritual practices across various cultures. By examining common symbols found in different mythological traditions, we can identify universal themes and shared human experiences.

For instance, the sun is a potent symbol found in numerous mythologies worldwide. In ancient Egyptian religion, Ra is the solar deity associated with creation and cosmic order, represented by the sun disc or a man with a sun disc on his head. In Norse mythology, the god Baldur embodies the sun and light.

Similarly, the Hindu deity Surya represents the sun's radiant energy and life-giving power.

Another universal symbol found in diverse mythologies is the tree. In Norse mythology, the World Tree, Yggdrasil, connects different realms and serves as a symbol of cosmic order. The sacred fig tree, known as the Bodhi tree, holds great significance in Buddhism as the place where Siddhartha Gautama attained enlightenment. In Celtic mythology, the oak tree symbolizes strength, wisdom, and connection to the divine.

Exploration of the universal symbols and themes found in diverse cultural and religious contexts

As we delve deeper into the study of iconography and symbols, it becomes evident that certain symbols and themes transcend specific cultural and religious boundaries. These universal symbols reflect fundamental aspects of the human experience and the innate quest for spiritual understanding.

The Journey of Transformation:

One universal theme found in diverse mythological traditions is the hero's journey or the transformative quest. This theme is often symbolized by the image of a labyrinth or a winding path. In ancient Egyptian mythology, the soul's journey through the afterlife is depicted in the funerary texts and the imagery of the mummy's journey to the realm of Osiris. Similarly, in Greek mythology, the hero's journey is exemplified by the labyrinth of the Minotaur, where Theseus navigates the maze to confront his inner demons and emerge transformed.

The Sacred Feminine:

The presence of the divine feminine is another universal theme in mythology and religious traditions. Goddess figures representing fertility, wisdom, and nurturing aspects of the divine can be found across cultures. The Egyptian goddess Isis, the Greek goddess Athena, and the Hindu goddess Lakshmi are examples of revered feminine deities. Their symbols and iconography emphasize the power of creation, wisdom, and compassion.

The Symbolism of the Serpent:

The serpent is a symbol deeply rooted in mythologies around the world. In Egyptian mythology, the uraeus, a rearing cobra, represents the protective and regal power of the pharaohs. In Norse mythology, the world serpent Jormungandr encircles the earth, symbolizing the cyclical nature of life and the interconnectedness of all beings. The serpent also plays a significant role in Mesoamerican cultures, where Quetzalcoatl, the feathered serpent, represents wisdom and cosmic balance.

Exercises:

Choose two deities from different mythological traditions and compare their iconography. Identify similarities and differences, and discuss how the cultural context might have influenced their representations.

Select a universal symbol, such as the sun or the tree, and research its significance in different mythologies. Write an essay exploring the variations in symbolism and the underlying themes associated with the symbol across cultures.

Explore the concept of the hero's journey in different mythological traditions. Choose two heroes from different cultures and analyze the stages of their journeys, focusing on the symbols and challenges encountered along the way. Compare and contrast their transformative quests.

Conclusion

Throughout this chapter, we have explored the rich iconography and symbols associated with various deities in ancient Egyptian religion. We examined the depictions and symbols of Osiris, Isis, Horus, Hathor, Ra, and other major deities, uncovering the layers of meaning embedded in their visual representations. From the mummified figure of Osiris with a crook and flail to the throne-shaped headdress of Isis and the falcon-headed Horus, each deity's iconography offers a unique glimpse into their roles, attributes, and mythological significance.

Understanding the significance of visual representations in ancient Egyptian religion

The visual representations of deities in ancient Egyptian religion served multiple purposes and carried profound symbolic meaning. The ancient Egyptians believed that the images and symbols had the power to manifest the divine presence and facilitate communication with the gods. The careful selection of iconography and symbols was a means to convey specific qualities, roles, and associations of the deities. Understanding the visual language of ancient Egyptian religion allows us to grasp the complex interplay between the divine and human realms, as well as the cultural and religious values of the ancient Egyptians.

Reflection on the enduring symbolism and its relevance in contemporary spirituality

The enduring symbolism found in ancient Egyptian iconography continues to resonate in contemporary spirituality and various fields of study, including witchcraft, divination, herbalism, shamanism, and ecospirituality. These symbols and their associated meanings transcend time and cultural boundaries, tapping into universal archetypes and the collective unconscious.

For example, the symbol of the sun, embodied by deities like Ra, reflects the power of light, warmth, and cosmic order. This symbol can be found in various spiritual practices, where it represents illumination, personal growth, and the source of life. The divine feminine symbolism represented by goddesses like Isis and Hathor resonates with the revival of interest in feminine spirituality and the recognition of the sacred feminine in contemporary contexts.

Moreover, the study of ancient Egyptian iconography invites us to explore the deeper layers of symbolism and meaning in our own spiritual practices. By delving into the symbolism of different deities and their attributes, we can gain insights into our own spiritual journeys, cultivate a deeper connection with the natural world, and engage in a broader dialogue with diverse spiritual traditions.

In conclusion, the iconography and symbols associated with each deity in ancient Egyptian religion offer a profound window into the beliefs, values, and aspirations of this ancient civilization. The visual representations serve as a bridge between the earthly and the divine, allowing us to glimpse the mysteries of the cosmos and our place within it. By understanding and appreciating these symbols, we can enrich our own spiritual journeys and cultivate a deeper sense of connection to the sacred. The study of ancient Egyptian iconography invites us to explore the depths of human spirituality and the enduring power of symbols in shaping our understanding of the divine.

Exercises:

Select a deity discussed in this chapter and create your own artistic representation of their iconography. Reflect on the symbolism and meaning behind your artistic choices.

Research a contemporary spiritual practice or tradition that incorporates ancient Egyptian symbolism. Compare and contrast the use of symbols in both ancient Egyptian religion and the contemporary context, examining how they have been adapted and interpreted.

Engage in a group discussion or debate on the relevance of ancient Egyptian iconography in modern spirituality. Explore differing perspectives and opinions, considering the cultural appropriation of symbols and the ethical implications of using ancient religious imagery in contemporary contexts.

Chapter 14: Religious Rituals and Temples

In the intricate tapestry of ancient Egyptian religion, rituals held a significant place as profound expressions of devotion and means of establishing and maintaining connections with the divine. Defined as a prescribed set of actions, gestures, and words performed in a formalized manner, religious rituals formed an essential component of the religious and spiritual practices of the ancient Egyptians.

Rituals played a vital role in the lives of the ancient Egyptians, permeating every aspect of their existence. These rituals encompassed various forms, ranging from daily observances to grand seasonal festivals and sacred funerary ceremonies. Each ritual was imbued with symbolic meaning, reflecting the fundamental beliefs, cosmology, and cultural values of the ancient Egyptian civilization.

Role of Rituals in Establishing and Maintaining Divine Connections

Religious rituals served as the bridge between the human and divine realms, facilitating communication and communion with the gods. They were performed to honor and appease the deities, seeking their blessings, protection, and guidance. By engaging in specific actions and reciting sacred incantations, the ancient Egyptians believed they could establish a direct and reciprocal relationship with the divine forces.

Rituals were considered sacred acts, often performed by specially designated priests and priestesses who acted as intermediaries between the mortal world and the realm of the gods. These religious professionals meticulously followed prescribed procedures, ensuring the correct execution of rituals to maintain the cosmic balance and uphold the divine order.

The efficacy of rituals rested upon the belief that the gods actively participated in the ceremonies, responding to the prayers, offerings, and symbolic actions performed by the participants. Rituals were seen as potent vehicles for invoking the divine presence and receiving divine blessings, granting favor, protection, and prosperity to the individual worshipers, the community, and the entire kingdom.

The ancient Egyptians regarded rituals not merely as empty formalities, but as powerful transformative acts that could bring about tangible effects in the physical and spiritual realms. Through rituals, individuals sought purification, spiritual enlightenment, and harmony with the divine forces, fostering a sense of belonging and interconnectedness within the cosmic order.

The significance of rituals extended beyond the immediate connection with the gods. They played a crucial role in the collective identity and cohesion of the ancient Egyptian society. Rituals provided a communal framework for shared experiences, reinforcing social bonds and strengthening the ties between individuals, families, and the wider community. They were occasions for communal celebration, reflection, and collective reaffirmation of cultural values and religious beliefs.

By delving into the world of religious rituals in ancient Egyptian religion, we gain profound insights into the intricate tapestry of their spiritual and cultural landscape. Exploring the symbolism, practices, and beliefs associated with these rituals offers us a glimpse into the ancient Egyptians' quest for divine communion, their reverence for the gods, and their enduring desire for harmony with the cosmic forces that shaped their lives.

As we delve deeper into the subsequent sections of this chapter, we will examine the various types of rituals, their structures and components, the symbolism embedded within them, and their social and cultural significance. Through this exploration, we will uncover the richness and complexity of religious rituals in ancient Egyptian religion, inviting us to contemplate their relevance and enduring legacy in contemporary spiritual practices.

Exercises:

Reflect on a religious ritual or ceremony from a different cultural or spiritual tradition. Compare and contrast its purpose, symbolism, and role in establishing a connection with the divine with the rituals in ancient Egyptian religion.

Choose an aspect of your daily life or routine and create a simple ritual around it. Consider the actions, objects, and words you would incorporate to infuse meaning and intention into the ritual. Reflect on how this ritual could help you establish a deeper connection with yourself or the divine.

Types of Religious Rituals

Daily Rituals

✧   Morning and Evening Offerings

In ancient Egyptian religion, daily rituals formed an integral part of the religious practices, serving as a means to establish a connection with the divine on a regular basis. Among these daily rituals, morning and evening offerings held a prominent place.

Every morning, individuals would present offerings to the gods as a gesture of gratitude, seeking their blessings and protection for the day ahead. These offerings typically included food, beverages, incense, and flowers, symbolizing sustenance, nourishment, and beauty. The act of offering was accompanied by prayers and recitations, expressing reverence and devotion to the gods.

Similarly, in the evening, individuals would perform another round of offerings, expressing gratitude for the blessings received throughout the day and seeking divine protection during the night. The evening offerings aimed to maintain a harmonious relationship with the gods and ensure their continued favor and support.

✧ Purification Rituals

Purification rituals played a vital role in the daily religious practices of the ancient Egyptians. These rituals were performed to cleanse oneself of impurities and restore a state of spiritual purity, which was essential for engaging with the divine forces.

Various purification rituals were conducted, such as ritual bathing, anointing with oils, and recitation of sacred spells and incantations. These actions symbolized the removal of physical and spiritual impurities, enabling individuals to approach the gods in a state of ritual cleanliness.

Purification rituals were not only performed by individuals as part of their personal religious practices but also formed an important aspect of temple rituals and ceremonies. The priests and priestesses would undergo purification before conducting rituals on behalf of the community, ensuring their spiritual readiness and purity.

Seasonal Rituals

✧ Opet Festival

The Opet Festival was one of the grandest and most significant seasonal rituals in ancient Egyptian religion. It celebrated the rejuvenation and renewal of the kingship, symbolizing the revitalization of cosmic order and the divine connection between the pharaoh and the gods.

The festival spanned several weeks and involved elaborate processions, temple rituals, and communal celebrations. The highlight of the Opet Festival was the sacred boat procession, during which the image of the deity, usually Amun, was carried in a magnificent barque from the temple to a nearby sacred site.

The Opet Festival embodied the ancient Egyptian belief in the cyclical nature of time, the renewal of life, and the eternal bond between the divine and human realms. It served as a means to reaffirm the divine kingship, seek blessings for the kingdom's prosperity, and engage the community in collective worship and celebration.

✦ Sed Festival
The Sed Festival was another significant seasonal ritual associated with the kingship and the pharaoh's reign. It was held to commemorate the pharaoh's thirty-year jubilee and to renew their divine authority and vitality.

The Sed Festival encompassed a series of ceremonies and rituals, including the pharaoh's symbolic renewal of youth and strength. The pharaoh would perform a ritual race and engage in various physical activities, symbolizing their continued ability to rule with vigor and wisdom.

The Sed Festival was a momentous occasion for the kingdom, as it reaffirmed the pharaoh's legitimacy, marked a milestone in their reign, and invoked the gods' blessings for the kingdom's continued prosperity and stability.

Funerary Rituals

✦ Opening of the Mouth Ceremony
The Opening of the Mouth ceremony was a crucial funerary ritual performed to ensure the deceased's rebirth and enable their transition into the afterlife. It was believed that the deceased's mouth and senses needed to be restored to facilitate their ability to eat, drink, speak, and perceive in the realm of the spirits.

During the ceremony, a priest would use special tools and perform specific gestures and incantations to touch the deceased's mouth, ears, eyes, and nose, symbolically restoring their faculties and awakening their spiritual senses. This ritual act aimed to revitalize the deceased's ka (life force) and reconnect them with the divine forces that sustained the afterlife.

✧   Funerary Processions and Rituals

Funerary processions and rituals were conducted to accompany the deceased on their journey to the afterlife and ensure a proper burial and commemoration. These rituals involved the participation of family members, priests, and mourners, who would enact various symbolic gestures and recite prayers and spells.

The processions would typically involve the transportation of the deceased's mummy to the burial site, accompanied by mourners and priests carrying offerings, sacred objects, and ritual tools. The rituals performed at the burial site included the dedication of funerary offerings, the recitation of spells for protection, and the pouring of libations to nourish the deceased's ka.

Funerary rituals were essential in ancient Egyptian culture, as they provided a means to honor the deceased, ensure their safe passage into the afterlife, and maintain a lasting connection between the living and the dead.

By understanding the significance and practices of these various types of religious rituals in ancient Egyptian religion, we gain insight into the complex spiritual worldview of the ancient Egyptians and the profound role that rituals played in their daily lives and communal worship. These rituals fostered a sense of connection, reverence, and harmony between the human and divine realms, allowing individuals to partake in the sacred mysteries and experience a profound sense of spiritual fulfillment.

Structure and Components of Religious Rituals

The ancient Egyptian religious system was highly organized and structured, with priests and priestesses playing a central role in conducting rituals and maintaining the divine connection between the human and divine realms. These individuals held esteemed positions within society and were responsible for the performance of various religious ceremonies and practices.

Priests and priestesses served as intermediaries between the people and the gods, facilitating communication and interaction with the divine forces. They underwent rigorous training and education in religious texts, rituals, and sacred practices, ensuring their expertise in the performance of religious duties.

The priests and priestesses were associated with specific temples and dedicated to the service of particular deities. They were responsible for the daily rituals and maintenance of the temple, including the preparation of offerings, the performance of purification rites, and the recitation of prayers and spells.

Priests and priestesses also played a vital role in providing spiritual guidance and counseling to the community. They offered interpretations of dreams, provided advice on religious matters, and participated in healing rituals and ceremonies. Their presence and involvement in the rituals instilled a sense of divine authority and ensured the proper conduct of religious practices.

Offering Rituals and Their Symbolic Significance

Offering rituals held great symbolic significance in ancient Egyptian religious practices. The act of making offerings to the gods was believed to establish a reciprocal relationship between the human and divine realms, where humans expressed gratitude and reverence, and the gods bestowed their blessings and protection in return.

Offerings included a wide range of items, such as food, beverages, incense, flowers, and precious objects. These offerings represented sustenance, nourishment, and beauty, symbolizing the provision of the gods and their benevolence towards humanity.

The type of offering and the manner in which it was presented varied depending on the deity and the specific purpose of the ritual. For example, offerings of bread and beer were commonly made, as they were staple foods in the Egyptian diet. Offerings of meat, vegetables, fruits, and dairy products were also common, reflecting the agricultural abundance of the Nile Valley.

The act of offering itself was performed with utmost care and reverence. Priests and priestesses would approach the sacred altar or shrine, reciting prayers and invocations, and presenting the offerings with clean hands and pure intentions. The offerings were often placed on altars or in designated areas within the temple, allowing the gods to partake of their essence while the physical items were later distributed among the temple staff and sometimes returned to the donors as blessed objects.

Through offering rituals, the ancient Egyptians sought to nourish and please the gods, acknowledging their divine presence and their role as the benefactors of life and creation. These rituals served as a means to establish and maintain a harmonious relationship with the gods, ensuring their continued favor and support for the well-being and prosperity of the community.

Incantations and Invocations During Rituals

Incantations and invocations formed an integral part of ancient Egyptian rituals, serving as powerful tools to invoke the presence and assistance of the gods. These sacred utterances, often accompanied by gestures and ritual actions, were believed to have the ability to call forth divine forces and evoke their intervention in the human realm.

Priests and priestesses were highly skilled in the recitation of these incantations, having memorized and studied the sacred texts that contained the knowledge of the gods' names, attributes, and actions. The precise pronunciation and intonation of the words were considered crucial, as they were believed to carry the inherent power of the divine.

Incantations and invocations served different purposes depending on the ritual context. They could be used to invoke the specific deity being honored, to request divine blessings, to seek protection against malevolent forces, or to express gratitude and praise. These utterances were often poetic and rhythmic, following prescribed formulas and structures that were passed down through generations.

By uttering these sacred words, the priests and priestesses sought to establish a direct line of communication with the gods, transcending the boundaries between the mortal and divine realms. The power of language and sound was believed to hold inherent magical qualities, capable of influencing and shaping the spiritual forces that governed the universe.

Ritual Tools and Objects Used in Ceremonies

Rituals in ancient Egyptian religion involved the use of various tools and objects that held symbolic significance and facilitated the performance of religious ceremonies. These items were carefully crafted and imbued with sacred power, representing the connection between the earthly realm and the divine.

One essential tool used in rituals was the sistrum, a musical instrument associated with the goddess Hathor. The sistrum was a rattle-like instrument with a handle and a metal frame adorned with metal discs or crescents. It was believed to produce a sound that pleased the gods and could ward off evil spirits. The sistrum was often shaken by priestesses during rituals and processions, creating a rhythmic and melodic accompaniment to the prayers and invocations.

Another important ritual object was the ankh, the symbol of life and divine power. The ankh resembled a cross with a loop at the top, representing the eternal cycle of life and death. The ankh was frequently depicted in the hands of gods and goddesses, and it was often held by priests during rituals as a symbol of their connection to the divine and their role in facilitating the flow of life force energy.

Ritual knives, known as ritual blades or flint knives, were also employed in religious ceremonies. These knives, made of flint or other precious materials, were associated with the cutting and offering of food and the symbolic slaying of enemies of the gods. They were ritually purified and consecrated before use and were handled with great care and reverence.

Other ritual objects included sacred vessels for holding and pouring libations, such as the canopic jars used in funerary rituals, and ritual statuettes representing deities or deceased individuals, which were believed to house the divine presence during ceremonies.

These ritual tools and objects were not mere symbols or props but were considered to possess inherent divine power. Their use in rituals facilitated the physical and spiritual connection between the human and divine realms, allowing the priests and priestesses to embody and channel the energies and qualities of the gods they served.

In conclusion, religious rituals in ancient Egyptian culture were facilitated by priests and priestesses who held significant roles in conducting ceremonies and maintaining the divine connection. Offering rituals, accompanied by incantations and invocations, served as a means to establish a reciprocal relationship with the gods, while the use of ritual tools and objects enhanced the symbolic and spiritual dimensions of the rituals. Understanding the roles, symbolism, and practices associated with these elements enriches our understanding of the ancient Egyptian religious experience and underscores the profound importance of rituals in fostering a sense of connection, reverence, and spiritual fulfillment.

Temples: Sacred Spaces for Rituals

Temples held a central and revered position in ancient Egyptian religion, serving as sacred spaces dedicated to the worship of deities and the performance of religious rituals. These architectural marvels were not merely physical structures but were believed to be the dwelling places of the gods themselves, where the divine and mortal realms intersected.

The primary purpose of temples was to provide a dedicated space for the rituals and ceremonies that formed the core of Egyptian religious practice. These rituals were believed to maintain cosmic order and harmony, ensuring the continued functioning of the universe and the well-being of both gods and humans.

Temples were considered the earthly abodes of the gods, serving as gateways for divine energy and presence to manifest in the human realm. They were meticulously designed and constructed to reflect the grandeur and power of the gods they honored, creating a conducive environment for communication and communion with the divine.

Architecture and Layout of Temples

The architecture and layout of temples in ancient Egypt were carefully planned and executed, embodying both religious symbolism and practical functionality. Temples were often monumental structures characterized by massive stone walls, towering pylons, and elaborate entrance gateways.

The temple complex typically consisted of several key components, including an outer courtyard, a hypostyle hall, a sanctuary, and sometimes additional chapels, shrines, and storage areas. The layout was designed to facilitate the movement of priests, ritual participants, and sacred objects throughout the various stages of the religious ceremonies.

The entrance to the temple was marked by monumental pylons, colossal statues, and intricate relief carvings that depicted scenes of religious significance. The outer courtyard served as a gathering space for worshippers, where they could participate in public ceremonies and observe the rituals performed by the priests.

The hypostyle hall, characterized by rows of massive columns, provided a transition between the outer world and the sacred inner sanctuaries. This space was used for communal rituals and processions, with the columns symbolizing the primeval reeds from which the world was believed to have emerged.

The sanctuary, also known as the Holy of Holies, housed the cult image of the deity to whom the temple was dedicated. Access to this sacred inner sanctum was strictly limited to the high-ranking priests, who would perform rituals and offer prayers directly in the presence of the deity. The sanctity of the sanctuary was emphasized through dim lighting, veiled entrances, and the use of precious materials and ornamentation.

Roles and Responsibilities of Temple Personnel

Temples required a dedicated workforce to ensure the smooth functioning of rituals and daily operations. The personnel associated with temples included priests, priestesses, temple staff, and craftsmen. Each individual had specific roles and responsibilities that contributed to the overall functioning and maintenance of the temple.

Priests and priestesses were the primary religious functionaries within the temple. They were responsible for conducting rituals, offering prayers and invocations, and maintaining the sacred spaces and objects. Priests underwent rigorous training in religious texts, rituals, and the proper performance of ceremonies.

Temple staff included scribes, musicians, singers, and attendants who supported the priests and priestesses in their duties. Scribes recorded the details of rituals and maintained temple records, while musicians and singers provided melodic accompaniment to the rituals, enhancing their spiritual ambiance. Attendants were responsible for the upkeep of the temple, including cleaning, provisioning, and organizing ritual objects.

Craftsmen played a crucial role in temple construction and maintenance. They were skilled artisans who carved reliefs, sculpted statues, painted murals, and crafted ritual objects. Their expertise ensured the aesthetic beauty and symbolic significance of the temple's artistic elements, contributing to the overall spiritual atmosphere of the sacred space.

Temple Rituals and their Connection to Cosmic Order

The rituals performed within temples were intricately connected to the concept of cosmic order and the Egyptian understanding of the universe. These rituals aimed to maintain maat, the fundamental principle of harmony and balance in Egyptian cosmology.

The rituals conducted in temples were seen as microcosmic reflections of the cosmic order. Through precise and meticulous performances, the priests sought to reenact the divine acts that had established the world, reestablishing and reinforcing the harmonious relationship between the gods and humanity.

Key temple rituals included daily offerings, purification ceremonies, processions, and festivals dedicated to specific deities. Daily offerings consisted of food, drink, and incense presented to the gods as a gesture of sustenance, gratitude, and devotion. Purification rituals involved cleansing the sacred spaces, the priests, and the ritual objects to ensure their spiritual purity and readiness for contact with the divine.

Processions, both within the temple complex and outside in public spaces, allowed for the active participation of the community in religious celebrations. These processions often involved carrying the cult image of the deity, accompanied by music, chanting, and elaborate displays of religious iconography.

Festivals held at specific times throughout the year were grand events that brought together the entire community in celebration of the deities. These festivals included rituals, performances, and processions that honored the gods, commemorated significant mythological events, and reaffirmed the cyclical nature of the cosmos.

Through these rituals, the temple served as a microcosm of the cosmos, a place where the divine and human realms intersected, and where the principles of maat were upheld and celebrated.

In conclusion, temples in ancient Egyptian religion held immense significance as sacred spaces dedicated to the performance of religious rituals. Their architecture and layout were meticulously designed to facilitate the movement of worshippers and the communication between the human and divine realms. The roles of priests, priestesses, and temple personnel were crucial in ensuring the smooth functioning of rituals and the maintenance of sacred spaces. Temple rituals, deeply intertwined with the concept of cosmic order, were enacted to uphold maat and establish a harmonious relationship between the gods and humanity. Understanding the purpose, symbolism, and practices associated with temples provides valuable insights into the religious beliefs and practices of ancient Egypt, fostering a deeper appreciation for their rich and complex spiritual traditions.

Symbolism and Symbolic Actions in Rituals

Rituals in ancient Egyptian religion were replete with symbolic gestures and movements that conveyed profound meanings and facilitated a connection between the participants and the divine realm. These symbolic actions were carefully choreographed and performed with intention and precision.

One notable example of symbolic gestures is the act of prostration or bowing. Bowing down before deities or sacred objects demonstrated humility, reverence, and submission to the divine authority. It symbolized the acknowledgment of the gods' power and the supplicant's willingness to surrender to their will.

Another symbolic movement commonly observed in Egyptian rituals was the act of circumambulation. Participants would walk in a circular path around a sacred object or space, such as a shrine or an altar. This circular motion symbolized the cyclical nature of life, the eternal nature of the cosmos, and the unending cycle of birth, death, and rebirth.

Hand gestures, known as mudras, were also employed to convey specific meanings during rituals. For instance, the ankh gesture, where the thumb and forefinger are held together while the other fingers are extended, symbolized life and fertility. By performing these mudras, participants invoked the symbolic power associated with the gestures, aligning themselves with the intended qualities or energies.

Symbolic Objects and their Roles in Rituals

Symbolic objects played a significant role in Egyptian rituals, representing various aspects of the divine and embodying the qualities and powers associated with specific deities. These objects were carefully selected, crafted, and consecrated to enhance the ritual experience and facilitate the communication between the human and divine realms.

One such object is the sistrum, a musical instrument resembling a metal hoop with metal crossbars and jingling discs. The sistrum was often associated with the goddess Hathor and was used in her worship rituals. Its sound was believed to ward off evil and bring about divine blessings. The rhythmic shaking of the sistrum during rituals created a unique auditory experience, symbolizing the presence of the goddess and invoking her protective and nurturing qualities.

Another symbolic object frequently employed in rituals was the ritual knife, known as a khopesh. The khopesh, with its curved blade and ceremonial decorations, symbolized the power and authority of the priests and the gods. It was used in purification rituals and sacrifices, representing the act of cutting away impurities and offering them to the divine.

Symbolic Meanings of Offerings and their Connections to Deities

Offerings were a fundamental aspect of Egyptian rituals, and the choice of offerings held deep symbolic significance. Different types of offerings were associated with specific deities, reflecting their domains, characteristics, and desires.

Food offerings, such as bread, meat, and fruits, were commonly presented to the gods. Bread, for example, symbolized sustenance and nourishment, and its offering represented the provision of sustenance to the gods and the reciprocity of their blessings. Meat offerings were associated with sacrifice, signifying the giving of life to sustain the divine and establishing a reciprocal relationship between humans and the gods.

Libations, the pouring of liquids such as water, milk, wine, or oil, were another important form of offering. Libations represented the act of pouring forth life-giving substances and were believed to convey the essence of these substances to the gods. The choice of liquid and the manner of pouring held symbolic meaning. For instance, water represented purity and regeneration, while wine symbolized joy and celebration.

Offerings also extended beyond physical objects and included symbolic gestures and acts. Lighting incense, for instance, symbolized the purification of the ritual space and the ascent of prayers to the heavens. Burning candles represented illumination, enlightenment, and the presence of the divine light.

Understanding the symbolism and symbolic actions in rituals provides insight into the complex layers of meaning and intention behind ancient Egyptian religious practices. By engaging in symbolic gestures, utilizing symbolic objects, and offering items with symbolic significance, participants actively participated in the ritual process and established a connection with the divine realm. These symbols and actions served as powerful tools for expressing devotion, invoking divine presence, and aligning oneself with the cosmic order of the universe.

Examples:

Problem: Analyze the symbolic gestures and movements performed during an ancient Egyptian ritual. What meanings do these gestures convey? How do they contribute to the overall ritual experience?

Exercise: Choose a deity from another mythological tradition and explore the symbolic objects associated with them. Compare and contrast these objects with those used in ancient Egyptian rituals. How do they differ in terms of symbolism and cultural context?

Discussion: Discuss the symbolic meanings behind specific offerings in ancient Egyptian rituals. How do these offerings establish a connection between humans and the deities? Can you think of any modern-day rituals or practices that involve symbolic offerings?

Religious Rituals and Social Order

Religious rituals in ancient societies, including those of ancient Egypt, played a crucial role in shaping and maintaining social order. These rituals were not merely expressions of personal piety or devotion but were deeply embedded in the social fabric of the civilization. They served as powerful mechanisms for reinforcing social hierarchies, defining group identities, and exerting control over individuals and communities. This section will explore the intricate relationship between religious rituals and social order, focusing on the reinforcing of social hierarchies, inclusiveness and exclusivity, and the use of rituals for political and ideological control.

Rituals as a Means of Reinforcing Social Hierarchies

Religious rituals in ancient Egypt were intricately connected to the prevailing social hierarchies of the time. The performance of rituals and the participation in specific rites were often contingent upon an individual's social status and role within the community. High-ranking officials, priests, and members of the royal family would have exclusive access to certain rituals and ceremonies, while the general population had limited participation.

For example, during the Sed Festival, a major ritual associated with kingship, only the reigning pharaoh could engage in the most significant aspects of the ceremony. This emphasized the divine authority and special status of the king, solidifying his position as the central figure in religious and social life. The participation of lower-ranking officials and the general public was limited to specific roles and spectating, reinforcing the hierarchical structure of society.

Inclusiveness and Exclusivity in Religious Rituals

While religious rituals often reinforced social hierarchies, they also had elements of inclusiveness and exclusivity. Certain rituals and festivals were designed to involve the broader community, allowing individuals from various social strata to participate and share in the collective religious experience.

For instance, during the Festival of Bastet, individuals from all walks of life could partake in the festivities, offering their devotion to the goddess Bastet. This inclusivity fostered a sense of unity and shared identity among the participants, transcending social divisions and promoting a sense of community.

However, it is important to note that even in inclusive rituals, there were often limitations and restrictions based on gender, age, and social status. For instance, certain rituals may have been exclusively reserved for men or women, or only certain age groups were allowed to actively participate. These exclusions reinforced social norms and maintained the existing social order within the religious context.

Rituals as a Tool for Political and Ideological Control

Religious rituals were not only mechanisms for reinforcing social hierarchies but also served as powerful tools for political and ideological control. The ruling elite often utilized rituals to legitimize their authority and consolidate their power over the populace. By associating themselves with the deities and performing rituals in their honor, rulers could claim a divine mandate, bolster their legitimacy, and justify their political dominance.

For example, pharaohs were not only seen as political leaders but also as divine representatives on Earth. Through elaborate rituals and ceremonies, pharaohs established their connection to the gods, reinforcing the belief in their divine right to rule. The performance of rituals, such as the Heb-Sed or the Coronation Ritual, emphasized the pharaoh's central role in maintaining cosmic balance and upholding Maat, the divine order.

Furthermore, religious rituals were often utilized to promote specific ideologies and propagate certain values and beliefs. Temples, as centers of religious life, became platforms for disseminating ideological messages to the masses. Through rituals and inscriptions, temple priests and officials could shape public opinion, reinforce societal norms, and maintain the existing power structures.

Examples:

Problem: Analyze the role of religious rituals in reinforcing social hierarchies in ancient Egypt. Discuss how different social groups had varying degrees of access and participation in rituals. Provide examples to support your argument.

Exercise: Research a specific religious ritual from another ancient civilization and compare its role in reinforcing social order to that of ancient Egypt. Identify similarities and differences in how rituals were used to shape social hierarchies and maintain stability.

Discussion: Discuss the ethical implications of using religious rituals as a tool for political and ideological control. Consider the potential benefits and drawbacks of such practices, drawing examples from historical and contemporary contexts.

Changes in Religious Rituals over Time

Religious rituals, like any cultural practice, are not static but evolve and change over time. In the case of ancient Egypt, the religious rituals underwent significant transformations from the Old Kingdom to the New Kingdom, influenced by external factors and internal developments. This section will explore the changes in religious rituals over time, focusing on the evolution from the Old Kingdom to the New Kingdom, the influence of foreign cultures on Egyptian religious practices, and the decline and transformation of rituals in late Egyptian history.

Evolution of Religious Rituals from the Old Kingdom to the New Kingdom

The religious rituals of ancient Egypt evolved and adapted throughout its long history. The Old Kingdom (2686-2181 BCE) was marked by a focus on mortuary rituals and the worship of the sun god Ra. Temples during this period were relatively simple structures dedicated to the pharaohs and their funerary cults.

However, with the rise of the New Kingdom (1550-1070 BCE), there was a shift in religious practices. The pharaohs, particularly during the reign of Amenhotep IV/Akhenaten, introduced a new monotheistic religious system centered around the worship of the Aten, the sun disc. This period witnessed significant changes in ritual practices, including the construction of new temples and the reorganization of religious hierarchies.

Influence of Foreign Cultures on Egyptian Religious Practices

Egypt's interactions with foreign cultures, through trade, conquest, and diplomacy, had a profound impact on its religious rituals. The influx of foreign ideas and deities led to syncretism, the merging of Egyptian and foreign religious beliefs and practices. For example, during the Greco-Roman period, Egyptian religious practices became intertwined with Hellenistic and Roman religious traditions.

The cult of Isis, originating in Egypt but widely popular in the Greco-Roman world, exemplifies this syncretism. Egyptian rituals associated with Isis underwent adaptations and assimilated aspects of Greek and Roman religious practices. The spread of these syncretic rituals demonstrates the dynamic nature of religious practices and the ability of ancient Egyptian religion to absorb and incorporate foreign influences.

Decline and Transformation of Religious Rituals in Late Egyptian History

In the later periods of Egyptian history, such as the Third Intermediate Period (1070-664 BCE) and the Late Period (664-332 BCE), the religious landscape of Egypt underwent further changes. Political instability, foreign invasions, and the decline of central authority impacted religious rituals.

During these periods, the authority of the pharaoh diminished, and the role of local cults and priesthoods gained prominence. Temples and rituals became more localized, with a focus on regional deities and practices. This decentralization led to variations in religious rituals across different regions of Egypt.

The conquest of Egypt by Alexander the Great and the subsequent rule of the Ptolemies brought significant Greek influence to Egyptian religious practices. Greek deities were syncretized with Egyptian gods, resulting in new rituals and cults that reflected this cultural fusion.

Examples:

Problem: Compare and contrast the religious rituals of the Old Kingdom and the New Kingdom. Discuss the key changes and developments that occurred during this period, highlighting the shift in focus and ritual practices.

Exercise: Research and analyze the impact of the Atenist religious reforms introduced by Akhenaten. Discuss the changes in religious rituals, temple architecture, and the role of priests during this period.

Discussion: Debate the influence of foreign cultures on Egyptian religious rituals. Consider the positive and negative aspects of syncretism, using examples from the Greco-Roman period and the syncretic cults of Isis and Serapis.

Exercise: Select a specific late Egyptian period, such as the Third Intermediate Period or the Late Period, and examine the changes in religious rituals during this time. Discuss the reasons for the decline and transformation of rituals, including political and social factors.

Through the study of the evolution, influences, and decline of religious rituals in ancient Egypt, students can gain a deeper understanding of the dynamic nature of religious practices and their interaction with cultural, political, and social contexts.

Comparative Analysis of Rituals in Other Cultures

Religious rituals are not exclusive to ancient Egypt; they are found in various ancient civilizations and continue to be practiced in contemporary cultures around the world. This section will provide a comparative analysis of Egyptian rituals with rituals in other ancient civilizations and explore the universal elements and themes that transcend cultural boundaries.

Comparison of Egyptian Rituals with Rituals in Other Ancient Civilizations

✧ Mesopotamian Rituals:

Mesopotamia, the land between the Tigris and Euphrates rivers, was home to ancient civilizations like Sumer, Akkad, and Babylon. The religious rituals of these civilizations shared some similarities with Egyptian rituals, such as the use of temples as sacred spaces and the belief in the existence of multiple deities. However, there were also notable differences in the focus of rituals and the specific practices associated with them. For example, Mesopotamian rituals placed a strong emphasis on divination and the role of priests as intermediaries between humans and the gods.

✧ Greek Rituals:

Ancient Greek religious rituals revolved around the worship of various gods and goddesses, and they were characterized by elaborate ceremonies and sacrifices. While the Greeks had different deities and myths from the Egyptians, both cultures shared a belief in the importance of maintaining harmonious relationships with the divine through rituals. Greek rituals often took place in open-air sanctuaries, while Egyptian rituals were predominantly conducted in temple complexes. Additionally, the Greek concept of rituals focused more on civic and communal practices, whereas Egyptian rituals were closely tied to the pharaoh and his role as the intermediary between the divine and the people.

Exploration of Universal Elements and Themes in Religious Rituals

✧ Mythic Narratives:

Across different cultures, religious rituals often draw upon mythic narratives that explain the creation of the world, the actions of deities, and the relationship between humans and the divine. These narratives provide the foundation for rituals and serve to reinforce cultural and religious beliefs.

✧ Symbolic Actions:

Symbolism is a fundamental aspect of religious rituals worldwide. Symbolic actions, such as gestures, movements, and the use of ritual objects, are employed to communicate and enact spiritual concepts. These symbolic actions transcend cultural boundaries and serve as a means of connecting with the sacred.

✧ Communal Participation:

Religious rituals often involve communal participation, bringing individuals together as a collective body. Through shared rituals, communities reaffirm their shared beliefs, values, and social bonds. Whether it is the congregational prayers of Islam or the group chanting and dancing in Shamanic rituals, communal participation is a universal feature of religious rituals.

Examples:

Problem: Compare and contrast the rituals associated with the worship of deities in ancient Egypt and ancient Mesopotamia. Discuss the similarities and differences in terms of rituals, temple architecture, and the role of priests.

Exercise: Research and analyze a specific ritual, such as the annual Eleusinian Mysteries in ancient Greece, and compare it with an Egyptian ritual of your choice. Discuss the significance, symbolism, and participation in both rituals.

Discussion: Explore the universal themes and elements found in religious rituals across different cultures. Engage in a discussion on the importance of symbolism, mythic narratives, and communal participation in shaping and reinforcing religious practices.

Exercise: Choose a contemporary religious ritual or ceremony from a culture or tradition of your choice and identify the universal elements and themes present in the ritual. Reflect on how these universal elements connect the ritual to the broader human experience.

Conclusion

Throughout this chapter, we have delved into the intricate world of religious rituals in ancient Egypt. We explored the various types of rituals, from daily and seasonal ceremonies to funerary rites, and examined their significance within the context of ancient Egyptian religious beliefs and practices. The iconography, symbolism, and actions associated with these rituals provided a deeper understanding of the complex relationship between humans and the divine.

In ancient Egyptian religion, rituals played a pivotal role in establishing and maintaining connections with the gods. They were seen as pathways for communication, devotion, and seeking divine blessings. Through offerings, purifications, invocations, and symbolic actions, individuals and communities engaged in rituals to honor the gods, express gratitude, seek protection, and ensure cosmic harmony. The visual representations and symbolic objects used in these rituals served as powerful conduits for spiritual experiences and transformative encounters with the divine.

Reflection on the Enduring Significance of Rituals in Contemporary Spiritual Practices

While ancient Egyptian religion may belong to the distant past, the enduring significance of religious rituals is evident in contemporary spiritual practices across various traditions. Rituals continue to serve as profound ways to connect with the divine, cultivate spiritual experiences, and reinforce a sense of belonging and purpose within communities.

In the realms of Witchcraft, Divination, Herbalism, Shamanism, and Ecospirituality, rituals are integral to the spiritual journey. Whether it is the casting of spells, the reading of Tarot cards, the creation of herbal remedies, the trance-inducing practices of shamans, or the sacred ceremonies honoring the Earth, rituals provide a container for intention, energy, and transformation. They facilitate a sense of connection with the spiritual realm, the natural world, and the self.

Exercises and Activities to Deepen Understanding and Engagement with Religious Rituals

To deepen your understanding and engagement with religious rituals, here are some exercises and activities to explore:

✧ Ritual Observation and Analysis:
Choose a ritual from a specific tradition or culture and attend or observe it, either in person or through video recordings. Analyze the various elements, symbols, and actions involved. Reflect on the intention behind each aspect of the ritual and its significance within the broader religious context.

✧ Personal Ritual Creation:
Create your own personal ritual for a specific intention or purpose. Consider the symbols, actions, and objects you would incorporate and the steps you would follow. Reflect on how this self-created ritual helps you establish a connection with the divine or the spiritual realm.

✧ Comparative Analysis:
Select two different religious traditions or cultures and compare their rituals. Explore the similarities and differences in terms of symbolism, actions, and the role of participants. Reflect on the cultural, historical, and theological factors that shape these rituals.

✧ Ethical Considerations:
Engage in a discussion or written reflection on the ethical implications of religious rituals. Consider topics such as inclusivity, cultural appropriation, and power dynamics within ritual spaces. Reflect on how rituals can foster understanding and respect while navigating potential challenges.

By actively engaging with these exercises and activities, you will not only deepen your understanding of religious rituals but also cultivate a more profound connection with your own spiritual journey. The exploration of rituals invites us to reflect on our relationship with the divine, the natural world, and ourselves, fostering personal growth, and collective transformation.

In conclusion, religious rituals have been and continue to be powerful vehicles for spiritual connection, transformation, and the affirmation of cultural and communal identities. By studying the rituals of ancient Egypt and exploring their significance in contemporary spiritual practices, we gain insights into the diverse ways in which humans seek to engage with the sacred, honor their beliefs, and navigate the mysteries of existence. Through these rituals, we bridge the gap between the physical and the spiritual, and embrace the profound wisdom that lies within the realm of religious experience.

Part 5: Overview of Religious Rituals and Ceremonies in Ancient Egypt

In Part 5 of our exploration into the multifaceted world of ancient Egyptian religion, we embark on a comprehensive overview of the religious rituals and ceremonies that formed the backbone of this rich and intricate belief system. From the daily practices to the grand annual celebrations, these rituals were not only essential for maintaining divine connections but also played a vital role in shaping social order, political structures, and cultural identity.

Ancient Egypt was a civilization deeply rooted in religious devotion and the belief in the interplay between the mortal and the divine. The rituals and ceremonies performed by the ancient Egyptians were not superficial gestures but intricate and purposeful actions that sought to establish and nurture a profound connection with the gods and goddesses who governed various aspects of life.

Our journey into the realm of ancient Egyptian religious rituals begins with an exploration of the daily practices and offerings that formed the foundation of religious life. These rituals, such as morning and evening offerings and purification rites, were performed by individuals and communities to express reverence, gratitude, and seek blessings for themselves, their families, and the kingdom as a whole.

Moving beyond the daily routines, we delve into the grandeur of Egyptian temples, the sacred spaces where the rituals and ceremonies unfolded. These architectural marvels were not only awe-inspiring in their design but also played a pivotal role in fostering the connection between humans and the divine. We study their purpose, architectural features, and the responsibilities of the temple personnel who oversaw these sacred spaces.

No exploration of ancient Egyptian religion would be complete without an in-depth analysis of the festivals and annual religious celebrations that marked the calendar year. These festive occasions were characterized by elaborate rituals, processions, and communal gatherings, all designed to honor the gods, rejuvenate cosmic energies, and reinforce social cohesion.

Our investigation further leads us to the unique institution of divine kingship, where the pharaohs were seen as living embodiments of divine power. We explore the rituals and ceremonies associated with the pharaoh's role as a deity and the interplay between political authority and religious responsibility.

Moreover, we uncover the profound connection between the pharaohs and the gods, examining the rituals and cultic statues that embodied this sacred bond. We analyze the spiritual and political dimensions of this relationship and its implications for ancient Egyptian society.

Expanding our scope, we investigate the influence of Egyptian religion on other cultures, exploring the syncretism and exchanges that occurred with neighboring civilizations. Through this comparative analysis, we gain a deeper understanding of the interconnectedness of ancient belief systems and the cross-cultural fertilization of religious ideas.

Finally, we reflect on the enduring legacy of ancient Egyptian religious rituals in contemporary spirituality and the ways in which they continue to inspire and influence modern interpretations. We engage in critical thinking and discussion, exploring exercises and activities that allow us to deepen our understanding and connection with the profound rituals and ceremonies of ancient Egypt.

In Part 5, we invite you to journey through the sacred rituals and ceremonies of ancient Egypt, unraveling their significance, symbolism, and enduring impact on the lives of the ancient Egyptians and the broader human experience.

Chapter 15: Role of Temples as Sacred Spaces and Their Architectural Features

The ancient Egyptian civilization is renowned for its elaborate and magnificent temples, which served as sacred spaces dedicated to the worship of the gods. These temples were not merely architectural marvels but held immense religious, social, and cultural significance in the ancient Egyptian society. In this chapter, we will delve into the role of temples as sacred spaces and explore their architectural features, shedding light on their profound impact on the religious practices of the ancient Egyptians.

Significance of Temples in Ancient Egyptian Religion

Divine Abodes: Temples were considered the earthly abodes of the gods, where their presence was believed to reside. These sacred spaces were constructed with meticulous precision and adorned with intricate carvings and paintings, symbolizing the divine nature of the deities worshipped within.

Center of Religious Life: Temples served as the focal points of religious life in ancient Egypt. They were the sites of daily rituals, offerings, and ceremonies performed by the priests and priestesses on behalf of the pharaoh and the community. These rituals aimed to establish and maintain a connection between the human and divine realms, ensuring the harmony and well-being of the cosmos.

Gateway to the Afterlife: Temples were closely associated with the concept of the afterlife in ancient Egyptian belief. They housed sacred chapels and shrines dedicated to the veneration of deceased ancestors and provided a space for funerary rituals and offerings. Temples played a crucial role in facilitating the journey of the soul to the realm of the gods and ensured the eternal sustenance of the deceased.

Role of Sacred Spaces in Religious Practices

Sanctity and Purity: Temples were regarded as sanctified spaces, separated from the mundane world. They were constructed with careful consideration of sacred geometry and aligned with cosmic principles. The architecture, layout, and decoration of the temples reflected the cosmic order and aimed to create an atmosphere of purity and divine presence.

Ritual Performance: Temples served as stages for the performance of intricate religious rituals. These rituals involved purification ceremonies, processions, offerings, incantations, and invocations, all meticulously orchestrated to honor the gods and maintain cosmic balance. The architectural features of temples, such as colonnades, courtyards, and inner chambers, were designed to accommodate and enhance the ceremonial activities.

Community Gathering: Temples were not only places of worship but also centers for communal gathering and social cohesion. People from all walks of life, including priests, nobles, and commoners, participated in temple rituals and festivals. Temples provided a sense of community and served as venues for social interaction, where individuals could come together to celebrate, seek divine guidance, and engage in acts of devotion.

In this chapter, we will explore the architectural elements of ancient Egyptian temples, such as pylons, hypostyle halls, courtyards, and sanctuaries, examining their symbolic meanings and functional roles within the religious context. We will also analyze the spatial organization of temples and their alignment with astronomical phenomena, highlighting the ancient Egyptians' profound understanding of cosmology and their desire to reflect the celestial order in earthly structures.

Through the study of temples as sacred spaces and their architectural features, we gain a deeper appreciation for the central role of religious practices in ancient Egyptian society. We come to understand the intricate relationship between the physical and the spiritual, the human and the divine, and the enduring legacy of these magnificent structures that continue to captivate and inspire awe in the modern world.

Purpose and Function of Temples

In ancient Egypt, temples served as sacred spaces dedicated to the worship of the gods. They were constructed as physical manifestations of the divine presence, with the primary purpose of housing the statues or cult images representing the deities. These statues were believed to embody the essence and power of the gods, and their presence within the temple sanctuaries established a direct connection between the earthly realm and the divine realm.

Housing the Divine Statues

Temples were designed with specific areas known as sanctuaries or naos to house the divine statues. These sanctuaries were usually located at the innermost part of the temple, accessible only to the highest-ranking priests. The statues were meticulously carved and adorned with precious materials, representing the gods in their iconic forms. The statues were considered the physical embodiment of the gods and were believed to receive the prayers, offerings, and rituals performed by the priests on behalf of the community.

Establishing a Direct Connection with the Divine

By housing the divine statues, temples provided a physical space where the gods could be approached and worshipped. Ancient Egyptians believed that the presence of the gods resided within the sanctuaries, and rituals conducted within these spaces were believed to establish a direct connection between the human and divine realms. Through offerings, prayers, and ceremonial acts, the priests aimed to maintain the cosmic order and seek divine favor, ensuring the well-being of both the human and divine worlds.

Centers of Administration and Economic Activities

Temples in ancient Egypt played a multifaceted role beyond their religious functions. They were not only places of worship but also served as centers of administration and economic activities.

Role of Temples in Managing Land and Resources

The temples were bestowed with vast land holdings, often granted as divine gifts or acquired through donations and endowments from the pharaoh, nobility, and the general populace. The temple estates encompassed agricultural lands, orchards, vineyards, and livestock. Temples administered these lands and managed the labor necessary for their cultivation. The produce and resources generated from these lands were used to support the temple operations, including the provision of offerings to the gods, maintenance of the temple structures, and support for the clergy.

Support from the Community through Donations

Temples relied on the support and contributions from the community for their sustenance. The ancient Egyptian society recognized the importance of maintaining the temples and the divine favor associated with them. Individuals, both wealthy and humble, made regular donations of goods, offerings, and even financial resources to the temples. These donations ranged from simple foodstuffs to valuable treasures, and they were seen as acts of devotion and a means to earn favor from the gods. In return, the temples provided various services to the community, such as healing, oracles, and blessings, reinforcing the reciprocal relationship between the temples and the people.

Through the study of the purpose and function of temples in ancient Egypt, we gain insight into the complex interplay between religion, administration, and economy in ancient Egyptian society. Temples were not only centers of religious devotion but also vital institutions that facilitated the governance of land and resources, as well as the fostering of communal cohesion through acts of generosity and support. The temples stood as prominent symbols of divine presence and power, serving as pillars of stability and order in the ancient Egyptian civilization.

Examples:

Problem: Analyze the role of the divine statues in the sanctuaries of ancient Egyptian temples. How did these statues contribute to the religious practices and the relationship between the human and divine realms?

Exercise: Imagine you are a high-ranking priest responsible for the administration of a temple. Develop a plan outlining strategies to manage the temple's land holdings effectively and ensure the economic stability of the institution. Consider factors such as agricultural practices, labor management, and resource allocation.

Discussion: Engage in a group discussion on the significance of community donations to the temples. Discuss the motivations behind these acts of generosity and their impact on the temple's operations and the relationship between the temples and the community.

By engaging with these examples, problems, and exercises, students can critically analyze the multifaceted nature of temples in ancient Egypt and explore the intricate connections between religion, administration, and community dynamics.

Architectural Features of Temples

The temples of ancient Egypt were meticulously designed and constructed with careful attention to their layout and architectural features. These architectural elements played a significant role in creating sacred spaces and facilitating the rituals and ceremonies conducted within the temple complex.

Axis of Symmetry and Sacred Geometry

One of the key design principles observed in ancient Egyptian temple architecture was the concept of axis of symmetry. Temples were often aligned along an east-west axis, with the main entrance facing east to greet the rising sun. This alignment symbolized the connection between the divine and cosmic forces, as the sun was associated with the powerful solar deities.

Sacred geometry, based on precise mathematical proportions and ratios, also influenced the temple layout. The use of geometric principles, such as the golden ratio or the application of harmonic ratios, was believed to imbue the structures with harmonious and divine qualities. These geometric principles were applied to the proportions of the temple's columns, walls, and courtyards, creating a sense of balance and aesthetic harmony.

Different Sections of the Temple Complex

Temple complexes were typically composed of several distinct sections, each serving a specific purpose in the religious and administrative functions of the temple.

a. Pylon and Courtyard: The entrance to the temple complex was often marked by large monumental gateways known as pylons. These gateways were adorned with intricate reliefs and carvings depicting scenes of religious significance. Beyond the pylons, there was an expansive courtyard where various rituals and processions took place. The courtyard was an open space that allowed worshippers to gather and participate in religious activities.

b. Hypostyle Hall: Moving further into the temple complex, one would enter the hypostyle hall. This grand hall was characterized by rows of massive columns supporting the roof. The columns were often intricately decorated with reliefs and hieroglyphic inscriptions, narrating mythological stories and emphasizing the divine nature of the temple.

c. Sanctuary and Inner Chambers: At the heart of the temple complex lay the sanctuary, also known as the naos, which housed the cult statues of the gods. The sanctuary was a restricted area accessible only to the highest-ranking priests. It contained the most sacred shrine and was believed to be the dwelling place of the deity. Surrounding the sanctuary, there were additional chambers used for storing ritual objects and performing specific ceremonies.

d. Offering Chapels and Secondary Structures: Temples often had separate chapels dedicated to specific deities or to honor the pharaoh. These chapels were smaller in size and served as spaces for offering prayers and making offerings to the gods. Additionally, temples had secondary structures such as storerooms, administrative offices, and workshops to support the daily operations of the temple complex.

Examples:

Problem: Analyze the significance of the east-west alignment in ancient Egyptian temple architecture. How did this alignment reflect the religious beliefs and cosmological concepts of the ancient Egyptians?

Exercise: Create a scaled model or architectural drawing of an ancient Egyptian temple, emphasizing the axis of symmetry and the geometric principles used in its design. Explain the rationale behind your design choices and how they relate to the religious and aesthetic principles of ancient Egyptian temple architecture.

Discussion: Engage in a group discussion on the symbolism and purpose of the different sections of a temple complex. Debate the role of the sanctuary and the restricted access to the inner chambers. Discuss the implications of this exclusivity on the relationship between the priesthood, the pharaoh, and the general worshipper.

Temple decorations and reliefs

The ancient Egyptian temples were adorned with intricate decorations and reliefs, which served as a visual language conveying religious and mythological concepts. Symbolism and iconography played a significant role in temple artwork, allowing worshippers to connect with the divine, understand complex religious narratives, and participate in rituals on a symbolic level.

Exploring the Esoteric Wisdom of Ancient Egypt for Modern Spirituality

Symbolism in temple artwork often revolved around the natural world and cosmic order. For example, the use of lotus flowers and papyrus plants represented the fertile and life-giving aspects of the Nile River. Animals such as falcons, snakes, and lions were associated with specific deities and symbolized their characteristics and powers. The representation of human figures in specific poses and with specific attributes conveyed their roles as deities, pharaohs, or priests.

Iconography in temple reliefs consisted of a standardized set of symbols and visual conventions that conveyed specific meanings. Hieroglyphic inscriptions accompanied many reliefs, providing textual explanations and adding another layer of significance to the artwork. Through the careful arrangement of symbols, poses, and hieroglyphs, the artists created a cohesive visual language that communicated the religious beliefs and mythological narratives of ancient Egypt.

Depictions of Rituals, Gods, and Divine Narratives

Temple reliefs often depicted various religious rituals, allowing worshippers to visually witness and participate in the sacred actions. These depictions served as instructional aids, guiding priests and worshippers in the proper performance of rituals and offering insights into the cosmological and spiritual significance of these practices.

Ritual scenes commonly depicted the different stages of rituals, including purification, offering, and invocation of the deity. The artists portrayed priests in specific attire and positions, engaging in precise gestures and actions that aligned with the established religious protocols. These scenes provided a visual representation of the correct procedures, ensuring the continuity and accuracy of the rituals across generations.

Gods and goddesses were prominent subjects in temple reliefs, showcasing their divine attributes, roles, and relationships. These representations were carefully crafted to highlight the distinct characteristics of each deity and communicate their specific powers and responsibilities. For example, the powerful sun god Ra might be depicted with a solar disk on his head, symbolizing his role as the bringer of light and life.

Divine narratives and mythological stories were also depicted on temple walls, often spanning multiple reliefs. These narratives included creation myths, tales of the gods' triumphs and conflicts, and stories of the pharaoh's divine lineage and interactions with the gods. By depicting these narratives, the temple reliefs served as visual storytelling devices, reinforcing the religious and cultural narratives that shaped the ancient Egyptian worldview.

Examples:

Problem: Analyze the symbolism and iconography in a specific temple relief, discussing how the arrangement of symbols and figures conveys religious and mythological concepts. Provide a detailed interpretation of the relief, considering the cultural and religious context.

Exercise: Choose a specific ritual depicted in a temple relief and recreate it through a series of drawings or a small-scale diorama. Explain the significance of each step in the ritual and the symbolism behind the gestures and offerings.

Discussion: Engage in a group discussion on the role of temple decorations and reliefs in fostering a spiritual connection between worshippers and the divine. Explore the challenges and opportunities of using visual representations to convey complex religious ideas. Discuss the potential variations in interpretations of temple artwork and the implications for our understanding of ancient Egyptian religion.

By actively participating in these examples, problems, and exercises, students can delve into the rich symbolism, iconography, and narrative representations found in temple decorations and reliefs. They can develop a deeper understanding of the religious beliefs, rituals, and mythological narratives of ancient Egypt, while also honing their critical thinking skills and engaging in meaningful discussions about the significance of visual representations in religious contexts.

Roles and Responsibilities of Temple Personnel

In ancient Egypt, the role of priests and priestesses was central to the functioning of temples and the performance of religious rituals. These individuals underwent rigorous training and education to prepare them for their sacred duties. Priests and priestesses were often selected from specific families or lineages, with the knowledge and traditions of priesthood passed down through generations.

The training of temple personnel involved the study of religious texts, rituals, and the proper performance of offerings and ceremonies. They learned the intricate details of temple protocols, including the purification rituals, the correct recitation of prayers and invocations, and the handling of sacred objects. The priests and priestesses also received instruction in the mythological narratives and cosmological beliefs that underpinned the religious practices.

Ritual Duties and Responsibilities

Priests and priestesses had various ritual duties and responsibilities within the temple. They were responsible for maintaining the sanctity of the temple and performing daily rituals to honor the gods and goddesses. This included the opening and closing of the temple, the purification of the sacred spaces, and the offering of food, incense, and other symbolic items to the deities.

Priests specialized in specific rituals associated with particular deities, while priestesses often had their own unique roles and responsibilities. For example, priestesses of the goddess Hathor played a significant role in music, dance, and fertility rituals. The high priest or priestess held a prestigious position and oversaw the temple's activities, ensuring the proper execution of rituals and the well-being of the temple community.

Temple Staff and Administration

Organization and Management of Temple Affairs

Apart from the priests and priestesses, the temples required a dedicated staff to manage the administrative and logistical aspects of temple affairs. This included scribes, accountants, and other administrative personnel who maintained records, managed the temple's finances, and coordinated the offerings and donations.

The organization of temple staff varied depending on the size and importance of the temple. Larger temples had a hierarchical structure, with different levels of administrators overseeing specific areas. The efficient management of resources, land, and finances was crucial to the temple's functioning and its ability to support the religious activities and the surrounding community.

Support Roles in Maintaining the Temple Complex

In addition to the priests, priestesses, and administrative personnel, there were numerous individuals involved in the upkeep and maintenance of the temple complex. These support roles were essential for the smooth operation of the temple and the preservation of its physical structure.

Craftsmen and artisans were responsible for the construction, repair, and embellishment of the temple's architectural features, such as statues, reliefs, and decorative elements. Servants and caretakers ensured the cleanliness and tidiness of the temple, while gardeners tended to the temple gardens and cultivated the plants used in rituals and offerings.

Examples:

Problem: Research and analyze the training and education of priests in ancient Egypt, comparing it with the training of religious practitioners in other cultures such as witchcraft, shamanism, or herbalism. Identify similarities and differences in the training methods and the role of lineage in these practices.

Exercise: Create a hypothetical temple administration structure for a specific ancient Egyptian deity, outlining the roles and responsibilities of different personnel within the temple complex. Justify your choices based on historical evidence and the cultural context.

Discussion: Engage in a group discussion on the significance of hierarchies and specialized roles within temple personnel. Explore the potential benefits and challenges of having a specialized priesthood in religious institutions, considering both historical and contemporary perspectives.

Chapter 16: Festivals and Annual Religious Celebrations

Festivals held a profound significance in the religious and cultural life of ancient Egypt. These vibrant and elaborate celebrations played a vital role in connecting the human realm with the divine, honoring the gods and goddesses, and reinforcing the cosmological order. Festivals were pivotal moments when the entire community came together to engage in religious rituals, communal activities, and social interactions.

Commemoration of Divine Events and Mythological Narratives

Festivals often commemorated significant events and mythological narratives associated with the gods and goddesses. These events could include the birth, coronation, or sacred marriage of a deity, as well as the triumph over chaos or other mythological battles. By reenacting these events through rituals, processions, and performances, the ancient Egyptians sought to connect with the divine world and ensure the continuous flow of cosmic harmony.

Expression of Devotion and Gratitude

Festivals provided a platform for the ancient Egyptians to express their devotion and gratitude to the gods and goddesses for their blessings and protection. Through offerings, prayers, and acts of worship, individuals and communities conveyed their reverence and sought the favor and benevolence of the deities. Festivals were occasions for both personal and collective piety, reinforcing the reciprocal relationship between humans and the divine.

Role of Annual Celebrations in Religious and Social Life

Annual celebrations formed an integral part of the religious and social fabric of ancient Egyptian society. These recurring events marked the passage of time, connected communities, and reinforced cultural values and traditions. They brought together people from different social classes, providing opportunities for social cohesion and collective identity.

Reinforcement of Cosmic Order and Maat

The annual celebrations in ancient Egypt were intricately linked to the concept of Maat, the cosmic order and harmony that governed the universe.

Through the rituals and ceremonies performed during these celebrations, the Egyptians sought to maintain the balance between the natural and supernatural realms, ensuring the continuation of Maat. By actively participating in the annual festivals, individuals affirmed their commitment to upholding moral and ethical principles, both individually and as a society.

Promotion of Social Cohesion and Community Engagement

Annual celebrations fostered a sense of community and belonging among the ancient Egyptians. These events provided opportunities for people to come together, interact, and forge social connections beyond their immediate circles. Festivals included processions, feasts, music, dance, and other communal activities that brought joy, entertainment, and a sense of unity. They allowed individuals to share experiences, exchange knowledge, and strengthen social bonds.

Opet Festival

The Opet Festival holds a significant place in the religious calendar of ancient Egypt, embodying profound spiritual beliefs and cultural traditions. This annual celebration, which spanned several centuries, was dedicated to the rejuvenation and renewal of the divine kingship, as well as the relationship between the pharaoh and the gods. Understanding the history and significance of the Opet Festival offers a glimpse into the complexities of ancient Egyptian religious practices.

The Opet Festival originated in the New Kingdom period, during the 18th dynasty, and continued to be celebrated until the Roman period. It was primarily associated with the god Amun, one of the most important deities in the Egyptian pantheon. The festival took place in the city of Thebes, particularly in the temples of Karnak and Luxor, which served as the focal points for the grand ceremonies.

The festival's significance lay in its role in reinforcing the divine legitimacy of the pharaoh and his connection to the gods. It symbolized the rejuvenation of the pharaoh's divine power and the restoration of Maat, the cosmic order. The Opet Festival also served as an opportunity for the pharaoh to interact with the deities, seek their blessings, and receive their guidance for the well-being and prosperity of the kingdom.

Rituals and Activities During the Festival

The Opet Festival encompassed a series of rituals and activities that unfolded over several weeks, captivating the city and its inhabitants with their grandeur and spiritual fervor. These rituals aimed to honor the gods, reaffirm the pharaoh's divine mandate, and engage the community in acts of devotion and celebration.

The Procession

The centerpiece of the Opet Festival was the grand procession that carried the sacred statues of Amun, Mut, and Khonsu from the Karnak Temple to the Luxor Temple. The statues were mounted on sacred barques, magnificently adorned and accompanied by priests, musicians, dancers, and enthusiastic crowds. The procession symbolized the gods' journey from their main sanctuary to visit the pharaoh, strengthening the bond between the divine and earthly realms.

Offerings and Rituals

At both the Karnak and Luxor Temples, elaborate rituals and offerings were conducted to honor the gods. These rituals included purification ceremonies, libations, incense offerings, and the presentation of food and precious objects. Priests and priestesses performed prayers and invocations, seeking the favor and blessings of the gods for the pharaoh, the royal family, and the community. These acts of worship and reverence were believed to ensure the continued protection and prosperity of the kingdom.

Symbolism and Themes of the Opet Festival

The Opet Festival was rich in symbolism and themes that reflected the ancient Egyptians' worldview, religious beliefs, and social structures. These symbols and themes offered profound insights into the complex interplay between the human, divine, and cosmic realms.

Renewal and Regeneration

The Opet Festival symbolized the rejuvenation and regeneration of the pharaoh's divine power and the renewal of cosmic harmony. The gods' visit to the pharaoh during the procession represented the revitalization of the pharaoh's role as the divine intermediary, ensuring the perpetuation of Maat and the well-being of the kingdom. The festival acted as a potent symbol of cyclical renewal and the eternal cycle of creation and rebirth.

Divine Kingship and Royal Authority

The Opet Festival underscored the concept of divine kingship, emphasizing the pharaoh's role as the earthly embodiment of the gods. Through the rituals and ceremonies, the pharaoh demonstrated his connection to the divine and his responsibility to uphold the cosmic order. The festival affirmed the pharaoh's divine mandate and served as a platform to reinforce his authority and legitimacy in the eyes of the gods and the people.

Examples:

Problem: Analyze the role of the Opet Festival in the religious and political life of ancient Egypt. Discuss the ways in which the festival served to consolidate the pharaoh's power and authority, and how it contributed to the overall stability and harmony of the kingdom.

Exercise: Imagine you are a participant in the Opet Festival. Write a descriptive essay detailing your experience during the procession. Include sensory details, emotions, and reflections on the significance of the festival for the community and the individual.

Discussion: Engage in a group discussion on the symbolism and themes of the Opet Festival. Compare the festival's themes with those found in other religious traditions, such as witchcraft, shamanism, or ecospirituality. Analyze the universality of these themes and their relevance in contemporary spiritual practices.

Sed Festival

The Sed Festival, also known as the Heb Sed or Jubilee Festival, was a significant event in ancient Egyptian religious and political life. This festival, celebrated by the pharaoh after reigning for approximately 30 years, served a dual purpose: to renew the king's strength and vitality and to reaffirm his kingship and connection to the gods. Understanding the purpose and historical context of the Sed Festival sheds light on the deep-rooted beliefs and rituals of ancient Egyptian civilization.

The Sed Festival originated in the early dynastic period and continued throughout the Pharaonic era. Its origins can be traced back to the myth of the sun god's rejuvenation and the pharaoh's association with this solar deity. The festival was a reflection of the cyclical nature of time and the pharaoh's role as the embodiment of divine power and cosmic order.

Rituals and Ceremonies Associated with the Sed Festival

The Sed Festival comprised a series of elaborate rituals and ceremonies, each with its own symbolic significance. These rituals aimed to renew the pharaoh's vitality, purify his body and spirit, and reaffirm his divine authority as the ruler of Egypt.

The Ritual Run

One of the central activities of the Sed Festival was the ritual run, in which the pharaoh would complete a circuit around a designated area. This run symbolized the pharaoh's physical and spiritual endurance, emphasizing his continued ability to govern and protect the kingdom. The run served as a public display of the pharaoh's strength and vitality, and it was a moment of celebration and jubilation for the entire community.

Coronation and Purification

During the Sed Festival, the pharaoh underwent a symbolic coronation and purification ceremony. These rituals involved the anointing of the pharaoh with sacred oils, the donning of ceremonial regalia, and the recitation of prayers and invocations. The coronation and purification rites symbolized the pharaoh's renewal and his reconnection with the divine, reaffirming his legitimacy and authority as the rightful ruler.

Symbolic Meaning of the Sed Festival

The Sed Festival was rich in symbolic meaning, reflecting the ancient Egyptians' cosmological beliefs and their understanding of kingship and divine power. The festival encompassed several themes and symbols that were deeply ingrained in the cultural and religious fabric of ancient Egypt.

Renewal and Rejuvenation

At its core, the Sed Festival represented the renewal and rejuvenation of the pharaoh's kingship. The rituals and ceremonies performed during the festival aimed to restore the pharaoh's energy, vitality, and divine favor. The festival symbolized the cyclical nature of kingship and the pharaoh's ability to rule effectively over an extended period.

Divine Authority and Cosmic Balance

The Sed Festival emphasized the pharaoh's divine authority and his role as the mediator between the earthly and divine realms. By undergoing the rituals and ceremonies of the festival, the pharaoh reaffirmed his connection to the gods and his responsibility to maintain cosmic balance and order. The Sed Festival underscored the pharaoh's role as the living embodiment of Maat, the principle of harmony and justice.

Examples:

Problem: Compare and contrast the Sed Festival with other similar jubilee celebrations in different cultures, such as the Roman lustrum or the Chinese imperial ascension rituals. Analyze the underlying themes and symbolic meanings of these festivals and their significance for the rulers and societies.

Exercise: Design a modern-day Sed Festival for a fictional ruler. Outline the key rituals, ceremonies, and symbolic elements that would be included in the festival. Reflect on the underlying meaning and purpose of each component.

Discussion: Engage in a group discussion on the symbolic meaning of the Sed Festival. Explore dissenting opinions and alternative interpretations of the festival's significance. Discuss how the symbolism and themes of the Sed Festival can be relevant in contemporary spiritual practices, such as witchcraft, divination, or herbalism.

Other Festivals and Celebrations

Heb Sed Festival

The Heb Sed Festival, also known as the Sed Festival, held great significance in ancient Egyptian culture. However, in addition to the Sed Festival, there were numerous other festivals and celebrations that played integral roles in the religious and social life of ancient Egypt. Understanding the context, rituals, and symbolic meanings of these festivals provides valuable insights into the diverse aspects of ancient Egyptian spirituality.

Wepet Renpet (New Year)

Wepet Renpet, meaning "Opening of the Year," marked the beginning of the agricultural and religious calendar in ancient Egypt. This festival typically fell in late July or early August, coinciding with the annual flooding of the Nile River. The Nile flood was essential for the fertility of the land and ensured a successful agricultural season. The Wepet Renpet festival celebrated this vital natural event and carried profound religious significance.

During the Wepet Renpet festival, people engaged in various rituals and ceremonies. These included purification rites, offerings to the gods, and processions to sacred sites. One of the central activities was the reenactment of the myth of the sun god's birth, symbolizing rejuvenation, new beginnings, and the cyclical nature of time. The festival also involved communal feasting, music, and dance, fostering a sense of unity and collective celebration.

Festival of Bastet

The Festival of Bastet honored the goddess Bastet, the feline deity associated with protection, joy, and fertility. Bastet was particularly revered in the city of Bubastis, where her main temple stood. The festival attracted pilgrims from all over Egypt who came to pay homage to the goddess and seek her blessings.

The Festival of Bastet was a vibrant and joyous celebration characterized by lively processions, music, dancing, and feasting. People adorned themselves with elaborate costumes and jewelry, and the streets of Bubastis bustled with excitement. The festival served as a time for communal bonding, religious devotion, and expressing gratitude to the benevolent goddess.

Examples:

Problem: Analyze the role of festivals in fostering social cohesion and community bonding in ancient Egypt. Compare the festivals of Wepet Renpet and the Festival of Bastet, highlighting similarities and differences in their communal aspects and their significance for individuals and society.

Exercise: Design a modern-day celebration inspired by the Wepet Renpet festival. Consider the symbolism and themes associated with the Nile flood and agricultural abundance. Create a detailed plan that includes rituals, decorations, and activities that would capture the essence of the ancient festival while adapting it to contemporary cultural and environmental contexts.

Discussion: Engage in a group discussion on the cultural and religious significance of the Festival of Bastet. Explore how the veneration of feline deities can be found in other spiritual traditions, such as witchcraft or shamanism.

Discuss the potential ecological implications and the importance of animal symbolism in contemporary ecospirituality.

Comparative Analysis of Festivals

When examining the festivals of ancient Egypt, it is enlightening to compare them with festivals from other cultures around the world. While each culture has its unique traditions and beliefs, there are often intriguing similarities and differences that shed light on shared human experiences and the universal need for spiritual expression.

One example of a festival with similarities to ancient Egyptian celebrations is the Beltane festival in modern Pagan and Wiccan traditions. Beltane, celebrated on May 1st, marks the beginning of summer and the fertility of the land. Just like the Wepet Renpet festival in ancient Egypt, Beltane involves purification rites, bonfires, and communal festivities. Both festivals celebrate the cycles of nature, the importance of fertility, and the renewal of life.

On the other hand, the Japanese festival of Obon showcases distinctive cultural elements while sharing some common themes with ancient Egyptian festivals. Obon, held in mid-August, is a time to honor ancestors and commemorate the spirits of the deceased. During this festival, people clean and decorate their ancestors' graves, light lanterns, and perform traditional dances. Although the specific rituals and beliefs differ, both Obon and the Sed Festival emphasize the connection between the living and the dead and provide an opportunity for spiritual reflection and remembrance.

Universal Elements and Themes in Religious Celebrations

Across different cultures and traditions, there are universal elements and themes that emerge in religious celebrations. These elements often tap into deep-seated human desires for connection, meaning, and transcendence. By examining these universal aspects, we can gain a deeper understanding of the human condition and the fundamental principles that underpin religious practices.

Rituals and Ceremonies: One commonality among religious celebrations is the presence of rituals and ceremonies. These structured actions and symbolic gestures provide a framework for participants to engage with the sacred and establish a sense of order and continuity. Whether it is the offering of incense in Egyptian temples or the casting of a circle in modern witchcraft rituals, rituals serve as a bridge between the mundane and the divine.

Communal Gathering: Festivals often serve as a focal point for communal gathering, fostering a sense of belonging and shared identity. People come together to celebrate, worship, and engage in collective activities. This communal aspect strengthens social bonds and creates a supportive environment for spiritual exploration. For example, the gathering of pilgrims in Bubastis during the Festival of Bastet reflects the power of collective worship and the sense of unity it fosters.

Symbolism and Myth: Symbolism and myth are prevalent in religious celebrations, providing a narrative framework through which participants can understand and engage with the divine. These symbols and stories carry deep cultural meanings and serve as a way to transmit religious teachings and values. In Egyptian temple reliefs, the depiction of rituals and divine narratives served to convey sacred knowledge and inspire reverence.

Examples:

Problem: Compare and contrast the rituals and symbolism of the Wepet Renpet festival in ancient Egypt with the Beltane festival in modern Pagan traditions. Discuss how both festivals reflect the cyclical nature of time and the importance of fertility, while also acknowledging the cultural specificities that distinguish them.

Exercise: Imagine you are organizing an interfaith gathering where representatives from different spiritual traditions, including Egyptian, Celtic, and Japanese, come together to share and celebrate their respective festivals. Design a program that incorporates elements of each tradition while emphasizing the universal themes of renewal, gratitude, and connection.

Discussion: Engage in a group discussion on the significance of communal gathering in religious celebrations. Explore how the experience of coming together in celebration impacts individual spirituality and fosters a sense of belonging and shared purpose. Draw examples from various cultural and spiritual contexts to support your arguments.

Chapter 17: Divine Kingship and Pharaoh as a Deity

In ancient Egypt, the concept of divine kingship played a central role in the religious, political, and social structures of the civilization. The belief in the divinity of the pharaoh, the ruling monarch, was deeply ingrained in the Egyptian worldview. According to this concept, the pharaoh was not merely a mortal ruler but was also considered a living embodiment of the divine.

The divine kingship ideology can be traced back to the earliest periods of Egyptian history, where the pharaohs were regarded as intermediaries between the human realm and the realm of the gods. The Egyptians believed that the pharaoh possessed a direct connection with the divine forces that governed the universe. This connection bestowed upon the pharaoh immense power, authority, and responsibility to ensure the prosperity and well-being of the kingdom.

Pharaoh's Role as a Representative of the Gods

As the representative of the gods, the pharaoh was considered the earthly counterpart of the divine order. The pharaoh's role encompassed both religious and political dimensions, intertwining the realms of the sacred and the secular. In his religious capacity, the pharaoh performed rituals, made offerings to the gods, and acted as the chief priest of the nation. Through these rituals, the pharaoh sought to maintain cosmic balance and harmony, ensuring the favor of the gods upon the kingdom and its people.

The pharaoh's divine status was reinforced through monumental architecture and elaborate ceremonies. Temples were built in honor of the pharaoh as a deity, serving as centers of worship and the site of important rituals. The construction of grand monuments such as the Great Pyramids of Giza exemplified the pharaoh's divine role and immortal legacy.

Moreover, the pharaoh's authority extended beyond religious matters to encompass governance and administration. As the ruler, the pharaoh was responsible for maintaining order, justice, and the welfare of the people. The concept of Ma'at, the cosmic principle of balance and harmony, was intricately tied to the pharaoh's role as a representative of the gods. By upholding Ma'at, the pharaoh ensured the proper functioning of society and the cosmic order.

Examples:

Problem: Compare the concept of divine kingship in ancient Egypt with the notion of sacred kingship in other cultures such as the Inca Empire or the Shang Dynasty in China. Discuss the similarities and differences in the understanding of the king's divine status and the implications for political and religious structures.

Exercise: Imagine you are an ancient Egyptian scribe tasked with composing a hymn praising the pharaoh as a deity. Write a hymn that captures the essence of the pharaoh's divine nature, his role as a representative of the gods, and the significance of his reign for the prosperity of the kingdom.

Discussion: Engage in a group discussion on the potential challenges and controversies surrounding the concept of divine kingship. Consider dissenting opinions and alternative perspectives that question the legitimacy and implications of attributing divine status to a mortal ruler. Explore the potential consequences, both positive and negative, of such a system of governance.

Origins and Development of Divine Kingship

The origins of divine kingship in ancient Egypt can be traced back to the earliest periods of the civilization. In these early stages, the belief in the divine nature of the ruler was rooted in animistic and shamanistic traditions. The king was seen as a mediator between the human and spiritual realms, possessing a special connection to the deities and the supernatural forces that governed the world.

During the Predynastic and Early Dynastic periods, the ruler was referred to as the "Horus," a title associated with the falcon god Horus. This connection with Horus symbolized the king's divine lineage and his role as the earthly embodiment of the falcon deity. The early kings were believed to possess the spirit and power of Horus, allowing them to wield authority over both the earthly and spiritual realms.

The Rise of Pharaonic Ideology

The development of pharaonic ideology marked a significant shift in the understanding of divine kingship in ancient Egypt. With the unification of Upper and Lower Egypt under a single ruler, known as the pharaoh, the concept of royal divinity became more formalized and elaborate. The pharaoh became not only a representative of the gods but also their earthly counterpart.

The rise of pharaonic ideology can be attributed to the political consolidation of the kingdom and the need to legitimize the authority of the ruler. The pharaoh was seen as a divine figure with a direct connection to the gods, embodying their power and wisdom. This ideology was reinforced through religious texts, rituals, and iconography that depicted the pharaoh in divine regalia and engaging in sacred activities.

Evolution of the Pharaoh's Divine Status

Over time, the pharaoh's divine status continued to evolve, reflecting changes in religious beliefs and political circumstances. The New Kingdom period witnessed a heightened emphasis on the pharaoh's association with the sun god, Amun-Ra. The pharaoh was considered the son of Amun-Ra, sharing in his divine essence and participating in his cosmic cycle.

During this period, the pharaoh's divine role expanded to include the concept of divine filiation, where the pharaoh was believed to be the biological offspring of the gods. This belief further solidified the pharaoh's divine lineage and legitimized his authority as a ruler.

Furthermore, the pharaoh's divine status was intricately linked to the concept of Ma'at, the cosmic principle of order, truth, and justice. The pharaoh was responsible for upholding Ma'at and maintaining cosmic balance through his actions and rituals. By doing so, the pharaoh ensured the well-being and prosperity of the kingdom and its people.

Examples:

Problem: Compare the early beliefs in royal divinity in ancient Egypt with similar concepts of divine kingship in other cultures, such as the concept of the "Mandate of Heaven" in ancient China or the belief in divine rulership in Mesopotamia. Discuss the commonalities and differences in the development and manifestation of divine kingship in these civilizations.

Exercise: Research and analyze the iconography and symbolism associated with the pharaoh's divine status in different periods of ancient Egyptian history. Select a specific artwork or artifact that represents the pharaoh as a deity and interpret its significance in relation to the evolving understanding of divine kingship.

Discussion: Engage in a group discussion on the potential implications of the pharaoh's divine status on the religious, political, and social fabric of ancient

Egyptian society. Consider different perspectives, including dissenting opinions, and explore the complexities and controversies surrounding the concentration of power and authority in the hands of a divine ruler.

Symbolism and Rituals of Pharaonic Authority

The crown and regalia worn by the pharaoh in ancient Egypt were rich in symbolism, representing the pharaoh's divine authority, power, and role as a mediator between the gods and the people. Each crown and regalia had its own significance and conveyed specific aspects of the pharaoh's divine identity.

The Double Crown (Pschent): The Double Crown was a composite crown consisting of the Red Crown of Lower Egypt (Desheret) and the White Crown of Upper Egypt (Hedjet). The combination of these two crowns symbolized the pharaoh's dominion over the entire kingdom, signifying the unification of the two lands. It represented the pharaoh's role as the ruler of a unified Egypt and the embodiment of its divine sovereignty.

The Nemes Headcloth: The Nemes headcloth was a striped headdress worn by the pharaoh, often associated with the image of Tutankhamun. It featured a striped pattern and a uraeus, a rearing cobra, on the forehead. The Nemes headdress represented the pharaoh's divine authority and kingship. The uraeus symbolized the pharaoh's power to ward off evil and protect the kingdom.

The Blue Crown (Khepresh): The Blue Crown, also known as the War Crown, was a ceremonial crown associated with military campaigns and battle. It had a distinctive shape and was adorned with divine symbols and motifs. The Blue Crown represented the pharaoh's martial power and his role as a warrior leader, protecting Egypt from external threats and maintaining order within the kingdom.

Pharaonic Rituals and Ceremonies

Pharaonic rituals and ceremonies played a crucial role in reinforcing the pharaoh's authority and divine status. These rituals were performed by priests and attended by the royal court and the general populace, showcasing the grandeur and sanctity of the pharaoh's rule.

Coronation Ceremony: The coronation ceremony marked the formal accession of the pharaoh to the throne. It included rituals such as the purification of the pharaoh, the anointing with sacred oils, and the crowning with the Double

Crown or the Nemes headcloth. The ceremony symbolized the pharaoh's divine legitimacy and his investiture with the authority to rule.

Heb-Sed Festival: The Heb-Sed Festival was a jubilee celebration held to commemorate the pharaoh's thirty-year reign. It involved various rituals and activities, including processions, offering rituals, and physical challenges that demonstrated the pharaoh's vitality and ability to continue ruling effectively. The festival reinforced the pharaoh's divine right to rule and his ongoing connection with the gods.

Sed Festival: The Sed Festival was another jubilee celebration held periodically to renew the pharaoh's divine authority and rejuvenate his rule. The festival involved rituals such as the "running of the sed" and the pharaoh's symbolic death and rebirth. Through these ceremonies, the pharaoh's vitality and power were restored, ensuring the continuity of his divine rule.

Cult of the Living Pharaoh

The Cult of the Living Pharaoh was a religious practice that revered the pharaoh as a living deity during his lifetime. It emphasized the pharaoh's divine nature and his ability to provide divine guidance and protection to his subjects.

Temple Worship: The pharaoh, as the living embodiment of the gods, received worship and offerings in temple complexes dedicated to his cult. People would come to pay homage to the pharaoh, seeking blessings, divine intervention, and protection.

Royal Processions: The pharaoh would often participate in grand processions, parading through the streets in ceremonial regalia and accompanied by priests, officials, and musicians. These processions served as a public display of the pharaoh's divine authority and allowed the people to witness and celebrate his presence.

Oracle Consultations: The pharaoh, as the intermediary between the divine and human realms, was sought for his wisdom and guidance. People would consult the pharaoh or his designated oracles for divination and advice on important matters, relying on his divine insight to make decisions and resolve issues.

Pharaoh as a Deity

In ancient Egypt, the pharaoh was closely associated with specific gods, often considered the earthly manifestation of divine power and authority. This association served to reinforce the pharaoh's divine status and establish his legitimacy as a ruler. Different pharaohs may have been linked to different gods based on their family lineage or personal preferences. Examples of such associations include:

Amun-Ra: The pharaoh's association with Amun-Ra, the king of the gods, was prevalent throughout Egyptian history. The pharaoh was believed to be the son of Amun-Ra, symbolizing the divine lineage of the ruling family and the pharaoh's direct connection to the supreme deity.

Horus: The pharaoh was often identified with Horus, the falcon-headed god associated with kingship and the sky. The pharaoh was considered the living embodiment of Horus on Earth, with his rule representing the continuation of Horus' divine kingship.

Osiris: The pharaoh's association with Osiris, the god of the afterlife and resurrection, emphasized his role as a divine ruler who ensured the continuity of life and the preservation of cosmic order. The pharaoh was seen as the earthly representative of Osiris, responsible for maintaining the well-being and prosperity of the kingdom.

Pharaoh as the Intermediary between Gods and People

One of the fundamental roles of the pharaoh was to act as the intermediary between the gods and the people. The pharaoh was believed to have a unique connection to the divine realm, enabling him to communicate with the gods and receive their guidance on matters of governance and religious practice. This intermediary role was crucial in maintaining harmony between the human and divine realms. Examples of the pharaoh's role as an intermediary include:

Offering Rituals: The pharaoh performed elaborate offering rituals to the gods on behalf of the entire kingdom. Through these rituals, the pharaoh conveyed the people's gratitude and sought the gods' favor and protection. The pharaoh's actions were believed to influence the gods' decisions and ensure their continued support for the kingdom.

Oracle Consultations: The pharaoh, as the divine oracle, provided guidance and insights to the people by channeling the wisdom of the gods. People sought the pharaoh's counsel on matters of importance, such as military campaigns, agricultural practices, and personal affairs. The pharaoh's divinely inspired advice played a central role in decision-making and ensuring the well-being of the kingdom.

Pharaoh's Role in Maintaining Cosmic Order

The pharaoh's rule was intrinsically linked to the concept of Ma'at, the divine order that governed the universe. It was believed that the pharaoh had the responsibility to uphold and restore Ma'at, ensuring the stability and balance of the cosmos. The pharaoh's role in maintaining cosmic order manifested in various ways:

Rituals and Offerings: The pharaoh conducted rituals and offered regular sacrifices to the gods to maintain cosmic harmony. These rituals were believed to have a direct impact on the cosmic forces that influenced the well-being of the kingdom and its people.

Temple Construction and Maintenance: The pharaoh played a vital role in the construction and maintenance of temples dedicated to the gods. Temples were considered the sacred dwelling places of the gods, and their proper upkeep was essential to ensure the gods' favor and the continuous flow of divine energy.

Laws and Governance: The pharaoh enacted laws and governed the kingdom based on the principles of Ma'at. By establishing just and equitable governance, the pharaoh upheld the principles of cosmic order within the human realm, fostering stability and prosperity.

Challenges to Divine Kingship

While the concept of divine kingship was deeply ingrained in ancient Egyptian society, it was not without its challenges and dissenting opinions. Throughout history, there were individuals and groups who questioned the absolute authority of the pharaoh and sought alternative power structures. Some of the dissenting opinions and alternative power structures include:

Priesthood and Temple Authority: The powerful priesthood, particularly in the later periods of Egyptian history, held significant influence and could rival the pharaoh's authority. Temples were centers of religious and economic power, and the high priests enjoyed considerable autonomy and wealth. In some instances, the priesthood even claimed divine authority parallel to the pharaoh, challenging his exclusive right to communicate with the gods.

Regional Autonomy: Egypt was not a homogenous entity but comprised different regions and city-states with their local rulers and power structures. At times, these regional rulers asserted their autonomy and challenged the central authority of the pharaoh. While they acknowledged the pharaoh's divine status, they sought to maintain a degree of independence in their local governance.

Dissident Movements: Throughout Egyptian history, there were individuals and groups who rejected the divine status of the pharaoh altogether. These dissenting voices criticized the concentration of power in a single individual and proposed alternative systems of governance. Some advocated for a more egalitarian society where power was distributed among the people or where religious authority was decentralized.

Political and Social Dynamics Impacting the Authority of the Pharaoh

The authority of the pharaoh as a divine ruler was not immune to the political and social dynamics of ancient Egypt. Various factors influenced and shaped the pharaoh's authority, sometimes undermining or challenging it. Some of these dynamics include:

Succession and Legitimacy: The smooth transition of power from one pharaoh to the next was crucial for maintaining the divine authority of the monarchy. Instances of disputed succession or weak rulers could create instability and lead to challenges to the divine kingship. Questions of legitimacy could arise if a pharaoh was seen as unfit or lacked the support of key factions within the ruling elite.

Foreign Influences and Invasions: External threats, such as foreign invasions or the influence of foreign cultures, could impact the perception of the pharaoh's divine authority. In times of political turmoil or foreign dominance, the pharaoh's ability to protect Egypt and maintain cosmic order could be questioned, eroding confidence in his divine status.

Economic Challenges: Economic difficulties, such as famine or economic crises, could lead to social unrest and undermine the authority of the pharaoh. If the pharaoh was unable to ensure the prosperity and well-being of the people, it could create dissatisfaction and weaken belief in his divine mandate to govern.

Part 6: Belief in the Divine Nature of Pharaohs

Belief in the divine nature of pharaohs played a central role in ancient Egyptian society and religion. This belief system positioned the pharaoh as not only a mortal ruler but also as a divine being, bridging the gap between the earthly realm and the realm of the gods. Part 6 of our study delves into the fascinating world of pharaonic divinity, exploring the origins, development, and implications of this fundamental aspect of ancient Egyptian culture.

Origins of the Divine Nature of Pharaohs

The origins of the belief in the divine nature of pharaohs can be traced back to the early periods of ancient Egyptian history. It emerged from a complex interplay of religious, political, and cultural factors. The early Egyptians perceived their rulers as representatives of the gods on Earth, tasked with maintaining cosmic order and ensuring the prosperity and well-being of the kingdom. Over time, this perception evolved into the concept of divine kingship, wherein the pharaoh was considered a living embodiment of the gods and possessed a direct divine connection.

In this worldview, the pharaoh emerged as a central figure in maintaining cosmic order and ensuring the well-being of the kingdom. The pharaoh was seen as a representative of the gods on Earth, acting as a link between the divine realm and the mortal realm. This notion can be attributed to the Egyptians' desire for a stable and harmonious society, where the gods' favor and protection were essential.

The early Egyptians observed that their rulers possessed a unique ability to bring prosperity and stability to the kingdom. They witnessed the pharaoh's command over the natural resources and their ability to maintain law and order. This led to the belief that the pharaoh had a divine mandate, granted by the gods themselves, to rule over the people and ensure their welfare.

Over time, this perception of the pharaoh's role as a representative of the gods evolved into the concept of divine kingship. The ancient Egyptians began to regard the pharaoh not merely as a mortal ruler with the gods' endorsement, but as a living embodiment of the gods. This divine connection bestowed upon the pharaoh extraordinary powers and authority that surpassed those of ordinary individuals.

The concept of divine kingship became more firmly established as Egyptian civilization advanced. The religious rituals and ceremonies associated with the pharaoh's rule grew in complexity, emphasizing their divine nature. The construction of monumental temples dedicated to the worship of the pharaohs further reinforced their elevated status. These structures served as centers of religious and political power, where the pharaoh's divine role was prominently displayed and celebrated.

Moreover, the belief in the pharaoh's divine nature was intertwined with the cultural identity of the Egyptian people. It became an integral part of their collective consciousness and worldview, shaping their understanding of the cosmos, their rituals, and their social and political structures.

In summary, the origins of the belief in the divine nature of pharaohs can be traced back to the early periods of ancient Egyptian history. It emerged from a complex interplay of religious, political, and cultural factors, as the Egyptians perceived their rulers as representatives of the gods and recognized their vital role in maintaining cosmic order and ensuring the prosperity and well-being of the kingdom. Over time, this perception evolved into the concept of divine kingship, where the pharaoh was considered a living embodiment of the gods and possessed a direct divine connection.

Development of the Concept of Pharaonic Divinity

As Egyptian civilization developed and encountered new challenges, the concept of pharaonic divinity evolved and became more elaborate. The rise of complex religious rituals, the establishment of a priestly class, and the construction of monumental temples all contributed to the strengthening of the pharaoh's divine status. The pharaoh's association with specific gods became more pronounced, and the rituals and ceremonies surrounding the pharaoh's divine role became increasingly intricate and sophisticated.

One crucial aspect of the development of the concept of pharaonic divinity was the rise of complex religious rituals. As the religious system of ancient Egypt became more intricate, the pharaoh's role in these rituals became increasingly prominent. The pharaoh, as the living embodiment of the gods, played a central role in ensuring the favor and protection of the deities. Elaborate ceremonies were performed to maintain cosmic order, seek divine guidance, and demonstrate the pharaoh's divine connection. These rituals often involved the participation of priests, who acted as intermediaries between the pharaoh and the gods, and they took place in the grand temples dedicated to the worship of the pharaoh and the gods.

The establishment of a priestly class further contributed to the development of the pharaoh's divine status. Priests held significant religious and administrative positions within Egyptian society, and they played a crucial role in perpetuating the belief in the pharaoh's divine nature. They were responsible for conducting rituals, maintaining temple cults, and interpreting the will of the gods. The close association between the pharaoh and the priests reinforced the idea of the pharaoh as a divine figure, as the priests served as custodians of the pharaoh's divine authority and facilitated the communication between the earthly and divine realms.

Additionally, the construction of monumental temples served as a tangible expression of the pharaoh's divinity. These architectural marvels were grandiose structures dedicated to the worship of the gods and the glorification of the pharaoh. They were adorned with intricate carvings, inscriptions, and artwork depicting the pharaoh's divine role and connection to the gods. These temples became focal points of religious and political power, attracting pilgrims from all corners of the kingdom and symbolizing the pharaoh's authority as a divine ruler.

Furthermore, the pharaoh's association with specific gods became more pronounced as the concept of pharaonic divinity developed. Different pharaohs aligned themselves with particular deities, often based on regional or family traditions. By aligning themselves with specific gods, the pharaohs strengthened their divine status and solidified their connection to the divine realm. For example, the pharaoh Amenhotep IV, later known as Akhenaten, introduced a monotheistic cult centered around the worship of the sun disk, Aten. This shift in religious practice reflected the pharaoh's desire to emphasize his unique divine connection.

In conclusion, the development of the concept of pharaonic divinity was shaped by various factors in ancient Egyptian society. The rise of complex religious rituals, the establishment of a priestly class, the construction of monumental temples, and the pharaoh's association with specific gods all contributed to the evolution and elaboration of the pharaoh's divine status. These developments highlighted the central role of the pharaoh as the living embodiment of the gods and further solidified their authority and divine connection within the religious and political framework of ancient Egypt.

Chapter 18: Connection between Pharaohs and Gods

The ancient Egyptian civilization had a unique and intricate belief system that emphasized the close connection between the pharaohs, the earthly rulers, and the gods, the divine beings worshipped by the ancient Egyptians. This connection between pharaohs and gods held great significance in the religious and political fabric of ancient Egypt, shaping the ideologies and practices of the society. Exploring the connection between pharaohs and gods allows us to gain a deeper understanding of the ancient Egyptian worldview and the role of divine rulership in their culture.

Significance of the Connection between Pharaohs and Gods in Ancient Egyptian Religion

In ancient Egyptian religion, the connection between pharaohs and gods played a pivotal role in maintaining cosmic order and ensuring the prosperity of the kingdom. The pharaoh, as the earthly representative of the gods, was seen as the linchpin that bridged the gap between the mortal realm and the divine realm. This connection was central to the religious and political ideologies of ancient Egypt, as it established the pharaoh's authority, legitimacy, and divine right to rule.

The ancient Egyptians believed that the gods governed every aspect of life, from the natural forces to the well-being of individuals and the prosperity of the kingdom. By aligning themselves with the gods, the pharaohs gained divine endorsement and support, allowing them to fulfill their duties as rulers effectively. The connection between pharaohs and gods was believed to grant the pharaohs the power and wisdom necessary to navigate the complexities of governance and maintain cosmic balance.

Moreover, the connection between pharaohs and gods had a symbolic and ritualistic significance. The pharaoh was seen as the living embodiment of the gods, carrying their divine essence within them. This belief not only elevated the status of the pharaoh but also imbued the ruler with a sense of sacredness and holiness. The rituals and ceremonies associated with the pharaoh's divine nature reinforced this connection and served as a means of communication and interaction between the mortal and divine realms.

Beliefs and Ideologies Surrounding the Divine Nature of Pharaohs

The divine nature of pharaohs was deeply rooted in the religious and cultural beliefs of ancient Egypt. According to these beliefs, the pharaoh was not merely a mortal ruler but rather a being of divine essence with a direct connection to the gods. This concept of divine kingship elevated the pharaoh to a position beyond that of a political leader, endowing them with a sacred and elevated status.

The ideologies surrounding the divine nature of pharaohs emphasized the pharaoh's role as the intermediary between the gods and the people. The pharaoh was perceived as the conduit through which the gods communicated their will and maintained cosmic order. The ancient Egyptians believed that the pharaoh's actions and decisions directly affected the harmony of the universe, and therefore, the ruler was responsible for upholding the moral and ethical principles dictated by the gods.

The divine nature of pharaohs also served as a unifying force in ancient Egyptian society. The belief in the pharaoh's divine authority and the connection to the gods provided a shared sense of identity and purpose among the people. It reinforced the notion that the pharaoh was not just an individual ruler but a divine figure who embodied the collective hopes, aspirations, and spiritual beliefs of the entire kingdom.

In conclusion, the connection between pharaohs and gods held immense significance in the religious and political framework of ancient Egypt. It ensured the pharaoh's authority and legitimacy as a ruler and provided a spiritual foundation for the governance and well-being of the kingdom. The beliefs and ideologies surrounding the divine nature of pharaohs shaped the ancient Egyptian worldview, influencing their religious practices, rituals, and societal cohesion. Exploring this connection offers valuable insights into the complex interplay between religion, politics, and culture in ancient Egypt.

Pharaoh as the Son of a God

The ancient Egyptians believed that pharaohs were not only connected to the gods but were often considered as the literal offspring of deities. Mythological narratives played a crucial role in establishing the divine lineage of pharaohs and further solidifying their authority. These myths depicted the pharaohs as the direct descendants of gods, emphasizing their divine heritage and positioning them as exceptional beings.

One prominent example of the mythological narratives surrounding the divine parentage of pharaohs is the story of Horus and Osiris. According to this myth, Osiris, the god of the underworld, ruled over Egypt before being murdered by his brother Seth. Osiris' wife, Isis, magically conceived their son Horus, who later became the rightful heir and avenger of his father's death. This narrative portrays the pharaoh as the legitimate successor to the divine lineage and reinforces the idea that they possess a divine essence derived from their godly parent.

Similarly, other pharaohs were associated with different gods through mythological narratives, such as Amun, Ra, or Ptah. These stories served to establish the pharaohs' divine connection and reinforce their authority. By aligning themselves with specific gods, the pharaohs symbolically merged their mortal existence with the divine, emphasizing their divine birthright to rule.

Implications of the Divine Lineage for Pharaohs' Authority

The belief in the pharaohs' divine parentage had significant implications for their authority and power within ancient Egyptian society. The divine lineage provided a strong foundation for the pharaohs' claim to rulership and justified their absolute authority over the kingdom. It was believed that their divine heritage bestowed upon them a unique wisdom, power, and legitimacy to govern and protect their people.

The association with gods through divine parentage elevated the pharaohs above ordinary mortals, establishing their exceptional status. This belief system created a hierarchical structure in which the pharaoh was considered closer to the divine realm than any other individual in the kingdom. It reinforced the notion that the pharaoh possessed a sacred duty to uphold the divine order and ensure the well-being of the land and its inhabitants.

Moreover, the divine lineage of pharaohs fostered a sense of continuity and stability in Egyptian society. The belief that each successive pharaoh was the direct descendant of the gods provided a seamless transition of power and reinforced the idea of dynastic rule. It assured the people that the pharaohs possessed an inherent divine right to rule, thereby minimizing challenges to their authority and promoting social cohesion.

However, it is important to note that the divine lineage of pharaohs also posed challenges and potential conflicts. Succession disputes could arise if multiple individuals claimed a legitimate divine lineage. Moreover, the association with gods and the divine lineage could lead to high expectations placed upon the pharaohs, requiring them to exemplify the qualities of their divine ancestors and maintain a harmonious relationship with the gods throughout their reign.

In conclusion, the belief in the pharaohs as the sons of gods through mythological narratives played a crucial role in shaping their authority and establishing their legitimacy as rulers. The divine lineage provided the pharaohs with an elevated status, exceptional wisdom, and a sense of divine purpose. It created a hierarchical structure within society, reinforced dynastic rule, and contributed to the stability of ancient Egyptian civilization. The implications of the divine lineage extended beyond the individual pharaoh, influencing the expectations placed upon them and the dynamics of succession.

Pharaoh as the Living Horus

One of the most significant associations in ancient Egyptian religion was that between the pharaoh and the god Horus. Horus was a central deity in Egyptian mythology, often depicted as a falcon-headed god or as a man with a falcon head. He was closely linked to kingship, protection, and divine authority. The pharaoh was believed to embody the essence of Horus, representing the living manifestation of this powerful deity.

The association between the pharaoh and Horus was rooted in the belief that the pharaoh inherited the kingship directly from the god. It was believed that the ruling pharaoh was the earthly incarnation of Horus and that the divine power and wisdom of Horus flowed through the pharaoh, empowering him to rule with legitimacy and effectiveness. This association established a direct link between the divine realm and the earthly realm, solidifying the pharaoh's authority as the divine ruler.

Symbolism and Rituals Highlighting the Pharaoh's Horus Connection

To emphasize the pharaoh's connection to Horus, various symbols and rituals were employed within ancient Egyptian culture. These symbols and rituals served as visual representations and enactments of the pharaoh's divine identity as the living Horus.

One prominent symbol associated with the pharaoh's Horus connection was the "serekh," a rectangular shape depicting the façade of a palace or shrine. The serekh featured a falcon perched on top, representing the presence of Horus. This symbol was frequently used in the pharaoh's name, signifying their divine association and legitimizing their rule. For example, the name of the pharaoh Khafre was written within a serekh, emphasizing his identification with Horus.

Rituals and ceremonies also played a significant role in highlighting the pharaoh's Horus connection. During important religious festivals and coronation rituals, the pharaoh would participate in reenactments that symbolized their divine identity. For example, the Heb Sed Festival, a jubilee celebration marking the pharaoh's thirty-year reign, included rituals where the pharaoh engaged in activities associated with Horus, such as the symbolic slaying of enemies or the renewal of their divine authority.

Additionally, the pharaoh's regalia and attire further emphasized their connection to Horus. The double crown, known as the Pschent, which combined the Red Crown of Lower Egypt and the White Crown of Upper Egypt, represented the pharaoh's dual kingship and their association with the gods Horus and Seth respectively. The use of falcon imagery and falcon-shaped headdresses also reinforced the pharaoh's Horus connection, visually aligning them with the divine falcon deity.

These symbols and rituals served to reinforce the pharaoh's divine authority and establish their connection to the god Horus. They visually and ceremonially expressed the pharaoh's divine lineage and affirmed their role as the living embodiment of Horus. The symbolism and rituals surrounding the pharaoh's Horus connection were integral to the religious and political ideologies of ancient Egypt, solidifying the pharaoh's authority and maintaining the cosmic order believed to be essential for the kingdom's prosperity and well-being.

In conclusion, the association of the pharaoh with the god Horus played a crucial role in ancient Egyptian religion and political ideology. The pharaoh was seen as the living embodiment of Horus, inheriting divine power and legitimacy directly from the god. Symbols such as the serekh and regalia, as well as rituals and ceremonies, highlighted the pharaoh's connection to Horus and visually represented their divine identity. These symbolic representations and enacted rituals reinforced the pharaoh's authority and affirmed their role as the divine ruler of Egypt. The association with Horus was central to the concept of pharaonic divinity and the maintenance of cosmic order within ancient Egyptian society.

Pharaoh as the God's Representative on Earth

In ancient Egyptian belief, the pharaoh held a pivotal role as the intermediary between the gods and the people, responsible for maintaining cosmic balance and ensuring the well-being of the kingdom. The pharaoh was believed to possess a divine mandate and acted as the earthly representative of the gods, serving as a crucial link in the cosmic order.

The pharaoh's primary responsibility was to uphold Ma'at, the fundamental principle of balance, harmony, and truth in Egyptian cosmology. Ma'at represented the natural order of the universe and encompassed concepts such as justice, morality, and cosmic stability. As the god's representative on Earth, the pharaoh's actions and decisions were believed to directly impact the maintenance of Ma'at.

The pharaoh's role in preserving cosmic balance extended beyond the human realm. It was believed that the gods relied on the pharaoh to perform rituals and ceremonies that would ensure the continued harmonious interaction between the divine and mortal realms. By maintaining a strong connection with the gods through offerings and rituals, the pharaoh played a crucial part in sustaining the cosmic order.

Rituals and Responsibilities Demonstrating the Pharaoh's Divine Mandate

To fulfill their role as the god's representative on Earth, the pharaoh was entrusted with specific rituals and responsibilities that demonstrated their divine mandate. These rituals and responsibilities served to reinforce the pharaoh's connection with the gods and reaffirm their authority as the divine ruler.

One of the key rituals performed by the pharaoh was the "Heb Sed" festival. This jubilee celebration marked the pharaoh's thirty-year reign and symbolized their renewal of divine authority. During the festival, the pharaoh would partake in various activities, including processions, offerings, and ceremonial races, demonstrating their physical and spiritual prowess as the chosen representative of the gods.

The pharaoh also had the responsibility of overseeing the construction and maintenance of temples dedicated to the gods. These temples served as sacred spaces where the pharaoh would perform rituals and offer sacrifices on behalf of the kingdom. By actively participating in these religious practices, the pharaoh reaffirmed their divine connection and solidified their role as the god's representative on Earth.

Furthermore, the pharaoh played a crucial role in the administration of justice. As the embodiment of Ma'at, the pharaoh was responsible for upholding fairness and order in society. This included hearing petitions, resolving disputes, and enacting laws that promoted justice and harmony. By serving as the ultimate arbiter of justice, the pharaoh demonstrated their divine mandate and their commitment to maintaining Ma'at.

In summary, the pharaoh served as the god's representative on Earth, entrusted with the task of maintaining cosmic balance and ensuring the well-being of the kingdom. Through their rituals and responsibilities, the pharaoh reinforced their divine mandate and solidified their role as the intermediary between the gods and the people. By upholding Ma'at, performing sacred rituals, overseeing temple construction, and administering justice, the pharaoh demonstrated their connection with the divine and their commitment to preserving the cosmic order. The pharaoh's role as the god's representative was integral to ancient Egyptian religious and political ideologies, establishing a divine authority that was essential for the kingdom's prosperity and stability.

Divine Rituals and Ceremonies for Pharaohs

The coronation rituals held significant importance in ancient Egypt as they marked the official ascension of the pharaoh to the throne and the establishment of their divine kingship. These rituals were highly symbolic and aimed to validate the pharaoh's authority as the ruler chosen by the gods.

One of the central elements of the coronation ceremony was the crowning of the pharaoh. The pharaoh would be adorned with the royal regalia, including the Double Crown, representing the unification of Upper and Lower Egypt, and the ceremonial beard, symbolizing divine wisdom and authority. The act of crowning signified the divine investiture of power and the pharaoh's transformation into a god-king.

Another vital aspect of the coronation ritual was the "Heb-Sed" ritual, which took place in the pharaoh's first year of rule. This ritual aimed to validate the pharaoh's ability to continue ruling effectively and maintaining cosmic balance. Through various activities, such as ceremonial races and offerings, the pharaoh would demonstrate their physical and spiritual prowess, reinforcing their divine mandate and ensuring the renewal of their rule.

Sed Festival and the Renewal of Pharaoh's Rule

The Sed Festival, known as the "Heb Sed" in ancient Egypt, was a significant ritual celebrated to mark the pharaoh's thirty-year reign and ensure the renewal of their rule. The festival was a culmination of the pharaoh's achievements and served as a testament to their enduring power and divine authority.

During the Sed Festival, the pharaoh would engage in various ceremonies and processions, often held in sacred spaces or temple complexes. These activities aimed to reaffirm the pharaoh's connection with the gods and their role as the divine ruler. The pharaoh would perform rituals, make offerings to the gods, and receive their blessings, symbolizing the continuous support of the divine in their rule.

The Sed Festival also provided an opportunity for the pharaoh to connect with their subjects. It was a time of celebration and unity, as people from different parts of the kingdom would gather to honor the pharaoh's reign. The festival emphasized the pharaoh's role as a unifying figure, bringing together the people under their divine authority and fostering a sense of national cohesion.

Funerary Rituals for Deceased Pharaohs

Funerary rituals held immense significance in ancient Egyptian culture, particularly for deceased pharaohs. These rituals were designed to ensure the successful transition of the pharaoh's spirit into the afterlife and to secure their eternal divine status.

Upon the death of a pharaoh, a complex series of funerary rituals would be conducted. The body of the pharaoh would undergo the process of mummification to preserve it for the journey into the afterlife. Elaborate funeral processions, accompanied by mourners, priests, and various symbolic objects, would escort the pharaoh's body to the final resting place, such as a royal tomb or pyramid.

Funerary rituals included the Opening of the Mouth ceremony, where the deceased pharaoh's mouth was symbolically opened to enable their spirit to eat and drink in the afterlife. This ritual was believed to restore the pharaoh's vital functions and ensure their sustenance in the divine realm.

Additionally, the pharaoh's tomb or pyramid would be filled with offerings, including food, drink, and personal belongings, to provide for the pharaoh's needs in the afterlife. These offerings were intended to sustain the pharaoh's divine existence and maintain their connection with the gods.

The funerary rituals for deceased pharaohs emphasized their continued divine status even beyond death. It was believed that the pharaoh would join the pantheon of gods, becoming an immortal deity and maintaining their role as a divine figure even in the afterlife.

In summary, divine rituals and ceremonies played a crucial role in ancient Egyptian society, particularly in relation to the pharaoh's divine authority. The coronation rituals established the pharaoh's divine kingship, while the Sed Festival ensured the renewal of their rule. Funerary rituals ensured the transition of deceased pharaohs into the afterlife, securing their eternal divine status. These rituals were imbued with symbolism and served to reinforce the pharaoh's connection with the gods, validating their authority and demonstrating their pivotal role as the divine ruler of ancient Egypt.

Challenges to Pharaohs' Divine Status

Despite the widespread belief in the divine nature of pharaohs in ancient Egypt, dissenting views and resistance to their divinity did exist within the society. While the pharaoh was revered as a living god, there were individuals and groups who questioned or rejected this perception. Such dissenting views often stemmed from different religious beliefs, political motivations, or social circumstances.

In ancient Egypt, the priests held significant religious authority and played a crucial role in the religious practices of the kingdom. Some priests and religious scholars might have challenged the notion of the pharaoh's divine status, considering it an exaggeration or promoting alternative religious beliefs. These dissenting views could arise from different interpretations of religious texts, local religious traditions, or even personal convictions. For example, in the later periods of Egyptian history, the rise of Atenism under Akhenaten challenged the traditional polytheistic beliefs and the pharaoh's divine status, focusing on the worship of the sun disk Aten as the supreme deity.

Additionally, there were instances of political opposition to the divine authority of pharaohs. Ambitious individuals or rival factions within the royal court or the nobility might have questioned the legitimacy of a particular pharaoh's divine lineage or sought to challenge their rule. This could manifest in attempts to depose or overthrow the pharaoh, either by rallying support among the nobles or inciting rebellions among the populace.

Political and Social Factors Impacting the Pharaohs' Legitimacy

The pharaoh's divine status and legitimacy were not solely determined by religious beliefs but were also influenced by political and social factors. The stability of the kingdom, the pharaoh's ability to maintain order, and their successful leadership played crucial roles in maintaining their perceived divine authority.

If a pharaoh faced significant political or military failures, such as territorial losses or economic downturns, it could undermine their legitimacy in the eyes of the people. Challenges from foreign powers, internal conflicts, or economic crises could lead to doubts regarding the pharaoh's divine favor and their ability to uphold Ma'at, the cosmic order that ensured harmony and prosperity.

Social factors, such as popular discontent or dissatisfaction with the ruling pharaoh's policies, could also impact their perceived divinity. If the common people experienced hardship or perceived injustices in their daily lives, they might question the pharaoh's divine mandate and believe that their ruler had lost the favor of the gods.

Furthermore, changes in religious beliefs and cultural shifts within Egyptian society could also influence the perception of the pharaoh's divine authority. For instance, during the Third Intermediate Period, when Egypt was fragmented and ruled by competing dynasties, the authority and divine status of individual pharaohs varied greatly, reflecting the political disunity and the decline of centralized power.

In conclusion, challenges to the divine status of pharaohs in ancient Egypt emerged from dissenting views, political opposition, and social factors. While the pharaoh was widely regarded as a living god, dissenting religious beliefs and political motivations could question or reject their divinity. Additionally, political and social factors such as political instability, military failures, or popular discontent could impact the pharaoh's legitimacy and their perceived divine authority. These challenges highlight the complex interplay between religious, political, and social dynamics within the ancient Egyptian society, shaping the understanding and acceptance of the pharaoh's divine status.

Chapter 19: Pharaonic Rituals and Religious Responsibilities

Rituals played a central role in the religious and ceremonial life of ancient Egypt, and the pharaoh, as the highest religious authority and living embodiment of the gods, had specific rituals and religious responsibilities that were unique to their divine position. These rituals encompassed a wide range of practices and ceremonies, each with its own significance and symbolism.

One of the most important rituals in the life of a pharaoh was the coronation ceremony, which marked the official ascension to the throne and the establishment of divine kingship. This elaborate and carefully orchestrated event involved various rituals, including the crowning of the pharaoh with the royal regalia, the anointing with sacred oils, and the presentation of ceremonial objects symbolizing their royal and divine authority. Through these rituals, the pharaoh was officially recognized as the ruler and representative of the gods on Earth.

Another significant ritual in the pharaoh's religious responsibilities was the Sed Festival, also known as the "Festival of the Tail." This festival was held to rejuvenate and renew the pharaoh's rule, typically after they had been in power for 30 years. It involved a series of ceremonies and processions, with the pharaoh engaging in physical activities to demonstrate their continued strength and vitality. The Sed Festival was a crucial moment for the pharaoh to reaffirm their divine authority and to assure the people of their ability to maintain order and prosperity.

Funerary rituals for deceased pharaohs were also of great importance in ancient Egypt. These rituals were conducted to ensure the smooth transition of the pharaoh's soul into the afterlife and to secure their eternal divine status. They involved elaborate burial ceremonies, mummification processes, and the construction of monumental tombs, such as the pyramids, to serve as eternal resting places for the pharaoh's physical remains. These funerary rituals were believed to facilitate the pharaoh's journey into the realm of the gods, where they would continue their divine existence.

Importance of Religious Responsibilities for Pharaohs

Religious responsibilities held immense significance for pharaohs in ancient Egypt, as they were believed to be the intermediaries between the gods and the people. The pharaoh's role in maintaining cosmic balance and order, known as Ma'at, was intricately tied to their religious responsibilities. It was believed that the pharaoh's adherence to religious rituals and the fulfillment of their religious duties directly impacted the well-being and prosperity of the kingdom.

The pharaoh's performance of religious rituals was not merely a ceremonial display but a vital aspect of their responsibilities as the divine ruler. By participating in these rituals, the pharaoh reaffirmed their connection to the gods, demonstrated their commitment to upholding Ma'at, and sought the divine blessings necessary for the harmony and stability of the kingdom.

Furthermore, the pharaoh's religious responsibilities extended beyond ceremonial rituals. They were expected to actively engage in the patronage and maintenance of temples, which served as the physical dwelling places of the gods and important centers of religious and social activities. The pharaoh oversaw the construction and restoration of temples, endowed them with offerings and resources, and appointed priests and priestesses to ensure the proper functioning of religious rituals and the continuous worship of the gods.

In conclusion, pharaonic rituals and religious responsibilities were integral to the divine role of the pharaoh in ancient Egypt. These rituals encompassed coronation ceremonies, Sed Festivals, and funerary rituals, among others, each with its own significance in affirming the pharaoh's divine authority and ensuring the well-being of the kingdom. The pharaoh's commitment to fulfilling their religious responsibilities was crucial in maintaining cosmic balance and upholding Ma'at. By actively participating in rituals and supporting temple activities, the pharaoh demonstrated their divine connection and played a vital role in the religious and ceremonial life of ancient Egypt.

Daily Rituals and Offerings by the Pharaoh

The pharaoh's role in daily religious practices was of utmost importance in ancient Egypt. As the divine ruler, the pharaoh was responsible for maintaining the cosmic balance and ensuring the gods' favor and protection over the kingdom. Daily rituals and offerings formed a crucial part of the pharaoh's religious responsibilities, allowing them to fulfill their divine duties and maintain the harmonious relationship between the human realm and the divine realm.

The pharaoh's day would typically begin with purification rituals to cleanse themselves before engaging in religious activities. This involved purifying the body through ritual bathing and adorning themselves with sacred regalia. The pharaoh would then proceed to the temple or designated sacred spaces within the palace, where they would lead and participate in various daily religious ceremonies.

One of the key rituals performed by the pharaoh was the act of making offerings to the gods. These offerings consisted of food, beverages, incense, and other valuable items that were believed to sustain and nourish the divine beings. The pharaoh would personally present these offerings as a gesture of reverence and gratitude to the gods, symbolizing their role as the intermediary between the human and divine realms.

Significance of Offerings Presented by the Pharaoh

The offerings presented by the pharaoh held deep symbolic and spiritual significance in ancient Egyptian religion. They were not merely material goods but acts of devotion and reciprocity, expressing the pharaoh's reverence and gratitude to the gods and seeking their benevolence in return.

The offerings provided sustenance to the gods, who were believed to rely on these offerings for their nourishment and well-being. By presenting food, beverages, and other valuable items, the pharaoh ensured that the gods remained satisfied and content, thereby safeguarding the cosmic balance and the prosperity of the kingdom.

Furthermore, offerings served as a means of establishing and maintaining a reciprocal relationship between the pharaoh and the gods. In ancient Egyptian belief, it was understood that the gods had a vested interest in the well-being and success of the pharaoh and the kingdom. Through offerings, the pharaoh demonstrated their commitment to fulfilling their divine responsibilities and sought the gods' continued protection, guidance, and favor.

The act of presenting offerings also had a symbolic significance. It represented the pharaoh's recognition of the gods' supreme authority and their own humble position as a servant and representative of the gods. It further emphasized the pharaoh's role as a mediator between the divine and mortal realms, bridging the gap and establishing a harmonious relationship between the two.

In conclusion, the daily rituals and offerings performed by the pharaoh were integral to their religious responsibilities and their role as the divine ruler of ancient Egypt. Through these rituals, the pharaoh expressed their devotion to the gods, maintained the cosmic balance, and sought divine blessings for the prosperity and well-being of the kingdom. The offerings presented by the pharaoh held both practical and symbolic significance, sustaining the gods and establishing a reciprocal relationship between the pharaoh and the divine beings.

Rituals for the Maintenance of Ma'at

The pharaoh's role in upholding cosmic order, known as Ma'at, was a fundamental aspect of their religious responsibilities in ancient Egypt. Ma'at represented the concept of divine harmony, balance, and justice that governed the universe. It encompassed principles such as truth, righteousness, balance, and order, and it was believed that the stability and prosperity of the kingdom depended on the pharaoh's ability to maintain Ma'at.

As the living embodiment of the gods, the pharaoh held the divine mandate to preserve and restore Ma'at. It was their sacred duty to ensure that the natural and social order remained in balance, free from chaos and disruption. The pharaoh's actions and adherence to Ma'at were believed to have a direct impact on the well-being of the kingdom and its inhabitants.

Rituals and Ceremonies to Maintain Balance and Harmony

To fulfill their responsibility in upholding Ma'at, the pharaoh engaged in a variety of rituals and ceremonies designed to maintain balance and harmony within the kingdom. These rituals were performed regularly and were often conducted in sacred spaces such as temples or designated ritual sites.

One important ritual for the maintenance of Ma'at was the daily offering ritual. As mentioned earlier, the pharaoh presented offerings to the gods as a means of sustaining their favor and maintaining the cosmic balance. These offerings were not only symbolic gestures of devotion but also practical actions that helped to nourish the gods and keep them satisfied.

Another significant ritual was the Heb Sed Festival, a jubilee celebration held to renew the pharaoh's rule and reaffirm their commitment to Ma'at. This festival involved elaborate ceremonies and rituals, including the pharaoh's symbolic reenactment of their coronation and their participation in various physical and intellectual challenges. The festival served as a public display of the pharaoh's power and authority, reinforcing their role as the guarantor of Ma'at.

Furthermore, the pharaoh participated in the ritual of the "stretching the cord" or "stretching the rope." This ritual involved the pharaoh holding a cord that symbolized the unity and stability of the kingdom, while priests and officials performed accompanying rituals and prayers. This act symbolized the pharaoh's commitment to maintaining the social and cosmic order, ensuring that the kingdom remained prosperous and harmonious.

Other rituals and ceremonies focused on specific aspects of Ma'at, such as justice and truth. The pharaoh would engage in rituals related to the administration of justice, offering prayers and supplications to ensure fair and equitable rulings. They would also participate in ceremonies that emphasized the importance of truth and integrity, as these virtues were considered essential for the maintenance of Ma'at.

In conclusion, the pharaoh's rituals and ceremonies for the maintenance of Ma'at were crucial for upholding cosmic order and ensuring the prosperity and stability of ancient Egyptian society. Through their participation in daily offering rituals, the Heb Sed Festival, and various other ceremonies, the pharaoh demonstrated their commitment to Ma'at and their role as the guardian of divine harmony. These rituals served as reminders of the pharaoh's responsibility to maintain balance and harmony, and they reinforced the interconnectedness between the pharaoh, the gods, and the well-being of the kingdom.

Pharaoh as the Chief Priest

In addition to their role as the political and divine leader of ancient Egypt, the pharaoh also held the position of the chief priest, responsible for overseeing and participating in temple rituals. The temples were considered the dwelling places of the gods and were central to the religious life of the kingdom. As the chief priest, the pharaoh played a vital role in the performance of these rituals, ensuring the connection between the earthly realm and the divine realm.

The pharaoh's involvement in temple rituals included leading and officiating at important ceremonies, making offerings to the gods, and performing sacred rites. They would enter the inner sanctuaries of the temples, where only the most high-ranking priests were allowed, to commune directly with the gods and seek their blessings.

The pharaoh's participation in temple rituals served multiple purposes. Firstly, it reaffirmed their status as the intermediary between the gods and the people. By actively engaging in the rituals, the pharaoh demonstrated their unique relationship with the divine and their ability to communicate with the gods on behalf of the entire kingdom. This further solidified the pharaoh's authority and legitimacy as the religious leader of Egypt.

Secondly, the pharaoh's involvement in temple rituals ensured the proper execution of the ceremonies and the correct performance of the sacred rites. The pharaoh's presence guaranteed that the rituals were carried out according to the established traditions and protocols, maintaining the integrity and authenticity of the religious practices. The pharaoh's active participation also set an example for other priests and devotees, emphasizing the importance of devotion and dedication in the worship of the gods.

Representation of the Pharaoh as the High Priest

In addition to their role as the chief priest, the pharaoh was also represented as the high priest in Egyptian religious ideology. This representation emphasized the pharaoh's unique connection with the gods and their ability to fulfill the priestly duties on behalf of the people.

As the high priest, the pharaoh embodied the ideal qualities and virtues associated with the priesthood. They were believed to possess divine wisdom, purity, and spiritual insight, making them uniquely qualified to perform sacred rituals and communicate with the gods. The pharaoh's status as the high priest further enhanced their religious authority and emphasized their role as the central figure in the religious life of ancient Egypt.

Furthermore, the pharaoh's representation as the high priest reinforced the concept of divine kingship. It conveyed the idea that the pharaoh not only held political power but also possessed the divine knowledge and spiritual insight necessary for the effective governance of the kingdom. By embodying both the roles of the political ruler and the high priest, the pharaoh symbolized the perfect union of temporal and spiritual authority.

The representation of the pharaoh as the high priest also had practical implications. It allowed the pharaoh to exert control over the temple priesthood and maintain a direct influence on religious matters. This ensured that the religious practices aligned with the pharaoh's vision and objectives, reinforcing their authority and further integrating religion and politics in ancient Egypt.

In conclusion, the pharaoh's role as the chief priest and their representation as the high priest underscored their involvement in temple rituals and their unique connection with the gods. The pharaoh's participation in temple ceremonies served to strengthen their religious authority and maintain the authenticity of the religious practices. The representation of the pharaoh as the high priest further emphasized their divine wisdom and spiritual insight, consolidating their position as the central figure in the religious and political life of ancient Egypt.

Rituals for the Success and Prosperity of the Kingdom

One of the prominent rituals associated with the success and prosperity of the kingdom in ancient Egypt was the Sed Festival. The Sed Festival was a jubilee celebration held to commemorate the pharaoh's thirty years on the throne and mark the renewal of their reign. This ritualistic event was of great importance as it symbolized the pharaoh's continued vigor, strength, and ability to rule effectively.

The Sed Festival served as a powerful affirmation of the pharaoh's legitimacy and divine mandate to govern. It was believed that through the performance of the Sed Festival, the pharaoh would be rejuvenated and granted an extended reign by the gods. The festival not only celebrated the pharaoh's achievements and longevity but also aimed to ensure the continuity and stability of the kingdom.

During the Sed Festival, elaborate ceremonies and rituals were conducted to reinforce the pharaoh's authority and ensure their continued success. The pharaoh would participate in a series of rituals, including processions, offerings, and symbolic acts, all aimed at renewing their divine connection and reaffirming their role as the protector and provider for the kingdom.

The Sed Festival also provided an opportunity for the pharaoh to display their power and magnificence to the people. The festivities were often accompanied by grand parades, performances, and public events, which allowed the pharaoh to showcase their wealth, prestige, and ability to rule. This spectacle served to instill a sense of awe and reverence among the populace, further reinforcing the pharaoh's position as the divine ruler and guarantor of prosperity.

Rituals to Ensure Fertility, Abundance, and Protection

The ancient Egyptians held a deep belief in the interdependence between the natural world and the well-being of the kingdom. To ensure fertility, abundance, and protection for the kingdom, various rituals were performed by the pharaoh and the priesthood.

One important ritual aimed at ensuring agricultural fertility was the "Flooding of the Fields" ceremony. This ritual involved the symbolic flooding of agricultural lands, mimicking the annual flooding of the Nile River. The pharaoh would oversee this ceremony, offering prayers and invocations for a bountiful harvest. This ritual symbolized the pharaoh's role as the provider of fertility and sustenance to the kingdom, ensuring the prosperity of the land and its people.

Another significant ritual was the "Offering to the Gods" ceremony, where the pharaoh would present offerings to the gods, expressing gratitude and seeking their blessings for the kingdom. These offerings included food, drink, incense, and precious objects, symbolizing the pharaoh's dedication and commitment to the gods. By making these offerings, the pharaoh aimed to maintain a harmonious relationship with the divine forces and ensure their favor and protection for the kingdom.

Additionally, rituals for protection played a crucial role in safeguarding the kingdom from external threats and maintaining its security. The "Ritual of the Protective Amulets" was performed by the pharaoh to invoke the power of specific protective deities. Amulets and charms representing these deities were worn by the pharaoh as symbols of divine protection. This ritual demonstrated the pharaoh's role as the guardian and defender of the kingdom, ensuring its safety and well-being.

These rituals for fertility, abundance, and protection were not only performed by the pharaoh but also involved the participation of priests, priestesses, and the wider community. Through their collective efforts, these rituals aimed to establish a harmonious relationship between the human, divine, and natural realms, thereby ensuring the success and prosperity of the kingdom.

In conclusion, the Sed Festival served as a significant ritual for the continuation of the pharaoh's reign and the stability of the kingdom. Rituals for fertility, abundance, and protection were conducted to ensure the well-being and prosperity of the kingdom. These rituals not only reinforced the pharaoh's authority and divine mandate but also established a connection between the earthly and divine realms, emphasizing the interdependence between human actions and the blessings of the gods.

Chapter 20: Influence of Egyptian Religion on Other Cultures

Ancient Egyptian religion exerted a significant influence on various cultures throughout history. Its impact extended beyond the borders of Egypt, reaching neighboring civilizations as well as distant lands. The beliefs, rituals, and symbols of ancient Egyptian religion resonated with people across different regions, shaping their spiritual practices and influencing the development of their own religious systems.

The widespread influence of Egyptian religion can be attributed to several factors. Firstly, Egypt's geographical location at the crossroads of Africa, Asia, and Europe facilitated cultural exchanges and trade routes, allowing the dissemination of religious ideas to neighboring civilizations. Additionally, Egypt's political and military power during certain periods further enhanced its cultural influence and made its religious concepts more accessible to other societies.

Egyptian religion was characterized by a complex pantheon of gods and goddesses, intricate rituals, and a strong emphasis on the afterlife. These distinct features of Egyptian religion captured the imagination of people from diverse backgrounds, leading to the adoption and adaptation of Egyptian religious concepts in different cultural contexts.

Cross-Cultural Exchanges and Transmission of Religious Concepts

The transmission of Egyptian religious concepts to other cultures was facilitated by various means, including trade, conquest, migration, and cultural interactions. As ancient civilizations came into contact with Egypt, they encountered its religious practices and often integrated elements of Egyptian religion into their own belief systems.

One notable example of the influence of Egyptian religion is its impact on the religious practices of the ancient Near East. The Egyptian concept of divine kingship, wherein the pharaoh was considered a god-king and the intermediary between the divine and earthly realms, influenced the development of similar concepts in Mesopotamia, Anatolia, and Canaan. For instance, in Mesopotamia, the idea of a ruler being divinely appointed and responsible for maintaining cosmic order can be traced back to the influence of Egyptian religion.

Egyptian religious symbols and motifs also found their way into the art and architecture of other cultures. The use of animal symbolism, such as the sphinx and the falcon, can be seen in the art of ancient Greece and Rome, where Egyptian motifs were incorporated into their own religious iconography. The fascination with Egyptian deities like Isis and Osiris also spread to the Greco-Roman world, where they were assimilated into the wider religious landscape.

Furthermore, the influence of Egyptian religion extended to the religious practices of Nubia, Kush, and Ethiopia. These neighboring regions, which had close cultural and trade ties with Egypt, adopted and adapted various aspects of Egyptian religious beliefs and rituals, integrating them into their own indigenous religious systems.

It is important to note that while Egyptian religion had a significant influence on other cultures, it was not a one-sided process. There were reciprocal exchanges and interactions, with foreign religious concepts and practices also influencing Egyptian religion to some extent. This dynamic process of cultural exchange and borrowing enriched the religious landscape of various civilizations and fostered a cross-cultural pollination of ideas.

In conclusion, ancient Egyptian religion left an indelible mark on the religious beliefs and practices of numerous cultures. Its widespread influence can be attributed to Egypt's geopolitical position, cultural interactions, and the appeal of its religious concepts. The transmission of Egyptian religious ideas occurred through trade networks, conquest, migration, and cultural exchanges, leading to the assimilation and adaptation of Egyptian religious elements by neighboring and distant civilizations. The cross-cultural fertilization of religious concepts enriched the spiritual traditions of these cultures and highlights the enduring legacy of ancient Egyptian religion.

Egyptian Religion and the Near East

The ancient Near East witnessed a dynamic exchange of religious ideas and practices between Egypt and Mesopotamia. While Egyptian and Mesopotamian religions had distinct characteristics, there were notable connections and shared concepts that emerged through cultural interactions.

One significant connection between Egyptian and Mesopotamian religious beliefs was the concept of divine kingship. In both civilizations, the ruler was considered a representative of the gods and held a crucial role in maintaining cosmic order. However, there were notable differences in how this concept was manifested. In Egypt, the pharaoh was seen as the living embodiment of the gods and possessed divine authority, while in Mesopotamia, the king was considered a servant of the gods and ruled with their blessing.

The influence of Egyptian religion on Mesopotamia can be observed in the adoption of certain Egyptian deities and religious practices. For instance, the goddess Ishtar, originally an Mesopotamian deity associated with love, fertility, and war, was influenced by the Egyptian goddess Isis. This syncretism resulted in a more expansive and multifaceted understanding of Ishtar, incorporating attributes from both cultures.

Furthermore, the spread of Egyptian religious motifs and iconography in Mesopotamia is evident in the art and architecture of the region. Egyptian symbols, such as the solar disk and the use of animal representations, influenced the artistic expressions of Mesopotamian cultures, demonstrating the cross-pollination of religious ideas.

Influence of Egyptian Religion on Canaanite and Phoenician Cultures

The influence of Egyptian religion extended beyond Mesopotamia to the cultures of Canaan and Phoenicia, which encompassed present-day Lebanon, Israel, Palestine, and parts of Syria. The geographical proximity and cultural interactions between Egypt and these regions played a significant role in the transmission of religious concepts.

In Canaanite culture, there was a significant adoption of Egyptian religious motifs and deities. The god Baal, a prominent deity in Canaanite religion associated with storms and fertility, shows some influence from Egyptian religious ideas. Baal's role as a provider of rain and fertility reflects similarities with the Egyptian god Osiris, who was associated with agriculture and the cycle of life and death.

Moreover, the spread of Egyptian religious practices is evident in the archaeological record of Canaanite sites. Temples dedicated to Egyptian deities, such as Hathor and Ptah, were established, showcasing the integration of Egyptian religious rituals into the religious landscape of the region.

The influence of Egyptian religion on Phoenician culture is also noteworthy. The Phoenicians, renowned for their seafaring prowess and extensive trade networks, interacted closely with Egyptian civilization. As a result, Egyptian religious ideas and practices were assimilated and adapted into Phoenician religious beliefs.

The goddess Astarte, worshipped in Phoenicia, exhibited parallels with the Egyptian goddess Isis. Astarte's association with fertility, love, and protection echoes the attributes of Isis, highlighting the influence of Egyptian religious concepts on Phoenician religious traditions.

Additionally, the Phoenician city of Byblos played a vital role in the transmission of Egyptian religious texts and knowledge to the wider Mediterranean world. The city's prominence as a center of trade and cultural exchange facilitated the dissemination of Egyptian religious ideas to other cultures in the region.

In conclusion, the connections between Egyptian and Mesopotamian religious beliefs as well as the influence of Egyptian religion on Canaanite and Phoenician cultures highlight the intricate web of cross-cultural exchanges in the ancient Near East. The adoption of Egyptian deities, the incorporation of Egyptian religious motifs in art and architecture, and the assimilation of Egyptian rituals into local religious practices demonstrate the enduring impact of Egyptian religion on neighboring civilizations. These influences contributed to the richness and diversity of religious beliefs and practices in the ancient Near East, showcasing the dynamic nature of cultural interactions and the interconnectedness of ancient civilizations.

Egyptian Religion and Greek Mythology

The influence of Egyptian religion on Greek mythology is evident through the incorporation of Egyptian deities into the Greek pantheon. As the ancient Greeks encountered Egyptian culture and religious practices, they identified parallels between Egyptian and Greek gods and sought to assimilate Egyptian deities into their own mythological framework.

One notable example is the identification of the Egyptian goddess Isis with the Greek goddess Demeter. Both goddesses were associated with fertility, agriculture, and the cycle of life and death. The Greek myth of Demeter and Persephone, which explains the changing of the seasons, bears similarities to the Egyptian myth of Isis and Osiris, which revolves around the themes of death and rebirth.

Another Egyptian deity that found a place in Greek mythology was the god Hermes, who became associated with the Egyptian god Thoth. Both gods were patrons of wisdom, writing, and magic. The Greek god Hermes inherited the attributes and roles of Thoth, becoming the messenger of the gods and the protector of travelers and thieves.

Impact of Egyptian Religious Motifs on Greek Religious Practices

The encounters between the Greeks and Egyptians also resulted in the adoption of Egyptian religious motifs and iconography in Greek religious practices. The artistic and architectural styles of ancient Egypt influenced Greek artistic expressions, leading to the incorporation of Egyptian elements into Greek temples and sculptures.

One prominent example is the use of the sphinx, a mythical creature with the body of a lion and the head of a human or animal, in Greek art and mythology. The Greek sphinx, often depicted with the head of a woman, drew inspiration from the Egyptian sphinx, which symbolized wisdom and guardianship. The most famous Greek myth featuring a sphinx is the story of Oedipus, who must solve the riddle posed by the sphinx to save the city of Thebes.

Additionally, the Greek city of Alexandria, founded by Alexander the Great in Egypt, became a center for the blending of Greek and Egyptian religious practices. The city's famous Library of Alexandria housed a vast collection of Egyptian religious texts and served as a hub for intellectual and cultural exchange. Greek scholars had the opportunity to study and interpret Egyptian religious ideas, which inevitably influenced their own religious beliefs.

It is important to note that while there were instances of Egyptian religious influence on Greek mythology and practices, the Greeks often adapted and assimilated these concepts into their own cultural and religious context. Greek mythology retained its distinct characteristics and narratives, incorporating Egyptian elements in a way that aligned with their existing religious framework.

In conclusion, the influence of Egyptian religion on Greek mythology is evident in the incorporation of Egyptian deities into the Greek pantheon and the adoption of Egyptian religious motifs and iconography. These interactions and exchanges enriched Greek religious practices, showcasing the interconnectedness of ancient civilizations and the impact of cultural encounters on the development of religious beliefs and mythologies.

Egyptian Religion and Nubian Cultures

The relationship between ancient Egypt and Nubia, located to the south of Egypt along the Nile River, involved a significant exchange of religious ideas. Nubia, also known as Kush, was influenced by Egyptian culture and religion due to its geographical proximity and historical interactions with Egypt. As a result, Nubian cultures adopted and adapted various elements of Egyptian religious practices.

The Nubians worshipped many of the same deities as the Egyptians, albeit with local variations. The gods and goddesses of the Egyptian pantheon, such as Amun, Isis, and Horus, were venerated in Nubia with their own Nubian names and distinctive characteristics. This suggests a syncretism between Egyptian and Nubian religious traditions, where the Nubians incorporated Egyptian deities into their own religious framework while maintaining their unique cultural identity.

Furthermore, the presence of Egyptian temples and cult centers in Nubia indicates the spread of Egyptian religious influence. The construction of temples dedicated to Egyptian gods, such as Amun-Ra, at sites like Napata and Meroe, attests to the Nubians' reverence for Egyptian religious practices. These temples served as religious centers where rituals and offerings were performed, and priests conducted ceremonies following Egyptian traditions.

Assimilation and Transformation of Egyptian Religious Practices in Nubian Cultures

While Nubian cultures adopted elements of Egyptian religion, they also transformed these practices to align with their own cultural beliefs and rituals. Nubian religious practices often incorporated indigenous deities and incorporated Nubian symbolism and iconography.

For example, the Nubians developed their own pantheon of gods and goddesses alongside the Egyptian deities they worshipped. These Nubian deities were often associated with specific Nubian cultural elements and natural phenomena, reflecting the Nubians' unique understanding of the divine.

Additionally, Nubian religious art and iconography demonstrated a blending of Egyptian and Nubian styles. The representations of deities and religious scenes combined Egyptian artistic conventions with Nubian features and symbols. This fusion of artistic traditions served to express the synthesis of Egyptian and Nubian religious beliefs and cultural identities.

The Nubians also adapted Egyptian religious rituals and ceremonies to suit their own context. While the general structure and purpose of the rituals may have mirrored those of the Egyptians, Nubian priests and devotees infused them with Nubian cultural elements and local traditions. This allowed for a distinct expression of religious devotion that incorporated both Egyptian and Nubian influences.

In conclusion, the relationship between ancient Egypt and Nubia involved a significant exchange of religious ideas, resulting in the assimilation and transformation of Egyptian religious practices in Nubian cultures. The Nubians adopted Egyptian deities, constructed temples following Egyptian architectural styles, and performed rituals influenced by Egyptian traditions. However, they also infused their own cultural elements, beliefs, and artistic expressions into these practices, creating a unique blend of Egyptian and Nubian religious traditions. This syncretism reflects the dynamic nature of cultural interactions and the ability of societies to adapt and incorporate foreign religious ideas while maintaining their own distinct identities.

Egyptian Religion and Mediterranean Cultures

The influence of Egyptian religious beliefs extended beyond the borders of Egypt and reached various Mediterranean cultures, leaving a lasting impact on their religious practices. The spread of Egyptian religion in the Mediterranean region can be attributed to factors such as trade, conquest, and cultural exchange.

Egypt's strategic location as a hub of trade and its status as a powerful empire facilitated the dissemination of its religious ideas to neighboring regions. Through trade networks and diplomatic interactions, Egyptian religious concepts and rituals were introduced to Mediterranean cultures such as the Greeks and the Romans.

Furthermore, the conquests of Alexander the Great and the subsequent Hellenistic period resulted in the fusion of Egyptian and Greek cultures, known as Greece-Egyptian syncretism. This cultural synthesis allowed for the integration of Egyptian religious beliefs and practices into the Hellenistic world, spreading Egyptian religious influence even further.

Influence of Egyptian Religious Iconography on Roman and Hellenistic Cultures

One of the significant ways in which Egyptian religion impacted Mediterranean cultures was through its religious iconography. Egyptian gods and goddesses were often depicted in human or animal form with distinctive attributes and symbols. These iconic representations found their way into the art and religious practices of Roman and Hellenistic societies.

In the Hellenistic period, Egyptian religious motifs and iconography were incorporated into Greek religious practices, resulting in the emergence of a hybrid style known as Egyptianizing art. This style involved the integration of Egyptian symbols and artistic conventions, such as the use of hieroglyphs, falcon-headed deities, and the portrayal of divine figures in the Egyptian artistic canon.

Similarly, Roman culture, particularly during the Roman Empire, was influenced by Egyptian religious iconography. The Romans, known for their assimilation of diverse cultures, adopted and adapted Egyptian artistic motifs in their depictions of deities and religious scenes. Egyptian gods and goddesses, such as Isis and Serapis, gained popularity in Roman religious syncretism, often associated with concepts of fertility, healing, and divine protection.

The influence of Egyptian religious iconography is evident in the architecture of Roman temples as well. The use of obelisks, an architectural feature borrowed from ancient Egypt, adorned various Roman cities as symbols of power and prestige. These obelisks served as both decorative elements and representations of the connection between the Roman Empire and the divine authority of the pharaohs.

In conclusion, Egyptian religion had a profound impact on Mediterranean cultures, spreading its beliefs and religious practices throughout the region. The dissemination of Egyptian religious ideas was facilitated by trade, conquest, and cultural exchange. The influence of Egyptian religious iconography, with its distinct symbolism and artistic conventions, can be observed in the art and religious practices of Roman and Hellenistic cultures. The integration of Egyptian religious motifs into Mediterranean societies reflects the enduring fascination with Egyptian spirituality and the ability of different cultures to incorporate and adapt foreign religious concepts into their own belief systems.

Part 7: Impact of Egyptian Religion on Neighboring Civilizations

The religious beliefs and practices of ancient Egypt had a profound influence on the civilizations that neighbored this great empire. From the Near East to Nubia, and even reaching Mediterranean cultures, Egyptian religion left an indelible mark on the religious landscape of these regions. This part explores the extensive impact of Egyptian religion on neighboring civilizations, delving into the connections, exchanges, and transformations that occurred as a result.

Egypt's religious system was a rich tapestry of gods, rituals, and cosmological concepts, deeply intertwined with the daily lives and worldview of the ancient Egyptians. As Egypt interacted with its neighboring cultures, both through trade and conquest, elements of its religious tradition were disseminated and adopted, shaping the religious practices and beliefs of these civilizations in significant ways.

The influence of Egyptian religion on neighboring civilizations was not a one-sided affair. While Egyptian beliefs and practices found resonance in these cultures, they also underwent adaptations and assimilations to align with the existing religious frameworks and traditions of these regions. This interplay of cultural exchange and synthesis resulted in a dynamic and diverse religious landscape, characterized by the fusion of Egyptian religious motifs and local religious systems.

This part will delve into various aspects of the impact of Egyptian religion on neighboring civilizations. It will examine the connections between Egyptian and Near Eastern religious beliefs, exploring the shared mythological narratives and the cross-pollination of religious concepts. The influence of Egyptian religion on the Canaanite and Phoenician cultures will also be explored, shedding light on the assimilation and transformation of Egyptian religious practices in these societies.

Furthermore, the impact of Egyptian religion on Greek mythology and religious practices will be examined. Greek mythology incorporated Egyptian deities, while Egyptian religious motifs influenced Greek religious art and rituals. The syncretism of Egyptian and Greek religious traditions resulted in a unique amalgamation of beliefs and practices that left a lasting impact on the religious landscape of the Mediterranean.

Lastly, the exchange of religious ideas between ancient Egypt and Nubia, a region to the south of Egypt, will be explored. The assimilation and transformation of Egyptian religious practices in Nubian cultures will be examined, highlighting the adaptability and flexibility of Egyptian religious beliefs as they encountered different cultural contexts.

By exploring the influence of Egyptian religion on neighboring civilizations, we gain a deeper understanding of the interconnectedness of ancient cultures and the enduring legacy of Egyptian spirituality. This exploration allows us to appreciate the complex dynamics of cultural exchange, adaptation, and synthesis that shaped the religious beliefs and practices of these civilizations, enriching their religious traditions and creating a tapestry of diverse spiritual expressions.

Join us as we embark on a journey through time and space, uncovering the fascinating impact of Egyptian religion on the beliefs and practices of neighboring civilizations. Through a careful examination of historical records, archaeological evidence, and cultural artifacts, we will unravel the intricate web of connections that linked these ancient societies and contributed to the vibrant religious tapestry of the ancient world.

Chapter 21: Exchanges and Syncretism with Other Ancient Religions

The religious landscape of the ancient world was not isolated but rather interconnected through a complex web of cultural exchanges and interactions. Among the civilizations that played a significant role in this interconnectedness was ancient Egypt, a civilization whose religious beliefs and practices had a profound impact on neighboring cultures.

Ancient Egypt, with its rich religious tradition and cosmological concepts, interacted with various neighboring civilizations through trade, diplomacy, and sometimes conquest. These interactions fostered the exchange of ideas, beliefs, and religious practices, creating a vibrant tapestry of cross-cultural influences and syncretism.

From the Near East and Nubia to the Mediterranean and beyond, ancient Egypt engaged with a diverse array of cultures, each with its own unique religious traditions. Through these encounters, Egyptian religious beliefs found resonance and assimilation, while simultaneously influencing and shaping the religious practices of these neighboring civilizations.

Importance of cultural exchanges and syncretism in religious practices

Cultural exchanges and syncretism, the blending of religious ideas and practices from different traditions, played a crucial role in the development and evolution of ancient religions. These exchanges allowed for the transmission of religious concepts, mythologies, rituals, and iconography across borders, fostering a rich tapestry of shared beliefs and practices.

The cultural encounters between ancient Egypt and its neighbors brought about a dynamic process of syncretism, where elements of Egyptian religion were integrated into the existing religious frameworks of other civilizations. This syncretism not only enriched the religious traditions of these cultures but also facilitated a deeper understanding and appreciation of the diverse spiritual expressions of the ancient world.

By exploring the exchanges and syncretism between ancient Egyptian religion and neighboring civilizations, we gain valuable insights into the interconnectedness of ancient cultures and the universality of certain religious themes and concepts. This exploration allows us to transcend the boundaries of individual civilizations and appreciate the collective spiritual heritage of humanity.

In this part, we will delve into the various exchanges and syncretic relationships that occurred between ancient Egyptian religion and neighboring cultures. We will explore the impact of Egyptian religious beliefs on the Near East, Nubia, and Mediterranean civilizations. Through a careful examination of historical records, archaeological evidence, and cultural artifacts, we will unravel the complex tapestry of interactions and influences that shaped the religious beliefs and practices of these ancient civilizations.

Join us on this journey of exploration as we trace the threads of ancient religious exchange and syncretism, shedding light on the interconnectedness of human spirituality and the enduring legacy of ancient Egyptian religion. By studying the multifaceted connections between these ancient cultures, we deepen our understanding of the complex and diverse tapestry of religious beliefs and practices that have shaped our world.

Egyptian Influence on Mesopotamian Religions

The ancient civilizations of Egypt and Mesopotamia, located in close proximity to each other, engaged in frequent contact and cultural exchanges. These interactions resulted in the sharing of religious concepts and the assimilation of certain deities into each other's pantheons.

Despite their geographical and cultural differences, Egypt and Mesopotamia shared some fundamental religious beliefs. Both civilizations recognized the existence of a pantheon of gods and goddesses who controlled various aspects of the natural world and human affairs. They believed in the divine order of the universe and the importance of maintaining cosmic balance.

Furthermore, some deities were recognized and worshiped in both Egyptian and Mesopotamian religious systems, although they often took on different names and attributes. For instance, the sky god Horus in Egyptian mythology bore similarities to the Mesopotamian god Marduk, both associated with kingship and divine authority. The goddess Isis in Egyptian mythology shared similarities with the Mesopotamian goddess Ishtar, both associated with love, fertility, and protection.

Examples of syncretism and cultural borrowing

The interactions between Egypt and Mesopotamia resulted in instances of syncretism and cultural borrowing, where religious concepts and practices were assimilated and integrated into the respective religious traditions. This syncretism is evident in various aspects of religious life, including mythology, iconography, and rituals.

One prominent example of syncretism between the two civilizations is the worship of the goddess Ishtar in Mesopotamia and her assimilation with the Egyptian goddess Isis. Over time, the attributes and symbolism of both deities merged, creating a syncretic goddess who embodied aspects of love, fertility, magic, and protection.

Another example is the adoption of Egyptian architectural and artistic styles in Mesopotamian temples and palaces. The grandeur and symbolism of Egyptian temples, characterized by colossal statues, obelisks, and elaborate wall reliefs, influenced the construction and ornamentation of Mesopotamian religious and royal structures.

The syncretic influence between Egypt and Mesopotamia was not limited to mythology and art but extended to religious rituals and practices as well. For instance, both civilizations engaged in offerings and sacrifices to appease and honor the gods. The rituals surrounding these practices, such as purification rites and the use of incense, show similarities and shared religious concepts.

By examining these examples of syncretism and cultural borrowing, we gain a deeper understanding of the interconnectedness of ancient civilizations and the fluidity of religious beliefs and practices. The exchange of ideas and the assimilation of foreign concepts enriched the religious traditions of both Egypt and Mesopotamia, creating a dynamic tapestry of shared beliefs and cultural influences.

In the following sections, we will explore further examples of syncretism and cultural borrowing between ancient Egyptian and Mesopotamian religions. Through the examination of textual evidence, archaeological findings, and artistic representations, we will uncover the intricate web of religious exchange and the enduring impact of these interactions on the spiritual landscape of both civilizations.

Interactions with Canaanite and Phoenician Religions

The ancient Egyptian civilization had significant interactions with the neighboring Canaanite and Phoenician cultures, located in the region known today as modern-day Lebanon, Israel, Palestine, and parts of Syria. These interactions facilitated the exchange of religious ideas, rituals, and beliefs between the Egyptians and the Canaanites and Phoenicians.

The proximity and trade routes between these civilizations fostered cultural and religious exchanges. Canaanite and Phoenician traders regularly visited Egypt, bringing with them their own religious practices and beliefs, which inevitably influenced and intermingled with the religious landscape of Egypt.

Syncretism and adaptation of Egyptian and Canaanite religious elements

The interactions between the Egyptian, Canaanite, and Phoenician cultures led to a process of syncretism, where elements from different religious traditions were merged or adapted to create a new and unique religious synthesis. This syncretism resulted in the assimilation of certain Egyptian deities into the Canaanite and Phoenician pantheons, as well as the incorporation of Canaanite and Phoenician religious motifs and practices into Egyptian religious rituals.

One notable example of syncretism is the assimilation of the Canaanite god Baal into the Egyptian religious framework. Baal, a prominent deity in Canaanite mythology associated with storms, fertility, and agricultural abundance, was integrated into the Egyptian pantheon under the name of Baal-Hadad. This syncretic deity represented the combined attributes of the Canaanite Baal and the Egyptian god Seth, who was associated with chaos and storms.

The Phoenicians, known for their seafaring and trade networks, also had significant religious exchanges with Egypt. The Phoenician goddess Astarte, associated with love, fertility, and war, was closely connected to the Egyptian goddess Isis. This syncretism resulted in the emergence of a hybrid deity known as Isis-Astarte, representing the amalgamation of both Egyptian and Phoenician religious traditions.

In addition to syncretism, the Egyptians also adapted certain Canaanite and Phoenician religious elements into their own rituals and practices. For example, the Canaanite and Phoenician tradition of sacred groves and nature worship influenced the Egyptian practice of associating specific trees and plants with deities and incorporating them into religious ceremonies.

These examples of syncretism and adaptation highlight the dynamic nature of ancient religious interactions and the ability of cultures to integrate and incorporate foreign religious elements into their own belief systems. The exchange of religious ideas between the Egyptians and the Canaanites and Phoenicians enriched the spiritual landscape of all involved, fostering a cross-pollination of religious motifs, rituals, and concepts.

In the subsequent sections, we will delve deeper into the specific instances of syncretism and adaptation between the Egyptian, Canaanite, and Phoenician religions. Through the examination of textual evidence, archaeological discoveries, and artistic representations, we will unravel the intricate tapestry of religious exchange and explore the enduring impact of these interactions on the religious beliefs and practices of these ancient cultures.

Hellenistic and Roman Influence on Egyptian Religion

During the Hellenistic and Roman periods, Egypt came under the influence of Greek and Roman conquerors who introduced their own religious beliefs and practices to the Egyptian society. The conquest of Egypt by Alexander the Great in 332 BCE marked the beginning of the Hellenistic era, during which Greek culture and religion greatly impacted Egyptian society. Subsequently, Egypt fell under Roman rule in 30 BCE after the death of Cleopatra VII.

The Greek conquerors, while recognizing the rich and ancient religious traditions of Egypt, also sought to integrate their own religious beliefs into the Egyptian context. This led to a process of syncretism, where Greek deities and religious concepts were combined with the existing Egyptian religious framework. Greek gods and goddesses such as Zeus, Hermes, and Aphrodite were identified with their Egyptian counterparts, resulting in the creation of new hybrid deities. For example, the Greek god Hermes was associated with the Egyptian god Thoth, resulting in the syncretic deity Hermes Trismegistus.

Similarly, the Roman conquerors brought their own religious practices to Egypt. The Roman pantheon of gods and goddesses, such as Jupiter, Mars, and Venus, found parallels and associations with the Egyptian deities. This led to the syncretic fusion of Roman and Egyptian religious elements, resulting in the emergence of new deities and rituals that incorporated both Roman and Egyptian characteristics.

Syncretism and integration of Greek and Egyptian deities and rituals

The interaction between Greek, Roman, and Egyptian religious traditions led to the syncretic blending of deities and rituals. This syncretism resulted in the emergence of new gods and goddesses who combined attributes from both Greek and Egyptian traditions. One prominent example is the syncretism of the Greek god Osiris with the Egyptian god Serapis, creating the deity Serapis-Osiris. Serapis-Osiris embodied the aspects of both Greek and Egyptian beliefs, serving as a bridge between the two cultures.

Greek and Roman rulers in Egypt also sought to affirm their authority by incorporating Egyptian religious practices and rituals into their own rule. This involved participating in traditional Egyptian ceremonies and portraying themselves as pharaohs, adopting the Egyptian iconography and regalia associated with divine kingship. The syncretism of Egyptian and Greek or Roman religious elements served to legitimize the rule of these foreign conquerors in the eyes of the Egyptian population.

Moreover, the integration of Greek and Egyptian religious beliefs was not limited to deities alone but also extended to religious rituals and practices. Egyptian temples, originally dedicated to Egyptian deities, began to incorporate Greek architectural styles and religious practices. Greek-style processions, festivals, and rituals became part of the religious calendar in Egypt, merging with existing Egyptian customs.

The syncretism and integration of Greek and Roman religious elements into Egyptian religion brought about a transformation in the religious landscape of ancient Egypt. This amalgamation of traditions allowed for the preservation of Egyptian religious practices, while also accommodating and adapting to the new cultural and religious influences brought by the Greek and Roman conquerors.

In the following sections, we will delve into specific examples of syncretism and the integration of Greek and Roman religious beliefs into Egyptian religion. Through the examination of archaeological evidence, inscriptions, and artistic representations, we will unravel the complexities of this interplay between cultures and explore the enduring impact of these interactions on the religious beliefs and practices of ancient Egypt.

African and Nubian Influences on Egyptian Religion

The interaction between ancient Egypt and Nubia, located to the south of Egypt along the Nile River, resulted in a significant exchange of religious concepts and practices. Nubia, known for its rich cultural heritage and long-standing connections with Egypt, played a crucial role in shaping Egyptian religion and vice versa.

The relationship between ancient Egypt and Nubia was characterized by both cultural exchange and political influence. As Egypt extended its influence southward, Nubia adopted many aspects of Egyptian culture, including religious beliefs and practices. Egyptian deities and religious motifs became incorporated into Nubian religious traditions, while Nubian deities and rituals also influenced Egyptian religion.

Syncretism and hybridization of Egyptian and Nubian religious traditions

The interaction between Egyptian and Nubian cultures led to the syncretism and hybridization of religious traditions. This syncretism involved the merging and adaptation of Egyptian and Nubian deities, rituals, and religious symbols, resulting in a unique blend of beliefs and practices.

One example of syncretism between Egyptian and Nubian religious traditions is the deity known as Mandulis. Mandulis was a solar deity worshiped in both Egypt and Nubia, associated with the sun and considered a symbol of royal power. In Nubia, Mandulis was particularly revered, and his cult centers, such as Kalabsha and Philae, played significant roles in Nubian religious life. The worship of Mandulis in Nubia incorporated elements from both Egyptian and Nubian religious traditions, reflecting the cultural exchange and syncretism between the two regions.

Similarly, the Nubian deity Apedemak, depicted as a lion-headed god, had strong connections to Egyptian religion. Apedemak was associated with war, protection, and fertility and was worshiped by the rulers of the Kushite kingdom in Nubia. The influence of Egyptian religion is evident in the iconography and symbols associated with Apedemak, which bear similarities to Egyptian deities such as Sekhmet and Amun.

The hybridization of Egyptian and Nubian religious traditions extended beyond deities to encompass rituals, symbols, and sacred sites. Temples and cult centers in Nubia, influenced by both Egyptian and Nubian religious practices, displayed a fusion of architectural styles and incorporated rituals from both cultures. For instance, the Temple of Amun at Jebel Barkal in Nubia featured Egyptian architectural elements alongside Nubian religious symbols and inscriptions, reflecting the syncretic nature of the religious practices in the region.

The syncretism and hybridization of Egyptian and Nubian religious traditions not only enriched the spiritual lives of the people but also played a significant role in the formation of cultural and political identities. These exchanges fostered a sense of shared religious heritage and helped forge closer ties between Egypt and Nubia.

In the following sections, we will explore specific examples of the exchange of religious concepts, the syncretism of deities and rituals, and the cultural influences between ancient Egypt and Nubia. Through the analysis of archaeological evidence, inscriptions, and artistic representations, we will unravel the complexities of this interplay and gain a deeper understanding of the mutual influence and hybridization of religious traditions in the ancient Nile Valley.

Chapter 22: Legacy and Enduring Influences of Egyptian Deities in Modern Spirituality

The ancient Egyptian civilization, with its rich mythology and pantheon of deities, continues to captivate and inspire individuals in modern times. The enduring influence of Egyptian deities can be observed in various forms of contemporary spirituality, including neo-paganism, occult practices, and New Age movements. The continued presence and relevance of Egyptian deities in modern spirituality highlight the timeless appeal and profound symbolism associated with these ancient gods and goddesses.

In contemporary spiritual practices, individuals often seek connection with ancient wisdom and archetypal energies. Egyptian deities offer a unique and compelling avenue for such exploration. Their distinct personalities, stories, and symbolic representations resonate with individuals on a personal and spiritual level, providing a framework for understanding the human experience and connecting with the divine.

For example, the goddess Isis, known as the mother goddess and a powerful magician, embodies qualities of nurturing, healing, and feminine power. In modern spiritual contexts, individuals may turn to Isis as a source of inspiration for personal growth, emotional healing, and the cultivation of inner strength. Similarly, the god Thoth, associated with wisdom, writing, and the moon, has found a place in modern spiritual practices related to knowledge, communication, and esoteric wisdom.

Egyptian deities are often incorporated into rituals, ceremonies, and magical practices by modern spiritual practitioners. They may be invoked for guidance, protection, or as sources of divine energy. The intricate symbolism associated with these deities provides a rich tapestry of archetypal energies that can be tapped into for personal transformation and spiritual development.

Overview of the enduring legacy of ancient Egyptian religion

The legacy of ancient Egyptian religion extends beyond its influence on contemporary spiritual practices. The cultural and artistic expressions of ancient Egypt continue to captivate scholars, artists, and enthusiasts around the world.

The monumental temples, intricate hieroglyphic inscriptions, and iconic representations of gods and goddesses serve as a testament to the deep spiritual beliefs and cultural significance of ancient Egyptian religion.

Furthermore, the impact of Egyptian religious concepts and symbolism can be observed in various fields of study, such as psychology, anthropology, and art history. The archetypal imagery, intricate cosmology, and belief in the interplay of divine forces in Egyptian religion have provided fertile ground for scholarly inquiry and exploration.

In art, the influence of ancient Egyptian aesthetics can be seen in modern design, architecture, and fashion. The stylized forms, geometric patterns, and symbolic motifs associated with Egyptian deities continue to inspire and inform contemporary artistic creations.

Moreover, the enduring legacy of Egyptian religion is also evident in popular culture. Egyptian mythology and iconography have been featured in literature, films, video games, and other forms of media, captivating audiences and igniting imaginations. This popularization of ancient Egyptian themes further solidifies the cultural impact and lasting fascination with this ancient civilization.

In the following sections, we will delve deeper into the ongoing presence and relevance of Egyptian deities in modern spirituality. We will explore specific examples of how these deities are incorporated into contemporary practices, examine the ways in which their symbolism resonates with individuals today, and analyze the enduring legacy of ancient Egyptian religion in various aspects of modern culture. Through this exploration, we will gain a deeper understanding of the enduring influence of Egyptian deities and their significance in shaping contemporary spiritual landscapes.

Egyptian Deities in Neopagan and Wiccan Traditions

In modern pagan traditions, such as Neopaganism and Wicca, the worship and veneration of ancient Egyptian deities have found a significant place alongside other pantheons and spiritual practices. The allure of Egyptian mythology, with its intricate cosmology and powerful archetypes, resonates with individuals seeking connection to the divine and a deeper understanding of the mysteries of life.

Within these traditions, practitioners may choose to honor specific Egyptian gods and goddesses based on personal affinity or resonance. For example, the goddess Isis, with her association with motherhood, magic, and healing, is often revered as a nurturing and protective figure. She is called upon for guidance, emotional support, and the cultivation of personal strength.

The god Horus, symbolizing divine kingship, protection, and spiritual vision, is another Egyptian deity frequently embraced by modern practitioners. Horus may be invoked for matters of spiritual growth, protection from negative energies, and the development of inner sight and intuition.

Incorporating Egyptian deities into pagan rituals and ceremonies allows practitioners to tap into the unique energy and symbolism associated with these ancient gods and goddesses. Offerings, prayers, invocations, and visualizations are often utilized to establish a connection with the chosen deity and to seek their blessings and guidance.

Interpretations and adaptations of ancient Egyptian rituals and symbolism

Contemporary pagan practices often adapt and reinterpret ancient Egyptian rituals and symbolism to fit within modern contexts and belief systems. While it is essential to approach these adaptations with respect and cultural sensitivity, they can serve as a means of connecting with the essence and archetypal energies of Egyptian deities.

One example of adaptation is the use of modernized versions of ancient Egyptian rituals, such as the "Opening of the Ways" or the "Ritual of the Opening of the Mouth," which were traditionally performed to awaken the spiritual senses and commune with the divine. In modern practice, these rituals may be adapted to suit individual or group needs, focusing on the invocation of specific deities or the establishment of sacred space.

Symbolism plays a vital role in modern interpretations of ancient Egyptian rituals. For instance, the use of sacred tools, such as the ankh (symbolizing life) or the djed pillar (representing stability and endurance), can be incorporated into rituals and altars to evoke the presence and blessings of relevant deities. Similarly, hieroglyphs and images associated with specific gods and goddesses may be used as visual representations or meditative focal points during spiritual practices.

It is important to note that these adaptations and interpretations are influenced by personal perspectives and the evolving nature of modern spirituality. They should be approached with a deep appreciation for the cultural context and symbolism of ancient Egyptian religion, as well as a commitment to honoring the historical legacy of this ancient civilization.

By incorporating Egyptian deities into Neopagan and Wiccan traditions, practitioners gain access to a rich tapestry of archetypal energies, symbolic wisdom, and spiritual connections. Through respectful engagement with ancient rituals and symbolism, modern practitioners can forge a personal relationship with Egyptian deities, drawing inspiration, guidance, and transformation from their timeless presence.

Egyptian Deities in New Age and Ecospirituality Movements

In the realm of New Age spirituality and self-development, Egyptian deities are often embraced as powerful archetypes that symbolize various aspects of the human psyche and spiritual journey. These deities are seen as embodiments of specific qualities and energies that individuals can invoke and integrate into their personal growth and transformation.

For example, the goddess Ma'at, with her association with truth, justice, and balance, is revered as an archetype of inner harmony and ethical conduct. Individuals may work with the energy of Ma'at to cultivate integrity, align their actions with their values, and seek balance in their relationships and daily life.

The god Thoth, known as the god of wisdom, writing, and magic, is often invoked as an archetype of intellectual pursuits and spiritual knowledge. Practitioners may draw upon Thoth's energy to enhance their learning, expand their consciousness, and access higher realms of wisdom and intuition.

These archetypal representations of Egyptian deities provide individuals with a framework for exploring and integrating various aspects of themselves. Through rituals, visualizations, and meditations, practitioners seek to establish a connection with the chosen deity, tapping into their unique qualities and wisdom.

Integration of ecological and environmental principles with Egyptian religious concepts

In the realm of ecospirituality, the wisdom and symbolism of ancient Egyptian religion have found resonance with those seeking to deepen their connection with nature and promote environmental consciousness. The concepts of Ma'at and the intricate relationship between humans and the natural world within Egyptian cosmology provide inspiration for ecological principles and practices.

The concept of Ma'at, representing cosmic order and harmony, can be interpreted as a call for humans to live in harmony with the natural world. The belief that human actions have an impact on the balance of the cosmos underscores the importance of environmental stewardship and sustainable living.

Incorporating Egyptian religious concepts into ecospiritual practices involves recognizing the interdependence between humans and nature and seeking to restore balance and harmony. Rituals and ceremonies may be performed to honor the land, water, and other elements of the natural world, invoking Egyptian deities associated with nature, such as Osiris (god of vegetation and fertility) or Hathor (goddess of joy and abundance).

Furthermore, the use of Egyptian symbols and iconography in ecological activism and awareness campaigns serves to evoke a sense of ancient wisdom and spiritual connection to the Earth. Egyptian motifs, such as the ankh or the lotus flower, may be employed as symbols of life, regeneration, and the interconnectedness of all living beings.

By integrating ecological and environmental principles with Egyptian religious concepts, practitioners of New Age and ecospirituality movements seek to create a holistic approach to their spiritual practice—one that honors the natural world, promotes sustainable living, and acknowledges the deep wisdom embedded in ancient Egyptian beliefs. Through this integration, individuals are encouraged to cultivate a profound connection with nature, live in harmony with the Earth, and contribute to the well-being of the planet.

Influence on Occult and Hermetic Traditions

The ancient Egyptian civilization had a profound influence on the development of occult traditions, particularly in the areas of magic and ritual practices. The rich and complex magical system of ancient Egypt, with its emphasis on the manipulation of divine forces and the use of ritual tools and spells, became a source of inspiration for occultists throughout history.

Egyptian magical practices involved invoking the power of various deities, working with symbols, and performing rituals aimed at influencing the natural and supernatural realms. These practices included divination, healing rituals, protective spells, and ceremonies for invoking specific deities or elemental forces. The knowledge and techniques of Egyptian magic were sought after and studied by occultists, leading to the incorporation of Egyptian elements into various occult traditions.

In the Western occult tradition, the Egyptian influence can be seen in systems such as Hermeticism, the Golden Dawn, and the Thelemic tradition. These traditions drew upon Egyptian magical practices and symbolism, integrating them with other esoteric teachings and philosophical frameworks.

Egyptian hieroglyphs, symbols, and deities were considered potent sources of spiritual and magical power. Occultists incorporated these symbols into their rituals, talismans, and magical workings, believing that they possessed inherent spiritual energy and the ability to connect with the divine realms.

Hermeticism and the study of ancient Egyptian wisdom and esotericism

Hermeticism, an occult tradition rooted in ancient Egypt and Greece, played a significant role in the study and dissemination of ancient Egyptian wisdom and esoteric teachings. The Corpus Hermeticum, a collection of philosophical and mystical writings attributed to Hermes Trismegistus, was highly influential in shaping the Hermetic tradition and its exploration of spiritual and metaphysical principles.

Within Hermeticism, the study of ancient Egyptian philosophy and spiritual practices was highly regarded. The teachings attributed to Hermes Trismegistus emphasized the pursuit of spiritual knowledge, the unity of all things, and the understanding of divine principles. These teachings reflected an amalgamation of Egyptian and Greek philosophical traditions, resulting in a unique synthesis of mystical thought.

Hermetic texts and teachings presented the ancient Egyptian gods and goddesses as embodiments of spiritual principles and archetypes. The deities were seen as symbols and channels through which divine wisdom could be accessed and understood. The study of ancient Egyptian myths, rituals, and symbolism became integral to the exploration of esoteric knowledge and spiritual transformation within Hermeticism.

Furthermore, the Egyptian concept of the soul and its journey through various realms of existence influenced the Hermetic understanding of the soul's ascent towards spiritual realization and union with the divine. The idea of spiritual evolution and the pursuit of gnosis (divine knowledge) were key elements in both ancient Egyptian and Hermetic philosophies.

The study of ancient Egyptian wisdom and esotericism continues to be an important aspect of occult traditions. Scholars and practitioners delve into the texts, rituals, and symbols of ancient Egypt, seeking insights into the mysteries of the universe and the nature of human consciousness. The enduring influence of ancient Egyptian spirituality on occult and Hermetic traditions demonstrates the timeless fascination with the wisdom and magical practices of this ancient civilization.

Representation in Art, Literature, and Popular Culture

The imagery and symbolism associated with Egyptian deities have long captivated artists and writers, leading to their depiction in various forms of visual arts and literature. From ancient times to the present day, Egyptian gods and goddesses have been a source of inspiration, their iconic representations evoking a sense of mystery, power, and timeless beauty.

In visual arts, Egyptian deities are often portrayed in sculptures, reliefs, and paintings. The art of ancient Egypt itself provides a wealth of examples, showcasing the intricate and stylized representations of gods such as Osiris, Isis, Horus, and Anubis. These depictions often feature distinct attributes and symbols associated with each deity, such as the falcon headdress of Horus or the crook and flail held by pharaohs representing their divine authority. The use of hieroglyphs and hieratic symbols further enriches the visual language of Egyptian art, conveying deeper meanings and connections to the divine.

Egyptian mythology and the stories of the gods have also been a fertile ground for literary exploration. Ancient Egyptian texts, such as the Book of the Dead and the Pyramid Texts, contain narratives and hymns dedicated to the deities, providing insights into their roles, relationships, and significance within the Egyptian cosmology. These texts have inspired countless adaptations, interpretations, and retellings in modern literature, from historical novels to fantasy and speculative fiction.

The enduring fascination with Egyptian deities in visual arts and literature can be attributed to the allure of their symbolism and the timeless themes they represent. The gods embody archetypal qualities and concepts, such as wisdom, power, fertility, and protection, which resonate with human experiences and aspirations. Their depictions in art and their presence in literature continue to captivate audiences, inviting them to explore the mysteries of ancient Egypt and engage with its spiritual and cultural heritage.

Symbolic significance and cultural impact of Egyptian gods in popular culture

The symbolism and iconography of Egyptian gods have permeated popular culture, becoming recognizable and often employed in various media and consumer products. The imagery of Egyptian deities can be found in movies, television shows, video games, fashion, and advertising, among other forms of popular culture. Their iconic representations have become shorthand for concepts such as power, mysticism, and exoticism.

In movies and television, Egyptian gods and themes have been featured prominently in productions ranging from classic films like "The Mummy" series to contemporary adaptations such as "Gods of Egypt." These portrayals often draw upon the grandeur and mystique of ancient Egypt, intertwining historical elements with fantasy and adventure.

Similarly, Egyptian gods have found their place in the world of video games, where they are often depicted as powerful beings with supernatural abilities. Games such as the "Assassin's Creed" series and the "Age of Mythology" franchise incorporate Egyptian deities as playable characters or influential entities within their narratives, allowing players to interact with and immerse themselves in the mythology of ancient Egypt.

The fashion industry has also been influenced by Egyptian symbolism, with designers incorporating Egyptian motifs and imagery into clothing, accessories, and jewelry. From stylized representations of Ankh symbols to hieroglyph-inspired patterns, these designs evoke a sense of exoticism and allure, appealing to consumers who are drawn to the aesthetic and cultural richness of ancient Egypt.

While the representation of Egyptian deities in popular culture can sometimes be sensationalized or simplified, it nonetheless demonstrates the enduring impact and fascination with ancient Egyptian mythology and spirituality. The gods' iconic imagery continues to resonate with people, serving as a visual shorthand for a range of meanings and associations. The cultural presence of Egyptian gods in popular culture serves as a testament to their enduring appeal and the enduring legacy of ancient Egyptian religion and symbolism in the modern world.

Chapter 23: Modern Interpretations and Relevance

Ancient Egyptian religion continues to inspire and influence various interpretations in modern times. The enduring fascination with the rich symbolism, mythology, and spiritual practices of ancient Egypt has led to the development of diverse approaches and reinterpretations of this ancient belief system.

In contemporary contexts, scholars, practitioners, and spiritual seekers have engaged with ancient Egyptian religion through various lenses, including historical, archaeological, anthropological, and esoteric perspectives. Academic research and scholarly studies shed light on the religious beliefs, rituals, and cosmology of ancient Egypt, providing a deeper understanding of its cultural and spiritual significance.

Moreover, modern practitioners of various spiritual paths, such as Neopaganism, Wicca, and eclectic spiritual traditions, have incorporated elements of ancient Egyptian religion into their practices. These individuals draw inspiration from the deities, rituals, symbols, and wisdom of ancient Egypt, adapting and integrating them into their own spiritual frameworks.

Relevance of ancient Egyptian concepts in contemporary contexts

The concepts and principles found in ancient Egyptian religion continue to hold relevance and resonance in contemporary contexts. The enduring legacy of ancient Egypt can be observed in the fields of psychology, self-development, and personal growth, where ancient Egyptian concepts are explored as archetypes and symbols for understanding the human psyche and spiritual journey.

For example, the concept of Ma'at, the ancient Egyptian principle of cosmic balance, order, and harmony, has found resonance in contemporary discussions on ethics, social justice, and ecological sustainability. The notion of aligning oneself with Ma'at and seeking balance in one's actions and relationships can be seen as a guiding principle for creating a more harmonious and just world.

Similarly, the symbolism and mythology of Egyptian deities continue to inspire artists, writers, and creators in various forms of art, literature, and popular culture. The timeless themes and archetypal qualities represented by these deities—such as the wisdom of Thoth, the nurturing nature of Isis, or the transformative power of Osiris—find expression in contemporary storytelling, providing avenues for exploration and personal meaning-making.

In addition, the study of ancient Egyptian religion and spirituality contributes to our understanding of human history, culture, and the evolution of religious thought. The exploration of ancient Egyptian beliefs and practices offers valuable insights into the development of religious concepts, the complexities of human spirituality, and the ways in which ancient cultures sought to connect with the divine.

Overall, the modern interpretations and relevance of ancient Egyptian religion reflect a continued appreciation for its rich symbolism, mythology, and spiritual wisdom. Whether through academic research, spiritual practices, artistic expressions, or cultural explorations, the legacy of ancient Egypt continues to inspire, inform, and offer valuable insights into our contemporary understanding of spirituality, human nature, and the quest for meaning and transcendence.

Psychological and Symbolic Interpretations

The myths and symbols of ancient Egypt offer a wealth of material for psychological analysis and interpretation. From a psychological perspective, Egyptian myths can be seen as narratives that reflect universal human experiences, struggles, and archetypal patterns of the human psyche.

Psychologists and scholars, such as Carl Jung, have explored the psychological significance of Egyptian myths and symbols. They have identified archetypal figures and themes within these myths that resonate with the collective unconscious—the deep, shared reservoir of human experiences and patterns of behavior.

For example, the myth of Osiris, Isis, and Horus can be interpreted as a symbolic representation of the human journey of death, rebirth, and individuation. Osiris, who is killed and later resurrected by Isis, symbolizes the transformative process of confronting and integrating the shadow aspects of the self. Isis, the nurturing mother figure, represents the healing and nurturing aspects of the psyche, while Horus embodies the potential for growth and the emergence of a new sense of self.

Symbolic analysis of Egyptian myths can also reveal insights into individual psychological processes. The journey of the soul through the various realms of the afterlife, as depicted in the Book of the Dead, can be seen as a metaphor for the transformative journey of the individual psyche. The challenges, trials, and rituals described in these texts reflect the psychological obstacles and tasks that individuals encounter on their own paths of self-discovery and personal growth.

Application of Egyptian symbolism in personal growth and transformation

The rich symbolism of ancient Egypt provides a powerful resource for personal growth and transformation in contemporary contexts. Many individuals draw inspiration from Egyptian symbols and incorporate them into practices aimed at self-development and spiritual exploration.

For example, the Ankh, an ancient Egyptian symbol representing life and vitality, is often used as a symbol of personal empowerment and connection to the divine. It can serve as a reminder to individuals to embrace and nurture their own life force, fostering a sense of purpose and vitality in their daily lives.

Similarly, the Eye of Horus, a symbol associated with protection and healing, is often utilized in energy healing practices and as a visual focus for meditation. It can be seen as a representation of inner strength, insight, and the ability to overcome challenges.

In addition, the imagery and symbolism of specific Egyptian deities, such as Thoth, the god of wisdom and knowledge, or Ma'at, the goddess of balance and truth, can be invoked to cultivate specific qualities or to explore particular aspects of the self. Individuals may engage in rituals, meditation, or creative practices inspired by these deities as a means of personal growth, self-reflection, and spiritual connection.

Furthermore, the exploration of Egyptian symbolism can help individuals gain insight into their own psychological patterns, unconscious desires, and areas of personal growth. By examining the symbols and archetypes present in Egyptian myths and applying them to personal experiences, individuals can deepen their self-awareness, explore hidden aspects of their psyche, and work towards personal transformation.

In summary, the psychological and symbolic interpretations of Egyptian myths and symbols offer valuable insights into the human psyche and can be applied to personal growth and transformation. By exploring the universal themes and archetypal patterns present in Egyptian mythology, individuals can gain a deeper understanding of themselves, cultivate personal empowerment, and embark on a journey of self-discovery and spiritual connection.

Archaeological and Academic Perspectives

Archaeological discoveries have played a pivotal role in deepening our understanding of ancient Egyptian religion. Through excavations of temples, tombs, and other religious sites, archaeologists have unearthed a wealth of artifacts, inscriptions, and architectural remains that provide valuable insights into the religious beliefs, rituals, and practices of the ancient Egyptians.

For example, the discovery of the Rosetta Stone in 1799, which contained inscriptions in multiple scripts including hieroglyphics, enabled the decipherment of ancient Egyptian writing. This breakthrough allowed scholars to access and interpret a vast corpus of religious texts, including hymns, rituals, funerary texts, and magical spells. These texts provide detailed information about the religious practices, cosmology, and mythology of ancient Egypt.

Archaeological excavations have also revealed intricate temple complexes dedicated to various gods and goddesses, providing physical evidence of the central role of religion in ancient Egyptian society. The layout and architecture of these temples, as well as the depictions and inscriptions found within them, offer valuable insights into the rituals, cult practices, and beliefs associated with specific deities.

Moreover, the discovery of tomb complexes, such as the Valley of the Kings, has provided important evidence about the funerary practices and beliefs concerning the afterlife in ancient Egypt. Elaborate burial rituals, tomb decorations, and the inclusion of funerary texts, such as the Book of the Dead, shed light on the complex religious beliefs and practices associated with death and the journey to the afterlife.

Academic research and interpretations of religious practices in ancient Egypt

Academic research has played a crucial role in interpreting and understanding the religious practices of ancient Egypt. Scholars from various disciplines, including Egyptology, archaeology, history, and religious studies, have dedicated their efforts to studying and analyzing the rich religious traditions of ancient Egypt.

One key focus of academic research has been the interpretation of religious texts and inscriptions. Scholars meticulously analyze and translate ancient Egyptian hieroglyphic texts, seeking to unravel their meaning, symbolism, and cultural context. Through this interdisciplinary approach, they aim to reconstruct the religious beliefs, rituals, and cosmology of ancient Egypt.

Academic research also examines the social and cultural dimensions of ancient Egyptian religion. Scholars explore the interplay between religion and other aspects of society, such as politics, economics, and social hierarchies. They investigate the roles and functions of priests, the organization of temple complexes, and the relationship between religious institutions and the ruling elite. By examining these broader social contexts, scholars gain a deeper understanding of how religious beliefs and practices shaped ancient Egyptian society.

Additionally, comparative studies with other ancient cultures and religions contribute to the academic understanding of ancient Egyptian religion. Scholars explore connections and similarities between Egyptian religious concepts and practices and those found in neighboring cultures, such as Mesopotamia, Canaan, and Greece. These comparative analyses shed light on cross-cultural influences, syncretism, and the broader religious landscape of the ancient Near East.

Overall, academic research and interpretations of ancient Egyptian religion are constantly evolving, driven by ongoing archaeological discoveries, new theoretical approaches, and interdisciplinary collaborations. Through their scholarly endeavors, researchers strive to unravel the complexities of ancient Egyptian religious practices, offering valuable insights into one of the world's oldest and most fascinating religious traditions.

Cultural and Identity Reclamation

In various contemporary contexts, the appropriation and utilization of Egyptian religious motifs have become powerful tools for cultural reclamation. This process involves reclaiming and revitalizing aspects of ancient Egyptian culture, including its religious traditions, as a means of asserting cultural identity, reconnecting with ancestral heritage, and challenging dominant narratives.

In diaspora communities, individuals and groups may incorporate Egyptian religious symbols, imagery, and practices into their cultural expressions as a way to reconnect with their roots and maintain a sense of cultural identity. For example, in African diaspora traditions such as Vodou and Afro-Caribbean religions, elements of Egyptian religious symbolism, such as references to deities like Osiris or the use of hieroglyphic-like symbols, can be found. These practices serve as a means of preserving cultural memory and forging connections with ancestral spiritual traditions.

Similarly, in the realm of contemporary spirituality and alternative religious movements, Egyptian religious motifs are often incorporated as a means of seeking spiritual connection and inspiration. Practices like Kemetic spirituality, which draws upon ancient Egyptian religious concepts and symbolism, have gained popularity among individuals seeking a connection to ancient wisdom and alternative spiritual paths. By engaging with Egyptian religious motifs, practitioners often express a desire to reclaim and re-contextualize these traditions within a contemporary framework.

Identity formation and religious expression in modern Egyptian society

In modern Egyptian society, religious expression plays a significant role in shaping individual and communal identities. While Islam is the predominant religion in Egypt, ancient Egyptian religious motifs and traditions continue to influence the cultural and religious landscape of the country.

For some Egyptians, a sense of national identity is deeply intertwined with ancient Egyptian heritage. The glorification of pharaonic history and symbolism can be seen in various aspects of Egyptian society, including architecture, art, and tourism. The use of ancient Egyptian motifs in national symbols, such as the emblem of the Egyptian flag featuring the golden eagle of Saladin, reflects the enduring presence of ancient Egyptian symbolism in shaping contemporary national identity.

Moreover, the coexistence of Islam and ancient Egyptian religious heritage has resulted in syncretic practices and beliefs. In certain contexts, individuals may integrate elements of ancient Egyptian spirituality, such as reverence for specific deities or the practice of divination, alongside their Islamic faith. These syncretic practices are often personal expressions of spirituality and can be found across a range of socio-economic backgrounds.

However, it is important to note that the use of ancient Egyptian religious motifs in modern Egyptian society is not without controversy and debate. Some argue that the appropriation and commercialization of ancient Egyptian symbolism in tourism or popular culture can trivialize or commodify the sacredness of these traditions. Others view the incorporation of ancient Egyptian motifs into religious practices as a departure from the original cultural and religious contexts in which they originated.

In conclusion, the utilization of Egyptian religious motifs as a means of cultural reclamation and identity formation is evident in various contemporary contexts. From diaspora communities seeking to reconnect with ancestral roots to individuals in modern Egyptian society expressing their religious and spiritual beliefs, the enduring presence of ancient Egyptian religious traditions continues to shape cultural identities and provide avenues for spiritual expression and exploration.

Ethical and Moral Frameworks

Ancient Egyptian religion encompassed a rich ethical and moral framework that guided the behavior and interactions of individuals within society. The examination of ethical principles derived from ancient Egyptian religious teachings provides valuable insights into the moral values upheld by the ancient Egyptians and offers potential guidance for contemporary ethical considerations.

Central to ancient Egyptian ethics was the concept of Ma'at, which can be understood as the balance, order, and harmony that governed the universe. Ma'at encompassed moral principles such as truth, justice, righteousness, and reciprocity. These principles formed the foundation of Egyptian society and were considered essential for maintaining cosmic balance and ensuring the well-being of individuals and the community.

The teachings of ancient Egyptian religion emphasized the importance of truth and honesty in all aspects of life. The value placed on truthfulness extended to personal conduct, relationships, and the administration of justice. Upholding truth and honesty was seen as a means to maintain harmony and integrity within oneself and the community.

Furthermore, justice and fairness were significant ethical principles in ancient Egyptian society. The ancient Egyptians believed in the divine judgment and the afterlife, where one's actions in life would be weighed against the principles of Ma'at. This belief system fostered a sense of responsibility and accountability for one's actions and reinforced the importance of treating others with fairness and equity.

Additionally, compassion, kindness, and respect for others were integral aspects of ancient Egyptian ethics. The concept of reciprocity guided social interactions, emphasizing the importance of treating others as one would wish to be treated. These moral values encouraged empathy, compassion, and the cultivation of harmonious relationships within the community.

Integration of Egyptian moral values in contemporary ethical frameworks

The ethical principles derived from ancient Egyptian religious teachings offer valuable insights that can be integrated into contemporary ethical frameworks. While modern ethical frameworks may differ in their philosophical underpinnings, the core principles of truth, justice, fairness, compassion, and reciprocity resonate across time and cultures.

In contemporary society, truth and honesty continue to be foundational ethical principles. Upholding truthfulness and honesty in personal and professional relationships fosters trust, transparency, and integrity. The ancient Egyptian emphasis on justice and fairness can inform contemporary debates on social justice, human rights, and distributive justice. The principles of fairness and equity can guide the development of inclusive and just systems and practices.

Moreover, the values of compassion and empathy can be integrated into contemporary ethical frameworks to promote kindness, understanding, and support for others. By considering the principles of reciprocity and treating others with respect and dignity, individuals can contribute to the cultivation of a more harmonious and compassionate society.

The integration of Egyptian moral values into contemporary ethical frameworks requires a nuanced approach that acknowledges the historical and cultural context of ancient Egypt while adapting these principles to address modern challenges and complexities. It is essential to critically engage with these teachings and explore their applicability to contemporary ethical dilemmas, considering the diverse perspectives and ethical frameworks present in our global society.

In conclusion, the examination of ethical principles derived from ancient Egyptian religious teachings offers valuable insights into moral values such as truth, justice, fairness, compassion, and reciprocity. Integrating these principles into contemporary ethical frameworks can contribute to the cultivation of a more just, compassionate, and harmonious society. By drawing upon the wisdom of ancient civilizations, we can enrich our understanding of ethics and moral values and apply them in navigating the complex ethical challenges of the modern world.

Chapter 24: Contemporary Perspectives on Ancient Egyptian Gods

The veneration and worship of ancient Egyptian gods have endured over millennia and continue to be practiced in various contemporary contexts. Despite the passage of time and the evolution of societies, the gods and goddesses of ancient Egypt maintain a significant presence and continue to inspire devotion, reverence, and spiritual connections among individuals and communities.

The enduring veneration of ancient Egyptian gods can be observed in various religious and spiritual traditions. In some cases, these traditions have been directly influenced by the ancient Egyptian religious practices and have sought to preserve and revive the worship of specific deities. These include modern revivalist movements, such as Kemeticism or Kemetic Reconstructionism, which aim to reconstruct and revive ancient Egyptian religious beliefs and practices.

Additionally, the continued veneration of Egyptian gods can be seen in syncretic traditions that blend elements of ancient Egyptian religion with other spiritual or esoteric practices. These syncretic approaches often incorporate Egyptian deities into broader frameworks of spirituality, such as Neopaganism, Wicca, New Age, and various occult traditions. In these contexts, ancient Egyptian gods are revered alongside deities from other cultures, forming a diverse and eclectic spiritual tapestry.

Furthermore, the fascination with ancient Egyptian gods extends beyond organized religious or spiritual groups. Popular culture, literature, art, and entertainment often draw inspiration from Egyptian mythology and incorporate depictions of Egyptian deities. This fascination contributes to the continued visibility and interest in the ancient Egyptian pantheon, reaching a wide audience and sparking curiosity and exploration.

Exploration of contemporary perspectives and practices related to Egyptian deities

Contemporary perspectives and practices related to Egyptian deities encompass a wide range of interpretations, beliefs, and rituals. These perspectives vary among individuals and communities, reflecting personal connections, cultural contexts, and spiritual preferences.

For some, the veneration of Egyptian gods is approached as a form of cultural and historical appreciation. They may study ancient Egyptian mythology, symbolism, and rituals as a means of understanding and connecting with the rich heritage and wisdom of ancient Egypt. Such individuals may engage in educational pursuits, participate in cultural events, or visit museums and exhibitions dedicated to ancient Egyptian civilization.

Others embrace the worship of Egyptian gods as part of their spiritual or religious path, finding inspiration and guidance in the deities' archetypal qualities and mythological narratives. These individuals may establish personal relationships with specific deities, engage in devotional practices, and incorporate Egyptian rituals and symbolism into their spiritual routines.

Contemporary perspectives on Egyptian deities also include psychological and symbolic interpretations. Some individuals explore the psychological aspects of the gods and goddesses as representations of human emotions, behaviors, and archetypes. They may use Egyptian mythology and symbolism as tools for personal growth, self-reflection, and therapeutic practices.

Moreover, the environmental and ecological aspects of ancient Egyptian spirituality have gained significance in contemporary perspectives. The concepts of harmony with nature, balance, and sustainability present in ancient Egyptian beliefs resonate with the growing interest in ecospirituality and earth-centered practices. This connection often involves exploring the ecological wisdom embedded in ancient Egyptian texts and integrating it into environmental activism, eco-conscious lifestyles, and nature-based rituals.

In conclusion, the continued veneration and worship of ancient Egyptian gods can be observed in various contemporary contexts. From organized religious movements to syncretic practices and cultural appreciation, the Egyptian pantheon maintains a significant presence in the modern world. The exploration of contemporary perspectives and practices related to Egyptian deities encompasses diverse interpretations, beliefs, and rituals that reflect personal connections, cultural contexts, and spiritual preferences. These perspectives contribute to the ongoing relevance and spiritual significance of ancient Egyptian gods in contemporary society.

Traditional Egyptian Religious Practices

The continuity of traditional religious practices in Egypt provides a unique insight into the enduring legacy of ancient Egyptian beliefs and rituals. Despite the influence of external religions and cultural changes over the centuries, certain aspects of traditional Egyptian religious practices have persisted and continue to be observed by a dedicated community.

In modern Egypt, there exists a community of individuals known as the Copts who identify as descendants of the ancient Egyptians and maintain a connection to their ancestral religious traditions. The Coptic Orthodox Church, which traces its origins to the early Christian period in Egypt, incorporates elements of ancient Egyptian rituals and beliefs within its liturgical practices. These include the use of incense, processions, and symbolic gestures reminiscent of ancient Egyptian religious ceremonies.

Additionally, in rural areas of Egypt, particularly in the Nile Delta and Upper Egypt, there are communities that have preserved folk customs and rituals with roots in ancient Egyptian traditions. These practices often blend elements of pre-Islamic Egyptian religion, Islam, and local folk beliefs. They may involve pilgrimages to sacred sites associated with ancient Egyptian deities or the celebration of seasonal agricultural festivals linked to the cycle of the Nile River.

Rituals, festivals, and offerings dedicated to ancient Egyptian gods

Traditional Egyptian religious practices encompass a variety of rituals, festivals, and offerings dedicated to ancient Egyptian gods. These observances aim to honor and invoke the presence of the deities, seek their blessings, and maintain a harmonious relationship with the divine.

One prominent example is the celebration of Wepet Renpet, also known as the "Opening of the Year" or the Egyptian New Year. This festival marks the flooding of the Nile River, which was vital for the fertility of the land and the success of agriculture. During Wepet Renpet, offerings and rituals are performed to express gratitude to the gods for their beneficence and to ensure a bountiful harvest in the coming year.

Another significant religious practice is the performance of temple rituals. Although many ancient Egyptian temples have been lost or have undergone transformations over time, some temples, such as the Temple of Luxor and the Temple of Edfu, continue to be used for religious ceremonies. These rituals often involve the participation of priests who act as intermediaries between the human and divine realms, conducting offerings, purification rituals, and processions to honor specific deities.

Offerings play a central role in traditional Egyptian religious practices. These offerings can include food, flowers, incense, and symbolic objects. They are presented to the gods as a gesture of devotion and gratitude, with the belief that the offerings nourish and sustain the deities' divine essence. Offerings may be made at home altars, in temples, or at sacred sites associated with specific gods or goddesses.

It is important to note that traditional Egyptian religious practices exist alongside other dominant religious traditions in Egypt, such as Islam. The interplay between Islam and ancient Egyptian traditions has resulted in unique syncretic practices and a distinct cultural and religious identity among certain communities.

In conclusion, the continuity of traditional religious practices in Egypt highlights the resilience and significance of ancient Egyptian beliefs and rituals in contemporary times. The presence of the Coptic Orthodox Church, the preservation of folk customs, and the observance of rituals and offerings dedicated to ancient Egyptian gods all contribute to the rich tapestry of religious diversity in Egypt. These practices provide a living connection to the ancestral heritage and spiritual traditions of ancient Egypt, fostering a sense of cultural identity and continuity.

Reconstructionist and Revivalist Movements

In recent decades, there has been a growing interest among individuals and communities in reconstructing and reviving ancient Egyptian religion. These movements, often referred to as Reconstructionist or Revivalist movements, aim to recreate and reconnect with the religious practices, beliefs, and spirituality of ancient Egypt. While these movements vary in their approaches and interpretations, they share a common goal of seeking a deeper understanding and engagement with the ancient Egyptian religious tradition.

Reconstructionist movements draw on various sources of information, including ancient texts, inscriptions, archaeological findings, and scholarly research, to reconstruct and recreate rituals, beliefs, and temple practices. These movements emphasize historical accuracy and strive to adhere as closely as possible to the ancient Egyptian religious traditions. They focus on understanding the cultural and religious context of ancient Egypt and seek to incorporate these elements into their modern practices.

Revivalist movements, on the other hand, may not strictly adhere to historical accuracy but are more concerned with embracing the essence and symbolism of ancient Egyptian religion and adapting it to contemporary spiritual contexts. These movements often incorporate personal interpretations, spiritual experiences, and modern concepts into their practices while maintaining a reverence for the ancient Egyptian gods and the cultural heritage of Egypt.

Contemporary reconstruction of rituals, beliefs, and temple practices

Contemporary reconstructionist and revivalist movements engage in the reconstruction of rituals, beliefs, and temple practices to varying degrees. These efforts are driven by a desire to reconnect with the spiritual and cultural heritage of ancient Egypt and to create meaningful religious experiences in the modern world.

Rituals play a central role in these movements, as they provide a means to engage with the deities, express devotion, and seek spiritual connection. Reconstructionists often meticulously study and recreate ancient Egyptian rituals based on available historical sources, aiming to replicate the structure, gestures, chants, and offerings used in ancient times. Revivalist movements, while incorporating elements of historical rituals, may also adapt and modify practices to suit contemporary sensibilities and spiritual needs.

Beliefs in these movements are influenced by ancient Egyptian cosmology, mythology, and theological concepts. Participants may explore the roles and attributes of various gods and goddesses, the understanding of the afterlife, and the symbolism embedded in ancient Egyptian religious texts and iconography. While some adhere closely to ancient Egyptian theological frameworks, others may reinterpret or adapt these beliefs to align with their own spiritual philosophies and understandings.

The reconstruction and revival of temple practices pose unique challenges. In ancient Egypt, temples served as the focal points of religious and communal life, with elaborate rituals performed by priests and attended by devotees. Today, reconstructed temples or sacred spaces inspired by ancient Egyptian architecture and symbolism may serve as places for rituals, meditation, and communal gatherings. These spaces aim to evoke the sacred atmosphere of ancient Egyptian temples and provide a platform for spiritual engagement and exploration.

It is important to recognize that reconstructionist and revivalist movements vary in their methodologies, interpretations, and level of historical accuracy. These movements are diverse and dynamic, shaped by the individual practitioners, their experiences, and the available historical and archaeological evidence. Ultimately, they seek to bridge the gap between the ancient and the contemporary, offering a means for individuals and communities to connect with the spiritual wisdom and cultural legacy of ancient Egypt in a meaningful and relevant way.

Personal Devotion and Eclectic Approaches

Within the realm of contemporary perspectives on ancient Egyptian gods, personal devotion to specific deities holds significant importance. Many individuals feel a deep connection to particular Egyptian gods and goddesses and choose to focus their worship and spiritual practice on these deities. This personal devotion can manifest in various ways, including offering prayers, conducting rituals, creating sacred spaces or altars, and engaging in acts of devotion and service.

Devotees may study the myths and symbolism associated with their chosen deity, seeking to understand their attributes, roles, and relationships within the ancient Egyptian pantheon. They may draw inspiration from ancient texts, hymns, and prayers, or explore modern interpretations and writings that offer insights into the qualities and teachings of the deity.

Personal devotion often involves building a relationship with the deity through regular communication, meditation, and contemplation. Devotees may seek guidance, support, and blessings from the deity, expressing gratitude and seeking their presence and wisdom in their daily lives. This practice of personal devotion allows individuals to cultivate a deep spiritual connection and sense of intimacy with the deity of their choice.

Eclectic approaches blending elements of ancient Egyptian religion with other spiritual practices

In addition to individual devotion to specific Egyptian deities, many practitioners adopt eclectic approaches that blend elements of ancient Egyptian religion with other spiritual practices. These eclectic paths often arise from the recognition that ancient Egyptian religion can complement and enrich other spiritual traditions, allowing for a unique synthesis of beliefs and practices.

Eclectic practitioners may draw inspiration from a wide range of sources, including but not limited to ancient Egyptian religion, neopaganism, witchcraft, ceremonial magic, and various esoteric and occult traditions. They may integrate Egyptian deities into their rituals, incorporate Egyptian symbols and iconography into their magical workings, or incorporate aspects of Egyptian mythology and cosmology into their belief systems.

The blending of ancient Egyptian religion with other spiritual practices is a creative and personal endeavor, allowing individuals to explore and express their spirituality in a way that resonates with their unique path and experiences. This approach can provide a rich tapestry of spiritual symbolism, practices, and philosophies, offering practitioners the opportunity to cultivate a diverse and multifaceted spiritual practice.

It is important to note that eclectic approaches should be approached with respect, careful study, and a genuine understanding of the cultural and historical context of ancient Egypt. Responsible eclecticism involves acknowledging the origins and sources of the practices being incorporated and treating them with integrity and cultural sensitivity.

Overall, personal devotion to specific Egyptian deities and eclectic approaches that blend elements of ancient Egyptian religion with other spiritual practices reflect the diverse ways in which individuals engage with and interpret the wisdom and teachings of ancient Egypt in the modern world. These approaches offer a dynamic and flexible framework for spiritual exploration, growth, and connection with the enduring legacy of Egyptian gods and goddesses.

Online Communities and Digital Offerings

The advent of the internet and the rise of digital technologies have facilitated the creation of virtual communities and online platforms dedicated to the worship and exploration of Egyptian gods. These digital spaces provide opportunities for individuals with shared interests in ancient Egyptian religion to connect, exchange knowledge, and engage in discussions and practices related to their spiritual beliefs.

Virtual communities focused on Egyptian gods can take the form of forums, social media groups, websites, or even dedicated online temples. They provide a platform for individuals to share experiences, ask questions, seek guidance, and find support in their spiritual journey. Members of these communities may come from diverse backgrounds and geographical locations, transcending physical boundaries to form a global network of devotees.

These online platforms often serve as valuable resources for learning and research, offering access to a wealth of information, scholarly articles, translations of ancient texts, and recommended reading lists. They may also host virtual rituals, workshops, and webinars led by experienced practitioners or scholars, providing opportunities for communal worship and shared spiritual experiences.

Digital offerings and rituals in contemporary religious practices

In the realm of contemporary religious practices, digital offerings and rituals have emerged as innovative ways to engage with Egyptian deities and maintain a spiritual connection in the digital age. While physical offerings were traditionally made at temples or sacred sites, digital offerings allow individuals to express their devotion and gratitude to the gods through virtual means.

Digital offerings can take various forms, such as virtual flowers, candles, food, or symbolic representations of offerings. These offerings are typically presented through digital images or animations, accompanied by prayers, intentions, or affirmations typed or spoken by the individual. While they do not have the physical substance of traditional offerings, they are seen as symbolic gestures of reverence and dedication.

Contemporary rituals conducted in digital spaces often involve the use of video conferencing platforms, livestreams, or prerecorded videos. These rituals can include guided meditations, invocations, chanting, or the recitation of prayers specific to Egyptian deities. Participants can engage in these rituals synchronously or asynchronously, allowing for flexibility and participation from different time zones and locations.

Digital offerings and rituals provide accessibility and inclusivity, as individuals who are unable to physically visit temples or participate in traditional rituals due to distance, physical limitations, or other constraints can still actively engage in spiritual practices and connect with the divine. While they may not replicate the full sensory experience of traditional practices, they offer a means for contemporary practitioners to express their devotion and maintain a sense of spiritual connection in the digital realm.

It is important to approach digital offerings and rituals with reverence and intention, treating them as sacred acts and respecting the cultural and symbolic significance of the ancient Egyptian religious traditions.

Chapter 25: Egyptian-Inspired Spirituality and Alternative Religious Movements

The rich and enduring legacy of ancient Egyptian religion has inspired a diverse array of alternative religious movements and spiritual practices. Drawing upon the symbolism, mythology, and rituals of ancient Egypt, these contemporary expressions of spirituality offer individuals a unique way to connect with the wisdom and power associated with the ancient Egyptian gods and goddesses.

Egyptian-inspired spirituality encompasses a wide range of belief systems and practices. Some individuals and groups seek to reconstruct and revive the religious traditions of ancient Egypt, aiming to faithfully recreate the rituals, beliefs, and temple practices of the past. Others approach Egyptian spirituality from a more eclectic perspective, blending elements of ancient Egyptian religion with other spiritual traditions, creating syncretic paths that resonate with their personal beliefs and experiences.

These alternative religious movements and spiritual practices often provide a sense of connection to ancient wisdom, offering individuals a pathway to explore their own spirituality outside the confines of mainstream religious institutions. They may draw inspiration from ancient Egyptian cosmology, mythology, symbolism, or the principles of ma'at (cosmic order and balance). Through rituals, meditation, divination, or other spiritual practices, practitioners seek to tap into the archetypal energies of the Egyptian pantheon and align themselves with the forces of creation and transformation.

Overview of the motivations and principles of Egyptian-inspired spirituality

The motivations for engaging in Egyptian-inspired spirituality are varied and personal. Some individuals are drawn to the beauty and mystique of ancient Egyptian culture, finding resonance in the grandeur of the temples, the intricate symbolism of hieroglyphs, and the artistry of ancient artifacts. Others are captivated by the profound wisdom and spiritual teachings encoded in the myths and religious texts of ancient Egypt.

Central to Egyptian-inspired spirituality are the principles and values exemplified in ancient Egyptian religion. These principles include the pursuit of balance, harmony, and interconnectedness with the natural world. The concept of ma'at, which emphasizes order, truth, justice, and ethical living, serves as a guiding principle for many practitioners. The gods and goddesses of ancient Egypt are seen as archetypal forces embodying different aspects of the human experience and cosmic energies, offering guidance and inspiration for personal growth and transformation.

Egyptian-inspired spirituality also places importance on the cultivation of a deep reverence and respect for the divine. Rituals, offerings, and devotional practices are employed to establish a sacred connection with the Egyptian deities, seeking their guidance, blessings, and protection. Meditation, visualization, and dreamwork may be utilized to deepen this connection and tap into the spiritual realms associated with the ancient Egyptian pantheon.

Furthermore, Egyptian-inspired spirituality often encourages a holistic approach to life, encompassing physical, emotional, mental, and spiritual well-being. Practices such as energy healing, crystal work, herbalism, and divination may be incorporated into spiritual rituals and daily life, drawing upon the wisdom of ancient Egyptian practices and beliefs.

In the following chapters, we will delve deeper into specific aspects of Egyptian-inspired spirituality, exploring rituals, practices, and beliefs that are commonly associated with this alternative religious movement. Through this exploration, we aim to provide a comprehensive understanding of the motivations, principles, and transformative potential of Egyptian-inspired spirituality in contemporary times.

Kemeticism and Kemetic Reconstructionism

Kemeticism, also known as Kemetic Reconstructionism, is a modern religious movement that seeks to revive and reconstruct the religious practices and beliefs of ancient Egypt. With a focus on historical accuracy and scholarly research, Kemeticism aims to create a contemporary expression of ancient Egyptian religion that is rooted in the cultural and religious context of its time.

Overview of the Kemetic religious movement and its emphasis on historical accuracy

Kemeticism takes its name from "Kemet," the ancient Egyptian term for Egypt. It emerged in the late 20th century as a response to the growing interest in ancient Egyptian spirituality and a desire to reconnect with the religious traditions of the past. Kemetic practitioners study and draw inspiration from a wide range of ancient Egyptian sources, including hieroglyphic texts, temple inscriptions, religious artifacts, and scholarly research.

One of the distinguishing features of Kemeticism is its emphasis on historical accuracy and academic rigor. Kemetic practitioners strive to base their beliefs and practices on the available historical evidence and scholarly interpretations of ancient Egyptian religion. They engage in extensive research, studying ancient texts and archaeological findings to gain a deep understanding of the religious rituals, cosmology, mythology, and symbolism of ancient Egypt.

Kemeticism recognizes the complexity and diversity of ancient Egyptian religious practices, acknowledging regional variations and the evolution of religious beliefs over time. This approach allows for a nuanced and multifaceted understanding of the ancient Egyptian pantheon and its associated rituals and deities.

Reconstruction of ancient Egyptian rituals and beliefs in modern contexts

Central to Kemeticism is the reconstruction of ancient Egyptian rituals and beliefs in modern contexts. Kemetic practitioners seek to faithfully recreate the rituals and practices of the ancient Egyptian religion, adapting them to contemporary settings while maintaining historical accuracy. These rituals may include offerings, libations, prayers, hymns, and other forms of devotion and worship.

Kemetic rituals often take place in private or communal settings, such as home shrines or dedicated temple spaces. They may involve the use of ritual tools, symbols, and sacred objects, such as statues or images representing the Egyptian deities. The rituals aim to establish a connection with the gods and goddesses, seeking their guidance, blessings, and presence.

Reconstructing ancient Egyptian beliefs involves studying the myths, cosmology, and religious texts of ancient Egypt and interpreting them in a way that resonates with modern practitioners. Kemetic practitioners explore the symbolism and archetypal meanings associated with the Egyptian deities, incorporating these insights into their personal and communal spiritual practices.

In addition to religious rituals, Kemeticism emphasizes ethical living and the principles of ma'at, which include concepts of justice, truth, harmony, and balance. Kemetic practitioners strive to embody these principles in their daily lives, fostering personal growth, social responsibility, and environmental stewardship.

Through the reconstruction of ancient Egyptian rituals and beliefs, Kemeticism offers a way to connect with the spiritual heritage of ancient Egypt and to forge a meaningful relationship with the gods and goddesses of that tradition. It provides a pathway for modern individuals to explore the wisdom, symbolism, and transformative potential of ancient Egyptian religion in a contemporary context.

In the following chapters, we will delve deeper into the specific rituals, practices, and beliefs of Kemeticism, providing a comprehensive understanding of this religious movement and its significance in the modern world

Magical and Esoteric Traditions

Egyptian magical practices have a long and rich history that dates back to ancient times. The ancient Egyptians believed in the power of magic and its ability to influence the natural and supernatural realms. They developed a complex system of magical spells, rituals, and amulets to achieve various goals, including protection, healing, love, and divination.

In contemporary occult traditions, such as modern witchcraft and ceremonial magic, there is a significant interest in Egyptian magical practices and their incorporation into magical systems. Many practitioners draw inspiration from ancient Egyptian magical texts, such as the "Book of the Dead" and the "Magical Papyri," to explore the rituals, spells, and symbols used by the ancient Egyptians.

These practices often involve the invocation and evocation of Egyptian deities, the use of hieroglyphic symbols and sacred words, and the employment of ritual tools and talismans associated with ancient Egyptian magic. Practitioners may adapt and modify these ancient practices to suit their individual or group magical traditions, integrating them into a broader system of magical work.

The integration of Egyptian magical practices into contemporary occult traditions not only provides a connection to the mystical and esoteric traditions of ancient Egypt but also adds depth and diversity to modern magical practices. It allows practitioners to explore different forms of magic, tap into the wisdom of the ancient Egyptian priesthood, and work with the powerful archetypes and energies associated with the Egyptian pantheon.

Esoteric interpretations of ancient Egyptian religious concepts and symbolism

Esoteric interpretations of ancient Egyptian religious concepts and symbolism have also played a significant role in contemporary spiritual and mystical traditions. Esotericism refers to the inner, hidden, or symbolic meanings attributed to religious texts, rituals, and symbols. It involves the exploration of deeper spiritual truths and the pursuit of personal transformation and enlightenment.

Within the realm of esotericism, various interpretations and systems have been developed that draw upon ancient Egyptian religious concepts and symbolism. These interpretations may delve into the mystical teachings of the Egyptian priesthood, explore the symbolic meanings of Egyptian deities and mythological narratives, or examine the esoteric dimensions of Egyptian cosmology and rituals.

Esoteric practitioners may engage in meditative practices, visualizations, or pathworking exercises that aim to connect with the archetypal energies and wisdom embodied by the Egyptian deities. They may also study and contemplate the symbolism of ancient Egyptian art, architecture, and religious texts, seeking hidden insights and spiritual truths.

The esoteric interpretations of ancient Egyptian religious concepts and symbolism offer a pathway for individuals to explore the mysteries and spiritual depths of the ancient Egyptian tradition. They provide a framework for inner transformation, self-discovery, and the development of spiritual insight and wisdom.

In the following chapters, we will delve deeper into the magical and esoteric traditions associated with ancient Egypt, examining the practices, rituals, and symbolic interpretations that continue to inspire and guide contemporary occult and esoteric traditions.

Neo-Egyptian Mystical and Mystery Schools

In the realm of alternative religious and spiritual movements, there are mystical and mystery schools that draw inspiration from ancient Egypt. These schools seek to explore and transmit the spiritual and mystical wisdom of the ancient Egyptian civilization to contemporary practitioners.

These mystical and mystery schools often incorporate elements of Egyptian mythology, symbolism, and ritual practices into their teachings. They aim to provide a structured and initiatory path for individuals interested in delving deep into the mystical traditions and esoteric knowledge associated with ancient Egypt.

The schools may offer courses, workshops, and study programs that cover various aspects of Egyptian spirituality, including cosmology, mythology, ritual magic, and divination. They may explore the teachings and practices of the Egyptian priesthood, examining the roles of priests and priestesses in ancient Egyptian society and their connections to the gods and goddesses.

B. Initiatory practices and teachings influenced by Egyptian spirituality

Initiatory practices and teachings influenced by Egyptian spirituality are a significant component of these mystical and mystery schools. The initiatory process often involves a series of rituals, ceremonies, and teachings that aim to awaken spiritual insight, deepen the connection to the Egyptian deities, and facilitate personal transformation.

Initiates may go through stages or degrees that correspond to different aspects of Egyptian spiritual teachings. These stages often involve experiential learning, meditation, and the study of sacred texts and symbols. Initiates may also participate in group rituals, guided visualizations, and other practices aimed at cultivating a direct experience of the divine and unlocking inner wisdom.

The teachings of these schools may emphasize the principles of Ma'at, the Egyptian concept of cosmic order and balance, and the cultivation of virtues such as wisdom, compassion, and integrity. They may explore the symbolism of Egyptian gods and goddesses, their archetypal qualities, and their relevance to personal and spiritual growth.

Moreover, these initiatory practices may incorporate elements of Egyptian ritual magic, such as the use of symbols, invocations, and sacred objects. Initiates may learn techniques for working with energy, divination, and healing, drawing inspiration from the magical practices of the ancient Egyptian priesthood.

Overall, the mystical and mystery schools inspired by ancient Egyptian spirituality provide a framework for individuals seeking a deeper understanding and experience of the wisdom and mysteries of ancient Egypt. They offer a structured path for personal and spiritual development, connecting practitioners to the spiritual heritage of Egypt and the transformative power of its mystical traditions.

New Religious Movements and Hybrid Traditions

In contemporary spiritual and religious landscapes, there are various new religious movements that incorporate elements of ancient Egyptian religion. These movements are often characterized by a synthesis of Egyptian spirituality with modern beliefs, practices, and cultural influences. They seek to create unique religious systems that resonate with individuals who are drawn to the symbolism, mythology, and spiritual wisdom of ancient Egypt.

These new religious movements may draw inspiration from the reconstructionist approaches mentioned earlier, aiming to revive and recreate the religious practices of ancient Egypt in a modern context. They may strive for historical accuracy and scholarly research in their understanding and interpretation of Egyptian religious traditions.

Within these movements, rituals, prayers, and ceremonies are crafted to honor and connect with the Egyptian deities. Sacred texts and mythological narratives are studied and revered, providing guidance and inspiration for adherents. Followers may engage in individual and communal practices, such as meditation, offerings, and devotion, to establish a personal connection with the Egyptian gods and goddesses.

Blending of Egyptian spirituality with other belief systems and cultural influences

In addition to new religious movements directly inspired by ancient Egyptian religion, there are also hybrid traditions that blend elements of Egyptian spirituality with other belief systems and cultural influences. These traditions may incorporate Egyptian deities, rituals, or symbols into broader spiritual frameworks, creating syncretic practices that reflect a fusion of diverse religious and cultural elements.

For example, individuals may incorporate Egyptian deities into their eclectic spiritual practices, drawing from various religious and mystical traditions to create a personal spiritual path. These practitioners may combine Egyptian mythology and symbolism with concepts and practices from other belief systems, such as Wicca, Druidry, or Shamanism, to form a unique and personalized spiritual practice.

Similarly, there may be cross-cultural influences where Egyptian religious elements merge with indigenous traditions or practices from other cultures. This blending can result in the emergence of new syncretic traditions that incorporate Egyptian deities or concepts alongside the beliefs and practices of the host culture.

In these hybrid traditions, practitioners often find resonance and spiritual meaning by drawing from diverse sources and embracing the richness of different cultural and spiritual heritages. They may seek to find commonalities, universal principles, and shared symbolism across different traditions, while respecting the distinctiveness and integrity of each.

By blending Egyptian spirituality with other belief systems and cultural influences, these new religious movements and hybrid traditions create opportunities for spiritual exploration, creative expression, and personal growth. They reflect the evolving nature of spirituality and the human desire to find meaning and connection through the integration of diverse spiritual perspectives.

Chapter 26: Use of Egyptian Symbolism and Deities in Popular Culture

The ancient civilization of Egypt has captivated the imagination of people throughout history, and its rich symbolism and deities continue to permeate popular culture in various forms of media. From literature to film, music to fashion, and even video games and advertising, Egyptian themes and iconography are often utilized to evoke a sense of mystery, exoticism, and timeless fascination.

The prevalence of Egyptian symbolism and deities in popular culture can be attributed to their inherent visual appeal and the aura of mystique surrounding ancient Egypt. The striking imagery of pharaohs, pyramids, hieroglyphs, and deities such as Isis, Osiris, and Anubis has become instantly recognizable and serves as a visual shorthand for an air of ancient wisdom, power, and spirituality. These symbols and figures are often used to add a touch of mysticism, grandeur, and otherworldly allure to various creative works.

Analysis of the motivations and impact of using Egyptian themes in various media forms

The motivations behind incorporating Egyptian symbolism and deities in popular culture are diverse and multifaceted. One primary motive is the desire to tap into the timeless and universal fascination with ancient Egypt, as it provides a rich tapestry of mythology, history, and artistic inspiration. By using Egyptian themes, creators can tap into a vast cultural heritage that has endured for millennia, thus evoking a sense of depth, antiquity, and a connection to ancient wisdom.

Additionally, the use of Egyptian symbolism in popular culture often reflects a broader trend of cultural borrowing and cross-pollination. Egyptian motifs may be borrowed and recontextualized within contemporary narratives, serving as a way to infuse a sense of intrigue, mysticism, or even a touch of the exotic into the storyline. This blending of ancient and modern aesthetics and themes allows for the creation of visually stunning and evocative imagery.

The impact of incorporating Egyptian symbolism and deities in popular culture is significant. On one hand, it helps to keep the legacy of ancient Egypt alive in the collective consciousness, introducing new generations to the wonders and mysteries of this ancient civilization. It also fosters an appreciation for the art, architecture, and mythology of Egypt, and may even inspire individuals to delve deeper into the history and spirituality of ancient Egyptian culture.

However, it is essential to approach the use of Egyptian themes in popular culture with sensitivity and respect for the cultural heritage they represent. Misrepresentations, cultural appropriation, or shallow interpretations can diminish the profound historical and religious significance of Egyptian symbolism. Therefore, it is crucial for creators and consumers of popular culture to engage in responsible and informed portrayals of Egyptian themes, appreciating the richness and complexity of this ancient civilization.

In the following chapters, we will explore the diverse manifestations of Egyptian symbolism and deities in popular culture, analyzing their presence in literature, film, music, fashion, and other media forms. Through this exploration, we aim to gain a deeper understanding of the motivations behind their usage and the impact they have on contemporary society's perception and interpretation of ancient Egypt.

Egyptian Symbolism in Visual Arts

The visual arts have long been a medium through which Egyptian symbolism and iconography are celebrated and reimagined. Artists across different eras and styles have drawn inspiration from the striking visual elements of ancient Egypt, incorporating them into their works to convey a sense of mysticism, power, and aesthetic beauty.

In paintings, the use of Egyptian motifs can be seen in various forms. Artists may depict pharaohs, gods, and goddesses adorned with traditional headdresses, ornate jewelry, and distinctive regalia. The iconic imagery of pyramids, obelisks, and hieroglyphs often features prominently, providing a visual anchor to the ancient Egyptian civilization. These elements are skillfully combined with artistic techniques and styles of the respective time periods, resulting in a fusion of ancient and contemporary aesthetics.

Sculpture is another medium where Egyptian symbolism finds expression. From classical sculptures to modern installations, artists have explored the human form in the style of ancient Egyptian statuary. The distinctive poses, rigid frontal compositions, and elongated proportions characteristic of ancient Egyptian sculpture are often emulated or reinterpreted, capturing the timeless beauty and grandeur associated with the civilization.

Exploring the Esoteric Wisdom of Ancient Egypt for Modern Spirituality

In the realm of graphic design, Egyptian motifs and iconography have been utilized in a wide range of contexts. From book covers and album artwork to logos and advertising campaigns, the allure of Egyptian symbolism is leveraged to create visually captivating and culturally resonant designs. The use of hieroglyphs, stylized depictions of gods and goddesses, and intricate patterns inspired by ancient Egyptian art serve as powerful visual elements that grab attention and evoke a sense of mystery and wonder.

B. Symbolic meanings and cultural associations in the use of Egyptian symbolism

The use of Egyptian symbolism in visual arts carries with it a range of symbolic meanings and cultural associations. These symbols often transcend their original context and acquire new layers of interpretation and significance in contemporary art.

For example, the depiction of the Eye of Horus, an ancient Egyptian symbol representing protection, healing, and spiritual insight, is often used as a symbol of wisdom and knowledge in modern artworks. It may convey a sense of inner strength and divine guidance, resonating with individuals seeking personal growth and enlightenment.

The Ankh, a symbol resembling a cross with a loop at the top, is another powerful Egyptian symbol that has been appropriated in various ways. It is often associated with concepts of eternal life, fertility, and the union of male and female energies. In contemporary art, the Ankh may be used as a symbol of spiritual awakening, balance, and the interconnectedness of all life.

The use of Egyptian motifs and iconography also invokes cultural associations tied to the ancient Egyptian civilization. These symbols evoke a sense of the mystical, the exotic, and the enigmatic, inviting viewers to explore the secrets of an ancient world. The longevity and endurance of Egyptian symbolism in popular culture further contribute to its association with timelessness, a link to the distant past that remains relevant and captivating in the present.

In conclusion, the depiction of Egyptian symbolism in visual arts allows artists to tap into the powerful imagery and cultural heritage of ancient Egypt. Through paintings, sculptures, and graphic design, they create captivating works that convey a sense of mystery, grandeur, and spirituality. The symbolic meanings and cultural associations embedded in these artworks add depth and resonance to the visual representation of ancient Egyptian motifs, fostering an ongoing fascination with this rich and enduring civilization.

Egyptian Gods and Goddesses in Literature and Film

Egyptian gods and goddesses have long captured the imagination of writers and poets, inspiring them to incorporate these divine beings into their literary works. From ancient times to the present day, the rich and colorful pantheon of Egyptian deities has served as a source of inspiration for authors seeking to explore themes of mythology, magic, and the human-divine relationship.

In novels and prose, Egyptian gods and goddesses often appear as prominent characters, driving the plot and influencing the lives of mortal protagonists. Their distinctive personalities, powers, and mythological narratives are woven into the fabric of the stories, adding depth and intrigue. Authors may draw from ancient Egyptian texts, such as the Book of the Dead or the Pyramid Texts, to inform their portrayal of these deities and create a sense of authenticity.

Poets, too, have found inspiration in the divine figures of ancient Egypt. Through vivid imagery and lyrical language, they bring the gods and goddesses to life, capturing their majesty, beauty, and symbolic significance. Poems may explore themes of worship, love, and transcendence, invoking the names and attributes of Egyptian deities to evoke a sense of the sacred and the mystical.

Additionally, mythology-inspired literature, such as retellings or reinterpretations of ancient Egyptian myths, serves as a platform for authors to explore the complex relationships between gods, mortals, and the natural world. These works may reimagine familiar stories or delve into lesser-known aspects of Egyptian mythology, offering fresh perspectives and engaging readers in the timeless themes and lessons found within these ancient tales.

Representation of Egyptian gods and goddesses in movies and television shows

The fascination with Egyptian gods and goddesses extends to the realm of visual storytelling, with numerous movies and television shows featuring these divine beings as central characters or influential forces within the narrative. From epic historical dramas to fantasy adventures, the presence of Egyptian deities adds an element of mysticism, wonder, and cultural richness to the screen.

In cinematic adaptations of ancient Egyptian mythology, gods and goddesses are often depicted with larger-than-life personalities and extraordinary powers. Their conflicts, alliances, and interactions with mortal characters drive the plot and explore themes of power, destiny, and the consequences of human-divine encounters. These portrayals can be both faithful to the ancient myths and open to creative interpretations that resonate with contemporary audiences.

Beyond direct adaptations, Egyptian gods and goddesses may also find their way into modern fantasy or supernatural stories, where they are reimagined and integrated into fictional universes. These representations may draw on the symbolic attributes and iconic imagery associated with the deities, presenting them in visually striking and culturally resonant ways.

In both literature and film, the portrayal of Egyptian gods and goddesses provides a gateway for audiences to connect with the rich mythology and cultural heritage of ancient Egypt. These artistic interpretations allow for a deeper exploration of the timeless themes, complex characters, and profound symbolism associated with the Egyptian pantheon, fostering an ongoing fascination with these divine beings and their enduring relevance in contemporary storytelling.

In conclusion, the presence of Egyptian gods and goddesses in literature and film reflects the enduring allure and cultural impact of ancient Egyptian mythology. From novels and poetry to movies and television shows, these divine figures continue to captivate audiences and inspire creative works that explore themes of mythology, spirituality, and the human condition. Their portrayal in various artistic mediums adds depth, intrigue, and a touch of the divine to our modern storytelling landscape.

Music and Performance Art

The allure of ancient Egypt has found its way into the realm of music, inspiring artists to incorporate Egyptian themes, melodies, and aesthetics into various genres and live performances. From traditional Egyptian music to contemporary genres such as rock, pop, and electronic music, the influence of Egyptian culture adds a unique and captivating dimension to the sonic landscape.

In traditional Egyptian music, elements of ancient Egyptian musical styles and instruments can be heard. Musicians may use traditional instruments like the oud, qanun, or ney to recreate the sounds and melodies that hark back to ancient times. These traditional musical forms evoke a sense of nostalgia and cultural heritage, connecting listeners to the historical and mythological context of ancient Egypt.

In modern music genres, Egyptian themes and aesthetics often appear in different ways. Artists may incorporate Egyptian-inspired melodies, scales, or rhythmic patterns into their compositions, infusing their music with a distinct Egyptian flavor. Lyrics may draw on ancient Egyptian mythology, symbolism, or historical events, offering a musical exploration of the gods, pharaohs, or iconic stories from ancient Egypt.

Live performances provide another avenue for artists to bring Egyptian themes to life. Elaborate stage designs, set pieces, and costumes may evoke the grandeur and mysticism associated with ancient Egyptian temples, rituals, and mythology. Dancers and performers may incorporate traditional Egyptian dance movements or create new choreographies inspired by the art forms of ancient Egypt. These performances transport audiences into a world where the ancient and the contemporary merge, creating a captivating and immersive experience.

Ritualistic elements and spiritual symbolism in Egyptian-inspired performances

Egyptian-inspired performances often incorporate ritualistic elements and spiritual symbolism to evoke the sacred and mystical aspects of ancient Egyptian culture. Artists may draw from ancient rituals, ceremonies, and religious practices, infusing their performances with a sense of reverence and transcendence.

Through choreography, movement, and gestures, performers may emulate the symbolic movements associated with ancient Egyptian religious rites. These movements can signify offerings, prayers, or the embodiment of specific deities. The use of sacred objects, such as incense, ankh symbols, or ceremonial vessels, further enhances the ritualistic atmosphere, creating a connection between the performers, the audience, and the spiritual realm of ancient Egypt.

Music and lyrics in Egyptian-inspired performances often carry spiritual symbolism, conveying messages of transcendence, inner transformation, or connection with divine forces. Lyrics may incorporate ancient Egyptian religious texts or invoke the names of deities, inviting the audience to engage with the spiritual themes and narratives associated with ancient Egyptian culture.

Overall, the incorporation of Egyptian themes and aesthetics in music genres and live performances allows artists to tap into the mystique and cultural richness of ancient Egypt. Through the use of traditional instruments, melodies, and dance movements, as well as the integration of ritualistic elements and spiritual symbolism, these performances provide an immersive experience that resonates with audiences, connecting them with the timeless spirit of ancient Egypt and its enduring fascination in the modern world.

Fashion and Consumer Culture

The allure of ancient Egypt has long captivated the world of fashion, with designers drawing inspiration from Egyptian motifs to create stunning and iconic pieces. Egyptian symbolism, art, and aesthetics have found their way onto runways, red carpets, and retail shelves, shaping trends and leaving a lasting impact on the fashion industry.

Fashion designers often incorporate Egyptian motifs into their collections, utilizing elements such as hieroglyphics, pyramids, scarabs, and iconic symbols like the Eye of Horus or Ankh. These motifs are translated into patterns, prints, embroideries, or embellishments, adding a touch of mystique and exoticism to garments. Dresses, tops, and accessories adorned with intricate Egyptian-inspired designs evoke the grandeur and elegance associated with ancient Egyptian culture.

Accessories play a significant role in channeling Egyptian aesthetics. Statement jewelry pieces, such as elaborate collars, cuffs, and headpieces, draw inspiration from the opulent jewelry of ancient Egypt. These pieces often feature gold tones, intricate detailing, and gemstones reminiscent of the rich materials used in ancient Egyptian adornments. Handbags, shoes, and belts may also incorporate Egyptian motifs, adding a touch of exotic flair to everyday fashion.

Commercialization and commodification of Egyptian symbolism

The use of Egyptian symbolism in fashion has not been without controversy. The commercialization and commodification of Egyptian symbolism raise questions about cultural appropriation, respectful representation, and the ethical implications of turning cultural heritage into consumer products.

While the incorporation of Egyptian motifs in fashion allows for creative expression and cultural exchange, it is important to navigate this terrain with sensitivity and respect. Fashion brands and designers must be mindful of the historical and cultural significance of the symbols they use and ensure they are represented accurately and authentically. Collaboration with Egyptian artists, artisans, or cultural institutions can help foster a more respectful and collaborative approach.

The mass production and consumption of Egyptian-inspired fashion also raise concerns about the commodification of cultural symbols. When ancient Egyptian symbolism becomes a mere trend or fashion statement, divorced from its historical and spiritual context, it can be reduced to a superficial and fleeting trend. It is crucial for consumers and fashion enthusiasts to engage critically with the meaning and significance of these symbols, fostering a deeper appreciation for the rich cultural heritage they represent.

In conclusion, the utilization of Egyptian motifs in fashion design and accessories offers a gateway to the allure and mysticism of ancient Egypt. When done respectfully and with a conscious awareness of the cultural significance involved, fashion becomes a means of celebrating and honoring ancient Egyptian culture. By acknowledging the historical context and engaging in dialogue and collaboration, the fashion industry can ensure that Egyptian symbolism is represented with integrity, fostering a deeper appreciation for the cultural heritage it embodies.

Conclusion

In conclusion, the use of Egyptian symbolism and deities in popular culture has become a pervasive and influential phenomenon. From visual arts to literature, film, music, fashion, and consumer culture, ancient Egyptian themes have captured the imagination of creators and consumers alike. The motivations behind incorporating Egyptian symbolism vary, ranging from fascination with the mystique of ancient Egypt to the desire for aesthetic appeal or commercial success.

Throughout this exploration, it is important to consider the impact and potential implications of the representation of Egyptian symbolism in popular culture. On one hand, it provides an opportunity for individuals to engage with and appreciate the rich cultural heritage of ancient Egypt. It allows for the dissemination of knowledge and sparks curiosity about this ancient civilization. Furthermore, the use of Egyptian symbolism can be a source of inspiration, enabling artists, designers, and creators to craft unique and visually stunning works.

However, it is essential to approach the use of Egyptian symbolism with sensitivity and respect. The risk of cultural appropriation, misrepresentation, and commodification is present, especially when symbols are divorced from their historical and spiritual contexts. It is crucial for both creators and consumers to engage in critical analysis and reflection, questioning the intentions, impact, and potential consequences of their choices.

To foster a deeper understanding and promote meaningful discussions, exercises and activities can be implemented. For example, students can be encouraged to analyze and compare different representations of Egyptian symbolism in popular culture, examining how they align or diverge from historical sources. They can explore the cultural, historical, and spiritual significance of Egyptian symbols and deities, encouraging reflection on their appropriate use and respectful representation. Additionally, open-ended discussions can invite participants to share their perspectives and engage in thoughtful dialogue about the complexities surrounding the utilization of Egyptian symbolism in popular culture.

By actively engaging in critical analysis, cultural appreciation, and ethical considerations, the use of Egyptian symbolism in popular culture can be a means of fostering understanding, respect, and appreciation for ancient Egyptian culture. It is through thoughtful engagement and ongoing dialogue that we can navigate the intersection of ancient heritage and contemporary expression in a way that honors and celebrates the legacy of ancient Egypt.

Appendix

Summary of Key Points Discussed in the Book:

Origins and Beliefs: The book delved into the origins of the belief in the divine nature of pharaohs, tracing it back to early Egyptian history. It explored the complex interplay of religious, political, and cultural factors that contributed to the development of the concept of pharaonic divinity.

Rituals and Responsibilities: The book examined the various rituals and religious responsibilities of pharaohs in ancient Egypt. It discussed their role in maintaining cosmic balance, their participation in daily religious practices, and the significance of offerings and ceremonies in their divine mandate.

Influence on Neighboring Civilizations: The book explored the widespread influence of ancient Egyptian religion on neighboring civilizations, such as the Near East, Canaanite and Phoenician cultures, Greek mythology, Nubian cultures, and Mediterranean cultures. It discussed the exchange of religious ideas, syncretism, and the impact of Egyptian religious motifs on these cultures.

Modern Interpretations and Relevance: The book delved into modern interpretations of ancient Egyptian religion and its relevance in contemporary contexts. It explored psychological and symbolic interpretations, archaeological and academic perspectives, cultural and identity reclamation, ethical and moral frameworks, as well as its influence on various alternative religious movements and spiritual practices.

Popular Culture: The book examined the pervasive presence of Egyptian symbolism and deities in popular culture. It discussed their representation in visual arts, literature, film, music, fashion, and consumer culture. It highlighted both the artistic and commercial aspects of incorporating Egyptian themes and symbols in popular culture.

Reflection on the Enduring Significance of Ancient Egyptian Religion:

Throughout the book, it became evident that ancient Egyptian religion continues to hold enduring significance. Its complex mythology, rich symbolism, and spiritual teachings continue to captivate individuals and inspire diverse forms of expression. From the reverence of ancient deities to the exploration of

Egyptian magical practices and the reconstruction of ancient rituals, people find deep meaning and personal connection in the traditions of ancient Egypt.

The enduring significance of ancient Egyptian religion lies in its ability to resonate with individuals across time and cultures. It offers a unique lens through which to explore themes of divinity, cosmology, ethics, and human spirituality. Its rituals, symbols, and teachings provide a framework for personal growth, self-reflection, and the pursuit of spiritual enlightenment.

Final Thoughts on the Connection between Ancient Religions and Modern Spirituality:

The exploration of ancient Egyptian religion in this book revealed a profound connection between ancient religions and modern spirituality. Ancient religious beliefs and practices continue to inspire individuals seeking spiritual fulfillment in contemporary contexts. From the reconstruction of ancient rituals to the integration of ancient wisdom into modern ethical frameworks, the study and application of ancient religions offer insights and guidance for individuals on their spiritual paths.

Furthermore, the incorporation of ancient religious motifs and concepts in popular culture reflects a continued fascination with the mysteries of the past and a yearning for spiritual meaning in the present. The enduring presence of Egyptian symbolism and deities in various forms of media underscores the timeless appeal of ancient religious traditions and their ability to resonate with contemporary audiences.

Ultimately, the connection between ancient religions and modern spirituality highlights the universal human quest for understanding, meaning, and transcendence. By exploring and engaging with the wisdom and practices of ancient civilizations, individuals can discover new perspectives, deepen their spiritual understanding, and forge connections with the timeless mysteries of the human experience.

Glossery

Ancient: Referring to a period in the distant past, typically before the Middle Ages or the fall of the Roman Empire.

Archaeological: Relating to the study of human history and prehistory through the excavation and analysis of artifacts, structures, and other physical remains.

Beliefs: The acceptance or conviction that certain ideas or concepts are true, often based on faith, cultural traditions, or personal experiences.

Civilization: A complex and highly organized society characterized by advanced social, political, economic, and cultural development, often marked by urbanization and the presence of written language.

Connection: The state of being linked, associated, or related to something else, often involving a relationship or a bond between two or more entities, concepts, or individuals.Contemporary

Cosmology: The study or understanding of the origin, structure, and overall organization of the universe or cosmos.

Cultural: Relating to the customs, traditions, beliefs, values, practices, and artifacts that characterize a particular group or society.

Deities: Gods or goddesses in a religious or spiritual belief system, often possessing supernatural powers and worshipped or revered by followers.

Divinity: The state or quality of being divine, often associated with gods, goddesses, or the divine nature or essence.

Ethics: The branch of philosophy that deals with moral principles, values, and conduct, examining what is morally right or wrong and guiding individuals or societies in making ethical decisions.

Exploration: The act or process of traveling, investigating, or seeking to understand new places, concepts, or ideas, often involving discovery or uncovering new knowledge or insights.

Exploring the Esoteric Wisdom of Ancient Egypt for Modern Spirituality

Influence: The capacity or power of someone or something to have an effect on the thoughts, beliefs, actions, or development of others, often through persuasion, inspiration, or the exertion of authority.

Interpretations: The act or process of explaining or understanding something, often based on personal understanding, cultural context, or subjective analysis.

Mythology: A collection of myths, legends, or traditional stories that explain the beliefs, customs, rituals, and values of a particular culture or religious tradition.

Offerings: Objects, items, or acts presented or given as a gift, tribute, or religious offering to a deity or spiritual entity, often as a form of worship or reverence.

Pervasive: Existing or present in every part or aspect of something; widespread or prevalent.

Practices: Customs, rituals, actions, or behaviors that are regularly followed or performed, often based on cultural, religious, or traditional beliefs.

Relevance: The quality or state of being closely connected or applicable to a particular context, situation, or subject matter; having significance or importance.

Religion: A set of beliefs, practices, rituals, and values centered around the worship of a deity or deities, often involving moral and ethical principles and providing individuals or communities with a framework for understanding the world and their place in it.

Rituals: Formalized, structured, and often repetitive actions, ceremonies, or practices performed in a specific order and manner, often associated with religious, spiritual, or cultural traditions.

Significance: The importance, meaning, or value of something in a particular context or situation; the quality of being significant or meaningful.

Spirituality: The quality or state of being connected to or concerned with the spiritual or non-material aspects of life, often involving personal beliefs, values, experiences, and practices related to one's inner self, higher power, or the transcendent.

Symbolism: The use of symbols or symbolic representations to convey ideas, meanings, or concepts beyond their literal or tangible form, often used in religious, artistic, or cultural contexts.

Syncretism: The merging, blending, or combination of different beliefs, practices, or traditions from different cultural, religious, or philosophical backgrounds, resulting in a new synthesis or hybridization.

Teachings: The doctrines, principles, lessons, or instructions imparted or communicated by a teacher, religious leader, or spiritual guide, often intended to provide guidance, knowledge, or moral and ethical teachings.

Traditions: Customs, beliefs, practices, or behaviors that are passed down from generation to generation within a particular culture, society, or community, often with a sense of continuity and historical significance.

Worship: The act of reverently honoring, adoring, or showing devotion to a deity, higher power, or spiritual entity, often through rituals, prayers, offerings, or other forms of religious or spiritual practices.

www.ingramcontent.com/pod-product-compliance
Lightning Source LLC
Chambersburg PA
CBHW082138120626

46553CB00010B/2702